Also by Jim Mason

Animal Factories (with Peter Singer)

An Unnatural Order

Uncovering the

Roots of Our

Domination of

Nature and

Each Other

Jim Mason

Simon & Schuster

New York London Toronto

Sydney Tokyo Singapore

SIMON & SCHUSTER
Rockefeller Center
1230 Avenue of the Americas
New York, New York 10020

Designed by Pei Loi Koay
Manufactured in the United States of America

2   3   4   5   6   7   8   9   10

Library of Congress Cataloging-in-Publication Data

Mason, Jim
An unnatural order : uncovering the roots of our domination of
nature and each other / Jim Mason.
p.   cm.
Includes index.
1. Animal rights.   2. Man—Influence on nature.   3. Sexual
discrimination against women.   4. Racism.   5. Colonies.   I. Title.
HV4708.M37   1993
304.2—dc20   93-28951
CIP

ISBN: 0-671-76923-5

The author gratefully acknowledges permission to reprint excerpts from the following sources:
Oklahoma, A Bi-Centennial History, by H. Wayne Morgan and Anne Hodges Morgan, reprinted by permission of W. W. Norton & Company, Inc., New York. Copyright © 1977 by American Association for State and Local History.

Where the Sky Began, by John Madson. Copyright © 1982 by John Madson. Reprinted by permission of Houghton Mifflin Company, New York. All right reserved.

The Pentagon of Power: The Myth of the Machine, by Lewis Mumford. Copyright © 1970 by Lewis Mumford. Reprinted by permission of Harcourt Brace & Co., Orlando, Florida.

The Domination of Nature, by William Leiss. Copyright © 1972. Reprinted by permission of George Braziller, Inc., New York.

(*cont. on p. 320*)

Acknowledgments

For the ideas and insights in this book, I am indebted to many people. My work was sparked by Elizabeth Fisher's *Woman's Creation,* published in 1979. From her, I first learned that animal husbandry, which originated in the ancient Middle East, contributed much of the patriarchal model that dominates Western culture. I am indebted also to Selma Miriam, who informed me of *Woman's Creation.* Through friendship with her, Betsy Beaven, and Noel Furies, I have learned of most of the basic works and ideas discussed in this book.

In the earlier years of research, Laura Moretti, an editor, prompted me to write an essay, which set off a chain of insights, research, and further writing. In the last year, financial and moral support from Ron Scott and his sister Janet Scott enabled me to turn notes and outlines into a finished manuscript. Through Ron's support and influence, I was able to gain the able research services of Monica Karaba, a Princeton senior, who spent her summer in the library poring over books for me. Monica, Ron, and I thank the Princeton Project '55, an alumni group that sponsors summer internships, for their interest and support.

Finally, this book would not have been possible without the support of my longtime friend Noreen Mola, and the persistence and encouraging spirit of my agent, Julie Fallowfield. Much of the credit must go, too, to my editor, Dominick Anfuso, whose enthusiasm and guidance carried me through the tedium of research and writing. His help and that of his assistant, Casandra Jones, eased difficult work and added much to the value of this book.

In addition to these influences, I am indebted to a number of other writers whose books informed this one. James Serpell's *In the Company of Animals* says about as much in its last three chapters as I do here. Paul Shepard's books, especially *Thinking Animals,* also greatly informed this work, as you will see. For anyone who seeks more—and deeper—ideas on humans, animals, and nature, I recommend all of Shepard's works listed in the references at the end of this book. For insights about animal hating, I am indebted to John Rodman and Barry Lopez, although the construction of misothery is my own. For a general readable survey of Western views of animals and nature, I am indebted to Sir Keith Thomas, whose book *Man and the Natural World* is among the best. For a general survey of human cultural evolution, Joseph Campbell's series, *The Historical Atlas of World Mythology,* is among the best. Helpful also were Yi-Fu Tuan's *Dominance and Affection,* Mary Midgley's *Beast and Man,* and Francis Klingender's *Animals in Art and Thought.* One book in particular was helpful and deserves much more readership: Michael Cohen's *Prejudice Against Nature.*

There are a great many other books that have informed me and offer much more than I have written here toward the repair of culture, our relations with each other, and our relations with the living world. For further, better information, I recommend: Andree Collard with Joyce Contrucci, *Rape of the Wild* (Bloomington: Indiana University Press, 1989); Mary Daly, *Gyn/Ecology* (Boston: Beacon Press, 1978); Riane Eisler, *The Chalice and the Blade* (San Francisco: Perennial Library, Harper & Row, 1988); E. Dodson Gray, *Green Paradise Lost* (Wellesley, Mass.: Roundtable Press, 1981).

For my mother and father.

In memory of Linda Frances Hall.

Contents

Preface   **11**

1. Dominionism Identified   **21**

2. Before Agriculture: A World Alive and Ensouled   **50**

3. Animals: The Most Moving Things in the World   **91**

4. Agriculture: A New Relationship with Nature, a New World Order for Living Beings   **118**

5. Misothery and the Reduction of Animals and Nature   **158**

6. Misogyny and the Reduction of Women and Female Power   **186**

7. Racism and Colonialism: Dominating Lands and Others   **210**

8. Rituals of Dominionism—Then and Now   **242**

9. Beyond Dominionism   **269**

References   **299**

Index   **310**

Preface

This book is written in hope and celebration. My hope is that we have the strength to rid ourselves of the destructive strands in Western culture. I celebrate the plenty of good strands that can have greater room to grow in the spaces they leave.

Some think that human society seems to be steadily going insane. They note the ridiculous hatreds that keep us nearly constantly at war with each other. They see that we are fouling our global nest, wiping out much of the planet's life and making life more and more miserable for ourselves.

I don't think we are going insane; I think we have just not learned to look deeply enough into the causes of our current social and environmental problems.

I believe with a growing number of others that these problems began several millennia ago when our ancestors took up farming and broke the primal bonds with the living world and put human beings above all other life. Because of this we have no sense of kinship with other life on this planet, hence no good sense of belonging here. Our tradition is one of arrogance toward the living world around us; it is a thing beneath us—to be either used up or kept at bay. We are, as intellectuals say, alienated from nature.

The price of our supremacy is a very deep break in our relationship with the living world around us. Many know this and would like to fix it. They ask: What is the fitting role for humankind in the scheme of life on earth? In intellectual circles this has been called the Nature Question. It is now time to bring this question into popular discussion, and I hope this book is a start.

Answering the Nature Question will be an ongoing process. It will begin with people coming to understand the past and how we got where we are today. It will continue by understanding that our views of the world are not carved in stone, but are determined by belief, culture, and habit—each of which changes over time, as they always have. So there is no padlock on our current situation. There are no chains that tie us to human supremacy over an increasingly wounded and bleeding living world.

We must understand, too, that there is more at stake here than species extinction and rain forest destruction. Our problems with nature cause problems within human society itself. We are creatures of nature, yet there are those who are very uncomfortable with it. They want to be greater than nature—next to God. And many people, in fact, do believe they are closer to God. Those who so believe look down on the Others whom they see as closer to nature than themselves. They tend to see these Others as inferior, bestial beings and they regard them with much the same hatred and contempt they have for nature in general. They treat the Others as they do nature: They try to control them and keep them at bay.

We see some of nature in our selves, too, our bodies, our health, our sexuality, and the other physical aspects of living, and of course we are uncomfortable about it. Our culture gives us a lot of negative views about animal nature, so we have a great deal of negative views about the animal nature we see in ourselves. And we treat this animal nature within us as we do the rest of nature: We try to control it, to keep it at bay.

The central idea in this book is that we must heal our blind spot for animals. Only a handful of intellectuals seem to understand how essential animals are to human beings, how they are the most vital beings in nature—the soul and the moving parts of nature. Animals represent and symbolize the various features and forces of nature. They have always fed the human mind and culture; they have given us the means of understanding the cosmos. When seen as kin, as they once were, animals gave us a crucial bond and a sense of belonging to the living world. Currently, however, the animal part of the Nature Question is kept on the back burner through ridicule and trivialization as well as open hostility toward those who raise it. The Animal Question is regarded as peripheral, a silly distraction from efforts to address what environmental heavyweights think is the more important Nature Question.

I submit that the Animal Question is central and fundamental to the Nature Question. We simply will not be able to come to terms with nature unless we come to terms with animals and animality, because, for the human mind and culture, animals are the most important part of nature.

Finally, there is still time to put things right, but not much time. If we do not come to terms with nature soon, the mess will get much worse and will be much harder for our children to fix. Ultimately, we may not destroy all life in the world, but we are steadily destroying the quality of it. We may not be careening over the brink of existence, but we are surely sliding into a mud hole—a much messier and unhappier existence. There is time—if we can find the strength to look more deeply at and struggle harder with our own beliefs, habits, and cultural traditions. If we are willing to face these and see them honestly, the repairs can begin at once.

Despite years of reading and thinking about the links between our social and environmental problems, my ideas about their deep common root did not jell until three or four years ago when a traveling experience brought them together. I was driving across northern Oklahoma, where an October sky was silting in with low, black, brooding clouds. Underneath me, the highway flowed westward, undulating with the arid swells of the prairie, its faded asphalt rolling on to the panhandle, laying down like a ribbon on a country quilt of fields, fencerows, and dusty towns. I saw a quilt heavily cross-stitched with history—a history noble to some, sordid to others. It occurred to me that Oklahoma is a place where nearly all of American history—perhaps Western history—compresses, focuses.

So when that trip was over I began looking into Oklahoma's history. As have others before me, I saw an instant replay of Western people's invasion, then colonization, and, finally, complete domination of the lands and native peoples of the Americas.

Most vividly symbolic was Oklahoma's first "land run," where, at noon on April 22, 1889, to the blast of a cavalry bugle, 50,000 settlers raced each other to claim a quarter-section of cheap land. Of this event, Oklahoma's preeminent historian Angie Debo wrote that "in a flashing instant" the land run "telescoped nine generations of American frontier history." The event was a congressionally approved invasion of lands that had been promised to Native Americans relocated from around the country "for as long as the run rise and go down . . . as long as grass grew . . . as long as the water runs." Because they were in on the action in one way or another, all of Europe and the Americas ate up the drama of this spectacular land grab; they called it "Harrison's Horse Race" after President Benjamin Harrison, who approved it. In their book, *Oklahoma: A Bicentennial History,* historians Wayne and Anne Hodges Morgan describe the tensions in the pioneers' camps that April day in 1889:

"As twelve o'clock approached, the waiting crowds became quiet, poised for flight. Horsemen strained forward in their saddles, checking cinches already checked a hundred times. Men in wagons daubed one last extra swath of grease on axles already floating in grease and prayed that their conveyances would survive the bumpy trip over the prairie. Engineers in waiting trains gripped their throttles, and passengers clung to every space with any hold they could find. At high noon, the starting flag dropped, a bugle sounded, and cavalry guns along the line repeated the signal amid shouts of anticipation and relief.

"The trains quickly surged ahead of the ragged lines of horsemen, and excited claim seekers jumped from roofs and doors of cars. Those not seriously hurt raced east and west of the tracks. When the thousands hurrying southward caught up with them, the crowds became a hopeless jumble. The trains finally stopped at Guthrie where hundreds more poured out in excited confusion, some looking for town lots, others seeking farm land on the edge of the proposed townsite. . . .

"With astonishing speed, the new settlers destroyed the arcadian quality of the land in the name of triumphant progress and civilization. By twilight on the opening day, the feet of people and animals, the wheels of heavy-laden wagons, the new foundations of buildings, all had crushed the wild grasses and flowers. It was symbolic of the changes to come. . . ."

That was only the first land run in Oklahoma. After negotiations and deals were struck with the various tribes, a second run swallowed up the promised lands of the Iowa, Sac, Fox, Shawnee, and Potawatomi. Then in April 1892, 25,000 people swarmed onto the 3 million acres that belonged to the Cheyenne and the Arapaho.

But the most spectacular—and famous—land run occurred on September 16, 1893, when over 100,000 people stampeded into the Cherokee "Outlet," or "Strip," in blistering 100-degree heat. Here was some of the best land left, and land-hungry pioneers were getting desperate. Emotions and hormone levels ran high and violence often flared. By all accounts, it was not Western humanity's finest day. According to the Morgans, "One successful settler stumbled over the body of a man with a slit throat and crushed skull, hidden in a hollow soon after the opening. Another . . . met a man who appeared demented, wandering around in a circle and asking helplessly, 'Where can I stake a claim? I want to get a home!' Still another pioneer party boasted of frightening a Negro from a claim with threats of lynching. Their neighbors endorsed the act with cries of 'That's right: we don't want any niggers in this country.' "

Violence, hatred, and inhumanity aside, for Oklahomans, "the glory of having been in the [Cherokee Strip] Run cut a lot more ice in Enid than coming over in the Mayflower," according to *Time* magazine in 1945.

In short order, other land runs and openings followed and white pioneers took over the lands of the Kickapoo, Kiowa, Comanche, Apache, Wichita, and Caddo. All that remained for America's native tribal peoples were some reservation lands held in common, the lands of the Five Civilized Tribes at the eastern end of the region, and some land in the far northeast corner. The rest of the Territory was rapidly filling up with settlers from every direction, but mostly from the adjacent states of Texas, Arkansas, and Missouri. Their migrations coincided with the flood of immigration into the United States from Europe, and many of these new Americans soon heard all about the land and opportunities in Oklahoma. In the two decades after Harrison's Horse Race, 2,000 European immigrants a year headed for Indian Territory to get their share.

Within a single generation, the last of the Indian lands was bought, bartered, and otherwise taken away by white Euro-Americans. On a warm Saturday, November 16, 1907, Oklahoma became the forty-sixth state of the Union. Its name comes from the Choctaw language: *okla*, meaning "people," and *humma*, meaning "red." Of the original idea of an American continent divided between native peoples and European settlers, mythologist Joseph Campbell wrote that, with Oklahoma's statehood, "The whole cruel deception had disappeared as by a magician's sleight of hand."

I was raised near Oklahoma—in the southwest corner of Missouri. From visits with friends and relatives and from reading about Oklahoma, I learned that ecologically, too, Oklahoma is—or was—a microcosm of America. At its eastern end, the wooded hills grew green and lush and there was an abundance of springs and streams. Through its middle ran the great American prairie—the Sea of Grass that stretched from Canada to the Gulf of Mexico. Toward its western end, Oklahoma's prairie grasses turned short and sparse as they merged into the arid steppes and deserts of the West. Then, as pioneers had elsewhere, Oklahoma's land runners "broke" most of this wild prairie and imposed on its primal soils monotonous fields of wheat, cotton, and corn.

For biodiversity, the prairie was North America's rain forest. At its grassroots thrived a whole world, "a teeming lifeswarm," wrote John Madson in *Where the Sky Began*. A single gram of loam from the surface soil of a fertile prairie held as many as 2 million protozoans (single-celled animals) and their food: another 58 million bacteria (single-celled plants). These made the prairie's upper soil a region a dynamic processes, a seething mass of life forces doing the microbiological labors that produced deep deposits of the dark, organic dirt we call humus. Some 150 kinds of grasses thrived on it, especially the big bluestem, or turkey foot, which grew six to nine feet tall.

Next in order of dominance grew little bluestem, then Indian grass, sloughgrass, switch grass, prairie dropseed, and sideoats grama. Others—Canada wild rye, June grass, porcupine grass, the wheatgrasses, needle-and-thread, the needlegrasses—found lesser niches in the Sea of Grass. Forbs, nonwoody plants other than grasses, also grew in a rich variety, 150 kinds in all. They included compass plant, rattlesnake master, blazing star, yellow stargrass, blue-eyed grass, yellow cornflower, bottle gentian, black samson, white prairie clover, purple prairie clover, and various other wild legumes. And flowers: wild indigo, violets, wild daisies, roses, and lilies.

From this variety, the coloring of the prairie must have been spectacular: "From the first greening of spring to the full ripening of autumn," author John Madson wrote, "it is spangled by a vivid progression of flowers—a rainbow host that first enamels the burned slopes of early spring and ends months later with great nodding blooms that rise above a man's head."

But there was still more life in the prairie. Above and in the Sea of Grass flourished some 300 species of birds. Prairie skies and grasses teemed with swallow-tailed kites, red-tailed hawks, marsh hawks, sparrow hawks, prairie chickens, and bobwhite quail. They were home as well to sandhill cranes, upland plovers, mourning doves, short-eared owls, nighthawks, short-billed marsh wrens, loggerhead shrikes, bobolinks, eastern meadowlarks, dickcissels, grasshopper sparrows, Henslow's sparrows, and vesper sparrows.

And there were the mammals—about ninety species in all. The large ones are most familiar: buffalo, also called bison, wolves, and coyotes. At the edges, where the prairie merged with woodlands, roamed elk, black bear, puma, lynx, mule deer, white-tail deer, and pronghorn antelope. And down in the prairie grass and sod dwelled dozens of species of small animals—gophers, ground squirrels, foxes, weasels, shrews, badgers, skunks, snakes, and many kinds of mice, voles, and rats.

"The most spectacular members of the prairie bestiary were shot into oblivion," wrote Madson. "Others passed more quietly, fading with the original grasslands and vanishing by default rather than human intent. They lingered in widening croplands, their margin of survival shrinking, until they were buried forever by corn and commerce."

The technological breakthrough that reduced the Great Prairie to today's corn and wheat belts came in the 1830s with the introduction of the polished steel plow. John Lane, Sr., of Lockport, Illinois, invented it, and a blacksmith from Grand Detour, Illinois, named John Deere improved, mass-produced, and peddled it to the countryside.

After a succession of refinements, these plows made short work of busting the prairie sod. With cutting disks and edges sharp as knives, they sliced through the thick mat of native grassroots and turned the topsoil belly up to the sun, rain, and wind. You can almost hear the destruction of life in this description of steel plowing by authors David Costello and John Madson: "Costello has said that the plow cut through tough rootlets and plant spurs with a sound like fusillades of tiny pistol fire, all amplified by the tempered steel moldboard in a steady ringing hum that might last fourteen hours a day. In the wake of the plow was the confusion of the prairie's dispossessed: meadow mice, shrews, small snakes, insects, ground-dwelling bees, a whole multitude of minor citizens that dwelt in the grassroots, attended by clouds of wheeling Franklin's gulls that followed the plowman."

In about fifty years, not quite a human lifetime, prairie plowing and pioneering, from first to last, was virtually complete.

Early in the 1900s, Oklahoma's settlers began to have access to a growing arsenal of weapons for land conquest. In 1901, Charles Hart and Charles Parr turned out their first two-cylinder, 45-horsepower, gasoline-powered "tractor." They coined the word to distinguish their machine from the competition—the older steam-powered engines. In 1907, 600 gasoline-powered tractors were made in the United States, one third of them by Hart and Parr. On the eve of World War I, 14,000 tractors were at work on American soil; within one year after the Armistice, 158,000.

Equipped with more and more powerful gasoline engines, these tractors easily pulled plows through what remained of Oklahoma's wild prairie sod. Until the plowing, the long roots of the wild grasses had kept a firm grip on the soil and its moisture. Severed from its deep cover and roots, the soil would not bear up to the farmers' monocultures of field crops and grazing animals. It fell barren—naked to the elements, particularly the hot, dry winds that swept up steadily from the Southwest each summer.

Nevertheless, Oklahoma agriculture went rapidly from subsistence farming to intensive, cash-crop agriculture. By the turn of the century, cotton was the principal crop, with wheat or corn occasionally taking the lead. Elsewhere in the nation, demand was high for these crops because of a combination of European immigration, industrialization, urban growth, and growing markets abroad. The years between 1898 and 1920 were good ones for American farmers, and they jumped to adopt new, scientific practices that milked maximum yields from the soil. Oklahoma farmers were no different, and they ignored warnings about soil erosion and depletion. Like many American farmers elsewhere, they cleared, plowed, and overplanted wherever they could. When World War I ended in 1918, Oklahoma agriculture was headed for disaster. Cotton, a voracious consumer of soil fertility, was planted in every county. Wheat also filled the fields—on marginal soil in many counties.

By the early 1920s, Oklahoma's oil boom was promising but the agricultural situation was ominous. Careless farming practices had destroyed thousands of acres. Ugly red gullies gutted hillsides. Spindly crops drooped under the summer sun. Damage from flooding and erosion was as devastating as periodic drought. Yet farmers who had plowed marginal lands to reap wartime profits continued to overproduce. They did it to survive because prices had declined. In dire straits, they could not afford to think about the disasters that would come with any weather change. Droughts, they thought, would come and go, as they always had. In the fall of 1930, the *Oklahoma Farmer-Stockman* assured readers that "the dry weather and hard times are but temporary." But the dry years kept coming, and in 1932 and 1933 wheat seeds failed to sprout. In 1934, there was no rain from February to July—the growing season.

All the while, summer's hot, southwest winds blew steadily across the naked land and sucked from the soil whatever moisture remained. So soon after its death by plowing, the topsoil turned to powder and blew away. In the years between 1933 and 1937, there were 362 dust storms, an average of one every five days. The tables were turned on the pioneers; now they were at the mercy of nature. Great clouds of powdery dirt darkened skies hundreds of miles to the north, and dustbits of it settled in Alaska and other parts of the globe. Dust storms ranged over Kansas, Colorado, New Mexico, and Texas, but Oklahoma is the Dust Bowl in the public mind. The term *Dust Bowl* originated there, at Guymon, in an Associated Press story about the era's most spectacular dust storm—the "black blizzard" of April 14, 1935. So-called because thick dust clouds blackened out the sky, the storm added the terrors of darkness to those of suffocation. According to Oklahoma historians Wayne and Anne Morgan, "people became lost in their own backyards. Travelers stranded in darkness at noon crawled along fences to farmhouses, or groped for ruts in the roads with bare toes."

People weren't the only sufferers during these dust storms. The Morgans tell how blowing sand blinded cattle, who ran in circles until they fell exhausted and suffocated from inhaled dust. Newly born calves often died the next day. Birds fluttered helplessly against the force of the winds. Jackrabbits huddled close to the ground facing away from the storm, and the swirling dusts turned them into dirty mounds with a twitching nose at one end. They tell of Caroline Henderson, a farm wife in Eva, who recalled seeing plants sitting high above the surrounding earth, roots exposed by the wind's force.

Torn and tangled over soil, minerals, oil, liquor, and racial prejudices, Oklahoma, ever the microcosm of American society, stumbled from the pioneer era into the modern. It made it, so to speak, by broadening its base of exploitation. In the sixties and seventies, a modern breed of Boomers and their politicians ushered in an era of industrialism to expand Oklahoma's unsteady economy beyond its boom-or-bust base of farming, oil, and mining. The sagging boomtowns were enthusiastic about new jobs, new money, and another dose of the pride of production. Oklahoma rapidly became a manufacturer of everything from aerospace equipment to recreational goods. Hartshorne, once a worn-out coal town, became a producer of sophisticated electronic equipment used in guided missiles. Enid turned out bicycles under its looming, empty grain elevators. Forced to cope in the modern world, Oklahoma's Indian tribes bought a Western-hat company at Lawton and started a line of sporting goods and playtime products at factories at Shawnee, Ponca City, and Anadarko.

In a headlong rush toward industrialization, the Indian Territory became another New Jersey. According to the Morgans, Oklahoma's industrial complex included: "wind tunnels at Perkins; millwork at Ada; steel fabrication and petrochemicals at Wetumka; a uranium plant at Sallisaw; carpets at Pawhuska; sailboats at Henryetta; barbeque smokers at Boley; dresses at Caddo; rods and reels at Broken Arrow; optical lenses at Muskogee; and pecan harvesters at Madill were dramatic testimony to the diversity of the state's changing industrial economy. Frederick, in southwestern Oklahoma, seemed to sum up the whole trend. With a population of fewer than 10,000 people in 1966 and an area of four square miles, it hosted producers of helicopters, granite building materials, bras, leather goods, and was the site for a cattle feeding lot."

In Oklahoma, right at America's heart and gut, came one of Western society's last convulsions of frontierism. There, where the force-fields of history are strong and fresh, is a close-up of much that is typical of Western society, particularly its obsession with expansion and the conquest of peoples and lands. There, in stark focus, are the ideals, and values that have driven our culture and history. In Oklahoma, as elsewhere, we destroyed the native, the natural, and planted the seeds of our modern social and environmental angst.

1

Dominionism
Identified

"Man's task," wrote Sir Keith Thomas in *Man and the Natural World*, "in the words of Genesis (1:28), [is] to 'replenish the earth and subdue it': to level the woods, till the soil, drive off the predators, kill the vermin, plough up the bracken, drain the fens." Agriculture, he said, stands to land as does "cooking to raw meat"—that is, it makes raw, wild nature suitable for human use and consumption. Agriculture is the process of taming and ordering plants, animals, and natural forces to make them more productive and beneficial to human beings. It is often defined as the manipulation and control of nature for the benefit of "man," meaning human beings.

We usually think of agriculture in terms of plows, tractors, and other farm implements, but these are merely its visible and tangible tools. We think of it also as a body of accumulated knowledge about soil, plants, and animals; farming is a skill or profession. Sometimes we think of agriculture as a way of life, and we are prone to romanticize its sanctity and its allure. These aspects of agriculture are the conscious ones, the ones we can easily see and think about.

Beneath them all, however, is an aspect about which we are hardly aware: Agriculture's effect on the mind and culture. For nearly 10,000 years people of the West have farmed—that is, manipulated nature for human benefit. Ponder for a moment this long human experience and how deeply it influences our thinking and culture. This is a hundred centuries of controlling, shaping, and battling plants, animals, and natural processes—all things of the world around us that we put under the word *nature.* Controlling—and alternately battling—nature is a very old way of life to us. It is a stance with nature so deeply ingrained in us that we are rarely conscious of it. Controlling nature is second nature to us. We are people of an agrarian culture, and we have the eyes, ears, hearts, and minds of agriculturists. Whether or not you have ever been a farmer, or even a visitor at a farm, if you are a Westerner you are imbued with the culture of the farmer and it determines virtually everything you know and think about the living world around you. Let us begin to figure out how.

"Agri-Culture"

Agriculture, of course, always needs land. Historically, as the story of the American prairie illustrates, the most alluring land to agriculturists, especially those from crowded, overworked lands, has been "virgin" land—land in its natural, unplowed, uncultivated state. Virgin land has certain practical values: It is usually cheap, fertile, and empty, and thus easy to bring under cultivation. Its "emptiness," however, is more a matter of perception than of fact. Other living things besides people live on and in it. Yet the perceptions of the pioneer farmer are shaped by the agri-cultural culture, which tells him that any lives in residence on the land are unworthy of his consideration. They are not seen, not regarded, or if they are at all, it is only as contemptible pests—things to be eliminated to make way for crops and livestock. Under agrarian culture, farmers generally, and pioneers especially, see and value only the lay of the land and the quality of the soil—things that will make their farms and lives better. Land exists, in their view, strictly for human benefit. As author and conservationist A. S. Leopold said of the founder of the West's agrarian religion: "Abraham knew exactly what the land was for; it was to drip milk and honey into Abraham's mouth."

Besides its practical allure, virgin land has a less conscious, more emotional attraction that wells up from the deep springs of agricultural culture: Virgin land, the Westerner thinks, *needs* to be taken over and cultivated; it *needs* to be made productive for humankind. There is something immoral about leaving it alone, letting it lie there untouched, un*improved*. Under the West's "agri-culture," then, one has a moral obligation to make virgin land productive. "Uncultivated land meant uncultivated men," said Keith Thomas, referring to the outlook of early European pilgrims in North America, "and when seventeenth-century Englishmen moved to Massachusetts, part of their case for occupying Indian territory would be that those who did not themselves subdue and cultivate the land had no right to prevent others from doing so." Thus, from the European point of view, not only God but the laws of the jungle licensed the taking of land in the Americas.

A License for Conquest

At a very fundamental level, then, the West's ideals and religion pushed the native peoples of Oklahoma and the Americas (and other places, as we shall see in Chapter 7) from their lands, their food supply, and their traditions. The European neither saw nor regarded them as living beings. If he regarded them at all, it was as *things*—things in the way of the European's moralized urge to conquer, tame, and cultivate.

Coupled with that urge was another, moralistic urge: to get away from crowded, degenerate, strife-torn Europe; to leave the decadent Old World behind and start over, pure and upright, in the New World. Europeans wanted to leave all the war, poverty, and disease behind and go to a fresh, clean place to live right by their God.

Author and philosopher Lewis Mumford pointed out that Western peoples' attitudes toward the New World were contradictory. On the one hand, they were driven by a desire to escape the rot of the Old World along with its fossilized institutions—Christianity and royal power. On the other hand, they were driven by a desire to extend the influence of these institutions into the New World. The contradiction was especially flagrant in North America, where the very colonists who broke with England in the name of freedom, equality, and the right to the pursuit of happiness retained the institution of slavery and relentlessly used armies to push native peoples from their lands. Those who were not exterminated or overpowered militarily were systematically defrauded by phony land purchases and treaties, which were just as systematically ignored or broken.

Equally contradictory was the Old World's sense of morality in the wilderness to the west. On the one hand, there was the sacred duty to extend Christian morality and civilization into the wild, empty place. On the other hand, there was a feeling among those in the New World of being beyond the law, outside the jurisdiction of Europe's moral institutions, where the law of the jungle could prevail. This latter attitude, as we shall see in Chapter 7, fostered much of the cruel, genocidal exploration and colonization campaigns of the Europeans. Mumford said it well in *The Pentagon of Power*: "As it turned out, the wilderness that Western man had failed to explore was the dark continent of his own soul . . . released by its distance from Old World sanctions, throwing off archaic taboos, conventional wisdom, and religious inhibitions, and obliterating every trace of neighborly love and humility. Wherever Western man went, slavery, land robbery, lawlessness, culture-wrecking, and the outright extermination of both wild beasts and tame men went with him: for the only force that he now respected—an enemy with equal power to inflict damage on him—was lacking, once his feet were firmly established on the new soil. Within half a dozen years after Columbus's landing the Spaniards, a contemporary observer estimated, had killed off one and a half million natives."

America's native peoples did not fall; they were pushed. They were pushed quite physically by Euro-American pilgrims and pioneers and their armies. But the pushers were also heavily armed with religious and cultural firepower. Europe's pilgrims and pioneers followed the twin stars of Christian Rebirth and Manifest Destiny and they had hung them over the wilderness to the west. They went after them with missionary zeal. Their explorations, their penetrations and invasions had, Lewis Mumford said, "from the beginning a touch of defiant pride and demonic frenzy." But we gave them noble names, like Manifest Destiny and the American Pioneering Spirit. Something in the Western culture allowed, through the magic of words, the cruel business of conquering two continents, their peoples, and their ecosystems to be carried out as a spiritual mission ordained by God.

New Questions, New Directions

If the religion of the European invaders had been a genuine, functioning ethical system instead of a self-drawn license to plunder, perhaps the historical record might not be so bloodstained. We ought to ask how all this could have happened—not only for the sake of simple justice to native peoples, but for the healing it could bring to their people and to their relations with the Westerners in America.

And we ought to ask it because the religion of the European invaders is degenerating into vacant beliefs, hollow rituals, and empty ceremonies. The religion that fueled so many conquests in so many parts of the world, the ethos that destroyed so much wild nature and so many native peoples, is nearly spent. The West's spiritual wells are running dry.

Is there a correlation between the withering of our religion and our ruthlessness over other life? Have the ancient biblical mandates to "have dominion . . . over all of the earth" and to "fill the earth and subdue it . . ." cost us our souls? If we, the people of Western culture, want to revive our humanity and keep our juggernaut of materialism from destroying the living world, we had better try to understand how we came to follow this destructive mandate. Where did we get this death-dealing way of thinking about the world?

First, it will help to identify the way of thinking, the outlook on the world, with a name. This will make it easier to pull it out of ourselves, to hold it up high and look at it. Held up against the strong light of current knowledge, we should be able to see through it.

For a name, the word *dominionism* is most apt. A dictionary says that the word *dominion* means "a supremacy in determining and directing the actions of others . . . the exercise of such supremacy." This fairly describes Western peoples' proud, basic view of the world and our most sacred, fundamental policy on how to live on it. In regard to nature—the world, its living beings, forces, and processes—then, our culture, our outlook, and our ways of thinking are dominionist.

Then we will want to ask: How does it enter our learning and shape our knowledge as children? How does it determine our thinking as adults? How does dominionism determine the ways in which we see the entire world around us—all other peoples, beings, and things?

There are lots of other good questions, like: How does dominionism become the basic mind-set of a society—one that is common to political leaders, artists, philosophers, and all of the other culture-makers who shape and lend direction to human living?

Genesis: The West's Creation Myth

In his book *The Domination of Nature*, William Leiss wrote: "A common feature of the religions that dominated the ancient world was the belief that all natural objects and places possessed 'spirits.' These had to be honored in order to insure oneself against harm, and before appropriating natural objects for human use man was required to placate the spirits through gifts and ceremonies. The Judeo-Christian religion, however, maintained that 'spirit' was separate from nature and ruled over it from without; it also taught that to some extent man shared God's transcendence of nature. Only man of all earthly things possessed spirit, and thus he did not have to fear the resistance of an opposing will in nature;

the Bible seemed to indicate that the earth was designed to serve man's ends exclusively."

Leiss goes on to cite part of a now-famous 1967 essay by historian Lynn White, "The Historical Roots of Our Ecologic Crisis." In it, White said that ". . . by destroying pagan animism, Christianity made it possible to exploit nature in a mood of indifference to the feelings of natural objects."

Not only did Christianity make this possible, but indeed commanded it. "Christianity," said White, "not only established a dualism of man and nature but also insisted that it is God's will that man exploit nature for his proper ends."

Leiss and White are wrong about one thing, though: Dominionism did not begin with Christianity, nor did it begin earlier with Judaism. It began even earlier; it was already there when the Bible, even the oldest parts, were written.

Most of us, however, have learned about the idea of "man's dominion" over the life on earth through the various passages of Genesis in the Old Testament. Genesis is often, if erroneously, cited as the source of dominionism. While it may not be the source in the historical or evolutionary sense, it is the source in the bibliographical sense. It is widely believed to be the Sacred Document containing God's gift to humanity of supreme authority over the world. Genesis is, in the words of Keith Thomas, "the Old Testament charter upon which human rule over nature [is] founded."

In beautiful language, Genesis tells the creation story—the fundamental myth—of Western civilization. From it, most of us learn our first and most basic understandings about who we are and how we came to be in the world—something all creation stories do. The Judeo-Christian creation story tells us that God made the heavens and the earth, then dry land and the waters, then plants, seasons, the sun, the stars, and the moon in four days. Then He made fish and sea creatures and birds of the air, urging them to "be fruitful and multiply, and fill the waters in the seas, and let the fowl multiply in the earth."

On the sixth day, God creates the land animals and the first man—in His own image. God then gives his first man "dominion over the fish of the sea, over the fowl of the air, and over the cattle, and over all the earth, and over every creeping thing that creepeth upon the earth." Note the significance of the order of creation. First, God makes everything in the world and then He makes a man to be in charge of it all. This sequence assists the belief that God created the world and all other forms of life just for man.

Then God directs His new man to: "be fruitful and multiply; and replenish [*fill*, in the Revised Standard Version] the earth, and subdue it." For the second time, He tells the man to "have dominion over the fish of the sea, and over the fowl of the air, and over every living thing that moveth upon the earth." After God rests for a day, He creates the Garden of Eden, gives His man the name Adam, and creates Eve.

As we all know, the serpent tempts Eve and she and Adam disobey God's command and eat fruit from the tree of knowledge of good and evil. God gets very angry at their disobedience and turns them out of the garden forever. He condemns the serpent to the lowest of conditions— crawling: "upon thy belly shalt thou go, and dust shalt thou eat all the days of thy life." He condemns "the woman" (still no name) and all women to suffer both pain in childbirth and the rule of men. God condemns Adam and all men to suffer at the hard labor of wrestling food from the earth.

The Fall, First Murder, and the Flood

This is the Fall from Grace, the punishment for having disobeyed God's command. It is a key passage in our culture's creation story because it is accepted as the explanation for the pain, toil, and hardship on earth. Thus it sets up a view of the world—and of human life in it—that is largely hardship and suffering. Note, then, two important associations that are set down by the Fall from Grace: First, life is hard and painful with much sweat, toil, and adversity.

Second, the soil, the earth, is base and low—something to rise above. The earth is not exactly evil, but it is low and contemptible—the serpent, as punishment for its wickedness, is condemned to crawl on its belly like a lowly worm of the earth. As to Adam: "Cursed is the ground for your sake, in toil you shall eat of it." And again, having sinned, Adam now has to die and turn into earth again: "In the sweat of thy face shalt thou eat bread, till thou return unto the ground; for out of it wast thou taken: for dust thou art and unto dust shalt thou return."

Note these associations well, for we will see them again and again in art, literature, music, and the other expressions of the "high," or agricultural, civilizations: Earth, flesh, and this life are seen as base, crude, and contemptible. On the other hand, heaven, spirit, and the next life are regarded as exalted, glorious, and desirable.

Expelled from the garden, Adam and Eve go out into the world and bear children. The first, Cain, becomes a "tiller of the ground," a planter or horticulturist, and the second, Abel, becomes a keeper of sheep, a herder, an animal husbandryman. Cain kills Abel in a jealous rage. Angry, God curses Cain and drives him away to be a fugitive and a vagabond in the world: "When thou tillest the ground, it shalt not henceforth yield unto thee her strength." Once again, God curses humanity and makes human life, especially the life of farmers, hard and frustrating.

After much begetting of children, there are many people in the world and troubles abound. God is sorry He made human beings and He sends a great flood to destroy them and all the beasts, birds, and other animals. God spares Noah, his family, and breeding pairs of each of the animals on an ark of gopherwood that God had commanded Noah to build.

After the flood, God grants, for the third time, dominion over the earth to human beings. God makes a covenant—a sacred agreement—with Noah, his family, and all human beings that spells out the basic relationship humans are to have with all the animals in the world: "And the fear of you and the dread of you shall be upon every beast of the earth, and upon every fowl of the air, upon all that moveth upon the earth, and upon all the fishes of the sea; into your hand are they delivered."

Some say that the Fall, the Flood, and the covenant mark the end of a "golden age" when life was peaceful and people and animals were not violent. To quibble over whether such a golden age existed in fact is to miss the essential message of our creation story: Something grave and sorrowful happened to human existence. Our civilization's most important myth, then, reflects human awareness of a major transition, a great change in the human way of life. Some think that the oldest oral versions of the myth were put together relatively early in the agricultural era, when much still remained of the earlier forager (hunter-gatherer) culture and lifeways. The overall theme of the myth expresses the longing of early agricultural people for their earlier, easier, freer forager way of life.

The Divine Mandate

Genesis, then, tells the sacred story of how we came to have dominion over all of nature. These passages are referred to throughout history as the Law, the Word, and they are given a sanctity that is beyond challenge or rebuttal. Three times God expressly grants human beings *dominion* over creation; very clearly, human mastery over nature is God's will. This, then, is the most basic of all the beliefs in Western religion, for the story of Genesis is included in each of the West's sacred books: the Torah, the

Bible, and the Qur'an. If the West's religions are likened to the legs of a three-legged stool, dominionism is the seat.

It is true that these sacred books contain plenty of passages about the proper care and humane treatment of animals, and many religious leaders point to these as evidence that human dominion is conditional in an attempt to soften the hard-line dominionism of Genesis. One example is the Presbyterian Animal Welfare Task Force, a study group put together in the mid-1980s by church congregations located in a major cattle, hog, and sheep production area of the Midwest. Their report states that "'the economy of our area is based almost entirely on agriculture and primarily on the raising of cattle, sheep and hogs." As Christians, they do not draw their ethics from secular moral philosophy, but from the Bible: "Ours is derived from knowing and attempting to do the will of God." In short, their report is an examination of biblical statements concerning the use, care, and treatment of animals. After restating the verses of Genesis giving human beings dominion over all living things, the authors conclude that life forms are ranked in a hierarchy with humanity at the top—closest to God.

From this position, human beings are clearly overlords and owners of other life. According to the task force's authors: "Although domestic animals remain the possession of the Creator on one level, on another they are considered human property, a highly desirable form of property. Proverbs 27:23–27 urges people to know and care for their herds because they represent the best kind of asset. A well-kept herd can provide for a family's present needs while at the same time increasing the family fortune as the herd grows. If managed properly, a herd can be a form of wealth that provides for a family generation after generation."

In this light we can see the true meaning of biblical passages that prescribe humane care and treatment. Their effect is not to limit human dominion in any way, but to subtly reinforce it by stating warnings and precautions about overuse and ill-treatment. The overall (and underlying) message to humanity is: *Use animals and other living things, and if you do it carefully, your wealth will increase.* The fact that the Bible contains so many passages about proper care and humane treatment suggests that poor care and overuse were common problems; so common that they were hurting the agrarian economy. Note, too, that the humane regard is limited to domestic animals—that is, people's property. The Bible does not direct people to extend humane care to wildlife and animals not owned. It seems clear, then, that Bible verses condemning cruelty were not intended to limit or condition dominionism in any way. Their real intent was to reinforce agrarian society's interests in reducing waste, managing resource, and increasing surpluses and wealth.

Dominionism in Other Cultures

Dominionism is also a fundamental belief in other societies that have a history of intensive agriculture. In these societies, foraging ways dwindled and agriculture rose to become the predominant means of subsistence thousands of years ago. This occurred in Africa, India, Southeast Asia, and, to a lesser extent, in parts of South and Central America. Thus, agrarian dominionism is a basic element in many religions and cultures around the world. In most of them, however, the principle of human dominion is rather less rampant and is often diluted by principles from the earlier, preagricultural religions—principles that had a better survival rate beyond the reach (initially) of the West's aggressive and rigidly monotheistic Judeo-Christian-Islamic Megareligion.

But I will not discuss the incidence of dominionism in these other agricultural religions and cultures. For one, being not of those traditions, it is too difficult for me to competently and fairly analyze them.

Second, it is the Western tradition that is the primary culprit in the destruction of the natural world, not the traditions of the Far East or the other major centers of agricultural civilization. Furthermore, most of the world, unfortunately, has become infected with Western culture and its dominionist ideas, even if all have not adopted the Judeo-Christian-Islamic religion. Japan, for example, has not bought heavily into Western religion, but its corporate, technocratic, industrial society is as chauvinistic about its right to exploit nature as any Christian European nation.

The Stewardship Apology

There are those who say that dominion over the earth does not mean ruthless conquest. They say it means benevolent stewardship. Predictably, the Presbyterian Task Force does this in an attempt to make dominion over animals seem less harsh and absolute. The authors' position: "Although domestic animals are a form of property, they are not property in the same sense as a building or land. They are made by God even as we have been. We accept them as a trust given to us by God. Our stewardship is a stewardship of care and protection for fellow creatures

God has blessed with the gift of life." This thinking is more and more common now that old-fashioned exploitation is coming under fire. Such thinkers are attempting to hold on to their divine right to use other life for human benefit by appearing to qualify and limit it somewhat. Their model is stewardship.

Essentially, stewardship advocates are apologists for dominionism, for they argue that dominion does not mean what people have thought it has meant over the past several thousand years. Now they tell us it was never supposed to have meant that humans should behave as ruthless lords over nature. They argue that the meaning of dominion has been distorted and mistranslated over the ages. They argue that we are supposed to act as gentle, humane shepherds and gardeners—tending, pruning, fertilizing, and cultivating the other life on earth. All that would be very nice, but it is too late. The dominionist dirty deeds have already been done.

In fact, dominion means just exactly what it has been taken to mean all these thousands of years: a license for boundless human exploitation of the rest of the living world. The task today is to get away from it now that we see how it destroys not only the living world but our quality of life within it.

The Authors of Genesis

One of the first orders of business, then, is to understand where Genesis came from, where the writers of Genesis got their ideas. What sorts of things were happening socially and economically in that part of the world that disturbed life so, forcing societies to develop myths to explain their existence? One thing is clear, Genesis was not written by the hand of God; it was written by *men*—real men in real cities in the Middle East on real days in history. (It is doubtful that women would have been allowed to compose these sacred writings. In *The Book of J*, however, Harold Bloom speculates that the principal author of Genesis was a woman, a *Gevurah* or "great lady" in court circles who worked closely with King Solomon's court historian. Even if "J" was female, she was a member of a patriarchal culture and her thinking and writing expressed its male-defined ideas and values.) These writers were no closer to God than were any other holy men anywhere else at any other time. Their ideas and their visions were no more direct from God than those of a Oglala Sioux shaman or a Celtic Druid priest. The religious system the Bible writers promulgated is not necessarily a better one for humanity than that of the

Nuer of northern Africa or the Aranda of central Australia. To persist in claiming that it is, is to persist in ethnic arrogance, which is a form of bigotry.

The writers of Genesis simply put down on paper—or sheepskin—what had been passed by word of mouth for centuries, the stories, fables, legends, and myths that had been told from generation to generation in verse, song, and ceremony. People moved about from place to place, and traders carried these stories and myths. While agriculturists preferred to stay in one place, wars, famines, drought, and other forces often caused dislocations. Scholars now think that there was a great deal of movement of people and commodities throughout northern Africa, Europe, and southern Asia (not to mention the Americas) and that this movement was going on for many centuries before the Hebrew scribes penned Genesis. In this way, fragments of a myth or a creation story from one tribe or region moved around to others. In time, perhaps some of the basic ones—myths that spoke to a common agricultural existence in a region—came to be adopted by societies in quite a large geographic area. In more time still, such myths might have grown into a religion.

Putting the Oral Tradition in Writing

After centuries of the oral tradition of myth-making and reshaping, writing began and religious leaders busied themselves with putting down the prevailing religious beliefs of their time. They wrote what their people had believed, in one form or another, for centuries, perhaps millennia.

Writing is believed to have begun around 3000 B.C. with the Sumerians, who lived just up the river from what is now modern Kuwait. We have, then, only about 5,000 years of history; all before that is prehistory—prewriting. Because we have such an orientation toward history and written documents, we overemphasize the importance of our ancient written documents—especially the sacred texts. We tend to think of these documents as sources, beginnings, starting points of our civilization and its beliefs. In doing so, we cut ourselves off from the many centuries of human development and culture that occurred before writing.

Sumeria, Persia, Egypt, and the other great, early cultures were not the starting points of Western civilization; they were, rather, culminations of millennia of human economic, social, cultural, and ideological growth that occurred around the eastern end of the Mediterranean Sea. Scholars call this region the Near East; laypersons call it the Middle East. It is here, from a great, rich stew of agricultural peoples and cultures, that the idea of dominionism emerges. This region was the "cradle of civilization"—the Western version of it anyway. Here, by the time writing began, a very old, sedentary agrarian society had already fashioned most of the myths that celebrated humanity's ascent to mastery over nature. Dominionism was alive and well—if still a child—long before it was codified by the scribes of Genesis.

Secular Dominionism

But our dominionist culture does not come solely from sacred texts and religious leaders; it comes from secular influences as well. In Egypt, Persia, Greece, Rome, and other settled, wealthy, agricultural civilizations, philosophers and poets furthered the world outlook into which they were born, which was that nature, the living world, existed for humanity, and humanity should rule over it. These classical writers carried out the same role as their brothers, the scribes of the sacred texts; both merely elaborated on the prevailing nature-dominating worldview that was already very old in their day. Like the Bible and other sacred texts, these classical writings have great authority in Western culture and they are still seen as sources of, and bases for, the rules governing how people should live. As with Genesis, however, the dominionist outlook was well entrenched long before it was "'author-ized' by classical thinkers.

Aside from biblical writings, the other main source of Western thought about nature is ancient Greece. Classical Greek thought was not monolithic but was broken up into rival schools of thought, with the Platonic and the Pythagorean schools being dominant. Western tradition favors the thought of Plato and his disciple Aristotle over all other Greek thought. Aristotle's works, especially, provided fuel for medieval Christian doctrine as well as that of the Renaissance somewhat later. And Aristotle, of course, was a strong advocate of dominionism. For him, nature was a hierarchy of beings, and man, having superior mental capacities, reigned at the top. In *Politics*, Aristotle wrote: "Plants exist for the sake of animals, and brute beasts, for the sake of man—domestic animals for his use and food, wild ones (or at any rate most of them) for food and other accessories of life, such as clothing and various tools."

And, he says, "since nature makes nothing purposeless or in vain, it is undeniably true that she has made all animals for the sake of man." Elsewhere in his writings, Aristotle says that "all animals must have been made by nature for the sake of men." For Aristotle, this was the natural order of things and it required little argument. Whereas the Bible says that human dominion was granted by God, Aristotle says that it is granted by the laws of nature.

Although prominent Roman writers such as Ovid, Seneca, Porphyry, and Plutarch frequently denounced the killing of animals for food and entertainment, their views did not become dominant in Western thought. Indeed, such views are generally ignored by later students of their writings. In all other respects, however, agrarian Roman culture took human dominion over nature for granted. Cicero's summation of the Roman view is surprisingly modern: "We are absolute master of what the earth produces. We enjoy the mountains and the plains. The rivers are ours. We sow the seeds and plant the trees. We fertilize the earth. We stop, direct, and turn the rivers; in short, by our hands and various operations in this world we endeavor to make it as it were another nature."

The Modern Worldview—an Alloy of Religious and Secular Dominionism

Centuries later, St. Augustine and other Christian thinkers translated, restated, and refined the older dominionist doctrines from Greek and biblical texts and passed them around again in the language of European Catholicism. Their regurgitated dominionism is the one that prevails in most Western religious philosophy right up to the present. The most influential of these was the thirteenth-century Christian writer St. Thomas Aquinas. It goes without saying that Aquinas, a Dominican priest, enthusiastically embraced the biblical version of dominionism. He was just as enthusiastic about the ideas of Aristotle, to whom he referred simply as "the Philosopher." Aquinas, like Francis Bacon and René Descartes to follow, was a key player in the forging of modern Western dominionism, which is a mixture of the ideas of both the agrarian church and state. Aquinas welded together both sacred and secular ancient dominionism to form a harder, heavier new alloy. Its stainless-steel purity has lasted, in the Catholic church at least, over 700 years. The following passage from a modern American Roman Catholic text states Aquinas's views on nature; note how closely the language follows Aristotle: "In the order of nature, the imperfect is for the sake of the perfect, the irrational is to serve the rational. Man, as a rational animal, is permitted to use things below him in this order of nature for his proper needs."

Around 1500, as Europe's Renaissance bloomed and as new continents were "discovered," the idea of humanity's mastery over nature rose to new heights. It became a major guiding idea in the blossoming arts and sciences as Europe emerged from the dens of the Dark Ages and the medieval era, when the church and superstition dominated life. As William Leiss explains, "the domination of nature is regarded as an important part of the modern utopian outlook." The whole direction of science since its birth in the Renaissance has been to master and exploit nature for human benefit. Its direction, according to Leiss, has been set by science-loving "creators of utopias." He notes, quoting biologist Rene Dubos, that "they fostered the view that nature must be studied not so much to be understood as to be mastered and exploited by man." Another biologist writer, Paul B. Sears, noted the same rampant dominionism in the modern era: "From the time of Bacon or, to be quite fair, that of Aristotle, scientists have written of the possibilities of a more perfect human society. Of late there has been an increasing emphasis upon the 'conquest' or 'control' of nature as a means to that end."

A Swaggering, Updated Dominionism for the Industrial Age

Soon after the blooming of the Renaissance, Europe produced two men who, more than any others, breathed a new vigor into the old dominionism inherited from the Greeks and the church. Francis Bacon and René Descartes, whose lives overlapped around 1600, are considered the "fathers" of modern science. Their other main accomplishment was to update dominionism for the scientific, and ultimately the industrial, age. "Bacon's great achievement," Leiss comments, "was to formulate the concept of human mastery over nature much more clearly than had been done previously and to assign it a prominent place among men's [earthly] concerns." Because of Bacon, Leiss says, "the idea was made 'respectable.' " Dominionism, of course, was firmly entrenched in the Judeo-Christian tradition and was already thousands of years old in Bacon's time. But he gave it a new significance. Leiss again: "The precise way in which Bacon reformulated it was crucial, for Christianity's hold on the European consciousness remained strong even as the traditional social basis of organized religion was being eroded by capitalism. Bacon provided the formula whereby the idea of mastery over nature became widely acceptable, a formula which also was easily secularized as the cultural impact of religion gradually diminished."

Bacon's "formula" for popularizing and secularizing dominionism was simple: He linked it, through science, to human desires for health, wealth, and power. For Bacon, the ultimate goal of science was "the relief of man's estate"—that is, making human life easier and better. In his *Novum Organum*, Bacon bragged that "the legitimate goal of science is the endowment of human life with new inventions and riches." According to Lewis Mumford, "indeed the idea of riches and material abundance pervaded his thinking about science." These were rapidly becoming legitimate ends in European society as an increasingly urban and commercial world displaced the medieval emphasis on faith and church. Bacon's ideas succeeded because they paved a moral road for the materialism and obsessions with wealth that were to come with capitalism and the industrial revolution.

Secularist and materialist as Bacon was, he gave up none of the human supremacy and dominionism expressed in Genesis. If anything his human chauvinism was even more swaggering than the Hebrews when he wrote: "Man, if we look for final causes, may be regarded as the centre of the world, insomuch that if man were taken away from the world, the rest would seem to be all astray, without aim or purpose." Such a supremacist view gave humans virtual ownership of nature with a secular kind of right to do anything they pleased with it—as a slaveowner might do with his slaves. Indeed, Bacon had a master-slave model in mind when he wrote: "I am come in very truth leading to you Nature with all her children to bind her to your service and make her your slave."

The Joys, the Rewards of Nature Conquest

In addition, as William Leiss has noted, Bacon reveals feelings about mastery over nature that are passionate, aggressive, and full of machismo. Says Leiss: "The psychological dynamic of mastery over nature is still discernible to some extent in Bacon's language, offering some clues to the network of psychic associations in which the desire for 'power' over nature was enmeshed. The vital legacy of magic and alchemy is revealed in his terminology, which displays strong overtones of aggression (including the sexual aggression connected with the feminine gender of the noun and the use of 'her' as the pronoun): 'hounding,' 'vexing,' and 'subduing' nature." Such feelings indicate a whole new dimension in men's motivation to conquer "mother" nature, one that becomes more and more aggressively the driving force in the modern age.

It would have been bad enough if Bacon had simply renewed the old biblical license permitting humans mastery over nature. But he went a step further: for Bacon, conquering nature was a rewarding, glorious activity. From the religious sources we got the notion that conquering nature is permissible, but from Bacon we got the notion that it is *desirable*. Human ambition makes us want to do it, said Bacon. In pure scientific and philosophical fashion, he identified—and thereby legitimized—three kinds of ambitions or quests for power. The first was personal ambition, or the increase of one's personal power in one's own country. The second was national, or the increase of the power of one's country over others. The third, and most noble, was to enlarge the power and dominion of humanity "over the universe of things." These notions of human ambition and power, of course, played right into the hands of the bustling, warring, expanding Europe from Bacon's day on. "Knowledge is power," he said, which legalized and elevated the vigorous pursuit of both. Pursuit of power, especially power over nature, became an obsession, an end unto itself, in the scientific age. Nature conquerors, like military conquerors, said Lewis Mumford, use "the same ambitions, the same drives, indeed the same neurotic compulsions to sacrifice all the other occasions of life to the displays and demonstrations of power." He noted that this creates special bonds among the "more vulgar" kinds of conquerors—traders, inventors, explorer/conquistadors, and "driving industrialists," who are hell-bent on displacing nature's bounty and joys with things they can profitably sell.

Descartes, the Decapitator

At about the time of Francis Bacon's death, a French philosopher/priest named René Descartes published ideas that further strengthened the case for humanity's conquest of nature. Descartes's major contribution was to completely sever any connection between man and nature and to place an absolute gap between them. More than any other thinker, Descartes detached humanity from the natural world and set it up as the ruling class, aloof from and absolutely unrelated to its underlings. From him we get the thinking that prevails in the modern era—that of a human race so superior to the rest of organic nature that we are distinctly apart from it.

Descartes cut humanity loose from the rest of nature by reclassifying other living beings as insensible, soulless machines. He explained the movement and behavior of animals by arguing that they were "animated" mechanically, like clocks. They are mere machines, like *automata*—the automated toys and dolls of Descartes's era. Under his view, wrote Australian moral philosopher Peter Singer, animals "experience neither pleasure nor pain, nor anything else. Although they may squeal when cut with a knife or writhe in their efforts to escape contact with a hot iron, this does not, Descartes said, mean that they feel pain in these situations. They are governed by the same principles as a clock, and if their actions are more complex than those of a clock, it is because the clock is a machine made by humans, while animals are infinitely more complex machines, made by God."

His beast-machine view of nature put humans, with their intellect and souls, in a very special category. His "explicit aim," wrote Keith Thomas, "had been to make men 'lords and possessors of nature.' It fitted well with his intention that he should have portrayed other species as inert and lacking any spiritual dimension. In doing so he created an absolute break between man and the rest of nature, thus clearing the way very satisfactorily for the uninhibited exercise of human rule." Cartesian thinking paved the way particularly for the emerging science of biology, which required a lot of cutting open and "looking into" sentient, nonhuman animals. In addition, it was the best possible rationalization for the way humans actually treated animals—not only in science, but in agriculture, war, and other endeavors that made use of them. It justified the elevation of humans over nature by licensing them, as Descartes put it, from "any suspicion of crime, however often they may eat or kill animals."

A Renewed License to Kill—and to Exploit

Descartes's decoupling from, and desensitizing of, nature blew away any remains of timidity or remorse a person might have in carrying out the ruthless, often violent, deeds of nature conquest. Exploitation of lower beings didn't hurt *them* and it greatly helped humanity. This boosted Bacon's ideas about the rewards and riches that could come from nature conquest. The ideas of these two men combined to give dominionism plenty of secular justification. Indeed, they made it glorious and a moral imperative as well: nature conquerors were now noble improvers of the human condition. As Lewis Mumford noted, though, they did not foresee that their noble ideas about science and knowledge would be stolen and ruthlessly applied by all kinds of characters to advance their various shades and schemes of self-interest. The two men thought they were advancing the disciplines of science and reason, but in effect, they made them one and the same with the domination of the natural world. In the process. they gave much fuel and fodder to all kinds of expansionist ambitions as Europe "discovered," explored, and colonized the Americas, the Pacific, and the rest of the globe from the sixteenth century on.

"A fascination with nature," wrote William Leiss, "marks the intellectual life of seventeenth-century Europe. In popular tracts and learned tomes nature's praises are sung; the greatest scientists and philosophers vie with *litterateurs* and outright charlatans in estimating the prodigies of which nature is capable. The age is virtually obsessed with the notion that nature possesses 'secrets' of inestimable value, and men insist that new methods of thought are necessary so that the 'hunt' for them may be pressed into nature's hitherto unexplored lairs. Marvels and miracles were said to be locked up there, of such magnitude that once in possession of them men could imitate the operations of the Creator.

"The religious teaching that man completes and perfects the works of creation was reinterpreted along more 'activist' lines. Nature was said to require the superintendence of man in order to function well, and this was understood as meaning a thorough transformation of the natural environment, rather than mere occupation or nomadic passage. This idea was used to justify the conquest and resettlement of so-called backward areas, such as the New World of the Americas, where it was claimed the native populations were not improving sufficiently the regime of nature. The belief that an active relationship between man and nature was one of the crucial elements in human civilization steadily gained momentum. It was a favorite theme throughout the eighteenth century as well. . . ."

A Crusading Ideology

One after another, the movers and shakers in science and industry turned the Baconian/Cartesian creed of aggressive, probing, scientific dominionism into, in the words of Leiss, "a crusading ideology." Progress in the arts and sciences would establish *man*'s dominion over the earth, they thought and wrote. The goal of human society, Leiss wrote quoting Joseph Glanvill (1688), was that "*Nature* being *known*, it may be *master'd, managed,* and *used* in the Services of humane Life." Similar phrases showed up in the writings of nearly all of the big names of Western civilization after Bacon and Descartes. The "conquest of nature" became such a buzzword that it was no longer questioned and was used as a rationale for most everything. After the seventeenth century, says Leiss, "few thinkers have felt the necessity of analyzing 'mastery of nature' as a separate phenomenon. The meaning of that phrase has ossified, so to speak, by virtue of endless repetition within a widely accepted context. . . ."

In short, nature domination became the intellectual bandwagon of the modern age—for its scientists and technocrats and its social reformers and radicals as well. In the nineteenth century, followers of French Socialist philosopher Claude Henri Saint-Simon used it to paint a glowing picture of how the industrial age could transform human society: "The exploitation of man by man has come to its end. . . . The exploitation of the globe, of external nature, becomes henceforth the sole end of man's physical activity. . . ." Karl Marx and Friedrich Engels, for all their revolutionary ideas, also toed the old nature-conquest line. For Marx, the realization of freedom would come from socialist human beings "rationally regulating their material interchange with nature and bringing it under their common control, instead of allowing it to rule them as a blind force." Engels added that under socialism humans would, for the first time, become "true masters of nature, because and insofar as they become masters of their own process of socialization." Other Marxist writers picked up the same theme and elevated it to the ultimate goal of the perfect communist state. In the 1950s the British Marxist Maurice Cornforth, for example, expressed a dominionist, human supremacist outlook at least as absolute as that of Genesis, Aquinas, Bacon, and the rest. In a section entitled, "Man's Mastery of Nature," Cornforth wrote: "It is the mastery of nature, achieved by intelligent work, that distinguishes the human way of life from that of the lower animals. . . . Increasing mastery of nature is, indeed, the essential content of material progress. In mastering natural forces men learn their laws of operation and so make use of those laws for human purposes." In doing so, he said, we "turn them from enemies to servants. . . ." In a Communist society, Cornforth said, "People now go forward without hindrance to know and control the forces of nature, to use them as servants, to remake nature, cooperating with nature to make the world a human world *since humanity is nature's highest product*" (emphasis added).

Dominionism Left and Right

Those who would have turned the world upside down still would have kept humanity at the top, and in control with an iron hand. The left's campaign against slavery and exploitation has stopped well short of humans' relations with the rest of the living world. A stark example is longshoreman/philosopher/union-hero Eric Hoffer, who in the 1960s wrote of his hopes that technological man could completely and finally conquer nature. With working-class honesty and directness, Hoffer echoes Bacon's aggressive machismo as he explains how to achieve paradise on earth: "wipe out the jungles, turn deserts and swamps into arable land, terrace barren mountains, regulate rivers, eradicate all pests, control the weather, and make the whole land mass a fit habitation for man." Hoffer, in other words, would totally destroy nature in order to make the world more comfortable for human beings. The view is so dominionist, alienated, and ruthless that it would have made even Aquinas and Descartes wince.

So deep and basic is the ideology of dominionism that it feeds the entire length of the modern political spectrum. During Ronald Reagan's presidency, his secretary of the interior, James Watt, used his born-again Christian ideology to justify turning over much of America's remaining wilderness areas to the oil, mining, and lumber industries. According to Watt, it was God's Will that human beings dominate nature and take what they needed. Nature was, after all, just a pile of untapped resources. At roughly the same time, technocrat/philosopher Buckminster Fuller was commanding huge fees telling college audiences all about his plans for geodesic domes, space capsules, and other high-tech contraptions that would allow humans perfect isolation from nature's effects. For neo-Cartesian Fuller, nature was negligible, obsolete; a messy, disorderly, unpredictable thing—quite female—to be avoided, controlled, or contained. Another folk-hero of the mid-twentieth century, B. F. Skinner, achieved fame for his most modern of utopias, *Walden Two*. In his book, Skinner's language repeats the dominionist rhetoric of the modern age: "the conquest of nature," "triumph over nature," "scientific conquest of the world," and "the urge to control the forces of nature."

Of course the modern, Baconian breed of dominionism is the guiding ideology of the business world. Its advertising frequently uses nature-conquest themes dressed up in the slick lingo of Madison Avenue. A leading chemical company, for example, follows Bacon when it brags of its efforts to offer us "better living through chemistry." Thus, what is primarily a tireless drive for ever-increasing profit, dividends to shareholders, and corporate power is presented to the public as a noble effort. Other firms are more direct: "We harness the elements of nature for the productive benefit of man," boasts Texasgulf, a manufacturer of "superior quality feed phosphates." In a newspaper editorial, a Colorado academic who bills himself as a "professor of business law and ethics." (a compound oxymoron) pontificates against animal rights protesters: "people are generally seen as made in the image of God . . . it is only people who occupy this exalted status. The things of the earth, including animals, are given by God for the benefit of people. So most religions describe a three-tiered hierarchy: God, people and everything else." The professor goes on with freeze-dried arguments packaged long ago by Aristotle, Aquinas, and Descartes.

Nuclear Dominionism

"The idea of mastery implicit in the Western worldview and the implication of dominion and control through power and knowledge give technology as we know it a malignant life of its own," noted Paul Shepard and Daniel McKinley in their book *The Subversive Science.*

The malignant life of our dominionist-driven technology came to a huge, ugly head in 1945 in an isolated stretch of desert near Alamogordo, New Mexico. The dead, dry flats there had been named Jornada del Muerto (Journey of Death) by the Spanish conquistadors four centuries before. It was the right kind of place to experiment with a wholly new order of death-dealing science and technology. Here a partnership of warriors and scientists (many of them, ironically, winners of the Nobel Peace Prize) put together their superweapon and named it Trinity.

The entire project was heavily shrouded in secrecy. Only a handful of men knew the whole picture, and they, of course, were in no position to back out of it. For those who worked in militarily managed ignorance, the effort was driven by, in the words of one writer, a "shared sense of adventure" out there in the western mountains and desert. The scientific spirit, as Lewis Mumford and others have noted, operates from the same dominionist base as the pioneer spirit. And that spirit was ever-present at Los Alamos and Alamogordo. The wife of one Trinity team member wrote: "I felt akin to the pioneer women accompanying their husbands across uncharted plains westward, alert to dangers, resigned to the fact that they journeyed, for weal or woe, into the Unknown." This pioneer/conqueror mentality pervaded the project from the beginning. When Enrico Fermi successfully controlled a nuclear chain reaction in his graphite "pile" at the University of Chicago on December 2, 1942, a famous physicist present phoned another to give the message: "Jim, you'll be interested to know that the Italian navigator has just landed in the New World." Of course, this may have been coded language, but the choice of metaphor is revealing.

At 5:29:45 A.M. Mountain War Time, Trinity was detonated and man-made nuclear rage began its Journey of Death.

After the "success" at Alamogordo, the race was on to bomb the Japanese into submission. At roughly the same time Trinity exploded in the New Mexico desert that July 16, another bomb, this one named Little Boy, was being loaded aboard the cruiser *Indianapolis* at San Francisco to begin a journey of death to Hiroshima, Japan. Three weeks later, on August 6, an air force bomber released Little Boy over the city and detonated it at an altitude of just under 2,000 feet.

Hiroshima—a Cartesian Laboratory

Army generals in charge chose Hiroshima as the target because it had not been "previously damaged by air raids." The choice was made by Brig. Gen. Leslie R. Groves, who explained: "It was desirable that the first target be of such size that the damage would be confined within it, so that we could more definitely determine the power of the bomb." Part military operation and part scientific experiment to measure the new weapon's killing power, Little Boy was, in those cruel contexts, a huge success: According to John Newhouse, journalist and author of *War and Peace in the Nuclear Age*, "The blast and fire . . . destroyed over 62,000 of the metropolitan area's 90,000 buildings. Roughly 30 percent of the population—an estimated 71,000 people—died that day, and many more died later from injury and radiation."

The bomb's enormous power and heat instantly vaporized many thousands of people. "There are photographs," wrote physician and peace activist Dr. Helen Caldicott, "of shadows of people on pavements in Hiroshima—that is all they left behind them." Thousands of others glanced at the flash and had their eyes melted, according to journalist and Pulitzer Prize–winning novelist John Hersey. In *Hiroshima*, he wrote: "There were about thirty men . . . all in exactly the same nightmarish state: Their faces were wholly burned; their eye sockets were hollow; the fluid from their melted eyes had run down their cheeks. . . . Their mouths were mere swollen, pus-covered wounds which they could not bear to stretch enough to admit the spout of a teapot. . . ."

Three days later, on August 9, the air force dropped a second atomic bomb—named Fat Man for Winston Churchill—on the city of Nagasaki. It, too, was a huge success in scientific/military terms: in a split second it killed 35,000 people and injured 60,000 others. It destroyed 44 percent of Nagasaki. Military leaders had expected more destruction, but bad weather forced the bomb away from its aim point.

These were mere twenty-kiloton bombs—equivalent to 20,000 tons of TNT. The atomic bombs stashed around the world today range in size from one to twenty megatons. A one-megaton bomb produces an explosion with the force of a million tons of TNT.

At what is being heralded as the end of cold war just years ago, the Americans had 11,469 nuclear weapons ready to drop on the Soviet Union—7,855 of which could explode in thirty minutes or less. The Soviet Union had 8,794 strategic bombs ready to drop on America or other countries—8,094 of which could explode in thirty minutes or less. Sixty percent of Americans could have been annihilated with only 300 one-megaton bombs. Meanwhile, American war plans targeted all 20 major Soviet cities and 80 percent of the 886 cities with populations above 25,000. Sixty warheads were aimed at Moscow alone.

Today, of course, there is no Soviet Union and the cold war is said to be over. Nevertheless, a world nuclear arsenal still exists, and many of the warheads and launch buttons are now in the hands of an array of fractious leaders of feuding nations. Today, the threat of nuclear war has not been reduced, only made more complex and diffuse.

Caldicott cites a study by the Royal Swedish Academy of Sciences published in *Ambio* magazine in 1982 that explored the consequences of an all-out nuclear war among the various nuclear nations. With roughly 50,000 bombs among them, there are more than twice as many bombs in the world as there are appropriate target cities. According to Helen Caldicott, the study determined that "in a global nuclear war, of the 1.3 billion urbanized population in the Northern Hemisphere, 750 million people will be killed instantly from blast alone, and a further 340 million will be seriously injured. Within minutes, the urban population will be reduced to less than one third; more than half of the survivors will be injured."

In 1983, the World Health Organization published a report entitled *Effects of Nuclear War on Health and Health Services* that predicted, for a similar nuclear war scenario, one billion dead and one billion injured. All the world's nations endorsed this report, except for the United States and a few of its close allies.

Megadeaths, Mental Illness

Those are just the figures for the bombs' immediate effects. Then there are the numbers for the slow, painful deaths and destruction to follow. After a full-scale nuclear war, experts estimate that up to 90 percent of Americans could be dead within thirty days. Similar devastation would reach continental Europe and other regions.

Of course, the experts say that the terrible potential of these weapons guarantees that they will never be used. Such is the logic of the nuclear age. No one in their right mind, they say, would ever launch these things. *No one in their right mind.* The thought is haunting.

The nuclear age and its world-spanning arsenals of death are the ultimate expression of dominionism. The long, cancerous growth of our human supremacist, nature-conquering ethos—from Genesis to Aristotle to Descartes—culminates with it, and we find ourselves right up against a horribly fatal wall of our own making. Locked exclusively into human concerns and disconnected from the rest of the living world, we have become so blind that we run upon our own swords.

Just imagine our cosmic mistake: So obsessed with conquering nature, we have finally built the tools to destroy it and ourselves. Here we are, fully equipped to wipe out a living world millions of years in the making, all because of fifty years of cold war quarreling over how to divide up the bread and potatoes.

Whether or not any of the 50,000 nuclear bombs are ever used, the insanity of it all is still overwhelming. That they were even conceived and built is a mark of the insanity of dominionism.

Environmental Dominionism

We can take some comfort in the fact that the devastation of a nuclear war has not yet happened. It is a shocking kind of destruction to think about, but it is still only a potential—a dangerous potential. Destruction of the living world through normal, day-to-day human activities, on the other hand, is well under way. It is not the dramatic, sudden kind of killing and destruction as that of an all-out nuclear war, but it is killing and destroying slowly, silently, insidiously.

It is killing mostly nonhuman life, but more and more it is killing human beings as well. It is occurring simply because we are overrunning the planet with our numbers and our consumer demands. We are destroying nonhuman beings and their habitat in a futile effort to produce more to feed and supply human life. We are turning prairies, rain forests, and marshes into deserts and wastelands. In taking over more and more of nature for human life, we are, ironically, destroying more and more of the quality of human life. In our exploitation of the living world we find the same irony that I noted above in our struggle for "security" using nuclear weapons: We wrestled nature to get ahead, but in the process we got locked into dominionist thinking with all of its obsessions and habits. Now these are about to ruin the earth that feeds and sustains us.

On the eve of agriculture 10,000 years ago, the global human population ranged, by various estimates, from 5 to 10 million people. By the eve of Christianity, it had increased to about 250 million. It grew slowly but steadily, reaching a billion people with the arrival of the industrial age after 1800. Over the last two centuries, the human population has shot up to about 5.4 billion people worldwide. Experts predict that it should stabilize at between 10 and 12 billion people by the year 2100. A hundred centuries of agriculture have brought nearly a 1,000-fold increase in the human population on the planet.

To make matters worse, our toll on the earth is not just a matter of human numbers. Each person today uses many times more material and energy in a lifetime than did a typical forager before agriculture. Taking into account all the buildings, machines, highways, and other products used, the typical American, for example, probably drains more material and energy from the environment in a week than a Paleolithic forager did in a year. Let's call this use of energy and material *person-demand*, for it gives us a measure of actual human toll on the planet. If we take an average of person-demand in all the nations of the world, from the richest to the poorest, we can get some idea of how much more a human being in the world today uses than one did 10,000 years ago.

Biologists and population experts Anne and Paul Ehrlich have compared person-demand in America to that in the world's poorest nations. The average American has, for example, roughly fifty times the environmental impact of an average Bangladeshi. And, the Ehrlichs say, the American causes seventy times the environmental damage of a Ugandan or Laotian. Yet even poor Bangladeshis, Ugandans, and Laotians use more material and energy than did Paleolithic foragers. By conservative estimates, then, the average American uses probably a hundred times as much material and energy as did a forager before agriculture. Let us strike a mean among rich nations and poor nations, and guesstimate that the average human in today's world has fifty times the person-demand of a Paleolithic forager.

If we apply this factor to current human population numbers, we get a more telling figure for the huge increase in our burden on the planet. Looked at in these terms, the human impact on the planet today is the product of a 1,000-fold increase in numbers, and a 50-fold increase in person-demand.

In other words, the impact on the planet today of *Homo sapiens sapiens* is 50,000 times greater that it was on the eve of agriculture.

Let's express it another way: A human being today uses fifty times more material and energy than did an ancient forager. Thus, with the world human population today at 5.4 billion, we use as much as 270 billion Paleolithic foragers. As far as the living world is concerned, then, there are over a quarter of a trillion of us human foragers.

It will be half a trillion in another century.

How well will people live under these conditions? That is a matter of furious controversy. Many see no problem as they assume that science and technology will keep us well fed, housed, and supplied. They are locked into the millennia-old thinking begun by ancient agriculturists: intensify production to meet growing human needs and numbers.

A Downward Spiral

Many others doubt that this direction can go on indefinitely. The links among population growth, poverty, and environmental degradation are too well documented now. We are seeing what the Worldwatch Institute calls a Downward Spiral. The spiral begins when a growing number of people are forced to make a living on increasingly marginal land, which, in turn, causes deforestation, overgrazing, soil erosion, and an assortment of other problems arising from intensified exploitation. These, in turn, further exacerbate their poverty, ill health, and insecurity, and they often move on and repeat the process elsewhere. Some 1.2 billion people around the world are now living in absolute poverty. It is estimated that about half of these people are trapped in the self-reinforcing process known as the Downward Spiral.

But human beings are not the only victims, and poor people are not the only environmental destroyers. As the juggernaut of human numbers and demands grow, more and more land is exploited. More and more resources are taken, more and more natural habitat is destroyed, and more and more nonhuman life is wiped out. Entire species are disappearing as a direct result of human efforts to intensify exploitation of the planet. There have always been extinctions by natural causes, of course, but the present, human-caused kinds are occurring several hundred times faster. We are causing extinctions faster than nature can supply new species. Some biologists say that we are stopping the evolutionary process. According to biologist Michael Soule: "At best, the planet's macrobiota [larger organisms] is entering a kind of pause, an evolutionary lacuna, caused by the human usurpation of the land surface. For the survivors, the pause will last until the human population declines to a biologically tolerable level —a level at which land appropriated by humans is returned to nature, and extinction rates return to the [paleontological] background level."

What are we doing? In our Baconian drive to use science and technology to "improve mans' estate" we are rapidly destroying our "estate"— that is, the natural world around us. Surely the time has come to reevaluate dominionist thinking. Dominionism may have worked when our numbers and needs were small and the health of nature was great, but it clearly is not working in the present world. To a growing number of people, it looks like a global suicide course with a nonhuman holocaust thrown in for good measure.

Beyond Dominionism

How to undo the dominionist mind-set? The greatest obstacle, in my opinion, is the well-settled perception that it is "'the natural order of things." Recall that this has been the perception for a very long time. Aristotle, the biblical scribes, the Romans, and St. Thomas Aquinas all thought that human dominion over the earth was perfectly well and good. Bacon, Descartes, and others strengthened the view; indeed, they turned it up a few notches by stressing its material rewards and moral imperatives.

So today we have a dominionism that is not only very old, but very aggressive. Given the deteriorating conditions around us, it is likely to grow even more aggressive as its staunchest advocates continue to use it as a means of addressing the human/environmental/social crisis.

It will be necessary, then, to persuade most human beings that the dominionist ethos is not the natural order of things. However old and well settled it may be, it had a beginning; and thus it can have an end.

It will be helpful to know that its beginning was not exactly freely chosen, that many people resisted it, and that many people took other directions. There are many, many other human views of life and the world, so dominionism cannot be "the natural order of things," for if it were, all peoples in all places in all ages would have subscribed to it.

It will be helpful to know how and why dominionism began, to see how it caught on as a way of justifying and furthering efforts to intensify human production. It was just one cultural strategy for coping with growing human numbers, needs, and wants.

In retrospect, and in light of what we know today, there are better strategies.

2

Before Agriculture: A World Alive and Ensouled

Midway through the "Indian Wars" of the nineteenth century, a man named Smohalla of the Sokulk, a small tribe of Nez Percé people of the Columbia River in eastern Washington, began preaching about a return to native spiritual concepts. His message attracted many followers and came to be known as the Dreamer religion. It embraced the idea of the benign Earth mother and rejected white European civilization and its principles. At the time, the U.S. government's strategy for dealing with "the Indian problem" was one of outright cultural genocide. Semi-nomadic people with no sense of property or boundaries in land interfered with the peace and safety of white settlers, so Washington began programs to "civilize" Indian tribes. One plan was to get them to take up farming and other kinds of white people's work. The many native peoples who fought these efforts found a leader in Smohalla. One of his speeches expresses the feeling for, and sense of kinship with, the living earth: "My young men shall never work. Men who work cannot dream; and wisdom comes to us in dreams. You ask me to plow the ground. Shall I take a knife and tear my mother's breast? Then when I die she will not take me to her bosom to rest. You ask me to dig for stone. Shall I dig under her skin for her bones? Then when I die I cannot enter her body to be born again. You ask me to cut grass and make hay and sell it and be rich like white men. But how dare I cut off my mother's hair?"

Although most of North America's native people had well-developed agriculture long before the European invasion, many nevertheless clung to the much older, forager worldview in which God, human beings, and the living world were one and the same.

A World Alive and Full of Souls

Under the very old religions, what I will call the *primal* religions, people of North America and elsewhere felt a union with the living world around them. They never thought of themselves as having a religion in the modern sense of the word; their "religion" was more of an attitude about the world and a way of thinking and living. To them, the world around them was alive and full of souls.

Under the native American point of view, "the world did not consist of inanimate materials to be used and of animals to be butchered and eaten," wrote Ruth Underhill in *Red Man's Religion*. "It was alive, and everything in it could help or harm him." In other words, the entire world was alive and people were *in*, not above, that living fabric. To the native people, everything in the world around them had spirits or powers that had to be dealt with if their lives were to go well. Theirs was a living world, teeming with nonhuman spirits, powers, and souls. What elements were powerful depended on the environment or ecosystem where a people lived. If they were hunter-gatherers, in a barren desert area or in the frozen far north, animals would be the dominant powers in their thought. If they lived in the wide-open plains, animals would be powerful and would bring visions, but the bulk of ceremonial reverence would go to the great expanse of the earth and the sky, to the four directions of the world and the winds that personified them. From this worldview, said Underhill, "The world is full of distributed power so that man lives constantly among potential companions and helpers."

This is not simply a romanticization of Indians by ecologically conscious moderns. Native peoples' strong feeling for the living world and their respect for its spirit powers were well described over a hundred years ago by conservative elitist Francis Parkman in *France and England in North America*: "To the Indian," Parkman wrote, "the material world is sentient and intelligent. Birds, beasts and reptiles have ears for human prayers and are endowed with an influence on human destiny. A mysterious and inexplicable power resides in inanimate things. They, too, can listen to the voice of man, and influence life for evil or for good. Lakes, rivers, and waterfalls are sometimes the dwelling-place of spirits; but more frequently they are themselves living beings, to be propitiated by prayers and offerings. The lake has a soul; and so has the river, and the cataract. Each can hear the words of men, and each can be pleased or offended. In the silence of a forest, the gloom of a deep ravine, resides a living mystery, indefinite, but redoubtable."

Anthropologists call this religious view of the world *animism*, as it endows things in the world—lakes, rivers, and forests, but mainly animals—with souls of their own. As a worldview (or religion), it was, of course, no accident, for primal people lived not merely close to, but *in* and *with* nature. Food and materials came not by working the soil, not by controlling the lives and growth of plants and animals, but by incredibly detailed knowledge about them. They lived with daily reminders of their connections with the living beings around them and with constant awareness of how their taking from their world might affect their lives in it. All of this evolved into a set of beliefs and eventually into tribal religions, which have taken on many forms and variations. What they all have in common, though, is a deep emotional attachment to, and respect for, the living world that made changing or controlling it unthinkable.

For many years, this old way of living has been called hunting-gathering, but as we shall see, hunting has been exaggerated. Since the great bulk of the people's diet came from plant foods obtained by gathering, we should call them gatherer-hunters. A better term, however, and one I will use from here on, is *forager*. For the nearly 45,000 years of *Homo sapiens sapiens'* existence before agriculture began 10,000 years ago, people lived by foraging. Another note on terminology: forager peoples are often identified as "primitive" people or "primitive" societies, whether they lived 20,000 years ago or whether they live today in what is left of the wildernesses of Africa, South America, and Australia. The latter are often called "contemporary" primitive societies. The problem is that "primitive" has become a derogatory and emotionally loaded word. In modern use, it implies backward ways, underdevelopment, and, perhaps, stupidity and incompetence. I prefer to use the word *primal* to describe the lifeways of our ancestors before some took up agriculture 10,000 years ago. We can refer to them as primal peoples or societies, and we can say that they were foragers rather than farmers.

The Basic Human Lifeway

Many now agree with George B. Leonard, author of *The Transformation*, that the transition from forager to farmer was "'the seed of alienation between humankind and nature from which has grown pollution, defoliation, jungle busting and potential nuclear disaster." That transition began a mere 10,000 years ago, and I say "mere" because we have been foragers over the millions of years of our evolution since we parted ways with the other apes. Some say this "divergence" occurred about 15 million years ago. Others think it might have been as recently as 4 to 8 million years ago. To ease calculations, let us strike near the mean and assume that divergence occurred 10 million years ago. The ratio of the age of forager society to that of agricultural society, then, is 1,000 to one. If all of hominid existence is pressed into one calendar year, we have been foragers until the last eight hours and forty-five minutes. In this relatively brief span of human existence, then, we have put together a way of living with the rest of the world that stands in sharp contrast to the ways of living described by Smohalla. For most of the "year" of human evolution, we had good feelings and dealings with both animate and inanimate nature. Then suddenly, in the words of our agri-cultural God, "The fear of [human beings] and the dread of you shall be upon every beast of the earth, and upon every fowl of the air, upon all that moveth upon the earth. . . ."

Actually, the transition from foraging to farming did not occur suddenly in our modern, made-for-television sense of time. It took thousands of years—probably about 4,000 years, but that is rather sudden in the grander scale of evolutionary time. In any event, if we want to understand what was lost in the transition, we ought to look at the very old, primal human lifeways. They are not things of the past; they are the great base of human existence. If we try to understand them and to know the feelings for the world that went with them, we will be better able to understand how our culture took the turns that it did when we took up farming. In fact, we may discover that our primal ways are not at all "finished," that they are dormant and long-suppressed but not dead by any means.

Foragers with Tools

Anthropologists believe that our hominid ancestors branched off from the other apes around 10 million years ago, give or take a few million years. In those days, our ancestors, the proto-people, lived on fruit and seeds in the forests of eastern Africa. When the forests shrank, they took to grassy, brushy lands called savannahs where they foraged for just about everything edible. They learned to use sticks and stones to crack nuts, cut seed pods, and dig for roots. Some have argued that they were "killer apes" and lived primarily by killing and eating large animals. Others, more recently, believe that much of the flesh in their diets came from scavenging carcasses from the kills of predators until about 20,000 years ago, when true, planned hunting began. (The controversy over the role of hunting in human evolution rages more strongly than ever, so much so that we will look at it separately in a moment.) At any rate, simple tools and natural primate curiosity, intelligence, and adventurousness helped pre- and proto-humans get along in a variety of environments. This gave them mobility over a greater range than most animals. That and a varied, omnivorous diet provided a good package for an animal's survival, for they simultaneously increased its overall food supply and reduced population pressures. If an area became so crowded with prehumans that daily foragings brought back less and less food, small groups of families, called bands, moved on in search of better pickings.

Tool-making abilities gradually improved and took a leap about 2 million years ago when our hominid ancestors learned to create sharp edges and useful shapes in stone. Anthropologists call prehumans *Homo habilis*, or "handy man"—and woman—at this point in evolution. They ranged for thousands of miles up and down the eastern part of Africa and possibly beyond the continent, although that is disputed. They flourished for about 500,000 years, until the first Ice Age flooded their African home range with clouds and cold mists.

Out of Africa, with the Hearth

When the weather warmed again, the handy men and women were gone and a new, improved species of early humans stood in their place. More canny and adventurous, *Homo erectus*, or "erect man," made the first forays out of Africa. During their million years of success, they spread out all around the Mediterranean, into Europe and eastward into India and China. Somewhere along the way, they discovered how to maintain fire and use it for cooking and providing warmth in their shelters. Undoubtedly, it helped them make their way north into the cold regions of Europe and Asia and to survive the winters. Here in caves, modern archaeologists have found the oldest known home fires. The circular firepits containing ashes, charred bones, heat-cracked rocks, and other remains are roughly a million and a half years old. John E. Pfeiffer, author of *The Emergence of Society*, believes that the hearth, the campfire, gave erect people a new kind of life: "It created special settings in thousands of sheltered places throughout the world, circles of warmth and light on the coldest, darkest nights, a longer day for work and play and the sharing of ideas." The fire-building people were about a foot and a half taller than their predecessors, the handy people, twice as heavy and equipped with a brain about four times bigger—a brain size very nearly that of humans today. The erect people were also considerably more human—very nearly like the Neanderthal people who emerged as the first true *Homo sapiens* ("wise people") about 300,000 years ago.

With fire and their greater tool kits of wood, fiber, and stone, the erect people were equipped to rove and spread their numbers about—even in harsh, unfamiliar environments. Their survival success was not simply a matter of tools and fire, however, for they had the advantages of some social equipment as well. There was some advantage in moving in tightly knit groups where ingenuity, tool craft, and other skills and abilities could be pooled. And, of course, there was safety and strength in numbers. Since they were hominid primates, they already had this kind of group bonding in their extended families and kin groups. It enabled the related families of a band to pass on their tools, food-collection tricks, and other knowledge from one generation to the next. In this way, the band built up its stores of information and equipment for successful living in its world—a world becoming increasingly complex as these proto-humans began to move great distances, across ecosystems, and into regions with unfamiliar climates and changing seasons. Generation after generation, their collective knowledge grew; slowly, tradition grew. Over time, some of these erect people came to have well-developed tools, plans, and traditions.

They came, in other words, to have culture, which is to say they came to be *human* beings. Their brain had evolved into an organ with new layers of tissue, new nerve centers, and new capacities that permitted elaborate speech, rich memory, thinking in symbols, foresight, and other mental processes more complex than any other animal's.

A Mind for Dreaming, Storytelling, and Art

Once it became capable of thought, imagination, and rich expression, the budding human mind beheld the world around it and was fascinated. Eyes and ears received almost constant sensation, which, channeled to the mindful brain, produced constant wondering, thinking, and imagining. The world out there was full of things to behold, to watch, to listen to, to tell about. These things would appear in dreams now that the new human brain was capable, even in sleep, of a greater kind of consciousness. And these things would take on names, now that the brain was capable of speech. All the watching, listening, dreaming, naming, and storytelling made the world of our first fully human ancestors all the more mysterious, all the more powerful. Being human, their minds needed to describe, explain, and understand this world. Mythologist Joseph Campbell called this stage of human evolution "the awakening of awe" and anthropologists see it as the beginning of human culture. It was also the birthstage of myth—our attempts to understand the world through stories and religions.

The awakening of awe occurred, according to experts, when the human mind became conscious of death. I think it is likely, however, that the budding human mind was first awed by the *life* in the world, especially the movement and habits of the other animals around it. Of all the things in the environment, only these moved about, and, like humans, they had eyes, ears, blood, and entrails. They copulated, defecated, urinated, and bore young—all activities well known to human beings of the time, which would make them all the more wonderful and mysterious, that is to say, subjects of awe.

With the emergence of these early *Homo sapiens*, then, fully human beings with culture—myth, ceremony, and art—began to populate the earth. Although they are sometimes called archaic humans, their brains were as large as ours and they were able to cope with long ice-age winters in northern regions. Not many years ago, anthropologists called them *Homo neanderthalensis*, or Neanderthal people, but now they are considered a forerunner yet a full-fledged member of our species. They have been much maligned as a result of the prejudice and ignorance that prevailed when we discovered their bones and campsites years ago. Because of it, the word *neanderthal* may forever mean a backward, beetle-browed person—an ape-man, a throwback. But like all such stereotypes, this caveman image is out of synch with a people who obviously grieved over their dead and buried them with food and flowers. They, like human beings ever since, wondered about the world and groped for an understanding of its mysteries. From somewhere among them, fully modern human beings emerged about 45,000 years ago. This is our own species, formerly called Cro-Magnon people but now simply modern humans, or *Homo sapiens sapiens* for "wise, wise man." In view of our historical record, the accurate label would be *Homo dominus*, for "god man" or "master people." As for the people named after the Neader valley in

Germany (but who ranged over Europe, Asia, and Africa), some say they did not completely die out, but that some of them merged with the new breed and their genes are with us today.

The Creative Explosion

Picture a corridor beginning in eastern Africa then fanning out to the north toward modern Turkey and to the east toward modern Iran and India. For some 10,000 centuries, this was the main thoroughfare for early humans pouring out of Africa into the rest of the world. Along its length occurred what John E. Pfeiffer calls the "creative explosion" of human culture, an event that began nearly 45,000 years ago and reveals the new, modern breed of humans as quite a different animal. It brings the emergence of art—"a spectacular emergence," Pfeiffer wrote—that reached a peak about 15,000 years ago in the paintings on cave walls in France and Spain. The exploding creativity shown by markedly more varied and sophisticated tools, the sudden appearance of ornaments and fine arts, and larger group sizes indicate greater social complexity, some social organization (government?), and more use of symbols. Pfeiffer and others believe that the creative explosion also brought a great leap in the evolution of language. The new human beings were well equipped for a highly mobile life-style of foraging and exploring new environments. They had the intelligence and an ever-growing body of skills and traditions to deal with changing seasons, climates, and environments. They had brains and ability enough to flourish, and then some. With their "surplus" mind, the new, modern humans could create art, myths, and a great range of practical inventions.

In the Living World

Alienated as we are from the natural world, our modern minds are too maimed to fully grasp how thoroughly this new, improved human mind was fed by its environment—particularly by the moving, living beings in it. The emerging cultural human mind literally took its shape and substance, its basic images and ideas, from the plants and animals around it. It came to know which plants out of hundreds made the best foods, medicines, and materials. It came to know the life cycles and day-to-day habits of dozens of kinds of animals intimately enough to be able to predict when and where a hunt might be most successful. It came to know how all of the above might be affected by wind, rain, seasons, and the other elements and forces in nature. From such living the people knew the land, their foraging territory, probably better than any modern ecologist could. They had, after all, generations of wisdom and experience in living in it, and, most of all, a feeling for it that no books nor journal can ever convey.

According to Pfeiffer, forager people "know their land in incredible detail. They know in their mind's eye, without conscious thought, the appearance of several hundred square miles of territory, often flat semi-desert spaces with no markers detectable to strangers. They know their territory so well, so precisely, that they can meet one another at a specified place as reliably as two New Yorkers meeting on the southeast corner of Fifth Avenue and Fifty-seventh street. Their minds contain atlases of maps. For the benefit of inquiring anthropologists they can make maps showing the locations of rivers, streams, lakes, ponds, bays, islands—maps that compare amazingly, feature by feature, with official surveyor's maps."

But mental mapping is only the beginning of what foragers knew. Their lives depended on alertness to and memory of the subtlest signs of living things. In her book *The Harmless People*, Elizabeth Marshall Thomas tells how a !Kung man walked straight to a spot in a barren plain with not a bush or a tree for reference where he pointed to a blade of grass with a tiny thread of vine wrapped around it. He knew that vine from months before when it grew green from the rainy season. Now that it was dry and he was thirsty, he dug at the spot, exposed a juicy root about two feet down, and quenched his thirst.

"The Australian aborigines are capable of similar feats," Pfeiffer wrote. "Richard Gould of the University of Hawaii, who has lived with them for long periods in the Western Desert, estimates that the average hunter knows the locations of more than 400 places with water. The list included perhaps half a dozen 'native wells' or permanent water holes, a larger number of water holes which may be used for limited periods and are dry the rest of the year, and a great many more obscure sources such as pools hidden in rock clefts and rainwater trapped in the crotches of trees."

Forager Health and Diet

Our "civilized" agricultural society holds many prejudices about forager peoples, but none more inaccurate, none more pervasive than the belief that their lives were full of starvation, hardship,and deprivation. This prejudice gets a hard going over by Mark Nathan Cohen in his book *Health and the Rise of Civilization*. "In the popular mind," he says, "to be primitive is to be poor, ill, and malnourished." In the course of our history we have assumed, says Cohen, "that the human work load became lighter, our nutrition better, our diseases fewer as civilization emerged."

In fact, it appears that ancient primal people enjoyed relatively high standards of living. Archaeological evidence from what scientists call the upper Paleolithic period—from about 30,000 years ago to 10,000 years ago—indicate that they had good diets and health. Skeletal remains provide some clues. Using such indicators as average height, number of teeth missing, and age at the time of death, archaeologists can assess human health over the centuries. They have found that only in recent times have people enjoyed the state of health that our Paleolithic ancestors did 30,000 years ago. In *Cannibals and Kings*, anthropologist Marvin Harris estimates the average human lifespan during the Upper Paleolithic at 28.7 years for females and 33.3 years for males. Looking at contemporary forager people, studies of !Kung women showed life expectancy at birth to be 32.5 years, a lifespan that compares favorably with that of people in many modern developing nations in Africa and Asia today. Bear in mind that the life expectancy at birth for nonwhite males in the United States did not reach 32.5 years until around 1900.

Among the most studied of contemporary forager peoples are the !Kung San or "Bushmen" of southern Africa because it is believed that their foraging practices tell us something about ancient lifeways. Studies of their diets show not only how well they ate but also that "hunters" is an inappropriate label for them. Cohen cites the pioneering studies of the !Kung economy by Richard Lee of the University of Toronto, who found that wild vegetable foods made up roughly 75 to 80 percent of the food consumed, and hunted meat made up the rest. Lee noted that the !Kung diet was highly varied and surprisingly selective from a large range of edible plants and animals. While we might not enjoy some of their dietary choices, it became obvious from Lee's work that the San people were by no means starving, primitive foragers who would eat anything.

Lee concluded that the !Kung people were reasonably well nourished. The nutritional quality of their vegetable foods compared well to all but the most nutritious of modern domestic foods. Mongongo nuts, a staple of the !Kung diet, rank with peanuts and soybeans in quality of protein, vitamins, and minerals. Some of their vegetable foods are known to be rich sources of vitamins. Lee found that the !Kung consumed 93 grams of protein per person per day, of which 34 grams came from animal sources. This puts them well within recommended daily allowances and well above Third World averages. Similarly, Lee calculated that the !Kung diet exceeded recommended dietary standards for all minerals and vitamins. Finally, at 2,140 kilocalories per person per day, the !Kung diet was a low-calorie one by our standards but average by Third World standards and adequate for people of small stature and moderate work load.

The Primal Life-style: Short Workdays

Now let us take a hard look at the popular belief that forager peoples spent all their time searching and struggling for food. Richard Lee also kept a record of how much time the modern !Kung spent foraging for food. Although they live at the edge of the Kalahari desert (a region much less lush than that of France during the Upper Paleolithic period), each adult needed less than three hours a day to provide a diet balanced in proteins and other essential nutrients. Lee found also that in a day of foraging, women gathered enough food to feed their families for three days and then spent the rest of their time resting, entertaining visitors, doing embroidery, or visiting other camps.

From this and the knowledge that gathering by women provided 75 to 80 percent of the !Kung's food, we can suppose that !Kung men generally had very light days. Evidence from other contemporary forager peoples suggests more of the same: Nonagricultural human beings, especially men, need to "work" only a few hours a day to make ends meet. No wonder Smohalla and other native Americans of the last century resisted the U.S. government's efforts to "civilize" them to the European way of dawn-to-dusk drudgery on farms.

Complex Primal Societies

Lately, we have learned that not all foraging lifeways were as simple and low key as the !Kung model. Anthropologists are rapidly discovering what they call "complexity" in human societies that existed long before agriculture began 10,000 years ago. In 1988, the *New York Times* reported that a "flood of new insights" has come in a rush and made Stone-Age complexity "one of the hottest topics in archaeology." Scientists are finding that for several thousand years before agriculture began, forager peoples had trade, elaborate implements, beads and ornaments, and settled communities with complex social organizations. They have found in Europe evidence of ornaments produced by assembly-line methods about 32,000 years ago. These were used, apparently, to identify leaders or other individuals or importance. In central Russia, foragers built villages and houses of Mammoth bones—the most available building material on the treeless steppes—some 20,000 years ago. In the Middle East, foragers built rather elaborate villages, buildings, and storage facilities about 13,000 years ago.

These new finds are knocking down old myths about Stone-Age forager peoples. They show that the people had much more cultural diversity and social organization than had been thought. Some people tended to stay in one place. Their settlements became villages with established decision-making hierarchies. They used rituals and other means to regulate social relations and behavior. In addition, Stone-Age foragers developed banking systems to store food surpluses, and apparently some people owned more than others. They traded goods over great distances and they crafted a considerable number and variety of tools and implements. And they still had time to create luxury goods, ceramics, and art.

Life in the Stone Age, apparently, was anything but "short, nasty and brutish," as Thomas Hobbes philosophized in the seventeenth century.

Primal Band on the Run

But we are getting ahead of ourselves. However exciting these new studies, such *complex* ancient forager societies are the exceptions to the rule because few ancient bands and tribes lived around a constant, rich supply of plants or animals. Most of the planet's surface did not offer such natural pantries. In general, foods from the wild were sparsely distributed and so were the people who foraged for them. Bear in mind, too, that they had no means of transportation other than their feet and that even with nets and baskets they could carry very little over distances. To get around to the food, then, the elementary human community—the band—had to stay small and mobile. Band size was as small as a dozen individuals in an extended family. Around the world, though, according to Pfeiffer, "it tends to hover around the 'magic number' of twenty-five."

Most of the bands observed by anthropologists in recent times moved their camps every few days or weeks, depending on the season. How often they moved seemed to be determined by both depletion and by their desire for new foods. Here, present-day biases toward our homes, neighborhoods, and sedentary life-styles click in again and give us a negative view of a forager nomadism. We think: "Poor folks! Always running and searching for something to eat." But interviews with contemporary foragers indicate that they love their mobility and cannot even think of living in one place all the time. We can assume that ancient foragers felt the same way, for when agriculture became "available," most did not rush to adopt it. Indeed, well into historic times forager people always resisted efforts to agriculturalize them.

In primal times again, people's mobility did more than keep up the supply of food. It added to their knowledge of their environment, which added to their security against enemies. Frequent moves stimulated and entertained, relieving the monotony and tensions of the camp. It also spread refuse and filth about so that they did not build up and become reservoirs for disease. Most importantly, though, mobility and ease in obtaining wild foods served to relieve conflicts both within and between bands. If a band got so large that disputes became frequent, it broke up and the factions went their separate ways. If two bands locked horns over a foraging ground, one could move on. In either event, the forager people knew so much about their world that moving on was no problem.

Foragers' Food Maps

The ease with which foragers gathered food is unbelievable to most urban moderns, who know of only one source of foodstuffs—the supermarket. Most of us know trees and plants only from a city park, and we are probably oblivious to which ones bear fruit or nuts. In our nature-alienated environmental ignorance, we can't imagine a band of twenty-five people being able to feed itself while wandering across the land.

For one thing, forager bands did not aimlessly wander about looking for food. They knew where the groves of nut trees stood, and they knew when the nuts ripened. If they were exploring an unfamiliar territory, they knew where the nut trees would be most likely to grow. I know this much from my own meager "forager" background—a childhood on a farm in the Missouri Ozarks. Every spring, when the gooseberries were ripe, grandmother, aunt, mother, and children took to the woods and fields carrying buckets. We knew the locations of our gooseberry bushes, for we had picked them clean for years before. We knew them as a city dweller knows where to find the local diner or convenience store. Gooseberries could usually be found at the edge of any stand of woods, where they grew low out into the clearing as if a landscaper had planted them to soften the lines of the tree trunks.

Then, around the fourth of July, the blackberries were ready for picking. And every fall we rounded up a few bags of walnuts and a bowl or two of hazelnuts. Some of the rarer and more special fruits, like wild pear or crabapple, came from trees more carefully mapped, and once one was found its placement by direction and nearby landmarks was locked into memory. With every change in the season came time to pick another kind of fruit, nut, or berry.

From memory—a collective mental map of our land and the surrounding countryside—the Mason family knew the locations of about two dozen kinds of wild plant foods. We did not have to hunt for them; we knew their ripening seasons, and we knew exactly where they lived. And we were not even real foragers. We learned our nut trees and berry bushes in a matter of years, within a single generation. Certainly, then, the real foragers who preceded us on that land centuries ago must have known ten or a hundred times as much as we did about what was edible, when it was edible, and where it could be found. They, after all, lived in the region many more generations than we did, which gave them much more collective experience and many more mental maps than we had. And although they covered a much greater expanse of land than we did, they surely knew about berry bushes at the edge of the woods, about walnut trees on a north slope. Primal peoples knew well the edible parts of their environment—so well that they did not even bother to gather in quantities and store the surplus for a "rainy day." To their way of thinking, nature stored it for them and it was out there waiting for them whenever they were hungry.

The New, Greater Human Mind Sees the Living World

Let us go back now and consider for a moment what was likely to have been happening in the minds of our distant ancestors—the new breed of modern humans—as they foraged in their environments some 40,000 years ago. We know that they had extensive, detailed knowledge of the plants and animals and other natural elements around them. After all, they did not just drop out of the sky one day and ignorantly start to poke about for food and shelter. Even though they were what we have been calling a "new breed," they were nevertheless an extension, an evolution of the longer, older line of hominid living. They evolved into a new breed all right, but with hundreds of thousands of years of forager experience and tradition. Very much of this food-foraging culture was already there when they came to have their new, improved brains with their capacities for wondering, dreaming, and speech. They had, as we have seen, brains to spare and lots of "time off." Probably much of this new, "surplus" mind ran to frequent thoughts, dreams, and speech about the amazing living world so close at hand, Well-equipped mentally, they wondered, dreamed, spoke, and sang about the many forms of plant life, about their changes through the seasons, their eternal silence, their inscrutable motionlessness. For a people so highly sensitive to the forms and the forces of living things in the world about them, the plant world must have seemed very mysterious indeed.

The animal world, on the other hand, offered sounds, movement, body shapes, and behavior that were strikingly similar to that of human beings. The bear or the ape stood on its hind legs and lifted morsels to its mouth with "hands." Bison, elk, wolves, beavers, and many other animals called to each other and foraged, moved, and lived in groups like people. Much more compelling to the human mind, though, would have been the obvious similarities of sexual acts and bodily functions. We are so very squeamish and silly about these because our dominionist culture works to separate and alienate us from animals and nature. My suggestion here makes us laugh and feel uncomfortable at the thought of animal sex and elimination. Our primal ancestors, however, were intimate with the living world, not alienated and hostile to it. When they stalked a bison herd and watched a bull, penis red and dripping with semen, mount and move his loins against a cow they would surely vividly recall their own sexual experiences. On their daily foraging rounds, they were likely to see animals of one sort or another defecating or urinating—acts that are daily human experiences as well.

Because these and other aspects of animals' existence were so very much like their own, primal people regarded them not as inferior beings, as we now do, but as other kinds of people with villages and languages of their own. Under the current dominionist mind-set, their straightforward, unadulterated, very primal view of animals is virtually impossible to accept or to understand because our emotional loading about animals is so very much different today.

Awe of the Animal Powers

At the same time, animals intrigued human beings with their size, speed, strength, habits, and other features. They were believed to have powers that humans did not have. For primal humans—especially those with the suddenly flowering mind, consciousness and culture of modern *Homo sapiens sapiens* about 45,000 years ago—the animals in their foraging lands were the most impressive, the most fascinating living beings in the world. Measured in terms of the amount of human wonder they caused, animals were the most wonderful things out there in the world. We see, for example, that the earliest known human art, painted nearly 20,000 years ago on cave walls in France, consists largely of animal figures. In his groundbreaking book *Thinking Animals*, biologist Paul Shepard notes that in these static images, the animals manifest "that invisible otherness." The animals are very much like us, yet different, and this puzzled primal people and goaded questions, such as: Who are they? Who are we? Shepard notes, by the way, that these caves were the first "churches" or temples—that is, places of mystery where people celebrated powers greater than themselves.

It would be wrong to think, however, that primal people *worshiped* these powers in the same sense and manner that we now go to church, praying and bowing to the mighty man-shaped agricultural God. As we shall see in more detail in Chapter 4, modern "worship" is based on the model of the early agrarian nation-state wherein the lowly vassal pledged loyalty and patriotic devotion to his or her all-powerful king. It is a dependent and paternalistic relationship in which the king is a super-father, presumably loving and protective, but often angry and vengeful. In contrast, the primal relationship with the powers of the living world was more of a partnership in which the human beings had *inter*actions and a strong sense of *inter*dependence with them.

Woman the Gatherer

We have been taught that ours has always been a "man's world," that fierce males have always hunted, brought in the food, and in general, ran things. In cartoons and comic books, early humans are usually depicted as big-game-hunting "cavemen" who carry either a club or a hunk of meat in one hand and drag a woman or two by the hair with the other. This false view, like so many other speculations about primal human society, is a prime example of how we tend to imagine the past by drawing on the present as a model. Like a fungus, our current values and prejudices creep in and stain the picture of human life in earlier times. Even our scholars carry this fungus, and it taints their scientific papers and history books. Not so long ago, virtually all the "finds" in anthropology and archaeology were made by men—often men of means and rank who could finance or finagle their own studies and expeditions. In many cases, their efforts were at least as much upper-class male hobby as they were disciplined science. This "old-boy network" sketched out much of the picture of early humanity that went out to the public in newspapers, popular magazines, and films. This picture has, unfortunately, taken on a life of its own because it has such great popular appeal.

A much different picture emerges now that more scientific tools and methods—and more women—have come to anthropology. Now we are finding that primal humans did not live by male-provided flesh alone. More thorough investigations such as Richard Lee's reveal that plant foods provided the great bulk of the diet—as much as 80 percent in most regions, and that it was gathered largely by women and children. From the earliest stages of human evolution right on up to present-day forager (hunter-gatherer) peoples, females have been the main food providers by a wide margin.

There is a fossil evidence that plant foods provided 80 to 90 percent of the diet of our very early hominid ancestors as they went through the transition from ape to human. The few insects, eggs, lizards, and other animal foods in their diets came from opportunistic finds—that is, picked up in the course of foraging for favorite plant foods. Not yet mighty hunters, they also probably scavenged meat and bones from the carcasses of animals killed by true predators. This was, in all likelihood, where humans acquired their taste for animal flesh. But gathering plants for subsistence was, according to University of California anthropologist Nancy Makepeace Tanner, "an activity far more certain of result than predation on or hunting of animals." She maintains that it was of such basic importance to early hominids' food quest that it is "simply amazing" that there has been so little study of its invention and development. (Tanner is being diplomatic, of course. She says it is *amazing*; I would say it is *telling*.) She adds: "One thing seems clear: Plant gathering was and is an arena in which females exercised their ingenuity and expended their energy."

Woman the Creator

Although the myth of man as the mighty hunter looms large and still hits a lot of chords today, it is slipping as a way of understanding how we branched off from the other apes and evolved toward (some degree of) humanity. Tanner and others say that the better evidence and scientific sense point to plant gathering by females as the "key innovation central to hominid divergence."

How radical this is! Our early ancestors were not flashy, heroic hunters, but mundane, boring leaf- and berry-pickers? It certainly doesn't fit our romantic notions of ourselves.

We have been taught that men made us human when they started killing other animals because they had to develop wits, tools, signals, and cooperation to carry out consistently successful hunts. Many, of course, want to believe this and will continue to believe it. Again, it comfortably fits into prevailing notions. But Tanner and others give excellent reasons for proposing that "gathering plants (and small animals such as insects) by mothers for sharing with their offspring was that key innovation." For one thing, this is the predominant foraging and feeding practice among both our next of kin, the apes, and most of the non-Western, tropical gathering-hunting peoples today. Its universality in time and place suggest that it is the great base of primate/hominid subsistence. For another, the kinds of proteins in our saliva are still those of plant eaters.

Furthermore, Tanner argues: "The innovation that produced more food would be most likely to occur initially among those on whom there was the most nutritional stress. These are women. It is women who bear babies and nurse infants. Above and beyond such physical nutritional stress on females, it was also early women who had the most responsibility for the survival of the next generation. Mothers' sharing of food with offspring—well documented for both chimpanzees and humans—meant that the gathering innovation made the utmost sense. By gathering with tools, early mothers could obtain enough food for themselves and to share with their young, even on the savanna."

By natural selection, then, these innovative, tool-using mothers were more successful in rearing their young, and their young were more likely to learn their ways and pass them on to succeeding generations. As half the children were males, men, too, picked up the innovations and skills with tools. If they were good at food collecting and sharing, they tended to stay with the kin group longer and live longer, which furthered their chances of mating with one of the females. The less proficient males probably became marginal to the group, less likely to reach adulthood and hence less likely to reproduce. Thus, both sexual selection and natural selection worked together to produce the same new breed of tool-using, food-sharing primate/hominid.

It is much later on in evolution before true, planned hunting appears, some now think as recently as 20,000 years ago—well after modern *Homo sapiens sapiens* appeared. Hunting now becomes relevant because this is our cultural as well as biological ancestor. Anthropologists generally agree that primal men tended to range farther from the home camp in pursuit of animals while women and children tended to stay closer in, making shorter forays with their children to gather plant foods and smaller prey. Even so, all evidence indicates that plant food collected, prepared, and shared by women still provided the overwhelming bulk of the diet. The exceptions are found mostly in extreme northern regions where the climate made animal flesh the most available food year-round.

Awe of the Female Powers

Even millennia before agriculture, then, there was this rough division of labor between the sexes. Never think for a moment, though, that the women of these societies were relegated to inferior, submissive roles. Their roles as child bearers, midwives, food gatherers, food preparers, food sharers, healers, shamans, and all-around nurturers contributed to considerable female power and status. In an age when the kin group was everything, females carried on the life of the kin group—via children, food, herbal medicines, and much of the knowledge of the magical powers in the world that could help or hurt her kinfolk. The mother role was central, of course, but it was bolstered by women's embeddedness in the weave of primal lifeways. To be female was to be in continuum with the major mysteries: childbirth, the silent but potent plant world, the fecundity of other animals, and the growth and regeneration of the living world (which we now sterilize and make into an abstraction with the words *nature* or *environment*).

Of all these roles, the procreative was the most compelling in primal times. It gave women a strong sense of personal identity and security as well as power and status within the group. "The female gender identity is automatically defined," wrote University of Pennsylvania anthropologist Peggy Reeves Sanday, ". . . by childbearing and nursing." She adds: "What comes to women naturally and provides them with a set of discernibly female activities comes to men more artificially. Perhaps because women have ways of signaling their womanhood, men must have ways to display their manhood."

Put another way by University of Virginia social anthropologist Henry S. Sharp in his study of northern Canada's Chipewyan people, "to be female is to be power, to be male is to acquire power. Men *may* have power but women *are* power just by being women." In primal society, men's power and status, then, had to come from rituals and planned activities, for they had no natural link to procreation yet.

We must bear in mind that primal people had no way of understanding reproductive and birth cycles. Jacquetta Hawkes and other anthropologists have noted that Australian and other "primitive peoples [do] not understand biologic paternity or accept a necessary connection between sexual intercourse and conception." With nine months separating the act of coitus from the birth event, it is unlikely that primal humans could have connected the two. From hunting, they had intimate and specialized knowledge of the habits of animals for the purpose of locating and following them to make a kill. It is unlikely, however, that they could have maintained contact with one animal or a few specific animals over a long enough period of time to see how copulation is linked to birth. The "discovery" of fatherhood would have to wait until people began to domesticate animals and to live continuously with the same few individual animals or herd over a long period of time.

But before human societies learned about the male role in sex and procreation, however, women "owned" it all and it gave them considerable status in primal societies. Because the birth of a human baby was an intense experience and an important event for the group, women's ability to bear children was impressive, mysterious, and surrounded by beliefs that females had special powers and connections. James Frazer, Margaret Mead, and a number of anthropologists have shown that since primal people did not associate men and coitus with childbirth, "the female was revered as the giver of life." The primal "explanation" of the compelling mystery—the miracle—of childbirth was that women had close connections to the awesome powers of nature. Indeed, people believed that women were *part of* these mysterious forces of nature that could either sustain or destroy, that could either bring forth human life or take it away.

These female powers inspired the other type of first art: the "Venus" figurines or "naked goddesses" of the late Stone Age. They, too, reflect what was most fascinating to the primal mind, what things were seen as the most powerful forces in the world. Whereas the cave paintings depicted the animal powers, these first sculptures depicted the mysteries of the female—pregnancy, childbirth, and fecundity. One such figurine found in a burial site suggests a female role in receiving the dead and the delivering of their souls to rebirth. We do not know exactly how primal people used these figurines. They may have used them as fetishes to aid childbirth, as idol/protectresses of the family hearth, or as sacred objects in ceremonies having to do with the life and fecundity of the kin group. Nevertheless, archaeologists have found them all across Europe and into Asia in sites that date from thousands of years before agriculture begins. They are evidence of an emerging mythology in which the outstanding human powers and their form were female. This mythology flourished until well into the agricultural period when the Naked Goddess came to be called Lady of the Wild Things, Protectress of the Hearth, Consort of the Moonbull, and many other names.

Ancient Hunting, Modern Mythology

We came to be human, the popular story goes, "because for millions upon millions of evolving years we killed for a living." So wrote Robert Ardrey, the best known of the popularizers, in his 1976 best-seller *The Hunting Hypothesis*. From earliest "man," he wrote, "we had to be preadapted to a diet consisting exclusively of meat, and equipped with skills of the chase that could guarantee survival." Ardrey claimed to have "hard evidence . . . from the field and the laboratory" that hunting and carnivory shaped humanity.

Robert Ardrey was not alone in these views. Many men of science have said essentially the same thing. Their books thicken the sections on anthropology and human evolution in most libraries. Typical is *Man and Wildlife*, a 1970 book by Swiss-born Dr. C. A. W. Guggisberg, a "distinguished zoologist and a world authority on conservation," according to the jacket copy. In a chapter entitled "Man the Hunter," Guggisberg sums up all of human evolution (and, by implication, his views of human "nature"): "Man," he said, has been "a predator and a ruthless killer for as long as he has existed." Where scientists usually make careful, guarded statements, Guggisberg states with heavy-handed certainty: "There is no doubt that of all human activities, hunting has to be regarded as by far the most ancient, and out of it grew what was to become our culture and civilization." He said of "Man the Hunter": "His entire existence was based on hunting."

Similar sweeping statements occur in just about any account of human evolution and existence. In his recent five-volume work on world mythology, Joseph Campbell, another great popularizer, wrote: " 'Man,' as Spengler has reminded us, 'is a beast of prey,' or, as is more usually said, 'a hunter.' " The same mythology is regular fare as well in coffee-table-book versions of our evolution. Said one: "It would be hard to exaggerate the importance of predation—or hunting—in the development of man." Apparently it is not hard at all, because everyone from nameless editors to famous writers to eminent scholars does it all the time.

Now and then, hunt-exaggeration goes so far that it becomes a joke. In story, film, and other popular forms, it is stated so crudely that it comes across as tacky propaganda, a parody of itself. I have two recent examples in mind. While I was finishing up my reading for this book, I accepted an invitation from relatives to house-sit their place in the country for two weeks. After full days of total immersion in heavy material, I would unwind on late-night television fare. In a single week, I managed to see two films that would surely break all records for exaggeration of the man-the-mighty-hunter myth. In one, *Missing Link*, the title character was a hairy, male ape-man who seemed to be lost, for he was always alone, frightened, and either running or hiding. I watched most of it and never saw a female or child character. According to the film, early human life boiled down to two activities: Either large, vicious animals were trying to kill Link and eat him, or Link was trying to kill large vicious animals and eat them. The other film, *Primal Man: The Killer Instinct*, gave the same basic picture of our prehistoric ancestors. The "plot" centered around a group of about six ape-men—all males and all very hairy. Again, no females, children, or family kin-group. The ape-man spent most of their time running, hiding, and fighting with each other over meat. Theirs, too, was a dog-eat-dog, kill-or-be-killed world. The film's thrill-a-minute action consisted entirely of killing and meat-eating—either by large, vicious predatory animals or by the six ape-men.

These are cartoonish dramas, of course, but they are drawn from a great body of literature—some academic, some popular. Of the popular works, playwright Robert Ardrey's *The Hunting Hypothesis* and his other books—*African Genesis* (1961), *The Territorial Imperative* (1966), and *The Social Contract*—were the most influential. There were other popularizers, too: Desmond Morris, who wrote *The Naked Ape* (1968) and *The Human Zoo* (1969). Man-the-mighty-hunter mythology was inflated a great deal by a pair of anthropologists, Robin Fox and Lionel Tiger, both of whom wrote books and articles for popular readership. Their book together, *The Imperial Animal* (1972), rivals Ardrey for its macho-hunter view of human existence: "We have been hunters ninety-nine per cent of our existence, and it was in this context that our behavior was selected."

All of these writers drew heavily, in turn, from the works of a group of scientists ranging from Konrad Lorenz and Raymond Dart back to philos-

Ha!

ophers. Oswald Spengler, Thomas Hobbes, and the misinterpreters of Charles Darwin. To be fair to them, they had crude scientific tools and scant evidence from which to draw. How could they trace a true, accurate picture of human evolution? Perhaps they did the best they could under the circumstances, but today their picture of the human past seems ludicrous because it so overdraws the importance of men, hunting, and meat-eating.

another rebuttal point

Biases Behind the Myth

It is true that our primal ancestors learned to improve the tools and techniques of hunting and became successful killers of animals for food. It is not true, as we have seen, that they hunted and ate meat to the exclusion of everything else. In the far northern climates, where plant foods were not available during much of the year, hunting and meat-eating did provide the base of human existence. But these societies are, evolutionary speaking, recent developments—late human adaptations, which makes them virtually irrelevant to understanding ourselves and the course of our evolution from tropical primates.

Neither is it true that we have been mighty hunters throughout that evolution. Some anthropologists now believe that humans probably first took to meat-eating as scavengers, occasionally grabbing a bit of meat and bone left among the remains of animals killed by true predators. That and the occasional killing of rodents, lizards, and other small animals surprised in the course of foraging kept animal flesh in the diet for millions of years. Evidence now suggests that true, planned, coordinated hunting of large animals began only about 20,000 years ago—some 25,000 years after the emergence of modern *Homo sapiens sapiens*.

Why do we cling to this myth? Why do we like to see humanity built on hunting and meat-eating? Why have we made our major cultural hero a predatory male with killer instincts? Why, to put it as simply as possible, have we overplayed hunting so? We ought to probe for causes because we will find out many things about ourselves that we need to understand if we want to come to better terms with each other and with the rest of the living world.

There are layers of causes. First and most obvious is the set of biases carried by scientific investigators. We must bear in mind that although the scientific *method* is value-free, scientists themselves are not. They hold values, or biases, that tend to color the more subjective parts of scientific

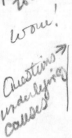

another rebuttal point

humans as scavengers & opportunists not preda- tors

W true!

Questions underlying causes

Bias

investigation, such as choice of subject, design of the investigation, inter-
pretation of data, and statement of conclusions. In the study of human
beings, then, prejudices about sex, race, diet, work, tools, intelligence,
life-style, and many other matters creep in and color the findings of
anthropologists. Some of our picture of the past, then, is merely a distorted imprint of today's prejudices.

Male Bias

Male chauvinism, as we have seen, has long been at work in the field
of anthropology. Male anthropologists have tended to play up male con-
tributions to humanity and to ignore those of the female. Women, they
assumed, were too busy nursing babies and tending the home fires to get
involved in art, technology, and culture. Until recently, for example, male-
dominated anthropology had not bothered to study and catalog the large
numbers of grinding stones that women used. The study of (presumed)
male tools, on the other hand, went to obsessive proportions. Nearly
everything with a sharp edge got identified as an early great hunter's
spearhead. Then thousands of these "spearheads" were classified into
types and subtypes upon subtypes. From this perspective, it looked as if
men were sophisticated tool-makers and -users, while women were all
thumbs. Lately, better analysis has revealed that many of these "spearheads" were actually digging, stripping, and chopping tools—probably
made and used by women.

When they studied contemporary tribal people, male anthropologists
again tended to follow male interests. Reviews of their studies show that
male anthropologists spent more time talking and being with men than
with women. When they studied relations between men and women,
male scientists tended to inject their own notions of power, hierarchy, and
intersexual dynamics. After such biased spadework by male scientists,
male popularizers like Ardrey, Morris, Tiger, and Fox carried the man-as-
hunter myth another step or two. Their speculations and interpretations
came largely from the realm of the subjective—a place where biases can
run unnoticed and unchecked.

Studies of People in Marginal Ecosystems

And there are other biases that have served to elevate the importance
of hunting. Anthropologists T. Douglas Price and James A. Brown argue

that their colleagues have relied too much on studies of today's surviving tribal peoples as models of ancient forager lifeways. This skews the data toward the hunter side of hunter-gatherer. According to Price and Brown, farmers and herders displaced forager societies early on in the temperate regions where plant foods provided the great bulk of the forager diet. The foragers were either wiped out or they migrated into marginal regions—deserts and the extreme north or south—where climate keeps plant food sparse or seasonal.

The !Kung people of southern Africa's Kalahari desert are one case in point. At the end of the Ice Age, their ancestors occupied the fertile grassy plains that stretched across northern Africa, where the Sahara desert now lies. As agriculture spread in waves outward from the Mediterranean and the Nile valley, the !Kung migrated down into southeastern Africa. They moved again after 500 A.D. in response to a rapid expansion of the Bantu people, who had acquired an improved horticulture based on domesticated yams, taro, and bananas brought to Africa by migrating Malayo-Polynesians.

Australia's "aboriginal" peoples are another case in point. At the end of the Ice Age, their homeland stretched from the middle of India eastward into southeast Asia and as far south as Indonesia and nearby islands. As agriculture spread from its centers in southeast Asia, these pre-Australoid forager people moved farther southward to New Guinea and Australia.

If we look at the !Kung or Australia's forager people today, then, we are looking at people who have been pressed into marginal econiches, where hunting often offers more food than plant-gathering. (Even so, as we saw earlier, the !Kung diet is about three fourths plant food; yet anthropologists still refer to them as "hunters of the Kalahari desert"!)

More bias toward hunting occurs because anthropologists tend to study foragers in far northern regions, especially in Canada and Siberia, where hunting is the dominant base of subsistence. The anthropologists have no choice, really, because true forager societies are nearly extinct in more temperate climates. Suppose you are beginning your career and you want to do field studies of some as-yet-unstudied and -unsullied tribe of forager people. Where would you look for them? Not in the continental United States or Europe. Not on tropical islands and shores now lined with cabanas and tourist hotels. You would have to look to the most barren, inaccessible places on earth, where "progress" has not yet destroyed ancient primal ways of life. You would have to go to the frozen extremes of land and ice to the far north, where neither farmers nor tourists wish to go, where foragers live primarily by hunting.

Built into modern ethnography (the study of a particular ethnic group), then, is a search for remote, isolated peoples—that is to say, far northern peoples. This bias shows up in anthropology's "standard cross-cultural sample," which contains 35 forager societies out of 186 societies overall. This sample, or parts of it, has been used in many kinds of comparative studies. The same societies are included in the Ethnographic Atlas and most of them are included in the Human Relations Area Files. These two compendiums are major reference works in the field of anthropology. Very often, when scholars make a statement about "most foragers," they are actually speaking about these thirty-five forager societies. In the standard cross-cultural sample, they are arranged in numerical order by geographic region. Africa has only three forager peoples in the sample; Eurasia, five; the Pacific, two; and South America, four. North America has a whopping twenty-one, most of them Canadian, in the sample. Hunter-oriented foragers, then, are greatly overrepresented in anthropology's basic reference works.

Bias in the Popular Appeal

This skew toward hunting in the basic anthropological materials takes a turn for the worse when popularizers draw from them and put even more spin on them. Male writers, especially, are prone to this. We can see it at work in Joseph Campbell's five-part *Historical Atlas of World Mythology*. In the first two parts especially, Campbell emphasizes the importance of hunting over every other means of subsistence. For him, human life from the end of the Ice Age to the advent of agriculture was one big, long hunt—he calls it "the Paleolithic Great Hunt." For Campbell, the ice receded, the climate warmed, grassy plains spread, animal herds proliferated, and humans lived off them. It is true that tribal people from Europe to the Far East followed the reblooming of plant and animal life as the edge of the glacier crept slowly northward and the tundra turned to plains. Many probably even became specialized hunters—that is, they learned the efficiency of living off a particular species, perhaps a particular herd. But this picture gives us no inkling of the great diversity of human lifeways in the other ecosystems around the globe. We grow up thinking that all culture and humanity sprang from these Euro-Asian Ice Age mastodon hunters.

Much of this bias stems from simple Eurocentric prejudice. Ever since the first "great art" was found in the caves of France depicting bulls, stags,

people, and other figures in scenes that have been interpreted—predictably—as "big-game" hunts, professors and popularizers have put great
emphasis on the caves, the art, the "hunters," and the meaning of it all. As
usual, what is found in Europe is assumed to be representative of the rest
of the world, and European events are assumed to be the prime movers
of life all around the world. Under a steady diet of such assumptions, the
rest of us are trained to think that what happened in Ice Age Europe
happened everywhere else as well.

Biased Interpretations of Fossil Remains

Much of the man-the-mighty-hunter myth is based, literally, on bone
piles. Anthropologists have pointed to "bone beds"—deposits of animal
bones showing signs of human tool use—as proof that primal humans
were skilled hunters. They simply assumed that humans killed the animals, ate the flesh, and left the skeletal remains. Lately, some of these
bone beds are proving to be a house of cards for the case that humans
have long been mighty hunters.

In the past two decades, anthropologists have been taking a fresh look
at fossil remains with new methods of investigation. These *taphonomic*
studies carefully examine all the kinds of processes that can affect a mass
of bones between the time the animal dies and it becomes fossilized. The
elements of this new approach are spelled out in *The Evolution of Human
Hunting*, a collection of symposium papers edited by Matthew H. and
Doris V. Nitecki. These investigators explain the many ways in which
bones are altered and bone beds are formed. For example, the animals
may have died of natural causes and the bones assembled by natural
causes. Floods could have killed the animals and then the current moved
them to narrow stream channels, brushy shores, and other places where
the carcasses piled up. One investigator documented how bone piles
accumulate on the plains of Africa today. She watched predators drag
their kills to the shade of a lone tree, where they could eat and rest out of
the boiling equatorial sun. After years of this activity, skeletal remains
would build up around the tree. Eventually the tree would die and disappear, leaving a mysterious mass of bones on the open plain. Bone beds
also tend to develop near watering holes and other areas where predation
is heavy. Normal predator activity, such as caching (burying) can be a
cause, as can the predator habit of bringing a piece of the kill back to a
den or other resting place. From these naturally caused bone piles, some

future archaeologist might conclude that humans did all the killing in these places.

Even the "working" or altering of bones in the beds can be done by natural agents, like water, sun, and trampling. In the Niteckis' *Evolution*, University of New Mexico anthropologist Lewis Binford takes his colleagues to task for their easy jumps to conclusions about such fossil remains. Everyone points to a bone bed at Torralba, Spain, he says, as evidence that humans were big-game hunters half a million years ago. The site is notable because it contained a great number of "worked" elephant bones. Torralba investigators dismissed natural and accidental forces and concluded that *Homo erectus* was a big-game hunter. Binford points out that "much of the bone from Torralba has been heavily modified by natural agents" and concludes: "Thus most of the early and spectacular claims for unique and provocative actions by hominids using bone tools turn out to be enthusiastic arguments made with little knowledge of patterns in nature. In short, middle-range studies did not anchor such interpretations; instead, 'what else could it be?' arguments warranted romantic views of the Torralba hominids."

There are human tools and other artifacts present at Torralba and many other bone beds. Even this is no proof that humans used those tools to kill the animals. What probably happened, according to paleoanthropologist Erick Trinkaus in the Nitecki book, is that "*Homo erectus* was only one of the agents that collected and processed portions of carcasses" half a million years ago. In other words, erect man and woman got more of their meat from scavenging carcasses than from killing animals, especially large animals. Trinkaus, Binford, and others also believe that early *Homo sapiens* (Neanderthal people) did not hunt, as has been thought. Trinkaus says that they "were preying primarily upon small to medium-sized and/or weak individuals, avoiding large and dangerous prey and scavenging considerable proportions of the animal products in their diets." Organized, planned, *true* big-game hunting, they believe, did not begin until about the time of the last Glacial Maximum, or about 20,000 years ago. This is at least 20,000 years *after* the emergence of modern humans, *Homo sapiens sapiens*.

The Baboon Model

Today's most well-known and widely read popularizer, Joseph Campbell refers again and again to Oswald Spengler, a German historian who wrote earlier in this century. A leading intellectual with great influence, Spengler wrote in *Jahre der Entscheidung* (Years of Decision, 1933) the following: "The human race ranks highly because it belongs to the class of beasts of prey. . . . [Man] lives engaged in aggression, killing, annihilation. He wants to be a master in as much as he exists. . . . Man is a beast of prey. I shall say it again and again. The traders in virtue, the champions of social ethics, are but beasts of prey with their teeth broken." Spengler's views may well be based on the historical record, for it does reveal wall-to-wall warfare and violence; biologically, however, he is wrong. Actually, our species belongs to the class of great apes—chimpanzees and gorillas. We are almost as closely related to the Asian apes, orangutans and gibbons. We are amazingly closely related to chimpanzees, according to Nancy Tanner: "Comparative studies of proteins through amino acid sequencing and immunology show that 'the average human polypeptide (i.e., protein molecule) is more than 99 percent identical to its chimpanzee counterpart.' This molecular similarity indicates common ancestry and divergence so recent that relatively few genetic changes (of the sort that code for the amino acid sequences of proteins) have had a chance to occur. The relatedness of chimpanzees and humans and the time of their divergence can therefore be judged in the same context as for other closely related pairs (horse-donkey; water buffalo–cape buffalo; cat-lion, etc.), all of which are thought to have diverged in Pleistocene or recent times—that is, within the last 2 million years."

Nevertheless, until primatologist Jane Goodall, most experts chose the baboon as the model for our ancestors' behavior. At first, they spent much time studying savanna baboons and baboons in zoos. One reason was that it was much easier for researchers to see the animals' behavior in these settings. Primates, they assumed, were all alike. Another reason given was that our early ancestors faced problems similar to baboons on the savanna—problems such as predators, scattered food sources, and lack of protective cover. More recently, however, most researchers have dropped the baboon model because they realize that these animals are simply too remote from our evolutionary line to provide relevant information about our past. The experts might as well have chosen zebras to see how an animal copes with the savanna. But the baboon model got plenty of play—especially from the popularizers. Robert Ardrey used it, as did Desmond Morris. Baboons provided the evidence they wanted, which was that humans are, by nature, bloodthirsty, aggressive, territorial meat eaters with physically powerful males ruling the roost and controlling the females.

[Margin annotations: "Concession"; "Chimps are our closest relative"; "Why baboons were used (& then dropped) as a model of our behavior & nature adaptation"; "attack on evidence for 'man-the-hunter' myth"]

That, of course, is the key reason why the baboon model was chosen in the first place and why it made the popularizers' books so popular. People, as we know, tend to believe what they want to believe. They especially love myths that make the status quo more comfortable. These myths work best when they are loaded with imagery and metaphors that key into the prevailing culture. This is how slogans like "survival of the fittest" or Tennyson's line about "nature red in tooth and claw" do their dirty work. Similarly, the image of a baboon troupe killing, fighting over flesh and females, and paying homage to a fearless, burly leader fits squarely with popular beliefs about the facts of life. It sells—in more ways than one. It has a built-in broad popularity that practically guarantees the media and entertainment industries huge profits and no political controversy. It pleases everyone and all sectors of society cooperate in passing it on to others, in classrooms, boardrooms, barrooms—even bedrooms. The baboon model, of course, fits hand-in-glove with its major spin-off: the idea that humans are killer apes who have always hunted and eaten flesh. There are other spin-offs: males are dominant, females submissive; warfare and violence are inevitable due to the aggression in our genes; some men are born to rule over others.

A Modern, Secular Religion—Complete with Creation Myth

Funny, isn't it, how these ideas sound like the proclamations of Rush Limbaugh, the ultraconservative talk show host? They are, indeed, the rightist's basic worldview. Unpleasant as it may be for right-wingers to think about, their articles of faith are essentially spin-offs of wrong ideas about baboons.

Wrong or not, they work well in the dog-eat-dog culture of industrial capitalism. As Nancy Tanner says, they "serve to interpret and justify aspects of the Western economic system and some of Western society's particularly chauvinistic, hierarchical, and warlike characteristics." Not only are they popular and handy, but they have the compelling authority of science. They stem, in fact, from Charles Darwin's and Alfred Russell Wallace's theories of evolution—or rather, from politically biased misinterpretations of them. Put together in a package, they make up a political outlook known as Social Darwinism. It is a quasi-scientific attempt to take some of the principles from the theory of evolution and use them to explain and justify social and economic inequities. Social Darwinists especially love the slogan "survival of the fittest," as it is politically useful in explaining how some people have considerably more wealth, power, and social privilege than others. Greed and exploitation, then, become "natural" and guilt-free.

This outlook is, unfortunately, very powerful and deeply woven into modern culture. It has become the major mythology of the industrial capitalist era. In any age people lean on mythologies that give some meaning to their lives and offer guidelines for their behavior in the conflicts and problems at hand. The Social Darwinist beliefs do all of this very well in the modern age. They fit well together. They "add up." They appear to make sense of the world. They confirm what people know and understand. They speak to concerns about good and evil.

In other words, they are a secular religion. Every religion, of course, needs an origin myth—a creation story—that lays down a society's basic world outlook in the form of a story. Because it tells how the society began and how it evolved, it is accepted as "the nature of things" and it serves as a guide for the society's future. I agree with Nancy Tanner, who believes that the baboon model for prehuman society and the man-the-mighty-hunter myth serve as the creation story for the Social Darwinist secular religion. It makes killer apes and male hunters the prime actors, the movers and shakers, in human evolution. Like Adam and Eve, they are the die from which humanity is molded. If aggressive male killer/hunters created all of humanity, then male supremacy, class conflict, competition, warfare, and all the ills of modern life are simply the basic nature of the world. Our task in life, then, is not to try to change things but to get with the program and try to come out on top. Implicit in this worldview, obviously, is the idea that those who come out on top—the fittest to survive—are the best, the chosen who shape the future. This establishes a hierarchy of being: some humans are better than others, and all humans are better than other forms of life.

Meat-Eater Bias

Just above we discussed Nancy Tanner's insight, which I want to re-emphasize because it explains so much: The man-the-mighty-hunter myth is the secular creation story—the Genesis—for the modern worldview. In it, we have a story about our beginnings that helps rationalize the power, violence, male dominance, and exploitation in the present world. Let us extend Tanner's insight a bit farther and deeper. Our idea of "the present world" should not be limited exclusively to human affairs—to the conflicts and hierarchy in relations between nations, races, or sexes. Human power, violence, and exploitation are not limited to interhuman relations but extend well beyond our species to our relations with nature and the living world. Moreover, a worldview, in any society, includes not only relations *among* people but also the relations human beings have with the rest of the world. So, although Tanner perhaps did not intend this, the hunter-creation myth probably helps service and rationalize human action on the rest of the world. I believe it does, particularly with respect to the exploitation of animals for meat. The secular creation myth says that we began as killer apes and evolved into Man, the Mighty Hunter. It says that killing and meat eating made us human, which makes them virtual sacraments in our culture.

Deeply ingrained in our culture, then, are some very strong values that favor killing and consuming animals for food. How could they *not* have affected studies of human diet, food collection, and evolution?

Surely our own culture's meat-eater values have been a factor in the exaggeration of the hunter role in human evolution in the same way that its patriarchal values have been a factor in the exaggeration of the male role in evolution. Indeed, both of these cultural biases worked well together in promoting the man-the-mighty-hunter model of human evolution. Hunting, as men's work, was highly valued by anthropology's mostly male investigators. And since hunting provided meat, it was doubly valued by meat-eating investigators.

The hunter-creation myth also helps a meat-eating society with a very troublesome problem. People, generally, are more than a little uncomfortable with killing animals for food. Most would probably not be willing to kill an animal themselves, except in dire circumstances. Even northern hunting peoples surrounded their hunting and butchering activities with ritual—much of it, as we shall see, to ease anxiety and discomfort. In the modern world, we are distant from these activities but we still have some vague awareness of them. Nevertheless, we don't like to think about them very directly or very often. Not only do we keep our distance from the slaughter, we keep our distance from even thinking about it if we want to stay comfortable and keep our appetites. We use many such habits of thinking to help us deal with the whole unpleasant business of killing animals for meat.

We also maintain some fictions and ideas that make it all easier—for example, Spengler's (and others') idea that "man is a beast of prey." Many of these strongly influence our understanding of the living world and our part in it. Their keystone idea, though, is the hunter-creation myth, for it tells us that hunting for meat is what made us human, which, in turn, raises both hunting and meat-eating to a sacred, mythic status.

Beyond the Biases

If we strip away the biases and the exaggerations that surround hunting and meat-eating, we can see a more accurate picture of our evolution. We see an essentially vegetarian species—like our closest kin, chimpanzees and gorillas. As noted earlier, even if chimpanzees everywhere kill and eat meat with the frequency of the stressed population Jane Goodall observed at her Gombe preserve in Africa, then it is still a very minor fraction of their entire range of chimp food-related behavior. Primatologist Geza Teleki has calculated that meat forms only 1 to 4 percent of the Gombe chimps' diet. Other studies of unprovisioned, untamed, forest chimps revealed no evidence of predation. At Gombe, most of the kills have been other monkeys, especially red colobus monkeys—a pattern more suggestive of social and territorial competition than of true hunting, predation, and food acquisition. Chimp killing followed by meat eating at Gombe may very well be an aberration induced by human presence or some other stress. Nevertheless, it got great play in sensational stories in the *New York Times* and in countless other popular newspapers and magazines. Gombe chimp meat-eating has been thoroughly popularized, perhaps canonized, by Western society. It is only the latest of a series of "proofs," or straws, clutched by an anxious, meat-eating human society to rationalize its habit.

Tellingly, the public and the popular press ignore the case of gorillas. As they are the most powerful and fearsome of our ape cousins, these animals seem to be the perfect heroes for our Rambo society. The problem is, they are strictly plant eaters, which ruins them for big coverage in the *Times* Science section and the other popular media. So far, the public has not wanted a gentle, food-sharing hero no matter how big his arms are.

If we want to see the great base of human evolution and subsistence, the picture is pretty clear: Gorillas are strict vegetarians. Chimpanzees—Gombe or not—forage for and consume plant food by an overwhelming majority. Archaeological evidence shows ancient "hunter"-gatherer, or forager, peoples depended more on plants than animals for food and materials. The same picture emerges from ethnographic studies of contemporary foragers like the !Kung of southern Africa. Only in the far North, far from our evolutionary home, do animals substantially outweigh plants as providers of human subsistence.

Man, the mighty big-game hunter, it seems, is more the creation of male-dominated anthropology and the popular press than the reality of human evolution. Woman, the Generous Gatherer, is a title much more descriptive of the overwhelming bulk of human evolution and subsistence. Now anthropology is finding out that early humans were more scavenger/collectors than hunters and that true hunting, especially of large animals, did not begin until about 20,000 years ago—well into our evolution as modern humans. Let us now look at hunting in this new light and see if we can understand how it might have begun and evolved.

Why Hunt "Big Game"?

Everywhere we look, it seems hunting has been exaggerated—even in the Old Stone Age when men were supposedly stalking and killing huge, hairy mammoths for a living. In his 1962 book *Primitive Social Organization: An Evolutionary Perspective*, anthropologist Elman R. Service reminds us that not all human societies in all regions around the world were big-game hunters during the Stone Age. He points out that they get the most attention from investigators probably because their life-style leaves the most nearly permanent evidence behind—bone beds and stone and bone tools. Hunters, then, leave a stacked deck at archaeological sites.

The hunters themselves may have exaggerated their successes with big-game animals, according to Lawrence Guy Straus (in Nitecki, *Evolution of Human Hunting*). Straus, a student of late Upper Paleolithic hunting in Europe, says many kinds of herd animals flourished on the great plains that expanded as the ice receded. Of these, wild horses and cattle were probably the toughest, most dangerous because of their size, speed, and fighting spirit. Significantly, however, they are the favorite motif of the Paleolithic cave art, Straus says, "not the more banal, safer reindeer and red deer" whose bone piles indicate that they were the most common prey." Another anthropologist, Richard S. MacNeish, renowned for his work in the cultures of early Central America, suggests the same: "These [earliest] people in the so-called 'big-game-hunting stage' or 'mammoth-hunting period' were far from being the great hunters they are supposed to have been. As one of my colleagues said, 'they probably found one mammoth in a lifetime and never got over talking about it.'"

If true, planned and coordinated hunting is more recent than has been supposed, we ought to ask: Why did successful foragers suddenly go to great risk and trouble to stalk and kill large, dangerous animals? Joseph

Campbell and quite a few others say that Ice Age conditions greatly expanded prairies and savannas across the continents of the Northern Hemisphere, which, in turn, gave rise to great, migrating herds of cattle, horses, deer, and other hoofed animals. These herds provided easy opportunities for foragers with basic hunting tools and skills. Many groups probably became specialized hunters—that is, they tended to prey on one or two species much in the same way that the Lakota Sioux and other tribes hunted buffalo on the North American plains centuries ago. Some hunter-forager groups may have followed a specific herd along its migrations throughout the seasons. In this way, a group of people could become highly efficient at meeting their dietary and material needs. The year-round hunting of large herd animals would also have given them greater mobility and range than before. On a plant-based diet, they probably would have stayed in a familiar ecosystem with familiar plant species, moving about with the seasons but never moving very far from the home range. As specialized herd hunters, they could travel as far as the herd ranged, even into unfamiliar ecosystems, and never be far from food and materials. They could also survive in cold climates, where plant food is scarce during much of the year. These opportunities, together with population growth and social competition in the warmer regions, probably drew some forager groups toward more hunting and more movement northward.

Enhancing the Male Powers

This strictly utilitarian view may not, however, tell the whole story. It does not consider what might have been going on in the minds and culture of those fully modern humans some 20,000 years ago. They may not have been such dull pragmatists as the above model suggests. Perhaps some of them "tilted" toward hunting, at least in part, because of cultural values that prevailed at the time. I have in mind two rather large areas of prevailing ideas: ideas about animals and ideas about the sexes. We saw above how these two areas provoked the most fascination, the most awe in ancient human culture. They were the only two subjects of our earliest art—a sure sign of much fascination and wondering.

I am suggesting something touchy, something sure to raise hackles: Men took up hunting, in part, to enhance their own status in the group. We have seen how women's roles in procreation and food provision gave them a sense of embeddedness in the group, which gave them a sense of security and identity that men lacked. These roles, as author and anthropologist Peggy Sanday and others have said, gave females in primal society an automatically defined gender identity and status. Male identity and status, on the other hand, had to be built through some sort of work or activity. While women had natural powers in primal times, men had to contrive theirs. Men, then, must have had some fear and jealousy of the female powers. Jungian psychologist Bruno Bettelheim suggests as much in *Symbolic Wounds*. He says that "the procreational ability of women gave them a relatively more important role" so that "men . . . go far in asserting their superiority." He was writing of patriarchal society, which comes after primal times in the agricultural period, but I believe this very same sexual psychology has its roots in the earlier, forager societies. Male inferiority, Bettelheim says, caused men to compensate through "aggressive manipulation of nature by means of technological inventions." They needed displays of power because "they despaired of being able, by magic manipulation of their genitals, to bear children."

Even anthropologists as conservative and chauvinistic as Robin Fox note this basic gender tension in primal times. In *Encounter with Anthropology*, Fox says: "Women participated in the natural world through childbirth; men stood apart from the natural world, mostly through the hunt and war. Women created life; men destroyed it. A good deal of the male religion involved a careful attempt, through hunt rituals and scalp ceremonies, to restore this balance."

There are many examples of male power balancing. The ritual of the vision quest was largely confined to men. The secrecy of preparations and rituals surrounding the hunt and the total exclusion of women from them created a mystique that empowered men and elevated their prestige within the group. Men probably advanced menstrual taboos as a way of compensating for female power. Menstrual blood was one of the more compelling manifestations of female power and of women's continuum with the mysterious forces of nature. As it symbolized female power, it was a threat to male power and it was feared in hunting societies. Many of them surrounded menstruating women with taboos and avoidances. Menstrual blood itself was especially powerful and feared as harmful to war and hunting expeditions. A hunter or warrior had to be careful to keep his weapons away from menstruating women or their blood. In hunter-forager groups today, men are the main performers in ceremonies and rituals in general. This has puzzled some anthropologists, and some, injecting their own gender biases, have interpreted it as evidence of male dominance. An anecdote shows how wrong they are: An ethnographer of a North American tribe noted the mostly male ceremonies and wondered if the females were being excluded somehow. When she asked a few of the women why they did not participate in tribal ceremonies, they told her: "We don't need to."

Taking the Animals' Powers

In the jargon of psychology, then, primal men had feelings of gender insecurity and lack of status in the group because of their societies' general awe of the female powers. Males needed some means of compensating for the power imbalance. I believe that their primary means of compensation was hunting—especially the hunting of large, powerful animals.

As discussed on page 64, animals impressed primal people with more than their mere physical size, strength, and speed. These mechanical "horsepower" notions are modern. More impressive to the primal mind were animals' perceived supernatural powers. As Joseph Campbell wrote: "Like the sun, the moon, and the stars, animals [were] aspects of the natural order, every species endowed with a power of its own, which [was] manifest in its individuals." Animals were the moving parts of the living world. They fed, bred, and bled like people. They shared the mysteries of birth, life, and death. They gave people a sense of continuum with the cycles, mysteries, and powers of the living world. As Campbell suggests, individual animals embodied this mysterious power. For primal men, then, successfully stalking and killing an animal was an experience with, as well as a dramatic display of, power. This is true even today, apparently, among some contemporary hunting peoples. In *Arctic Dreams*, Barry Lopez tells of Eskimo hunters' encounters with polar bears: ". . . some were deliberately courted, by men on the verge of manhood. These were not simply terrifying moments but moments of awe and apotheosis. These were moments that kept alive within the culture the overarching presence of a being held in fearful esteem. Tôrnârssuk, the Polar Eskimo called him, "the one who gives power."

The hunt, in other words, was not so much about nutrition as it was about acquiring power—the animal's power. Taking the carcass back and eating it with one's family and kinfolk enabled the whole group to share in the taking of the animal's power. Their attitude was probably similar to that of cannibals, who eat the flesh of their enemies and heroes to acquire their power, not their protein.

Hunting and sharing meat, then, gave men many more opportunities to balance women's powers in primal society. By perfecting weapons and stalking techniques, by conducting elaborate prehunt preparations, by surrounding it all in secret ceremonies, initiation rites, and menstrual taboos, men attempted to match the powers that came naturally to women.

Aside from the prestige gained by taking on an animal's power, hunting also gave men some role, and hence some status, as food providers.

Women's foraging provided food more consistently and in greater quantities, but it brought no excitement. The drama surrounding the hunt, more than volume of food produced, created the power and the positive image for male hunters. The excitement, of course, grew out of people's emotional conflicts, which grew out of their views of animals and their powers. Hunting them undoubtedly stirred strong feelings among members of the group. Over time, the group developed rituals to mollify these feelings. These rituals and preparations might go on for days; some were for men only, others involved the whole group. After the ceremonies, the hunters would depart and be gone for days—their very absence creating mystery and wonder in the minds of those who remained behind in the camp. When the hunters returned, especially if they brought the body of a large animal, they provided a thrilling, spectacular climax. This drama and the excitement provided by stories of the hunt must have brought the male hunters much favorable attention from the mundane world of a camp-bound group of people. In this way, male hunting provided a change from the boring, day-to-day routine of gathering roots, shoots, nuts, and the like.

Richard Leakey, son of famed anthropologist Louis and Mary Leakey, observed all of the above firsthand in the !Kung people: ". . . there was almost certainly more excitement about the men's contribution than the women's, even though the plant foods essentially kept everyone alive. There is a mystique about hunting: men pit their wits and skill against another animal, producing the silent tension of stalking, the burst of energy and adrenaline of the chase, and the elation of success at the kill. The challenge of a hunt is overt and visually impressive, the more so the bigger and fiercer the prey. Meanwhile the undoubted cerebral skills in mapping the distribution of plant foods, and knowing which will be ripe when, are much more calm, covert, and apparently unimpressive."

Foragers Deromanticized

Hunting, then, for myriad reasons, dominates our views of forager peoples and of human life before agriculture. Hunt-exaggeration distorts our understanding of human evolution, which, in turn, distorts our understanding of human nature. Equally distorting is our tendency to romanticize forager existence. Forager peoples, we think, are naked, innocent, childlike, and know no crime. The ambivalence is obvious: On the one hand, we are killer apes, beasts of prey; on the other, we are harmless children. We flip-flop from one extreme to the other, depending on what we want to believe at the moment. What goes on here is our struggle with a very old question: Is humanity basically evil, or is it basically good? We have struggled with it in religion, in philosophy, and now, after Darwin and Spencer, we struggle with it in anthropology—the biology of human beings. And anthropology seems no more able to settle it.

It is agreed, however, that forager people were, and still are, no strangers to the forms of violence and social injustice that offend us today. Infanticide, especially of female infants, was rather common. According to Marvin Harris, Paleolithic foragers may have killed as many as half the babies born. Anthropologists have seen a comparable rate of infanticide among forager peoples in Australia. Among far northern hunting peoples where mobility is essential, old people too weak to move or work are expected to "commit suicide" so as not to be a burden on the group. In most cases, infants and elderly were not killed outright, but were left to die of starvation and exposure.

As immoral as these practices seem today, they were well within the worldview and values of forager peoples. For them, population control was essential. If the band or group grew too large, there could be too little to go around, moving could be too difficult, and there could be violent conflicts that might split the group. Over long experience, people chose various ways to regulate their numbers. Women knew herbs and other methods to prevent pregnancy and to induce abortion. Taboos helped space out a woman's pregnancies so that children came three or four years apart. As gatherers who had to move miles each day, they were strongly motivated to spread out their pregnancies and the burdens of nursing infants. As for infanticide and geronticide, primal views of life and death made these less terrible to forager peoples. Just as there was no clear line between humans and animals, there was no clear line between life and death. Under the animistic worldview, says Joseph Campbell, "there is no such thing as absolute death, only a passing of individuals back and forth . . . through a veil or screen of visibility, until—for one reason or another—they dissolve into an undifferentiated ground that is not of death, but of potential life, out of which new individuals appear."

Male chauvinism also marred the generally egalitarian forager society—

especially, according to Marvin Harris, in those where hunting dominated food production. In these societies, male supremacy could be so strong that it aggravated female infanticide and bolstered male hunting cults. As bands grew into tribes and populations grew more dense, these hunter cults and hunt rituals grew into warrior cults and war rituals. Both had in common rituals involving painful initiation rites, mutilation, and desensitization to cruelty and suffering—values that survive in masculine culture today. Hunter societies tended to develop these "strengths" probably as part of preparations for the hunt or for battle.

At any rate, hunters could border on cruelty. As Campbell has noted, they tend to have a "a quality of ferocity" about them that is grounded in their "recognition of the ferocity that is of life itself, which lives on life." In his study of the beginnings of the coastal Inuit, or Eskimo, whaling industry in A.D. 1000, anthropologist Glenn W. Sheehan says that these peoples were not at all the friendly, gracious hosts of modern myth. They were "more likely to attack a stranger than to talk to him." Their society was, like many hunting cultures, warlike, but with methods of warfare designed for "complete annihilation of the foe." Elsewhere in North America, the values and traditions of hunting peoples persisted in tribes that had developed agriculture, complex social organization, and semi-sedentary communities. The otherwise democratic, egalitarian Iroquois peoples, for example, practiced ritual torture and cannibalism of war captives. The Pawnee people tortured a young woman to death each year as part of the ceremonies in tribute to the morning star.

Although torture and sacrifice were infrequent and irregular, they did occur in primal society. According to Marvin Harris, these cruel rituals were part of the ideology of warrior cults that grew out of hunting cults. After a skirmish with a hated enemy, victorious warriors needed some dramatic proof of their bravery. Small raiding parties would bring back a scalp, hand, or other trophy from the enemy. Larger parties would bring a live captive back to the village, where torture became a spectacle so all could relive the violence and glory of the battle. Tribal values on pride and supremacy also exacerbated conflicts with "outsiders" and contributed to these tortures. By the time the captive was brought before the entire community, the people were usually quite worked up from the war ceremonies and days of anxieties over the outcome of the battle. In this atmosphere of hate, fear, and anger, the entire community would simply *feel like* abusing the enemy prisoner. Under ritual torture and killing, according to Harris, the prisoner was "to die a thousand deaths," which, for the community, amounted to killing a thousand enemies.

The Powers Close to Nature

There is no denying that our ancestors had some cruel, violent traditions that are offensive to us today. Romanticizing them away does not help us understand human existence; instead, it removes information and distorts knowledge. But the cruelty and violence in primal society is not the issue here. What is more important for us to understand, because it is more basic to our current problems, is their view of the living world and how it changed as agricultural civilization emerged.

I have tried to explain how people, when they lived *in* nature, held the living world in awe. Although they did not have a word or concept for nature as we do today, they knew it and loved it better than we may ever know. They didn't sit around reflecting on nature in the way Henry David Thoreau or Aldo Leopold did. The living world was not a thing or an abstraction to them. Neither was it a warehouse full of "resources," as we see it today. Nature, the world out there, was alive, full of beings and souls . . . and powers.

From this worldview, other living things, especially animals, were regarded simply as other kinds of beings with lives and spirits of their own. And powers of their own. Sometimes people saw animals as friendly, sometimes not; nevertheless they saw animals as harboring powerful spirits.

In primal culture, the deities—the powerful spirits or the sacred—were *in* and *of* the natural world. They dwelled in it. On occasion, they could take the form of an animal, plant, or other thing in nature. Under this view of the world, then, *things seen as close to nature shared the powers* and were given considerable status and respect. I emphasize this point because we will refer to it again and again as we follow the evolution of society and its changing worldviews. As we have just seen, women especially drew their identity, status, and generally powerful place in primal society from the perception that they were somehow close to the mysteries and powers in nature. Men acquired theirs by mastering ways to take nature's powers—in the form of large, impressive animals. In either case, being seen as close to nature was good and powerful.

3

Animals: The Most Moving Things in the World

Bethsabee, a six-year-old girl, had never spoken, never hugged. An autistic child, she had been in a foster home since birth. She was confined to a room, usually in bed, and was continually drugged. Bethsabee avoided touching or looking at anyone. When someone tried to touch her, she stiffened. She played only with objects—usually blocks—as she babbled unintelligible sounds. Crying was her only sign of feeling.

In her nursery school in Bordeaux, France, Bethsabee's treatment was recorded on film by Dr. Ange Condoret, a veterinarian who pioneered the therapeutic use of animals with disturbed children. One day, Dr. Condoret filmed Bethsabee as she met a dog for the first time in her life. She stiffened, then briefly touched the animal with a block. The child's eyes flickered for an instant, then she withdrew again to her blocks.

On another day, Condoret filmed the girl as a dove was brought into the nursery room. Again, no response. But moments later, something miraculous occurred. The film shows Bethsabee seated before the dove as it suddenly took flight. The moment is described by psychiatrist Aaron Katcher:

"The record of that event on film is one of the most striking human transformations imaginable. Her eyes followed the dove, and her face was illuminated by a smile, the first one anyone had seen from her. Looking at the film and reversing the projector to run through the scene again and again, one is struck with wonder each time the sequence appears. Her face loses the withdrawn, inward, immobile expression of a severely disturbed child, and she becomes an apparently normal girl radiating joy.

The dove was encouraged to repeat its flight, and Bethsabee's gaze again was drawn to it and again she smiled."

Katcher reports that from that moment on, Bethsabee began to come out of her shell. She reached out to touch the bird when it stood still. She began to accept touching from her teacher and her classmates. At times, she would take her teacher's hand and bring it to touch herself. Within months, Bethsabee was joining in games with other children and speaking her first words.

Then there is the case of Michael Williams, who, at eighteen, was nonverbally autistic—that is, he did not use human language. He began therapy sessions with Dr. Betsy Smith of Miami, Florida, who used the Seaquarium's dolphins to reach disturbed children. In Michael's second session with the dolphins, he began making the dolphin clicking sound to get one named Sharkey to play ball with him. From then on, Michael "clicked" with the dolphins during sessions. Whenever he saw a dolphin on television or on a billboard, he would "click" at the image.

Six months after his dolphin therapy project stopped, he was in a drugstore when he erupted into an outburst of clicking. He was "talking" to an inflatable water toy made to look like a dolphin. A year after the project stopped, he went with his classmates to Seaquarium. Michael broke away from the group to find his old friends. When the teacher and others found him, he was standing at a locked gate clicking to the dolphins on the other side.

A year and a half after the project stopped, a television crew captured Michael's reunion with the Seaquarium dolphins. He approached the tanks and started clicking as soon as he heard Sharkey's sounds. For the next three hours, he played and clicked with Sharkey. According to last reports, Michael Williams still clicks with dolphins whenever he sees them.

And there is the case of Donny Tomei, who suffered serious head injuries after being struck by a car. For ten days he lay in a coma at Yale–New Haven Hospital, showing few signs of life. Doctors, friends, and family made repeated efforts to revive him, but he showed no response. Then one day at Donny's bedside, his parents began talking about his dog, Rusty, a six-month-old mixed-breed mutt the family had adopted from the local animal shelter. "He misses you," one said. At once, Donny moved an arm and a leg—his first response since the accident. Encouraged, doctors and family arranged to bring Rusty to the boy's bedside. The moment the dog jumped on his bed, Donny reached out to hug him. As Rusty licked his face, the boy came to—laughing and smiling.

Within moments, Donny spoke his first words in almost two weeks. Within days, his condition improved and he started physical therapy.

Motors of the Mind

What is it about animals that they can "get through" to the most severely impaired children? Why do animals move a human mind unmoved by anything else?

It is because animals are, and always have been throughout our evolution as a species, the most stimulating, fascinating things in the world around us. Today, we don't readily think so. Dulled as we are by the products of high technology and the fast-paced modern life-style they bring, animals have drifted far into the background. Or so we are inclined to think.

We may not have animals consciously on our minds very often today, nevertheless they are wired into some of the basic circuits of our brains. They are still alive, well, and kicking at the deepest levels of our consciousness. They moved Bethsabee, Michael Williams, and Donny Tomei to touch, talk, and feel when nothing else could.

To understand why, we need to recognize that throughout the 10 or so million years of our evolution, we have lived closely amid animals. All the while, they fascinated us, impressed us. Animals moved our minds even as our minds were evolving.

Other things in nature impressed us, too, like dark forests, violent storms, rivers swollen by flood waters. Yet animals impressed us in ways that the rest of nature could not. Animals, like us, move freely; and they are more obviously like people than are trees, rivers, and other things in nature. Animals have eyes, ears, hair, and other organs like us; and they sleep, eat, defecate, copulate, give birth, play, fight, die, and carry on many of the same activities of life that we do. Somewhat similar to us yet somewhat different, animals forced comparisons, categories, and conclusions. Animals made us think. Animals drove and shaped human intelligence.

Because animals shaped our minds as a species, they shape our minds as individuals today. They are so basic to human thought processes that we would probably not be able to learn speech or thought without them.

Unfortunately, too few human beings fully understand this. Biologist Paul Shepard thoroughly explained it in his 1978 book *Thinking Animals: Animals and the Development of Human Intelligence*. "There is a profound, inescapable need for animals that is in all people everywhere," he wrote; as shapers of human mind and thought, there is "no substitute" for them.

This need for animals, Shepard says, "is no vague, romantic, or intangible yearning, no simple sop to our loneliness or nostalgia for Paradise. It is as hard and unavoidable as the compounds of our inner chemistry. It is universal but poorly recognized. It is the peculiar way that animals are used in the growth and development of the human person, in those most priceless qualities which we lump together as 'mind.' It is the role of animal images and forms in the shaping of personality, identity, and social consciousness. Animals are among the first inhabitants of the mind's eye. They are basic to the development of speech and thought. Because of their part in the growth of consciousness, they are inseparable from the series of events in each human life, indispensable to our becoming human in the fullest sense."

Food for Thought

It is important to try to understand just how crucial animals are to our mental development in childhood. Key to the development of intelligence, experts say, is the ability to sort and classify things. As we become aware of the world around us during infancy, we try to understand the confusion, we try to put things in order. We make mental categories of things, and we give them names. Historically (or evolutionarily), Shepard says, humans did this mainly by observing animals moving and doing things. Trees, rocks, mountains, and other objects offered the mind rather simple, straightforward things to categorize and name, but the activities and behavior of animals offered a way of making sense of concepts and intangible things. These were even more important to human culture— that is, the carrying of learning and human experience from one generation to the next. Culture is mainly information about nonobjects, things that cannot be seen, like hunger, patience, courage, selfishness. These invisible things, however, could be observed in animal behavior. Then, of course, the evolving human mind had a field day relating these traits to human experience. As Shepard says, "The different animals not only represented usable images for social categories and sensed experience, but evoked further thought about them. The ecology of the lion produced an ecology of thought. Its anger, hunger, or motherhood bore peripheral messages. These analogical images carried whole trains of connections." Animals, in other words, provoked deeper thoughts about the world, thoughts like "who are they?" and "who are we?" and the other whys and wherefores of existence. Animals were indeed food for thought. They offered a constant moving feast of wonders and puzzles for the mind.

This is why animals are so "good to think," as Claude Levi-Strauss, the pioneer in the science of child development, put it. Because the mind was built from animals, the infant brain still "wants" to sort, categorize, process—understand—the world around it primarily by, in Shepard's words, "reading and thinking animals." Animals still are, as he puts it, "a handle for abstractions." Modern infants, of course, are not exposed to varieties of animals as were primal infants. But their brains and thought processes still need them. The other kinds of things in the modern nursery are not as good in helping an infant "read" the world, Shepard believes. "It is clearly animals, and to a lesser extent our bodies and the things we make, to which we turn in order to give shape to such a haphazard spectacle."

From childhood on, animals give the human mind a frame of reference to the rest of the living world. Yale University's Dr. Stephen Kellert, for example, uses surveys of people's attitudes about animals as indicators of their attitudes about nature and the environment in general. Kellert says that attitudes about animals serve as a sort of "index" to attitudes about the natural world in general.

Nevertheless, animals stand out from the rest of the natural world. We relate to them emotionally in ways that we do not with the inanimate world. Psychiatrist Katcher, among others, notes that human beings have much more feeling and empathy for animals than they do for other things in nature. We know that the average person recoils at the sight of a mangled animal by the side of the road but passes a crushed box or tree limb without any emotional reaction. Katcher believes this is because of the human instincts for nurturing and social bonding, which "spill over" to animals. This spill-over effect is stronger toward animals closest to human size and shape. We tend to have stronger feelings of empathy for dogs, deer, seals, and apes than we do for mice, snakes, birds, and the like.

As movers of the mind, thought, and feeling, animals are very strong stuff to human beings. No wonder our ancestors believed they had souls and powers.

The Power of Animal Images

One of the best indicators of the presence of animals in our minds and culture is their prominence in art. Art historian Lord Kenneth Clark devoted an entire volume to animals in art, as did British sociologist and art historian Francis Klingender. As we mentioned before, animals inspired the first art on the cave walls of Europe and Asia. And there is more behind those paintings than the mere food wishes of foragers. The great bulk of their diet came from plants, yet animals were the main thing on our ancestors' minds. We ought to think about why they were so much more fascinated with deer than with acorns.

In all of art since the cave paintings, Lord Clark has estimated that animals are represented more often than any other class of things in nature. According to estimates by Paul Shepard, animals make up about one tenth of the subject matter of serious art and about one fifth of cartoon strips in newspapers. Animals, as artists are well aware, can be used to convey many kinds of messages—even those words cannot. In religious art, animals are often the major symbols for teachings and moral themes. The dove symbolizes peace, the lamb innocence and Christian compassion. The bestiaries, the moral storybooks of the Middle Ages, relied exclusively on animals in pictures and stories to teach their lessons.

In addition to their symbolic value, animals add drama to art. As any student of painting knows, animals often set the tone of a painting. In bucolic landscapes, it is the cows chewing their cuds and dozing in the shade that convey the utter tranquillity and dreaminess of countryside life. In paintings of battle scenes, it is the twisted bodies of horses with fear in their eyes that shout out the cruelty and violence of war. In his masterpiece *Guernica,* Pablo Picasso used such a figure to convey the horror of the Fascists' surprise bombing raid on a small village during the Spanish civil war. Many of our great works of art would not be nearly so powerful, or so tender, if the animals were removed.

If we turn to commercial art and advertising, animals are equally prominent. There, as totem animals for the corporate tribes of the capitalist world, they stir up images and associations in the public mind that sell products. One company's gas puts a "tiger in your tank"; another's tires are "tough as a rhino." A mighty-antlered stag sells the protection of life insurance; a fluffy, fluttering dove sells soft, gentle soap. A male African lion sells both MGM movies and the Dreyfus Fund's brokerage services. For decades, RCA was best known for its logo of a dog in front of a phonograph listening, with cocked ear, to "his master's voice." The best-selling cars of all time are jaguars, pintos, impalas, falcons, mustangs, skylarks, cougars, sting-rays, barracudas, and beetles. Following its notion of the laws of the jungle, capitalism even names its own mood swings after animal behavior: in a "bull" market, investors come out snorting and charging; in a "bear" market, they hole up and sleep. Though we are jaded, nature-alienated, and numbed by our urban/industrial mess, animals still move our minds and propel our actions in the world.

We see this mover/shaker effect especially in the sports arena. At high schools around the country, ball teams name themselves after tigers, cougars, bears, and other ferocious animals. Some choose an animal mascot for its colors, as, for example, the cardinal or the bluejay. College teams and professional teams tend to choose names that reflect regional or metropolitan character, but in many cases an animal does that best. That is why Florida has its 'Gators, Miami has its Dolphins, and Arkansas has its Razorbacks. Because they stir up so many strong feelings and associations with territory, speed, strength, temperament, and coloration, animals give the sports team a high-powered way to signal their identity and their winning spirit.

We have animals on our minds in more ways and at deeper levels than you might think. Evidence for this shows up in the strangest places. Just glance through the pages of the *National Enquirer, The Globe, The Sun,* and the other supermarket tabloids sometime. Some psychologists see these as a means of reading the great public mass mind. They note that the mass marketing strategy of tabloids requires story themes that pack the strongest and broadest mind-appeal. These boil down to about six or seven surefire themes that get big audiences every time. Animal stories—whether about freaks, cruelty, or heroism—are right up there with celebrity sex gossip, crime, babies, flying saucers, and life after death. Often, combinations of two or more themes multiply the appeal. Some typical covers feature headlines such as: "Amazing Parrot Sings Like Elvis" and "Duck-Billed Baby Found in Hen House" and "Mom Gives Birth to Dog Baby." Animals, motherhood, crime, and babies all combined in "Ape Mom Steals Baby," a story about an orangutan who, bereaved after animal traffickers snatched her baby, took matters into her own hands and stole a human baby from a small village.

The Power of Animal Stories

Language and folklore also depend heavily on animals to convey messages to the human mind. Joseph D. Clark's book *Beastly Folklore* reveals over 5,000 examples of animal-based expressions. He documents our tendency to describe human behavior by comparisons to animals. We say, for example, that a person is "mousey" or "horsey." People "grouse" about things or "badger" someone. There are hundreds upon hundreds of examples. They support the experts' belief that animals moved humans to take language beyond a narrow set of grunts and noises. At any rate, they surely make it lively today. According to Clark, no other set of things in the universe is found so often in speech. This constant animal presence in language, like that in art, tells us much about the importance of animals to the human mind.

Because they play into the "wiring," animal stories and images stimulate; they have kick and clout. Aesop, a Greek slave in the sixth century B.C., was one of the first to use their potency to get moral and political messages across to a wide, popular audience. Francis Klingender explains how Aesop's fables worked: "By evoking childhood memories of animal fairy-tales and, to some extent also, every-day observations, these new symbols could gain a powerful hold on the imagination. When they were used, as in Greece, first as a 'slave-language' for the guarded expression of 'dangerous thoughts' and then for sweetening the pill of moral instruction, they could help to produce a commonsense, matter-of-fact approach to life." So effective were Aesop's fables that Gautama, the Enlightened One, or Buddha, borrowed several of them for his own spiritual teachings. Of his "Birth Stories," or *Jatakas,* more than a hundred are animal fables of the same stock as Aesop's.

In the West, the rise of agrarian culture and its megareligion greatly reduced animals as teachers of morality and spirituality. There, as we shall see, the domestication of animals had a powerful influence on the economy and worldview of emerging agricultural societies. Enslavement drastically altered the age-old status of animals and their place in the world with human beings. The West's agrarian culture, more than any other, subjugated animals and exalted humankind. It required a view of animals that left them little authority to teach morality and spirituality—unless, of course, they were rather obvious stand-ins for human foibles, as in the bestiaries. There they are human characters in animal form. However reduced they are from intrinsically valuable, autonomous beings, they nevertheless carry the code that works best on the developing human mind. Psychically, at least, animals are dynamic, spirited.

This forces Western culture to try to have it both ways: Animals are to be down, inferior, and insignificant, yet they are to be handy, potent, and significant when we need them to enliven the messages in our art, language, and religion. Our dominionist culture denigrates animals, yet our brain/mind needs them as fertilizer. There is a clash here, and we all grow up with it, on it. It probably affects human development in ways we have not yet bothered to try to understand. We try to reconcile this fundamental clash with various mental or cultural tricks. Or we simply put it away somehow, out of mind. But these may not be doing the job adequately. The very fundamentality of the clash makes it one of the biggest, earliest cracks in our psyche. How, it might be helpful to know, does it affect the people and culture of the West?

First Dragons, Now Space Aliens

As if there weren't enough real animals to populate our minds, we create imaginary ones. Folklore and fable are loaded with stories about dragons, griffins, unicorns, chimeras, sea serpents, winged horses, and the like. These provide supercharged villains and heroes and a magical quality to stories that could not be supplied by known animals, however wild and woolly. Against them, the human characters become larger than life. St. George might not have gone down in history if he had slain a mere lion or a bear. Paul Shepard thinks that fabulous fauna dominate these stories because "society needs more forceful images of incongruity in order to make . . . danger clear and to stimulate analytic thought." So we mix up animals' anatomies, we put together claws, fangs, wings, and tails and produce animals that defy classification. As a result, they signify terrible danger, possibly chaos. On a deeper, less conscious level, they puzzle us, they put demands on our categorizing minds and make us wonder all the more.

Shepard may be right, but I lean more toward Stephen Kellert's idea that animals serve as indicators of our broader views of nature. Kellert thinks we use animals to give shape and form to our deeper, vaguer perceptions of the world out there. If we have, say, fears about nature's powers, we tend to express them in the form of fearsome, powerful animals. This was especially so before we had science, public schools, and print and broadcast media to explain everything. When natural events and disasters made nature seem freakish and extremely powerful, the mind turned out freakish and extremely powerful beasts—supernatural beasts.

This may be why the fears created by the nuclear age took the form of monsters from outer space. Significantly, they are now humanoid and their terrible power is not so much physical as it is technological. Space aliens generally have skinny bodies, big heads, and mind-boggling weapons and vehicles. The power they have is beyond comprehension, beyond symbolism in earthly forms. It is out-of-this-world-power, a power from the stars and the megadimensions of the universe. It is the power we fear we have unleashed on ourselves.

The First Inhabitants of the Mind

As adults thoroughly "educated" about the superiority of humans and the lower status of animals, it is difficult for most of us to grasp Paul Shepard's ideas on how vital animals are to the development of human speech and intelligence. We are too used to thinking of animals as important only in the economic sense—for food, materials, work, and, lately, as keys to finding cures for terrible diseases. These utilitarian notions of importance occupy our adult minds and they keep us from understanding the deeper importance animals have to human beings. That is the tragedy and irony of it. We are too impaired by utilitarian culture to be able to fully understand animals' *psychic importance*—that is, their vital role in the making of our minds. If we struggle hard enough, though, perhaps we can get a glimmer of that importance. We must, I think, if we want to get to the bottom of our angst against nature.

If Shepard's ideas seem at first too abstract and incomprehensible, perhaps we need to see some hard examples of what is meant by phrases like "animals are the first inhabitants of the mind," and "animals shape speech and intelligence." We can find plenty of them in the nursery. There, animals are the major furniture in the infant's environment. Early on, there are the teddy bears and assorted stuffed animals, the animal-shaped toys, and the animal figures on cribs, blankets, bassinets, pillows, sheets, and sleepsuits. Then, as the child begins to grapple with speech, animals dominate storybooks, songs, and bedtime stories. Soon the child's first play with others consists largely of "playing animal." At every step of the way, animals are the main other things in the child's world. As the child learns about the world around him or her, animals are the chief informants.

Why is this? Why animals? According to Shepard: "Every child is committed to the use of animal images in the shaping of his [her] own consciousness because thought arose in the past as an interaction between different animals and between people and animals." We need animals to learn to think because human brains and thought processes grew up on animals. As we saw above, the complexity of animals' movement and behavior gave the evolving human mind much more to ponder, much more to think and talk about. "The necessity of animals is psychological," says Shepard. "Its roots are in the history of intelligence." Much of that intelligence has to do with speech, with words for things so that they can be categorized, stored, and recalled. At about two years of age, the human infant begins to demand names for things. Through vocal imitation and repetition, the child "begins a compulsive collecting of kinds that will go on for a decade," Shepard says. "The process has that inexorable quality of the growth of plant tendrils and one can almost feel the neural cells putting out synapses like rows of garden bulbs putting down rootlets that organize the soil spaces beneath them." So the budding mind grows—on seeing things, sorting them, and naming them. At this age, though, imaginary animals are of no interest unless there are pictures. "The lust for seeing the creature," he says, "is as strong as that for naming it."

Imprinting Gives Us a "Full Deck"

But why should we care about what happened back in evolution? Why do we need to understand the relationship between the mind and the external world of animals? Paul Shepard gives a three-part answer: First, he says, what evolved in humans "was not intelligence, but a development process." Genetics sets down the equipment, the brain, nervous system, and so forth, but it does not complete the process. He gives vision as an example: "If a patch is put over the eye of a newborn animal, it fails to develop those final nerve connections in the absence of light and the creature remains blind, even after the patch is removed." Similarly, the human brain needs animal types to help it make the connections that put the mind (and the world) in order. The use of animal types became "part of the process for each individual," Shepard says. "It was incorporated as a necessary ingredient, like light shining on the eye of the newborn. From the standpoint of the developing brain, an assembly, say, of horse-like animals—donkey, tarpans, zebras, asses, and other groups of their odd-toed relatives (the Perissodactyla)—is as essential as blood, stable temperature, moisture, and tissue nutrients in its growth."

Second, in producing the human brain, natural selection did not turn out an organ "that could assimilate an infinitely complex world like a stomach digesting meat." Instead, natural selection produced a linking device, one that takes "advice" on types, categories, and the order of things from the types, categories, and order of things in the living world. "The clever brain employed the existing composition of plants and animals of the ecosystem itself as a master model," Shepard says. "To have done it differently would have involved vastly more information storage of DNA and cumbersome connections and tissues." We don't come into the world with a full deck, in other words; we have to print (or imprint) it ourselves. The price was that the development of the mind and intelligence had to become part of the development of each individual—to be done again and again with each new human life. Fortunately, each new life does not have to start completely from scratch as it is born into a family, a tribe, and a culture. From these, some of the cumulative wisdom about types, groups, names, and the order in the world gets passed on.

Third, this whole setup makes the human animal highly adaptable to variations in environment and culture. If we had been born with brains already loaded with fixed ideas geared to a specific ecosystem, they would have served us only in that ecosystem. When it changed with geologic and climatic events, we would have had no mental equipment to help us migrate or otherwise cope with the change. As it is, we have an organ, the brain, which has the capacity for speech, thought, and the other activities we call *mind* so long as it is properly imprinted or informed by its environment in the developing years. In this way, our minds enabled our ancestors to spread out all over the world and live in greatly varying environments. As lands varied, the "advice" and imprinting varied and consequently human beings produced a great many kinds of cumulative wisdom about the world. These are the great many cultures of the world. To the eye, they appear to differ greatly in their beliefs, rituals, arts, and tools, but these very differences flow from the same source—the spongelike brain/mind that takes its shape and finds its order by sopping up the images, categories, and order in the world immediately around it.

Why Not Trees or Rocks?

Again and again the question arises: Why animals? Why do animals figure so centrally to the process of mind formation? Why isn't the child moved by stuffed plants and figures of trees and rocks? We have answered this in part before, when we saw that animals, particularly the behavior of animals, give the mind a way to "see" invisible things like hunger, patience, and so on. In turn, speech can give these intangibles a name. Animals, more than any other things in nature, give us a way to handle abstractions and concepts. These, in turn, can be very useful in a number of ways in speech and in culture. Shepard gives other reasons why the mind feeds primarily on animals. They are more like us, so the analogies are easier for an infant. He suggests that much of it may have to do with the fact that we, too, are animals and our brain/minds, wonderful as they are, are simply extensions of the brain/minds of animals. Out of raw, biological kinship the human brain/mind prefers animals for the imprinting it needs to develop intelligence and consciousness.

More important, nature apart from animals is, he says, "distressingly continuous and blended." The terrain, the weather, the sky, and the other parts of inanimate nature are so random in shape that they are impossible to classify and sort. These things do not readily lead a developing mind to see types and order in the world. Plants and animals come in species— that is, sets of individuals that are alike. This is what the questioning, budding mind needs in order to "understand" and make order of its environment. But plants are still and silent; they do not demand attention as do lively, noisy animals. Animals play, fight, breed, and do things. They are fascinating to watch. Of all the things in nature, then, animals *stand out* most in ways needed by the developing brain/mind. Animals are strong, active, noisy, colorful characters—all of which makes them most informative. In contrast, the rest of nature is background—relatively amorphous, still, inscrutable, and not much help to the budding brain/mind, whether that of the species or the individual.

Animals Embedded

If it is still hard to see this, perhaps some examples will help. In *Thinking Animals,* Shepard tells about "concealed creatures" and "embedded figures." These are more evidence that animals are, to use computer-speak, wired into our minds. All animals, he says, are moved by other things in nature to flee, breed, feed, fight, and so forth. With our more complex minds, animals often mean not only a meal or danger, but clues, signs, symbols—a whole language embedded in our brains. He tells of an experiment in which a man was given a brief glimpse of a silhouette of a tree stump. Its roots, branches, and contours form the image of a duck. Asked what he saw, the man did not indicate that he saw the duck. Then he was asked to describe a scene or tell a story. The story he told was full of references to feathers, nests, flight, ponds, and other things related to ducks. Shepard notes that the researchers concluded, lamely, without further inquiry, that the man "saw" the duck subliminally or unconsciously. This kind of perceptual activity goes on all the time, Shepard says. "As adults, we see creatures to which we do not attend, and . . . we weave them continuously into the flow of thought, from which they shed telltale signs into our conscious life."

There are more examples of these embedded animals. It is known that people suffering from some forms of schizophrenia are especially prone to spotting them. In their withdrawal from the real world, perhaps the primitive, deeply embedded animal figures are more prominent in their minds. Shepard notes also how widely animal figures are used in intelligence tests, personality studies, psychological therapy, and perceptual research. "The whole realm of visual figure use in psychology, especially in the study of children, is shot through with animals," he says.

The most extraordinary thing about this "science" of the mind is that psychologists appear not to have a clue—or any interest—as to why animals are used so much. They never raise the question of the reason for using animals at all, Shepard says, except to say that children "identify more readily" with animals and that animals offer better disguises for people whom they "represent." Why, one wonders, would curious, probing scientists not pursue this? Why would they not follow the trail, and try to find out precisely why their field relies so heavily on animal figures and why people are so responsive to them in tests, studies, and experiments?

First, let us go to another example or two. Consider the Rorschach test, in which the subject describes a scene or tells a story after being shown various inkblots. Again, most subjects interpret them as animals. Shepard notes that "the journals, books, and papers on Rorschach theory devote little attention to the most fundamental question that it raises." That these meaningless shapes are commonly seen as animal shapes is simply accepted. Shepard is annoyed—as am I—that the field does not ask: "Why do we use animal pictures to elicit information about a child's relationship to parents, siblings, friends, strangers, old people, or babies?"

Animal Presence in Children's Literature

We find the same reliance on animals in children's books and stories. We also find more of the same indifference about it among the experts. In *Animal Land,* Margaret Blount explores the use of animals in children's literature. To the question, "why so many stories about animals if their purpose is to shape the child's understanding of people?" she sounds like the psychologists: "This is the kind of story adults seem to enjoy writing." This is an answer but not an explanation. She gets warm, however, when she continues: "An animal fantasy is a kind of imaginative launching ground that gives a built-in power of insight to narrative—one is half-way there before one has noticed." This begs the question: "Why do animals, in particular, have that 'built-in power'?" Blount apparently does not really want to know, for she wrote: "If one wonders how it works or investigates too hard, the whole thing may fail."

To be fair to Margaret Blount, she is a novelist, not an analyst, and it is not her job to tell us why animals figure so heavily in children's literature. Yet she leaves us wishing that more people would try. Perhaps only Paul Shepard has tried. He comes closer than anyone to answering the question with his theories in *Thinking Animals*. He sums those theories up by saying that, for children's literature, "Animals are like an infinite company of sign-bearers."

Having relied on Shepard's basic ideas so much, I should point out that I disagree with some of the directions he takes them. He criticizes the use of the "warm and cozy world of little furry creatures" in children's literature, saying that it misuses animal images "to protect the person from unwelcome reality." He refers to "hiding the killing of some animals by others." Then he argues: "Shielded from killing among animals (seen as struggle for power, increase in disorder), as well as from any understanding of war in human society, the child may even reverse the order-making analogical series as an adult by 'explaining' nature according to his social and political comprehension of war." I think he is saying, in so many words, that when we hide killing among animals from children, we keep them from understanding the reality of nature so that, as adults, views of nature are "ideologized"—that is, tainted by airy ideals and partisan "isms."

I submit that what is being hidden from children in books, stories, and so on is not so much the natural, one-on-one killing of animals by other animals as it is their mass, industrialized killing by human beings. This killing, as I suggested in the last chapter, is the one we are most uncomfortable with—and not the animal-to-animal killing. We have long been ill at ease with human-animal killing, and we have hidden, disguised, ritualized, rationalized, and ideologized it—pardon the expression—to death throughout the ages. (I will elaborate on this subsequently when we discuss primal society's hunt rituals.)

It is the mental baggage of these ideologies, more than any others, that taint our views of nature. They also produce the sugar-coating of animals in children's literature. Acting from them, we conspire to protect children from any mention of human-animal killing as long as possible. We will explain *that* (and the whole business about death) to them when they are "a little bit older." This sets children up for a two-step process by which we implant these ideologies in them. First, they commonly suffer an emotional upheaval when they learn the reality of human-animal killing; second, this leaves them needy for some comforting words, some understanding of this painful new fact of life. In this state, they are wide open to the dominionist explanations that have been passed down over the generations. If I am right, we may have to begin looking at this ideology-implanting process as a form of child abuse—emotional, psychic, and possibly cultural abuse.

Playing Animal

The other universal "use" of animals by children is in play. Once they are old enough to walk and run, children the world over get much of their fun and exercise by "playing animal"—that is, by imitating animal postures, sounds, and behavior. In my own first- and second-grade years, my playmates and I spent most of our recesses cavorting about the playground as the animal of the day. Some of us would play like wolves and chase after each other. A classmate named Carolyn specialized in the horse, and she usually went into character as soon as the bell rang. Sometimes she would gallop, buck, and rear for nearly the whole play period. When the bell rang again, Carolyn would return to her desk, trotting and whinnying.

This is just one more way in which animals inform us during our developing years. Much of the fun is the simple thrill of exercise and the joy of using our newly discovered hands, feet, muscles, and limbs. Play makes us try out our bodies and test them against gravity, space, and the other people and things around us. Playfulness in our "cub years" is one of the things we have in common with other mammals. The instinct for it is stamped into the mammalian genetic code because it has such tremendous survival value in aiding the development of muscles, senses, coordination, and agility.

In humans, however, the play-acting is an important part of another kind of growth as well. Because we are such conscious animals, we have awareness of not only our body but the vague, indefinable thing called "self." Thus, in humans, self-actualization—or figuring out the *self*—is an important part of growth and development. Here again, animals come in handy to us. Let us go to Paul Shepard again: "Anthropologist James Fernandez believes that [play-animal] games are part of normal growth, events by which the self and then the society are more fully realized. [Fernandez] speaks of the young child as inchoate or incomplete. Creature-mimicking brings the person into the animal, with whom he is for a few moments enjoined. A certain trait of the animal contacts a corresponding part of the human self and awakens it." Animal play, in other words, helps us discover our *selves* at an early age.

This awareness of the self in humans produces a corresponding awareness of the *Other,* the people and things around one's *Self.* So we have the psychic chore of coming to terms with not only the Self but the Other as well. Our collective failure to do so can lead to social problems—that is, problems among various people, or Selves. Shepard says that playing animal is universal in children as a means of mapping out the Self in relation to Others. "It clarifies the differences as well as the shared quality between the self and the other," he says. As we play-act the various animals by exaggerating their traits (as in leapfrog, horseplay, monkey-shines, fox-and geese, "chicken," etc.) we find out that they are really not us and we are really not them. We take their traits on and, at the same time, we put them off. In imitating the Other, we establish its reality as a separate being, for if we have to imitate it we cannot *be* it. All that the child is aware of here, of course, is laughter and great fun, but deeper down, the child is working out the psychic boundaries between the Self and Others.

Totemism and Human Society

Whenever we hear the word *totem,* most of us think of the "totem pole" of certain North American tribes. To us, it looks like a pile of grotesque, caricatured animal heads carved from a log. Being from a nontotemic culture, we are oblivious to its meaning and use. For all we know, it is just another wood carving, maybe used in connection with some sort of magic or ceremonies. Maybe it wards off "evil spirits," we think in typical, superficial nontotemic fashion.

Totemic culture is a bit more sophisticated than that. To fully understand it, we have to try to understand the worldview of forager people—something we tried to do in the previous chapter. At the core of this view of the world is, as always, a set of myths or stories about how the world came into being. Creation myths, we call them. In totemic culture, these stories usually explain not only how the world began, but also how the tribe came into being. They provide a base for a whole body of tribal legends and lore that give the tribe a sense of place and purpose in the world. This body of stories and ideas about the world is an extension of the child's process of self-actualization. It provides the social group, the tribe or clan, with an identity, a history, and a model for its lifeways. Just as the child uses animals to find its personal Self, the tribe uses animals (sometimes other natural beings, but primarily animals) to find its social Self.

Into adulthood, in totemic cultures at least, human beings continue to follow the teachings of animals—the most fascinating, informative beings in the world. As their creation myths suggest, totemic cultures see animals as First Beings, ancestors, and teachers. This view was best expressed by the Pawnee chieftain Letakots-Lesa when he told anthropologist Natalie Curtis in 1904: "In the beginning of all things, wisdom and knowledge were with the animals; for Tirawa, the One Above, did not speak directly to man. He sent certain animals to tell men that he showed himself through the beasts, and that from them, and from the stars and the sun and the moon, man should learn." (If the chief's expression "the One Above" sounds suspiciously like a monotheistic male God, we should bear in mind that by 1904 his culture had been subjected to a few centuries of Christian missionary influence. We have no way of knowing if he was leaning toward their beliefs; perhaps he was simply trying to explain his people's beliefs in terms that "white" Euro-Americans could understand.)

These creation stories are surprisingly similar the world over. In *Red Man's Religion,* anthropologist Ruth Underhill says that there are very few basic plots. Common in eastern Asia and North America is the story of the Earth Diver, in which the world at first is only water. The first beings are diving birds or mammals—usually one of the species in the tribe's domain lands. One of these divers brings up a piece of soil from which the earth is made. Then a First Being appears who commands the divers. In another plot, the solid earth was always here; it just required some shaping by the First Beings when they appear. In another, there is no world at all in the beginning; a First Being comes out of the nothingness and makes the earth and seas by force of will or by using pieces of its own body.

Whatever the origins of the land and seas, the First Beings in them are invariably animals. Typically, they are animals with human abilities: They are in animal forms, but they speak and behave like humans. The subject of a great many stories and tales, they are often the creatures who transformed and shaped the earth to its present condition, and in many cultures, they are the ancestors of human beings. Generally, this First Being is the most wily and intelligent animal in the tribal area. Among North American peoples, it is the mink, raven, or bluejay in the Northwest; in the Plains, it is coyote or grandmother spider; in the Northeast, it is the white arctic hare.

After these First Beings, human beings come to the world. In most creation stories they are practically helpless, like infants. The older, wiser animal-people teach them how to make fire, tools, clothing, how to find food and to cook. They also teach the first people how to perform the dances, chants, and ceremonies. Then, typically, the animal-people go back to the forests and streams and become animals as we know them. Their descendants are the animals of the tribe's homeland. The human beings, the tribe's human ancestors, are now on their own, but they must continue to live and perform the ceremonies as they were taught. If they do not, the world will fall out of order. The attention to lifeways and the ceremonies, then, is not so much worship in the modern religious sense as it is a sense of obligation. It is what the tribe must do to carry out its end of the ancestral deal with the First Beings.

Primal Guilt

What I have said about the awe and fascination toward animals—the sense of kinship with them, the reliance on them as teachers and world-shapers—begs an obvious question: If primal people had such feelings and ideas about animals, how could they hunt, kill, and eat them? We know that they had none of the sort of feelings toward animals that today we call humane or compassionate. But we do see evidence in the form of certain beliefs and rituals that they had some feelings of discomfort, or guilt, about hunting and killing. This may seem off base unless we remember that they viewed prey animals as equals and, in some cases, as kin. An Eskimo hunter's statement reveals this feeling: "The greatest peril in life lies in the fact that human food consists entirely of souls. All the creatures that we have to kill and eat, all those that we have to strike down and destroy to make clothes for ourselves, have souls, like we have, souls that do not perish with the body, and which must therefore be propitiated lest they should avenge themselves on us for taking away their bodies."

Joseph Campbell, among others, notes a sense of actual guilt among foragers who hunted and killed animals for food. It was set up, in part, by their view of animals as ancestors, kin, and fellow beings. From this, he says, "A psychology of tension is thereby established on many levels,

which it is the function of hunting rituals and their mythologies to resolve." These rites, he says, are "indeed symptomatic of guilt." Feelings of
guilt or apprehension were resolved, in part, by belief systems that allowed the killing to be either painless or permitted by the supernaturals.
Societies that rely primarily on hunting for subsistence usually have a
myth of a supernatural being known as the Master of the Animals. This
figure is like a chief of the animal to be hunted—say, the caribou. According to typical tribal legends, a tribal ancestor had long ago made an
agreement with the Master Animal that allowed the tribe to hunt and eat
the caribou so long as the ceremonies were performed to show proper
respect for the caribou herd. In *Of Wolves and Men,* Barry Lopez describes this belief among the Naskapi people of the Labrador peninsula in
eastern Canada: "The agreement is mythic in origin, made with an Owner
of the Animals. In the Naskapi world this is the Animal Master of the
caribou because the caribou is the mainstay of the Naskapi diet. The
Animal Master is a single animal in a great mythic herd. He is both timeless
and indestructible, an archetype of the species. It is he who 'gives' the
hunter the animal to be killed and who has the power to keep the animals
away from the hunter if he is unworthy. In the foundation myths of every
hunting culture there is a story of how all this came about."

Ritual Atonement

In other types of hunter belief systems, the hunters must perform ceremonies of purification before and after the hunt. These are, according to
mythologist Joseph Campbell, usually rituals of atonement indicative of
some feelings of guilt. Campbell notes that the guilt and its ceremonial
component is greater when the prey animal is closest to human size and
shape. He gives the example of the Ainu of Japan who have elaborate
atonement rituals for the killing of bears, whom they believe to be their
ancestors and kinfolk. Essentially, the ceremony expresses their belief that
the bear is a great spirit who wants to be freed from his earthly body so
he can return to his home in the spirit world. The Ainu word for this
sacrificial killing means, literally, "to send away." Campbell reports that
with all the ritual, the Ainu still show ambivalence about the killing. Often
the women who have suckled the bear cubs alternately laugh and cry
during the ceremonies.

In many of the other cultures with bear cult sacrifices, similar guilt-
reducing ceremonies are practiced. "When the bear has been slain,"
Campbell notes, "it is usual to disclaim responsibility for his death. In

northern Siberia today, the Ostyaks, Votyaks, Koryaks, Kamchadals, Gilyaks, Yakuts, Yukaghir, and Tungus will say: 'Grandfather, it wasn't I, it was the Russians, who made use of me, who killed you. I am sorry! Very sorry! Don't be angry with *me.'*"

Other evidence of feelings of actual guilt by tribal hunters is provided by British scholar James Serpell: "Although it varies in detail from place to place, the undercurrent of guilt and the need for some form of atonement for animal slaughter is common among hunting people. In certain African tribes, for example, hunters are obliged to undergo ceremonial acts of purification in order to remove the stain of murder from their consciences. In others, the hunter will beg the animal for forgiveness so that it doesn't bear a grudge. The Barasana Indians of Colombia regard the act of killing animals as spiritually dangerous, and believe that their flesh is poisonous unless ritually purified first. Generally speaking, their anxieties about killing and eating game increase the larger and more anthropomorphic the animal involved. Among the Moi of Indochina, expiatory offerings are made for any animal killed by hunters, because they believe that it has been taken by force from its spiritual guardian who may decide to seek revenge. Moi folklore abounds with cautionary tales of evil befalling hunters who have failed to make the necessary restitution. Significantly, if an animal is caught in a trap, no offering is required because the Moi believe that the spirit guardian deliberately pushed the animal in, in order to punish it for some misdeed. Similarly, the Chenchu hunters of India propitiate the spirit world for any animal killed by themselves, but consider it unnecessary if the prey is killed by their hunting dogs; presumably because the blame rests with the dogs, not with the hunters. The remains of animals after they have been eaten are also treated with ritual respect in many cultures. The bones are often carefully collected, reassembled in something like their original order and provided with a decent burial."

Another authority, the German sociologist and zoologist Richard Lewinsohn, also understood the conflicts hunting people feel about killing animals, whom they also saw as kin, teachers, and creators: "[Guilt and] fear of animal revenge is the great *leitmotiv* resounding in all the social and cultural prescripts lumped under totem and tabu."

Pet Mania

If we want more evidence that animals have an extraordinary appeal and fascination to human beings, we find it in the institution of pethood. Pet mania, we might call it. It is estimated that Americans own over 48 million dogs, 27 million cats, 25 million caged birds, 125 million small mammals and reptiles, and over a billion fish. And they spend, according to pet industry experts, over $4 billion a year to feed these animals and another $4 billion on collars, leashes, cages, tanks, and the other accessories of control and confinement. The same burgeoning pet populations are common to all Western industrialized, city-dwelling nations.

This modern pet mania shows the very great and irrepressible need people have for animals. As human numbers and density increase, we urbanize the planet and eliminate native animals (wildlife) through our ever-intensifying agricultural practices. If we are not wiping them out in the wild, we are surely putting great distances between their communities and ours. Contained in urban and suburban centers, most of us are no longer able to grow up around great numbers and varieties of nonhuman animals. But we still have that primal, psychic need for them. So we bring them into our suburban homes and city apartments; if we can't live among them in their natural habitat, we bring them to live among us in our unnatural habitat. One way or the other, we need to have them around.

In an industrialized world, some industry will always arise to cater to human needs. Hence we have a pet industry to supply our needs for animals in the modern home. It is composed of puppy mills, backyard breeders, trappers and smugglers of wild birds and other exotic animals, collectors and breeders of tropical fish, and, after them, echelons of manufacturers of feed and supplies, distributors, chain stores, groomers, trainers, veterinarians, and therapists. Animal companionship is a hot commodity.

Which has led many a social commentator from Thorstein Veblen on down to grouse about pampered pets in rhinestone collars dining on gourmet food. Such luxuries are deliberately conspicuous; the cruelties, neglect, and the downside of pethood, however, are inconspicuous—and just as deliberately so. For every dog that gets regular sessions at the grooming parlor, many others get dumped or chained to the backyard fence. Some have estimated that nearly a third of all dogs in the United States end their lives in pounds and shelters. The public pet mania apparently stops there, for the adoption rate runs only about 10 to 15 percent. The other 85 to 90 percent of animals in "shelters" are routinely destroyed to make room for the steady flow of those abandoned. Modern pet-keeping is a very mixed bag; it offers intense contrasts in people's motives and in the care and treatment they offer their animal companions. We will explore these and more of pet mania in Chapter 8 when we discuss some of the rituals of dominionism.

People and Pets—Another Universal

We tend to think that pet-keeping is strictly a phenomenon of modern, affluent society. It is not. The excesses and extremes of pet mania are creatures of our nature-alienated, modern, urban culture, but pet-keeping in general is common around the world. Its universality is more evidence of the special place animals have in human life. Pethood, and the earliest stage of domestication of animals, probably began about 15,000 years ago when wild canids took up living with nomadic foragers. This appears to have happened all around the world. After centuries of close association with tribal peoples, these subpopulations of canids became some of the earliest breeds of dogs. Authorities debate the exact nature of the relationship, but it probably included companionship and affection. There is a 12,000-year-old burial site in northern Israel that contains two skeletons: one of an elderly human, the other of a five-month-old dog. The puppy was apparently killed—dispatched—to accompany his or her human companion into the afterworld. While that may not seem so touching to us today, the burial arrangement does: The body of the deceased human was arranged so that his or her left hand rested, according to James Serpell, "in a timeless and eloquent gesture of attachment, on the puppy's shoulder."

Serpell and others who have looked find that the practice of capturing, taming, and keeping animals for companionship is widespread among both forager and early-stage agricultural peoples. He also notes that anthropologists generally avoid examining this primal pethood. Now this raises the familiar red flag again, because anthropology tends to study other such universals to death. Why is this one "off limits"? We saw just above how psychologists have avoided studies of the universality of humans' responses to animals in myth, art, children's literature, and psychological testing. The void in interest in these universals is simply shrugged off, yet it sticks out like a sore thumb. There is, obviously, something in the modern culture's—and more certainly, modern science's—view of human-animal relations that puts these subjects off limits. The excuse would probably be that they are too silly, too trivial, for further investigation. The excuse itself is a proper and pregnant subject for serious examination, for it probably rests on a great, shaky pile of prejudices, assumptions, guilt, and other discomforts about the realities of the human-animal relationship. The whole subject is truly an emotional and cultural can of worms and hence easy to put off.

Pet-keeping, like art, myth, and ceremony, seems to be a constant in human society around the world. Even where tribal societies have no true domestic animals, we find companion animals. The accounts of North American Indians by early explorers tell of tribes that kept tame raccoons, moose, bison, wolves, bears, and other species as well as the usual packs of nearly domesticated dogs. Explorers in South America found more of the same, although, of course, the species were different. A nineteenth-century naturalist counted twenty-two species of "quadrupeds" that had been tamed and kept as pets by Amazon rain forest peoples. The same patterns of taming and pet-keeping were found among tribal peoples in Australia, Polynesia, and other parts of the Old World. In all of these areas there were accounts of women nursing baby piglets, puppies, monkeys, opossums, and other young animals side by side with their own infants.

More recently, anthropologists have observed the same patterns where tribal peoples have been able to maintain their primal lifeways. Cynics and Cartesians will suggest that the animals were tamed and kept in the villages in order to fatten them for dinnertime. Apparently not, by most accounts. Even though the tribes hunted and ate many of the species from which they took their pets, the individual animals adopted enjoyed exemption from slaughter. The people apparently enjoyed their animals' antics as well as the simple pleasures of taking care of them. The personalities of some animals, observers say, made them a steady source of discussion and entertainment. People could be close to these animals. They ceased to be regarded as Others, and they were integrated as members of the village extended family.

Animals for What Ails You

Lately, the caretaking, nurturing aspect of pet-keeping has been getting serious attention by health care professionals. You have probably seen many stories by now about the budding new field of "pet-facilitated therapy." This school of thought in health care uses animals to "treat" various kinds of illness in human beings. Essentially, pet therapy amounts to giving the patient his or her own pet—a sort of living "pill" for whatever ails the person. Actually, the animal itself is not the pill or medicine; the "magic bullet" is the human-animal bond. The therapeutic effect comes from the psychic and emotional benefits of a relationship with an animal.

As difficult as it is to measure (and thereby satisfy scientists and skeptics), pet therapy surely works. As we saw at the opening of this chapter, pet therapy has proven effective in reaching severely withdrawn and disturbed people. It has also been used to improve morale, appetite, social activity, and other elements of well-being in elderly residents of nursing homes. It has been used with the same results in prisons. In the 1970s social worker David Lee introduced fish, caged birds, and small mammals to murderers, rapists, and other violent criminals at Lima State Hospital for the Criminally Insane in Lima, Ohio. Over time, these pets reduced the frequency of fights, stopped suicide attempts, and improved prisoner relations with guards and staff. In other experiments with people and their pets, talking to and petting animals lowered blood pressure in the human subjects. In another study, individuals with heart disease who had pets had better chances of longevity than those without pets.

Good Instincts

Animals, or, rather, the close relationship with them, produce this stress-relieving, therapeutic effect because, experts say, they help to fill our need to nurture. We touched on this earlier when we discussed psychiatrist Aaron Katcher's theory that our basic human instincts for empathy and nurturing "spill over" to some animals. He and others believe that these instincts evolved in humans because our species cares for its young much longer than any other. Without steady nurturing by the family and kin group in primal times, relatively helpless human children would not have survived to sexual maturity. They would have died early in life. No doubt many did. Those that survived, however, passed on things with survival value to the next generation and the next and so on. Some of these things were physical traits, like erect posture, opposable thumbs, good vision, body build, and so on, but others were behavioral, like the urges to eat, have sex, and avoid injury. They tend to direct behavior in ways that help us stay alive as individuals and as a species. These are called instincts and they are inherited rather than learned (although learning can certainly enhance one's success in carrying out instinctive urges).

Katcher and others believe that nurturance and empathy are among the basic human instincts. (In fact, they are probably basic to all primates and some other mammals; they are just a bit stronger in the human species.) Empathy and nurturance had tremendous survival value in humans because they tied the family and kin group to infants and children during the many years it takes for human animals to reach self-reliance and sexual maturity. It is these feelings of empathy toward and urges to take care of children that Katcher and some psychologists believe "spill over" to other living things.

In other words, our nurturing and empathetic urges do not discriminate on the basis of species. Only the wordy, rational, hair-splitting parts of our mind and culture do that. We *learn* to discriminate; the prevailing culture and our elders teach it to us.

If it is true that the older, deeper primal mind does not differentiate among animals and young, if it regards all living things as one and the same, we have a great source of hope. It means that, embedded in the deepest seats of our psyche, there is the humane impulse. You may not be able to measure it, but you may have experienced it. This is the instinct that produces feelings of shock and horror when we see a child or help-less animal in obvious suffering.

Unfortunately, since we have been actively using and killing animals for nearly 20,000 years, we have put together a hodge-podge of cultural devices that repress many of these feelings. The device-making began with the hunt rituals in primal society, but, as we saw, they barely con-cealed tribal people's actual feelings of guilt and discomfort. We shall soon see the next stages in the assembly of these cultural devices as we look at how agrarian society learned to exploit horses, cattle, goats, and other mammals to power its machines and provide meat for city dwellers.

To put it simply, I am suggesting that with the emergence of Western agrarian society people developed ways to contain and repress some of our better instincts. This repression has an extra dimension in Western culture because Western societies were the first and biggest investors in animal domestication. We chose the path of using animals for utility and benefit, paving the way with comforting mythologies and leaving some of our humanity behind, underdeveloped. If I am right—or even close—we begin to wonder about the path not taken. What might life be like if, instead, we had taken directions in economy and culture that had built upon this humane instinct? Never mind the mistakes of 10,000 years ago, could we search for that path now? I think we can. And we can uncover our nurture/empathy instincts. We can bring them out in the open. We can build a culture that will feed them and build upon them. We can acknowledge them openly, honestly, and we can teach children how to express, rather than repress, them.

The All-Importance, Omnipresence of Animals

Buried under the demands and devices of dominionist culture, the need for animals—as companions, as exercisers of human empathy and nurturance, as kindred beings in the unity of creation, as feeders and inform-ers of the psyche—is hard to see. Their importance in these ways is not (to use computer-ese again) easily called up on our screens. Our "soft-ware" today is dominionist and utilitarian, and it calls up only the value of animals as resources or tools. Nevertheless, the animal presence is well embedded in art, mythology, folklore, literature, children's games, and the rest of our culture.

Throughout our evolution, animals have made us wonder and have helped us come to terms with the world around us. When we were foragers with earth-bound religions, animals were the First Beings, world-shapers, and the teachers of human lifeways. Their patterns of living and behaving were *familiar* (*family, familial*) and offered human beings a sense of continuum, of belonging, in the sprawl and chaos of the living world.

When we became agriculturalists and looked to the heavens for in-struction about the seasons and the elements, animals continued to pop-ulate the imagination. We saw animal forms among the stars. Of the forty-eight ancient, Ptolemaic constellations, all but a few are organic and twenty-five are named for animals. Of the twenty-two more that were added in the seventeenth century, nineteen have animal names. When we built colossal earthworks to appeal to the powers in the heavens, we built them to resemble animal forms. Some in Peru are over a mile long. One famous one in Ohio is in the shape of a giant snake with an egg in its mouth.

Nature and its forces and mysteries have been conceived of in animal form the world over. In ancient Egypt, Hathor, the cow goddess of the sky, was believed to have given birth to the sun. The sky was seen as a giant cow, her legs the four corners of the world. Ancient astronomers explained the workings of the universe by reference to the zodiac, which means literally "the circle of animals." Universally, animals bond us to the rest of nature.

4

Agriculture: A New Relationship with Nature, a New World Order for Living Beings

From Dubuque, Iowa, U.S. Route 20 streaks due west toward Sioux City, cutting straight through the flat heartland of America. From here, the Great Tallgrass Prairie once sprawled across the plains for a thousand miles in most every direction. This is now the Corn Belt, Soybean Belt, Hog Belt, and Fattened Cattle Belt. Dubuque and the other cities along the Mississippi supply the machinery that cuts the soil and reaps the grains. Sioux City and other cities out to the west provide the machinery that kills the cattle and hogs and packages their remains. All around are the farms on which domestic animals are fed and fattened, their numbers siphoning nutrients from the soils of the prairielands.

But you do not see farm animals in the fields that stretch to the horizon. Every now and then you can see a few cattle, but no hogs, chickens, or turkeys. Today, their vast numbers are contained (even in these wide open spaces) in high-tech "confinement" buildings where feed, water, light, air, and nearly everything else are strictly controlled—largely by machines. Not long ago, restless herds roamed these sweeping plains, flocks of birds soared over them, and other creatures scurried about in the thick, grassy canopy. They are gone, and in their place are long, low-slung, windowless, steel buildings lying sullen and mysterious among the monocultured fields of corn and soybeans.

Yet the animal presence is overwhelming—especially on a hot day.

Every few miles, the road is shrouded in a breath-stopping, rancid smell from some nearby animal factory. It is a sickly, deathly smell (if you have been around healthy animals fed on hay or pasture you know the difference), like the smell of a concentration camp. Which, of course, the factory farm quite literally is, because it concentrates a large number of animals indoors and feeds them a steady diet of grain concentrates (the agribusiness word for corn, soybeans, and the energy-rich seed parts of other plants). In addition, it is a factory in which energy and nutrients from the sun and soil are concentrated by animals and turned into meat, milk, and eggs.

This is modern, intensive agriculture. The word *intensive* comes from the farm community and is used with pride. It describes our system for mass-producing field crops and animals for our tables. If they use enough energy, machines, chemicals, pharmaceuticals, and expertise, farmers can extract a great deal more produce from their land and animals than ever before. Their system is the end-product of nearly 10,000 years of human effort guided by one basic strategy: intensify food production to feed the growing numbers of human beings.

Somewhere along the way, the evolving agri-culture also spawned dominionism (that God-given right to exploit the living world exclusively for human ends) and nurtured it right along to its present robust form. From today's end of the evolutionary sequence, it looks like agri-culture created a monster. Perhaps a many-headed monster, for as we shall see, human society, especially the Western division, comes to exert dominion over not only animals and nature but other people and their lands and cultures. University of Texas historian Alfred W. Crosby calls it "ecological imperialism" in his book of the same name, and points to the ancient Middle East as its birthplace. "If we seek the roots of the success of European imperialism," he says, "we must be off to the Middle East, to Abraham, to Gilgamesh and the cultural ancestors of all of us who eat wheaten bread, smelt iron, or record our thoughts alphabetically."

Now then, how did all this begin?

The First Planters

About 13,000 years ago the earth's most recent great glacial ice cap was melting away because of a warming trend. No one knows for sure exactly how and why, but by about 10,000 years ago human groups at scattered locations from northern Africa eastward to India and Southeast Asia were gathering wild plant seeds, sowing them, tending their growth, and harvesting them. At about the same time, some of them were also beginning to tend herds of wild sheep and goats, and before long, pigs, cattle, and other animals.

Farming began—but in fits and starts. The first farmers still moved with the seasons in search of ripening fruit and berries, they still gathered wild foods and hunted animals for food and materials. But over time, foraging gave way to farming and people settled, built more permanent dwellings, and worked the soil for greater control over their food supply.

As anthropologists would say, human society *intensified* its methods of getting food and materials. They quibble a great deal over precisely why people did this, but all the various theories boil down to human population density as the prime mover. In some ecosystems—especially near springs, rivers, marshes, lakes, and places where there is rich plant and animal life—human numbers gradually crept upwards. People tended to gang up in the places where food and materials were relatively abundant. Over time, some groups became more and more dependent on these areas and gradually gave up some of their older, always-moving foraging ways. Some, in fact, became sedentary and lived in nearly permanent villages even before they took up farming. Some of these food-rich areas attracted more and more people who were gradually becoming less skilled and equipped to forage distant food sources. Little by little, they were "circumscribed"—that is, locked in by their neighbors. There they were: stuck among a lot of other people competing for food and materials. The situation drove them to intensify food gathering, to bring in greater varieties and amounts and store some of them for a rainy day.

At first, these semi-sedentary foragers simply expanded their shopping lists, so to speak. Anthropologists call this the "broad spectrum" revolution because people greatly diversified their diets and foraging activities. They turned from hunting a large animal—say, the red deer—and began to hunt for many kinds of smaller animals—such a sheep, goats, and gazelles. They preyed on burrowing animals, fish, shellfish, and snails, and they gathered a much greater variety of nuts, seeds, shoots, and plants than ever before.

Eventually, some of these semi-sedentary foragers began "cultivating" a favorite wild stand of edible plants. At first, they probably just pulled up the plants they could not eat, making "weeding" the first agricultural chore. They may have enlarged the wild stand by spreading seeds or shoots at the edges. They probably moved plants, seeds, or shoots to other locations—say, near water or nearer the village.

Unconscious Selection

In the Middle East, where foragers were harvesting stands of wild wheat well before agriculture began, scientists have traced the steps toward domestication. When these foragers harvested a field, many seedheads shattered, and the seeds were lost to birds, mice, and winter's elements. By natural variation, some plants had tighter seedheads and it would have been a greater proportion of these that made it through harvesting and handling and into the gatherers' baskets. If they were in a region where sedentism was creeping in, the same group of foragers may have harvested the same fields year after year. From long forager experience, they knew about plant growth and the progression from seeds to sprouts to shoots to plants. They knew enough to save some of their harvest to reseed the field in the spring. They may also have weeded the field during the growing season. In time and with a little bit of care and cultivation, their tight-headed wheat plants flourished and took over the fields. Quite unintentionally at first, these early farmers selected and fostered plants whose seedheads could withstand human handling. Gradually, they produced a new "improved" strain of wheat—one that was easier to harvest, that yielded more grain for the same toil.

This wheat was substantially different from the original wild variety; it was, in other words, *domestic* wheat.

From there, we can suppose that the wheat planters traded seeds with neighbors and gradually the "neighborhood" had a short list of newly domesticated plants.

Eventually, these early forager-farmers learned that some of their plants were better than others and that by some mystical means their seeds produced more of the same. They passed on their knowledge through stories about sacred seeds and the mysteries of plant fecundity. They were becoming true planters: deliberate, albeit through myth and ritual, refiners, shapers, and domesticators of plants.

This slow process of domestication occurred around the world wherever environments and human population pressures led to creeping sedentism, not because of any people's advanced intelligence. From region to region, continent to continent, only the plant species varied. In the Middle East, the first plants to be domesticated were wheat and barley; in Africa, sorghum and yams; in southeast Asia, rice and yams; and in the Americas, corn, sweet potatoes, and squash. Most experts think plant domestication began first in the Middle East—the crossroads of the ancient world—where population pressures rose earliest. Domestication occurs somewhat later in the New World because the population descended from highly mobile Siberian hunter-foragers who came over between 25,000 and 13,000 years ago. As relatively recent arrivals into two large, "empty" continents, they had plenty of room to disperse. That, and perhaps northern hunters' population-controlling traditions, gave them a long run of time before people pressures led to creeping sedentism and the "need" for intensification.

The First Herders

Near in time and place in the Middle East, but in the hilly regions, people who specialized in hunting wild sheep and goats began to assert greater control over the herds. They were probably responding to population pressures in the region, and they intensified what they already knew best—hunting. These hunters gradually began to stalk and kill certain animals—usually males and the younger animals. With these selective, systematic killings, the group began to practice a primitive form of herd "management." A band of hunter-foragers probably attached itself to a particular herd, which became "their" herd to follow, to cull, and to live from. (It was early herders, experts believe, who brought the idea of property to human society.) Along with culling, the group began to control movement of the herd to the best grazing and watering areas. Little by little, these first herders learned the rudiments of animal husbandry—that is, techniques for the deliberate control of the mobility, diet, growth, and reproductive lives of the animals.

Over time, a group's familiarity with its herd of animals taught them some revolutionary things about the facts of life. As hunters, they already knew a lot about the habits and movements of each species, but now they were living much more closely and constantly with one herd. They were around the same animals day after day. Now it was possible to become familiar with individual animals and to watch them behave and change over their lifetimes. From such closeness and familiarity, herding peoples gradually learned about the end-results of copulation, about the respective roles of males and females in procreation, and about estral, gestation, and birth cycles.

From this, early hunter-herders learned to enlarge their herd by culling and castrating males, which produced a herd of many females and only a few breeding males. This reduced male competition, which altered the herd's social-sexual dynamics and ensured that most females were impregnated by the few "chosen" males. From this, they learned about selective breeding—that is, the selection of breeding pairs to create off-spring that will have the same characteristics as the parent pair. Eventually they learned to produce strains of animals that best suited their needs and desires. A group may have been selected for a particular type of horn, coat color, or markings to help distinguish "their" animals from their neigh-bors. (Selective breeding and the development of "new" animals are, after property, Western agri-culture's oldest obsessions.)

While their planter neighbors were busy domesticating plant species, then, groups of hunter-herders looked to familiar prey animals as their way to intensify food production.

As far as we know, sheep were the first animal to be domesticated—nearly 11,000 years ago, at Karim Shahir in the Kurdish hill country of northeastern Iraq. In short order, goats were domesticated in roughly the same region. Not far away in the Middle East, pigs, then cattle were domesticated. In general, nomadic peoples domesticated sheep, goats, cattle, and the large animals that moved in herds, while sedentary forager-farmers domesticated pigs, fowl, and the smaller animals that could be more easily confined in their villages.

Eventually, of course, some of the herders became settled farmers and took up planting; and some of their planter neighbors began keeping livestock. Doggedly, early farmers refined their new breeds of plants and animals and added more and more species to the domestic list. After many centuries, farmers took the next great step in agricultural intensification when they harnessed their cattle to pull plows and carts. With domestic animal power, tougher sod could be cut open, new fields laid out, bigger fields tended, and bigger loads hauled to the granaries. Very slowly, almost imperceptibly, a wholly new way of living was emerging. It was—Alfred Crosby is blunt—"at its base a matter of the direct control and exploitation of many species for the sake of one: *Homo sapiens.*"

A Long, Slow Transition

It is tempting to look back on the beginnings of farming as a sudden event, as if it were such a brilliant idea that it instantly caught on and swept through the ancient world much like today's latest hit song or hot dance step. Many a writer has described it as a "revolution," implying rapid, drastic change and a complete replacement of the old lifeways with the new. This view furnishes some dramatic prose and exciting imagery.

We envision messengers running from village to village shouting out the news: "Look! Take these seeds! Plant them and you'll be rich!" The village men throw down their hunting weapons, the women their gathering baskets. In a frenzy, they all run to the nearest meadow and start ripping into the soil. After a dissolve and a musical interlude, the next scene opens on the village square, where, surrounded by bulging granaries, jubilant people are drinking, singing, dancing, and feasting on fatted calves. Their revelry suggests celebration, like a bunch of new graduates or winners of some big game.

Well, yes, the transition to farming was, overall, an earth- and mind-shaking event, but if it was an "event" it was one that took thousands of years. We might like to think of it as a Great Leap, but it actually occurred in slow, halting steps. We must remember that the first planters and herders did not suddenly drop their older lifeways. Along with attending to their handful of newly domesticated plants and animals, they still gathered, hunted, and foraged for "wild" foods. Even under conditions of creeping sedentism, foraged wild foods provided the bulk of the diet for most groups for many millennia after the domestication of wheat and sheep. It would take a thousand years before any group in the Middle East would become fully dependent on domesticated animals and plants. It would take another 3,000 years before their farming methods would reach all of Europe.

Toil, Trouble, and Tragedy

The usual account of the early history of Western civilization boasts of the glories and benefits of settled farming society. It is an all-good-news account, usually. But we know that life during the change from foraging to farming was not so rosy. In this transitional period, farming's pace was one step forward, two steps back. The new breeds of plants and animals were not very reliable providers of food and materials. Their genetic base narrowed by selection and grown in monocultures, domestic species were vulnerable to diseases and pests. Farming methods were crude and not very productive. Some years they brought good harvests, but just as often they brought on problems, shocks, and setbacks.

And all the while, nomadism and foraging were diminishing as options in the increasingly crowded Middle East. Slowly, creeping sedentism and farming took over, bringing drudgery, monotony, crowding, famine, disease, bad teeth, and lots of new grounds for violence between individuals and groups. From an early farmer's point of view, the new ways may well have been seen as a grudging necessity—more bane than brilliant idea. The agrarian view of life as perpetual punishment was taking shape centuries before Genesis was written.

In the farmers' villages, disease hit like never before. Infant death and childhood disease had long been facts of life to forager people, but most of those who lived past puberty could look forward to a fairly ripe old age. Yet once groups settled in farming villages and stayed in place year after year, human hygiene took a nosedive. Living in increasingly larger communities with less and less variety in their diets and piled, literally, on top of their own refuse and wastes, people fell to waves of epidemics, probably for the first time in human history. Parasites, insects, rodents, and other disease carriers established their life cycles in the new, human-made ecosystems of croplands, human/domestic animal hosts, and refuse heaps. The human immune system was surely not ready for the deadly diseases that flourished in the crowding and filth of early farming villages. Creeping sedentism, regional crowding, and increased trade ensured their spread from village to village.

At the same time, the move to sedentary life sharply changed the human diet. Left behind was the richly varied, nutritious diet of foragers and in its place farmer-villagers existed on bread, gruel, and a handful of starchy staples. Comparative studies of bones show that foragers had generally better health than farmers. About 30,000 years ago, at the peak of the glacial period, adult males averaged 177 centimeters (5 feet, 11 inches) in height and females about 165 centimeters (5 feet, 6 inches). About 10,000 years ago, when the first farming appeared, males had shrunk to the size of ice-age females and women averaged about 153 centimeters (5 feet, 0 inches). Preagricultural people also had better teeth. At the peak of the Ice Age, the average person died with only 2.2 teeth missing. By 6500 B.C., dental loss at death had risen to 3.5 teeth, and by Roman times it had risen to 6.6.

The evidence shows that not until quite recently did human health get substantially better than it was in forager times. According to anthropologist Mark Nathan Cohen, farming societies did not reduce infant and child mortality below forager levels until the last two centuries. Nor, he says, did adult life expectancy increase substantially beyond that of forager times until the past century.

Yet the human population grew steadily once society settled down to farm and live in villages. How could it have grown if the people's health was so bad? Cohen, anthropologist Marvin Harris, and others say that the growth in numbers came primarily because of cultural changes. "Human population increased after the adoption of sedentism and agriculture," says Cohen, "not because survival improved but because human populations—for natural or cultural reasons—produced more children." Harris suggests that sedentary living would have allowed relaxation of the taboos against frequent sexual activity and pregnancy. Children's births did not have to be spaced years apart because infants were no longer quite the burden they were when the forager band moved with the seasons. And surely the changes in view of sexuality and procreation that came with agri-culture helped to increase family size. Males, with one eye on their personal role in procreation and the other on their family's wealth and status in the agrarian village, advanced the values on many wives, many children that typify patriarchal society. Now that society knew about men's role in procreation, manliness came to be equated with male fecundity and it was measured, in part, by how many children a man "sired."

The Common Wealth

The trend toward more people, more villages, more intensification put strains on the land and the living world. With foraging less and less an option, there was pressure to produce surpluses to carry the village through winters and lean years. Planters built their surpluses by clearing land, expanding fields, and by diverting streams for irrigation. Herders built theirs by expanding their grazing lands and by increasing the size of their herds. In good years, planters and herders traded their surpluses with each other, and all of the region's farmers benefited from more goods, more variety. Good years or bad, surpluses came to be highly desirable. People strived for a wealth of them and praised them in song and ceremony.

Gradually, the push for surpluses became ingrained in their agri-culture and the quest for wealth took on a life of its own. Ironically, it propelled the farming region into a spiral of self-generated conflicts and tragedies. It pushed up all the factors; human numbers, density, disease, environmental depletion, and competition for land, water, and materials. In taking the plunge toward intensified production, the region had inadvertently intensified its social and environmental problems. Eventually, many villages and communities collapsed, their people wiped out by disease or warfare. Many early communities collapsed from famine when their crops failed from drought, disease, or soil depletion. Among them were irrigators, who enjoyed bountiful harvests for years until continuous cropping and the water's leaching action ruined their soils.

By this stage in the evolution of farming, there was no turning back, no place to revert to the simple life of nomadic foragers. Agricultural intensification marched onward, its steps coming increasingly surer and quicker. Despite the recurrent cycles of disease, famine, and other setbacks, the human population steadily rose. There were about 5 million human beings in the world on the eve of agriculture 10,000 years ago. Four thousand years later, as Egypt, Babylonia, Sumeria, and the other first, great, agrarian city-states arose, there were 87 million. In another 4,000 years, at the time of Jesus of Nazareth, there were roughly 250 million human beings (the present U.S. population) on the planet. By the early 1800s, our numbers reached a billion. Today, the number is 5.4 billion and growing—at a rate of 92 million each year.

The New Social Order—Towns and Chiefs

Once farming got started in the early Middle East, the situation was one of growing populations in an ecologically restricted space. Under pressure, people took on new strategies for survival. One was intensification—that is, increased agricultural production—which led to surpluses and notions of property and wealth, which, in turn, led to the emergence of subordinate classes of people ruled by rich, powerful elites. Another strategy was expansionism, which led to militarism, which, in turn, led to slavery, subordinate classes, and the rule of the rich and powerful few. Let us see how this new, agrarian social order came into being.

After the long settling-in period discussed above, farmers' villages grew and grew. The villagers built roads to connect their settlements and increased their trade in commodities. Some villages became market centers or temple towns, which drew great numbers of people from the countryside. Some of these towns arose as old tribal conflicts turned into constant warfare over farmland or grazing territory, driving great numbers of people to seek out places of safety. Some towns became the first refuge centers, and the citizens organized communal labor to erect walls and fortifications. At Jericho near the Jordan River, the first walls went up in 7200 B.C., a sign that agrarian warfare came very early in that region.

Whether in villages or towns, human groups grew larger than ever before. Sedentary farmer families grew larger—in part because of a need for more hands in food production. Moreover, the community of families grew larger. Even some of the very early agricultural villages contained as many as several hundred people. Further into the agricultural period, towns and cities of several thousand people were common. With this growth in the size and number of human settlements, new beliefs and governing systems were needed to control social conflicts over water, cropland, roving animals, trading of commodities, and all the other frictions that can arise in the larger, more dense human community.

From Big Men's Generosity to Royal Power

In the earliest agricultural period, when society was still regulated by forager traditions, tribal chiefs continued to carry out the government role. To help in maintaining order and control as foragers turned to farmers and produced surpluses, these early chiefs used their role as spiritual leaders to effect power over the hearts and minds of their people. At first they became what Marvin Harris and other anthropologists call "Big Men," and they maintained their power by being good providers for their tribe or village. Essentially, they served as redistributers of early agrarian wealth. They held huge feasts and managed networks of supporters, all of which helped to ensure that the agricultural surpluses "trickled down" to the rest of the community. As time passed and the community came to value their office, the Big Men enjoyed increasing power, wealth, and prestige. Beliefs and mythologies emerged that supported their special position in the tribe or community. Before long, the Big Men were kings, and eventually these kings maintained their positions with taxes and armies. By this time in the evolution of agricultural society, they began to share power with priests who helped develop the new agri-cultural religions. Generally, the priests ruled over the temples and the temple towns, where they coordinated communal labor to build huge plazas, temple complexes, and irrigation projects.

Soon, within the king's armies, military elites emerged alongside the temple elites, and they became an independent and rival force in the community. On occasion, the generals would take over the temple lands and herds and push the priests into the background. Some of them became strong enough to make or break the king. When they worked in concert under shared ideologies and strategies, though, kings, generals, and high priests could "unify" a region into a bustling city-state. Eventually, the strongest ruling elites subdued other regions, annexed them, and built nation-states. This nation-building stage was reached in Mesopotamia by about 2300 B.C. when Urukagina, ruler of the city-state of Lagash in Sumeria, was violently overthrown by another king, Lugalzaggizi of the city of Umma. The new king, however, had overreached, and he could not hold onto his new kingdom. In short order, he was overthrown by King Sargon of Akkad, who established a dynasty that ruled over sections of Sumeria, Ashur (Assyria), Elam, and the Euphrates valley for generations.

But old ways, especially the forager religious beliefs, die hard, and against their weight the newly emerging agrarian religious beliefs were not always strong enough to maintain social control. Raw, physical power was, and rulers built armies not only to protect their people but to ensure their loyalty to the realm. Traditional chiefs gradually lost power to warrior chiefs who built bigger armies to enable them to control more people, more lands. As the scale of society grew larger, warrior chiefs turned into warrior kings, and the richest and most powerful towns turned into the capitals of the early agrarian city-states. To help maintain social control, powerful kings employed not only armies of soldiers, but slaves, artisans, and overseers whose job it was to create monumental temples, plazas, and other visually impressive structures. These were monuments to the egos, power, and wealth of the ruling elite, of course, but they were also designed to simultaneously intimidate the citizenry and stir their feelings of national pride.

The Warrior State

Again, we usually marvel at the art and architecture—the material wealth—created by the early agrarian city-states. They had a grand style, all right. But their social side was something else. Warfare, too, took on a grand style: It grew bigger and it lasted longer than ever before. Forager society had warfare and warriors, of course, but in agrarian society war became an institution and warriors became heads of state.

As agriculture spread throughout the Middle East, some of these capitals of agrarian wealth, military power, and regional influence began to rival each other. In a world where everything was expanding, they were bound to come into conflict with each other over ownership of croplands, rivers, and domestic animals, but also over trade practices and religious beliefs. There were neither national laws nor treaties yet, and it fell to the kings, priests, and military leaders to resolve conflicts. A lot depended on the views and values of this ruling elite. If it was warlike and expansionist, they tended to prevail in most disputes. Some of these most domineering city-states rode herd over a wide region and grew into the capitals of early civilization in Mesopotamia. Marvin Harris calls these primary states, and they mark the beginnings of royal dynasties, taxation, standing armies, bureaucracies, and the other trappings of government.

In the same region, secondary states arose as people joined forces against the more domineering primary state. Some of these developed along lucrative trade routes, ports, or other key geographical features. Jericho, the early walled city, was probably one of these secondary city-states as it was located in an oasis in the Jordan River valley. Other secondary states were established by nomadic peoples, usually herds-keepers, who took up raiding their wealthy, settled neighbors—first probably for pasture, water, or freedom of travel, but eventually for slaves, booty, and other things. Turks, Mongols, Huns, Hebrews, Manchus, Arabs, and many other herding peoples built their states out of years of warfare and raiding against more settled and powerful primary states.

Warfare, conquest, and ruthlessness as means of conflict resolution, then, were built into the new agrarian order at the earliest stages. Even as the new social pyramid and the first outlines of the state were taking shape, a certain kind of people were rising, or fighting their way, to the top. They were, generally, the male war experts—the men who had the weapons, the skills, and the very old hunter-warrior culture to give them a substantial edge in power struggles. The hunting culture, as Lewis Mumford has said, "promoted a surgical hardness about inflicting pain and taking life," and, as we have noted, its rituals and preparations merged into a warrior subculture even before agricultural times. It is this warrior subculture, many experts believe, that produced the kings, priests, and the rest of the ruling elite who were most influential in putting together the new agrarian order and its primary and secondary states. Mumford says the warrior cults led quite naturally into a cult of kingship. As to the origin of the agrarian king's godlike supremacy and special powers, he says, "there is no room for doubt: it was hunting that cultivated the initiative, the self-confidence, the ruthlessness that kings must exercise to achieve and retain command; and it was the hunter's weapons that backed up his commands, whether rational or irrational, with the ultimate authority of armed force: above all, the readiness to kill."

This cultural continuity between hunters, warriors, and rulers is evident in the art of early Egypt and Mesopotamia. Scenes of lion and bull hunting are a common way of depicting the heroism and personal powers of archaic kings. In Western art and literature all the way to the European Renaissance, royal status, power, and privilege are asserted mainly through hunting scenes and stories.

Slavery, Genocide, Rape, and Mutilation

Slavery, too, emerges from the warrior culture as it takes control of state formation and carries on state wars of conquest. As we noted in Chapter 2, preagricultural hunter-warrior groups had a long tradition of taking enemy captives back to their villages for public torture and execution. This tradition continued into the agrarian era—and then some. With the increased social scale and complexity in agrarian regions, the tradition took a sharp turn for the worse. University of Wisconsin historian Gerda Lerner describes the mass enslavement, mutilation, and execution that went with the earliest international warfare in the ancient Middle East in her book *The Creation of Patriarchy*. In the earliest wars of conquest, she says, the conquerors usually killed all the adult males and took the women and children back home with them. The enemy's men were killed so they would no longer be a threat; the women were spared because they were valuable as human booty—for both immediate rape and longer-term sexual slavery. In the conqueror's homeland, the captive women and children were vulnerable and homeless, which made it easy to turn them into slaves and household servants. (Eventually, though, some might become citizens and settle among their former enemies.)

These practices became routine in warfare between city-states in Mesopotamia. Both men and women expected to be cast into slavery, to be dishonored, if they lost a war. In time, then, men came to be included in the slave class. But since male captives might be a threat within the walls of the conqueror's city, they were usually mutilated by blinding, amputation, or castration. Castration, according to Lerner, was rather widespread. It was a way of emphasizing a man's reduction to the slave class. Women could be most dishonored and humiliated by rape, men by genital mutilation. Significantly, dishonoring and reduction was emphasized primarily through sexual torture and abuse. Lerner says there is "overwhelming historical evidence for the prepondance of the practice of killing or mutilating male prisoners and for the large-scale enslavement and rape of female prisoners." Early on, large-scale human tragedy came to be part of the cost of conquering and maintaining huge nation-states and empires. Soon after King Sargon established the first Mesopotamian nation, his heir, Rimush, boasts of conquering several Babylonian cities, of killing several thousand men in each, and of taking thousands of captives. The Assyrians were especially ruthless victors in war. One temple inscription tells of their blinding 14,400 captives after a victorious military campaign.

The magnitude of such a "victory," the booty—slaves and new lands gained—gave kings and the ruling elite even more power. And it made life somewhat better for even the common people of a victorious nation. The slaves reduced their work load. The might of their rulers protected them from dishonor and enslavement by a rival nation. Soon, the whole nation's culture embraced militarism, celebrating the glories and honor of battle in its art and poetry. Along with surplus wealth, military victory became a mark of national excellence, a badge of its civilization. So thoroughly was warfare culturally sanctioned that it took on a life of its own. Before long, it was war for its own sake—whether or not there was a real enemy—and it became almost a sport to booming agrarian society in the ancient Middle East. It gave the king a chance to exercise and display his troops. It furnished his artisans and poets with stirring material. It gave the people that high tension of anticipation, of feelings torn between the thrill of victory and the terror of defeat. All around, warfare bolstered national pride and reinforced the king's authority before his people.

Human Sacrifice

As if nearly permanent warfare wasn't enough, agricultural civilization brought ritual murder as well. Joseph Campbell includes a map of human sacrifice and its relative, cannibalism, in his volume *The Way of the Seeded Earth*, which shows "a strong interrelationship between cannibalistic practices and the three agricultural matrices" of the Middle East–Africa, Southeast Asia–Oceania, and the Americas. In all areas, the thrust is essentially the same: Human sacrifice is practiced to promote a more abundant yield of crops.

Lewis Mumford explained the association between agriculture and human sacrifice in terms of beliefs in the magical powers of blood. From way back in forager times, people had associated blood with fecundity and life forces. As they became farmers, perhaps these same beliefs carried over into the emerging mythologies of planting. Perhaps the early forager-farmers believed that human bloodshed, with the right sort of ceremonies, would please the powers who made the soil fertile and caused plants to grow. There is more than a touch of this kind of belief in the religion of the Aztecs, who institutionalized human sacrifice and cannibalism on probably the largest scale in history. In simplest terms, the Aztecs believed that the Sun god, their supreme god, required human blood without which the sun would go out, the corn would die, and Aztec society would be destroyed.

Joseph Campbell, forever the Jungian, thought human sacrifice became a ritual for primitive agriculturalists when they began to recognize a First Being whose body turned into the universe and its life force. In typically wordy, poetic language, Campbell described this recognition of life feeding upon itself as a "nightmare" for early forager-farmers: "In the aboriginal festivals of those parts of the world where the silent cosmic feeding of the plant kingdom on the substances of its mother Earth is the one, ever-present, inescapable, immediate experience of the meaning of life in a living environment, there is always a moment of ultimate frightfulness, executed either in some hidden place, or in full view, as the pivotal climax of an enveloping, dreamlike revel of feasting and hilarity, masks, music and dance, in celebration of the sublime frenzy of this life which is rooted (if one is to see and speak truth) in a cannibal nightmare."

After catching our breath, we turn to Marvin Harris and psychologist Eli Sagan, both of whom have devoted more effort to an understanding of human sacrifice. They say that it grew out of warrior rituals, which, as we have seen, grew out of ancient hunting rituals. Sacrifice ritualizes the feeling, Sagan says, "that [one] is absorbing the manly virtue, the courage, and the energy of the slain warrior by eating him. He is transferring to himself the *mana* ('spiritual power') of his enemy." Both Harris and Sagan say that ritual killing (and occasionally eating) of another human being serves to help warriors build up the manly toughness needed to face and inflict violent death. In warrior cultures, Sagan says, "cannibalism [a form of human sacrifice] is encouraged among the young, especially among novice warriors, as an aid to becoming brave, strong and manly." It is one of many rituals used by warrior subcultures to blunt feelings and encourage aggressive actions—like warring, scalp-taking, raiding, killing, hunting, fighting, and competing with other men for victories in violent games. Marvin Harris believes also that warrior societies used human sacrifice as dramatic proof of battle success and victory. Captured enemies were brought back to the camp to be tortured, slowly killed, and, in some regions, eaten to prove their warrior manhood and to share the revenge with their community. Once ritualized, according to Sagan, "it seems probable that the warring, torturing, and eating are desired for their own sake."

Terrorism with the Stamp of Religion

What needs more explanation is why human sacrifice—and less consistently cannibalism and human head-, scalp-, and trophy-hunting—is associated with early agricultural people the world over. Some experts think they are linked in that both had a common cause: rising human population density, which created more social conflicts, stress, anxieties, and disruptions of older lifeways. When human numbers increased, people took up sedentism, agriculture, and more pitched and dramatic violence against each other. Simple, hit-and-run skirmishes would no longer do because there were too many people and no place to escape. One's semi-sedentary enemy neighbors had to be kept at bay, so the village warriors had to raise the ante. They needed ultraviolence. They brought back human scalps, hands, heads, or captives, which made warfare more dreadful—to both the enemy and to the folks back home. Over time, these became regular fixtures of warfare and they were, of course, institutionalized in stories, myths, ceremonies, and rituals. Once they were given the seal of religion, they stayed on and took on new dimensions. In some regions they went from being a crude way of "keeping the peace" to become a tool of state terrorism.

The Aztec sacrifices are a case in point. In their homeland—the geographically restricted isthmus of central America—human density and social complexity had been building up for thousands of years. There was a succession of agrarian civilizations: the Maya, the Toltecs, the Olmecs, and many lesser ones. The Aztec people were Johnny-come-latelies to the region—invaders from the north who took over the remains of the old cities and empires. In barely two centuries, they went from hunter-foragers living in semi-nomadic bands to raiding tribal warriors to emperors of a ruthless agrarian state. Anthropologist and author of *Man's Rise to Civilization,* Peter Farb says that "in their extraordinary rise to statehood, the Aztecs had not rid themselves completely of some features of the less complex levels of band, tribe, etc. Relics of more simple kinds of institutions persisted in all levels of Aztec society."

The Aztecs were agrarian kings with the hearts of hunters. Their warrioring plopped them down at the head of an empire that they were not culturally equipped to maintain, so they held it as best they could with what they knew: warring, raiding, hostage-taking, sacrifice, and cannibalism. In a region that was ecologically limited from the outset, thousands of years of agricultural intensification made it worse. Their capital among the lakes, Tenochtitlán, contained from 200,000 to 300,000 people when

Cortez came from Spain. It was perhaps the largest city in the world at the time.

The Aztecs were vulnerable, ecologically and culturally, and their anxieties were reflected in their religion. It was a doom-and-gloom view of the world in which the sun would go out and human beings would be exterminated. That anxious worldview, combined with the religious belief that the sun god needed human hearts and blood, fueled a form of worship (or appeasement) that included, some say, almost daily human sacrifice and ritual cannibalism. Most of the victims were male prisoners of war, but slaves were also sacrificed as well as the occasional youths and virgins. So for religious reasons (that familiar refrain), the Aztecs became predators against their neighbors.

War as a Substitute for Cannibalism

Did our cultural ancestors, the peoples of the ancient Middle East, practice human sacrifice and ritual cannibalism? Maybe, but the evidence is sketchy. As a result, Western scholars tend to downplay these abominations in our own tradition. But they are prone to finding, and exaggerating, them in the civilizations of Africa, Asia, Oceania, and, especially, the Aztecs and Mayas in the Americas. In these lands, we have eyewitness accounts—by, of course, Western explorer/conquerors.

It is known that many of these accounts exaggerated cannibalism because of the ulterior motives of the "witnesses." According to church policy, cannibals and homosexuals were beyond salvation—that is, explorers did not have to regard them as human beings. As abominables, they did not have to be spared and turned over to the Jesuits. Their lands and goods could be taken without guilt or red tape. It is not unusual, then, to find explorers' reports loaded with descriptions of native people as "sodomites" and cannibals, for these were sure to result in royal permission to conquer.

Exaggerations and Western bias aside, cannibalism, at least, appears to have been rare in the early agricultural societies of the Old World. There, according to Marvin Harris, domestic animals supplied the need for flesh, blood, and ritual sacrifice. "From Europe to China," he says, "it was animal not human flesh that was brought to the altars, ritually sacrificed, dismembered, redistributed and consumed in communal feasts." (More on animal sacrifice in a moment.) Human sacrifice, however, does appear on the West's record. Many Middle Eastern archaeological sites show royal burials where a king was buried along with his entire court, a retinue of servants, and domestic animals. At the Ziggurat, or great pyramid, at Ur, the capital of ancient Sumeria, sixteen of these "sacred regicides" with mass human sacrifice and burial occurred within the 150 years after 2500 B.C. The kings and queens were probably ceremonially slain; the others appear to have been buried alive. Our mythologies also tell us of human sacrifice in the ancient West. From the Old Testament, the stories of Passover and of Abraham and Isaac suggest that human sacrifice was a religious ritual in much earlier times. Greek mythology, too, is full of references to the practice.

This relative rarity of cannibalism and human sacrifice in the Western tradition is poor grounds for feelings of superiority, however. We should remember that the violent and aggressive traditions of our older hunter cultures were redirected and reritualized in other ways—primarily in animal sacrifice and wars of conquest, which included the mass executions, mutilations, rape, and slave-taking discussed above. For Westerners, cannibalism is revolting, but, as Eli Sagan says, "other forms of institutionalized aggression are not as easy [for us] to recognize, particularly when domination has replaced killing." In the cultures of the West, he says, "the desire to kill and eat has been sublimated into the desire to dominate and oppress."

In the cosmic scheme of things, then, which region's early farmers committed greater routine atrocities: Mesoamerica's anxious cannibals or Mesopotamia's ruthless warlords? And besides, how do you measure routine atrocities?

A Western Specialty: Expansionism

All of the early agrarian centers had some things in common, namely, creeping sedentism, growing human populations and densities, towns, cities, craft specialization and trade. We should include in the list huge temples, plazas, palaces, fortifications, irrigation systems, and other massive public works projects. All had also a steady buildup of laws, government, bureaucracy, and other institutions of social control. This is why we see in all of the budding agrarian civilizations the same emergence of powerful kings, priests, and elites and domineering city-states. In all the agrarian centers, the pattern is the same: The most ruthless few increase their wealth and power while the majority of people, whether as slaves or peasants, settle into poverty, drudgery, and subjugation.

Ruling elites used their armies and religions with mixed effects. On the one hand, they broke down tribalism, unified squabbling peoples, and maintained some measure of social peace in their realms. On the other, they inadvertently enlarged the scale of social conflicts—extending war, oppression, slavery, ritual torture, and mass killing from intertribal to international dimensions. There are many surprising, and depressing, similarities among all of the centers of early agrarian civilization.

The Middle Eastern center, the source of Western culture, however, stands out in one substantial respect: Its cultural heritage is markedly more expansionist and domineering than the others. The kings, armies, and religions of the West aggressively overran other regions and peoples—more consistently, more deliberately, and at greater distances than the other centers. The Egyptians, Incas, Mayas, Aztecs, Chinese, and the people of India built trade networks and empires, of course, but not quite to the same extent nor with the same driving, domineering spirit as did the Middle Eastern Sumerians, Assyrians, Persians, and their offspring, the Greeks and Romans. Centuries later, it would be the Middle East's cultural grandchildren, the Europeans and Americans, who explored, conquered, and colonized every continent—not the Chinese or the people of India. The other agrarian centers spawned great, universalizing, tribe-spanning religions, but none has the missionary zeal, none is driven to convert remote lands and peoples, quite as intensely as the West's three-headed religion. Christianity and Islam, especially, are marked by their aggressive "outreach" campaigns into the lands of the not-yet-faithful. Jews and followers of other major religions have been content to stick more or less with their own ethnic and linguistic groups and to stay closer to home, but not the believers in Jesus and Mohammed. They carry on crusades, jihads, and other holy wars; their God orders them to demolish all other gods and the beliefs that go with them.

A Western Specialty: Herder Culture

Why is the Middle East/Western tradition so aggressive, so domineering? I'll give you a short, straight answer: large animal domestication. The hunting, then the herding, and finally the enslavement of large, powerful animals, especially cattle and horses, put Western culture on a power trip that continues full force today.

As we saw in the last chapter, animals, especially large animals, made deep psychic impressions on forager people. Animals stirred and moved their minds and shaped their culture. And culture, of course, guides human society and behavior. No wonder foragers believed that animals were the First Beings, the ancestors and teachers of human beings.

Large animals that live in herds had special characteristics and behaviors ("powers") that "taught" the people who hunted them. The people identified with "their" herd, calling themselves the reindeer people, the buffalo people, or the like. In northern Iraq, they would have been the sheep people and the goat people. To the west and north, cattle people and horse people; to the south, camel people. And then, millennium by millennium, these specialized hunters began to domesticate their herds. They domesticated sheep and goats 10,000 years ago, cattle 2,000 years later, and horses and camels about 2,000 to 4,000 years later still.

During the long, slow process, the old hunter "teachings" continued to guide the domesticators—and for quite a while. As herding gradually replaced hunting, new teachings cropped up, but they never completely replaced the old hunter culture. They grew *up from* the old and they grew *over* the old; but, like a taproot, the hunter culture lay deep and invisible, feeding the herders' lifeways and ideas about the world.

All of these large animal herding cultures grew up in or around the Middle Eastern agricultural center—the West's birthplace. After a formative period there, they rapidly spread their herds, their ideas, and their influence eastward to India and China, southward to Egypt and Africa, and westward to Greece and Europe. The herding culture supplied the building of the agrarian order and it became integrated into the rise of civilization—first in the Middle East, then in Europe, Egypt, India, and the rest of Asia.

Deliberate Oversimplification

Anthropologists, historians, and other professional academics naturally scream and tear their hair at such ideas. They deplore single-cause theories because they oversimplify the complexities of human evolution and historical development. Academics, of course, like lawyers, have a vested interest in keeping things complex. One's field needs to be confusing and beyond the comprehension of the average person. The more angles and theories that can be imagined, the more papers and books that can be written expounding on them all. The more complex things can be made to seem, the more the need for specialization, which, of course, creates jobs. Careers can be maintained on the study of one style of pot made in one city during the reign of one king. After many generations and levels of specialization, no expert understands any other and the very simplest things become extremely complex. This is how academicians hold their orbits.

Some of us, then, need to simplify things in the hope that we might come to understand our cultural development, which helps us understand our current problems, which, in turn, helps us find solutions and better directions. So let us concede that getting to the bottom of the character of Western culture is a very risky, very complex chore. Granted, there were many forces, many factors that pushed it along its way. Like a river, it has many eddies, currents, and tributaries. But also like a river, a main channel lies somewhere underneath it all, and somewhere it has a principal source.

Herder Values

The Middle East was the epicenter of large animal domestication—specifically cattle, horses, camels, goats, and sheep. It originated there, not in any of the other agricultural centers, although after domestication these animals were eventually introduced in Africa, India, and Eastern Asia.

Two points: First, this put a unique ingredient into the development of Western culture from the very start. As Alfred Crosby says in his book *Ecological Imperialism,* "The most important contrast between the Sumerians and their heirs, on the one hand, and the rest of humanity, on the other, involves the matter of livestock."

Second, this ingredient created huge repercussions—results that are, as we shall see, way out of proportion to the beginnings. Like yeast, large animal domestication exploded the West's agrarian cultural dough into some very large, crusty loaves. As German sociologist and zoologist Richard Lewinsohn said in *Animals, Men, and Myths,* "the specific variations produced by domestication may be small in a zoological sense but they are enormous from the sociological point of view, for they have effected deep-reaching transformations in the history of both human beings and animals."

Anthropologists, of course, abhor generalizations, but even they would have to admit that herdspeople—pastoralists, they call them—the world over have some basic traits in common. They are obsessed with their sheep, goats, cattle, camels, or horses, as the case may be, for the animals are both their tribal identity and their livelihood. The herd is everything to the pastoralists, and nothing gets between it and the best pasture and water. If anything does, single-mindedness easily turns to ruthlessness, defiance to violence. In *Thinking Animals,* Paul Shepard ticks off the mainstays of herder cultures the world over: "Aggressive hostility to outsiders, the armed family, feuding and raiding in a male-centered hierarchical organization, the substitution of war for hunting, elaborate arts of sacrifice, monomaniacal pride and suspicion." These same attitudes were cataloged among tribes of the Middle East by Charles M. Doughty in *Deserta Arabia.*

Anthropologists have noted more of the same among the Chukchi reindeer herders of eastern Siberia. According to Anthony Leeds, the Chukchi carry ideologies that help them build up and maintain their herds—their wealth. In *Man, Culture and Animals,* he says that these are bolstered by values on "the 'strong' man, the 'good herdsman,' sheer physical strength, competitive physical accomplishment, violence." The Chukchi love to boast, Leeds says, of "feats of strength, acts of prowess, violent and heroic behavior, excessive endurance and expenditure of energy."

If you have noticed how much this sounds like the American cowboy or rodeo star, you understand the timelessness, the universality of the herdsman. Leeds notes that Chukchi herdsmen boast all the more when they tell stories of war, the ultimate aims of which are to get more reindeer, to capture the human herdskeepers attached to them, and to seize control of the grazing land. He says that the above are "permeating behavioral characteristics" of these Siberian herdspeople. Both anthropologists' reports and Chukchi stories are loaded with references to "quarrels, fights, rages, murders, violations, and madnesses," says Leeds.

The Herder Dilemma: War or Poverty

British anthropologist B. A. L. Cranstone corroborates these views of herder culture after looking at herdspeople in Melanesia, North Africa, Syria, and Russian Turkestan. Since animals are the only form of wealth that is self-mobile, he says, their keepers need to be constantly on guard. "People who depend heavily on animals are, therefore, usually warlike because they have to be prepared to defend their herds." Especially warlike are those who herd camels and horses, for these are powerful animals who can run far and fast. Less warlike, he says, are those who herd sheep, goats, and the smaller, more controllable animals.

Anthropologist and popular writer Marvin Harris has studied a variety of human cultures looking for common elements. In *Cannibals and Kings,* he noted that "most nomadic or seminomadic pre-state pastoral societies are expansionist and extremely militaristic." They are usually warlike and male-dominated because their wealth is "animals on the hoof rather than crops in the field." Given their herd-following ways, economic pressures force them into a life of ranging far and wide for water, pasture, and other herds to steal.

In another overview of the world's herding cultures, anthropologist Homer Aschmann noted, in Anthony Leeds and Andrew Vayda's *Man, Culture and Animals,* the same constant need for territorial expansion. It may be restrained at times, but "a vigorously developed pattern of individual and collective aggression, and supporting institutional and ethical structures, exist in most herding cultures."

Aschmann noted another dimension to the destructiveness of herding societies: Their tendency to increase their herds invariably damages their rangeland. "No primarily herding society has ever achieved a stable ecologic adjustment except at a lower level of productivity than the one that existed when pastoralism was introduced." The worst damage is done by the least mobile and warlike cultures, because they tend to stay in one place while they build up their herds. The fierce, warlike herders simply move around, riding herd on other people and using their lands.

However romantic it may seem (and our herder-based heritage does dress it up in song and poetry), the herding way of life presented a harsh dilemma. And both horns were equally destructive: If herdspeople were peaceful, they destroyed the land and ended up in illness and poverty. If they were warlike, they had the best land and living, but they destroyed their neighbors and the social peace. As Richard Lewinsohn says: "Only in pastoral poetry were shepherd folk peace-loving. In reality, they were not far behind hunters in rapacity and belligerence."

The Herder Heritage

Sir Keith Thomas, the British dean of the history of ideas about nature, thinks herder values contributed to the domineering side of Western culture. In *Man and the Natural World,* he wrote: "Some anthropologists believe that it was the management of herds of domestic animals which first gave rise to an interventionist and manipulative conception of political life. Inhabitants of societies which, like those of Polynesia, lived by vegetable-gardening and growing crops which require relatively little human intervention seem to have taken a relatively unambitious view of the ruler's function. They believed that nature should be left to take its course and that men could be trusted to fend for themselves without regulation from above. But the domestication of animals generated a more authoritarian attitude."

Some will object that dictatorship, warfare, and slave-taking, as we have seen, naturally accompany the growth of the agrarian state. These horrors occur even in Mesoamerica, where dogs and turkeys were probably the only domesticated animals. But in the Middle East, royal power, wars, and raiding take on extra dimensions because of the cultural influence of the early herding peoples there. Remember that these large animal domesticators came from a long tradition as specialized hunters, so they had their hunter-warrior skills intact. Obviously, these went a long way toward helping them build up their herds—their wealth and security. From the perspective of a hunter-warrior, how much more glorious (as well as easier and faster) it was to increase the herd by raiding than by slow, plodding husbandry. Warrior skills also helped keep the wealth, for a prosperous tribe had to be constantly on guard against raids by others. Remember, too, that herders were markedly more expansionist than ordinary farmers. Planter folks were confined to a few acres in a valley or along a river bank, and they expanded their fields relatively slowly—over years. Herders, on the other hand, arrogantly dominated an entire region through military force, thus ensuring access to the best rangeland and water sources. In the Middle Eastern center, then, herders were best positioned to fill the warrior class, out of which arose the ruling elites and kings. Consequently, the entire hierarchy and culture in the region was imbued with herders' fierce, expansionist values. When these became integrated into the agrarian state's religion, military and other governing institutions, they made for a ruthless nation hell-bent on wars of conquest.

Besides war-mongering and empire-building, herders contributed a great deal to the West's obsession with property and money. Some think that it began with the ancient herders' obsession with their animal herds, their wealth on the hoof. Richard Lewinsohn argues that the concept of money—or exchangeable wealth—began with herding specifically rather than agriculture in general. In his book *Animals, Men and Myths,* Lewinsohn wrote: "The concept of property arose from the power of disposal over the herds and was older and stronger than the property concept based on ownership of land, for arable land was plentiful, tamed animals scarce. Land spells production, cattle spell consumer goods. Only consumable property has tangible worth. Animals were the first form of capital (wealth). The word 'capital' stems from Latin 'capita,' relating to the head count of cattle by which a man's wealth was measured."

Similarly, at the root of our words *impecunious* and *pecuniary,* which pertain to money, is the Latin *pecu,* the old word for cattle. In the old Aryan language, the word for warfare translated literally into "a desire for more cattle." Cattle, or more probably sheep and goats, were the first form of portable, exchangeable wealth—that is, the first form of money. They were the first capitalists, those ancient herders, and they also put forth the first get-rich-quick scheme: raiding others and stealing their animals. At the time, it was the quickest way to build up the money supply—the herd of animals.

The Costs of Success

We ought to look at the flip side of the herders' haughty, powerful style. How much of it crept into Western culture? On the surface, herders were proud, brave, and free, but underneath, their lives were full of fear and tension. However glorious and profitable, raiding for wealth created many insecurities and conflicts. It put a premium on toughness, manly power, military skills, and aggressiveness, but it took a toll on the rest of the human spirit. Herder values put man against man (especially men) and pushed individualism to an extreme. A man had to go off on his own and prove his manhood. He had to go it alone against all odds, he had to show that he could outdo all others. Few, of course, can live up to the model. Anthropologist Anthony Leeds saw the results in the reindeer-herding Siberian Chukchi: "Men who cannot compete and quarrel in the ideal Chukchi manner are considered 'weak,' even 'soft to die.' Men who reject or cannot cope with the fierce competition may commit suicide, may become shamans, or may become transvestite [homosexual] 'wives' of 'stronger' [more aggressive and competitive] men."

Does some of this sound like a Louis L'Amour novel? A John Wayne movie? It should; this is the stuff of the American "Western." Its popularity, its lasting appeal testifies to the depth of herder values in our culture. Even today, our male heroes are still following the model set down thousands of years ago by Middle Eastern pastoral tribes.

The herder's hard-riding life-style also took a toll on social cooperation, justice, and general regard for one's neighbor. Herders were arrogant, individualistic, well-armed, and skilled at warfare. As nomads, they looked down on settled farmers, regarding their stinking villages and drudge-work with contempt. Herders, particularly those who kept horses and cattle, were the scourge of the ancient world. Their roving for pastures and water sources put them in frequent conflict with planters. And the herders could usually demand the better end of the bargain. They had, after all, visible ability to control herds of large animals, many of which had been wrestled from other warlike tribes. They were well equipped to control other people as well, and they merged easily into first the warrior classes, then the ruling elites of early Western civilization. As Richard Lewinsohn notes in *Animals, Men and Myths,* "the wooden fence marked the beginnings of the concentration camp and the cord was the first shackle."

The Shepherd-Flock Model for Society

Sir Keith Thomas says that "domestication thus became the archetypal pattern for other kinds of social subordination. The model was a paternal one, with the ruler a good shepherd, like the bishop with his pastoral staff. Loyal, docile animals obeying a considerate master were an example to all employees." This model and these pastoral images are pervasive in Western culture. We look reverently upon notions of the Good Shepherd and the benevolent patriarch, for we are still informed by ancient herder life-ways. The good, civilized man *shepherds,* or *husbands* his family and property, also his household, his community, his nation, and, by extension, the entire world. The idea of the great, good shepherd is a central idea in Christianity, of course. It is the central idea as well in the secular concept of stewardship, a euphemism, in my opinion, for dominance, control, and exploitation, but with as much visible kindness as economics will permit. Stewardship *is* dominionism, but with a nice face for public relations.

The herder culture created patriarchy—the primacy and rule of men in human affairs. According to anthropologist Peggy Reeves Sandy, animal husbandry and herdskeeping were mainly men's occupations. Societies that depended on herds, she says, tended to be patriarchal with generally male-dominant cultures. Such societies proliferated in the Middle East where most of the agricultural species were domesticated. Male-dominant, patriarchal herdskeeping culture, then, was prevalent throughout the region where Western history and civilization begin with the agrarian city-states.

Male-dominated herder culture gained its wealth and power by controlling and manipulating—like all farmers—natural processes. In this case, the natural processes were animals' lives, their sexuality, and procreativity. The Good Shepherd loves his sheep, but he also builds up his flock—by castrating, dehorning, and culling. Africa's Masai, for example, who have enjoyed extensive media hype as good shepherds, castrated their rams by pounding their testicles between two stones. Ancient tribes used equally brutal methods. Their control over animals—we well as nature in general—was frequently ruthless, but it brought human benefit, comfort, and progress. Control and manipulation of animals—their numbers, sizes, and shapes—became almost an obsession in herding cultures. In time, control came to be valued in and of itself. It was the way of the Good Shepherd, a patriarchal model for the guilt-free exploitation of animals and natural processes.

These shepherd values grew into a religion, of course. Generations of prophets, philosophers, poets, and preachers filled out, refined, and updated the model and some went down in history as the great men of our civilization. Cotton Mather preached the Good Shepherd model from his pulpit to colonial America, and generations used it to justify filling up the rest of the continent. In their view, they were all Good Shepherds, carrying out peaceful, herd-tending duties; they, in turn were the flock of a Great Shepherd, their all-wise, benevolent, paternal god. In this way, control, domination, manipulation, and exploitation had a moral "cover" under the Shepherd model—a model that had been burned into history centuries before by the herdskeeping peoples who co-founded the West's agrarian civilization.

From Powers to Commodities

Domestic animal husbandry brought economic advantages, but it also brought about an unsettling of very old and deeply held ways of seeing animals, human beings, and the natural world. The unsettling process took centuries, of course, but it eventually destroyed the older, primal view of the living world that held animals and natural forces in awe.

The primal worldview saw people in partnership with, and having respectful views of, animals and nature. Animals were admired for their cunning, power, speed, ferocity, and elusiveness. They were seen as ancestors, as kinfolk, as having souls like people. Animal life animated and ensouled the world, gave meaning to its mystery and order to its chaos.

After centuries of manipulative animal husbandry, however, men gained conscious control over animals and their life processes. In reducing them to physical submission, people reduced animals psychically as well. Castrated, yoked, harnessed, hobbled, penned, and shackled, domestic animals were thoroughly subdued. They had none of that wild, mysterious power that their ancestors had when they were stalked by hunter-foragers. Domestic animals were disempowered—made docile—by confinement, selective breeding, and familiarity with humans. They gradually came to be seen more with contempt than awe.

In reducing domestic animals, farmers reduced animals in general, and with them the living world that animals had symbolized. Farming in general helped reduce the animal/natural powers because crop-conscious farmers saw more and more species as pests, more and more natural elements as threats. But it was animal husbandry in particular that nudged people from seeing animals as powers to seeing them as commodities and tools. It was husbandry that drastically upset the ancient human-animal relationship, changing it from partnership to master and slave, from being kin *with* animal-nature to being lord *over* animal-nature.

This reduction of animals—the soul and the essence of the living world to the primal mind—reduced all of nature, creating, in the agriculturalist's mind, a view of the world where people were *over* and distinctly *apart from* nature. Animal reduction was key to the radically different worldview that came with the transition from foraging to farming, for more than any other agricultural development, it broke up the old ideas of kinship and continuity with the living world. This, more than any other factor, accelerated and accentuated human alienation from nature. It originated in the West's first agricultural center, it found its legs there, and then it spread to the other centers of civilization. Husbandry was, I think, the more influential side of farming that led, ultimately, to the agrarian worldview that we still hold today. As that worldview began to emerge thousands of years ago, wrote University of California historian Roderick Nash, "for the first time humans saw themselves as distinct from the rest of nature."

From Totem Animals to the Sacred Herd

The reduction of animals, however, did not come in one fell swoop. It came in fits and starts during the long transition from forager society to agrarian civilization. Well into historical times, agricultural societies had their bull gods, ram gods, and many other animal-shaped deities. These deities, experts say, were a carryover from the old totemic belief systems of forager times. Francis Klingender traced this continuity in the art and archaeology of Egypt and North Africa in *Animals and Art and Thought*. He found plenty of pottery, paintings, and other evidence to confirm that, "as the various clans began to breed cattle and live on their milk, they transferred to their herds the notions of sanctity and kinship which formerly belonged to species of wild animals."

As we have seen, foragers, especially those who tilted toward hunting, generally had religions, or views of the world, that we call totemic. Under these, a Master of the Animals, a supernatural animal who was a sort of chief of its species, usually gave a tribe permission to hunt and eat members of its flock or herd. In some cases, however, the tribe was not allowed to hunt or eat its totem animal except during special sacrificial rituals. These concepts held on well into the agricultural period, but, increasingly, they had to be modified to meet society's new living conditions. People, after all, were settling in towns and it was not possible for them to go out to the forest and hunt for meat very often. In fact, with the growth of the agrarian towns and cities, the populations grew so large and the croplands so extensive that game animals, as well as forests, were probably sparse for miles around. The hunt, obviously, could no longer supply settled farmers and city dwellers with meat for the table.

Gradually, then, as hunting turned to herding and as settled farmers began to maintain small herds of their own, totemic views and rituals of the hunt were forced to change. The sanctity of totem animals and the powers of animals in general went into gradual decline. Slowly, imperceptibly, agrarians reduced the animal powers as they enhanced their own. In the earliest stages, as animal domestication and husbandry emerged from hunter-herders, the Master of the Animals became the Sacred Bull or Ram. This imaginary animal was a deity who was the spirit of the herd who was worshiped (or appeased) to ensure the protection of the herd. In herder cultures, chief/kings often identified themselves with this sacred animal to enhance their power and prestige with the animal's cult followers. Eventually, the kings used the association to enhance their own pretensions to deity, so that the king himself was the human personification of the Sacred Bull or Ram. In their capital cities, these kings maintained sacred flocks of sheep or herds of cattle that could not be killed and eaten except through ritual sacrifice.

Animal Sacrifice

It must have been a confusing time for the mind and the stomach. People yearned for meat, but they still carried the vestiges of totemic values, especially the kinship with the sacred herd. As Lord Kenneth Clark wrote: "While men still felt a kinship with animals, to eat them was a crime against the group, and expiation could be achieved only by a ritual feast in which all were involved." So guilt-spreading and communion, or redistribution, were the first bases for animal sacrifice. As usual, the practice took on layer upon layer of religious importance over the centuries. The basic belief emerged that the gods could be pleased by the sacrifices and that they would protect the crops or the people from disasters. Eventually, as rulers associated themselves with the sacred herd and conspired with the priestly class to conduct the state religion, animal sacrifices became an assertion of royal and priestly authority.

Throughout the ancient world, animal sacrifice followed the same basic formula: the animal was delivered to the temple and, after a ceremony designed to make the animal appear willing to be slaughtered, a priest carried out the ritual killing. The priest then burned a small amount of the meat as an offering to the god or goddess. The rest of the animal's carcass was either returned to the owner, redistributed to cult followers, or sold to others.

Interestingly, the ritual had many guilt-reducing and -spreading elements. First, only the priest could do the killing, which protected the animal's owner or eater from direct responsibility. Second, the priest did the killing for religious reasons under elaborate rituals, which, again, reduced responsibility. The ceremony was set up to make the gods responsible, and who was going to fool with them? This "is no mere speculation," says James Serpell. "According to an ancient Babylonian text, the head priest actually bent down to the ear of the slaughtered [animal] victim and whispered, 'this deed was done by all the gods; I did not do it.' " This verbal device is identical to some of the older forms of ritual killing practiced by primal hunters, particularly, as we saw in the previous chapter, Japan's Ainu people, who, once a year, ritually kill a bear, their totem animal and ancestor.

As Marvin Harris and other anthropologists point out, these ritual sacrifices became more and more frequent as the kings and priests conspired to buy peace and public support through more and more lavish public feasts. In time, the king's sacred herd became less and less sacred and the temple where the ritual slaughtering was done took on more and more the character of a commercial slaughterhouse. The scale and frequency of the rituals, says Serpell, indicate that they were "little more than a transparent excuse for feasting." When the Israelites dedicated Solomon's temple at Jerusalem, 22,000 oxen and 120,000 sheep were slaughtered and, if prevailing customs were followed, roasted and eaten by the multitudes.

Serpell says that animal sacrifice was common throughout the ancient Western world, practiced by Egyptians, Phoenicians, Babylonians, Hebrews, Persians, Etruscans, and Romans. It spread to India, as well, by way of her conquerors, the warlike, cattle-breeding Aryans from Persia and Afghanistan. There the Aryan warlords held huge redistributive feasts, according to Harris, at which Brahman priests presided and performed the ritual killings. The priests turned it into a monopoly on killing and eventually into a privilege by which Brahams alone could eat meat. Their meat elitism was one of the bases for the Jainist and Buddhist reformist revolts around 600 B.C. And in classical Greece, animal sacrifices were so frequent that "the Parthenon is said to have stunk like a slaughterhouse," according to Lord Clark. Homer's *Odyssey,* Clark notes, tells us that "no feast, no landfall, no hospitable welcome, no gift-laden departure [was] conceivable without the sacrifice of animals."

Animal sacrifice, then, took the place of hunting as a means of putting meat on agrarian tables. As farming regions became more populous and as urban settlements of the agrarian city-state grew larger, hunting could not provide enough flesh to satisfy the masses. Domestic animals were at hand, but guilt and old beliefs did not permit their wholesale slaughter. Something had to give. Priests and kings made meat available through the state-sponsored religion, a move that strengthened their government in two ways: It furnished a food craved as much for power as palatability, and it removed the people's guilt about the slaughtering process. A side effect was that ownership of flocks and herds—and arguably the meat-eating privilege itself—came to be associated with the wealthy, powerful elite.

A Question of Emphasis

Have I given too much emphasis to the animal side of agriculture? I don't think so. For one, as I have said, large animal domestication and herder culture are what makes Western civilization different from all others. These two developments are uniquely Middle Eastern. They begin in that agricultural center and they are integral to the evolution of agriculture there from the very start. Some animal domestication originates in the other agricultural centers, but it is sparse, the animals are small and not herd animals (with the exception of the llama group in Peru, to be discussed) and in most cases it does not occur simultaneously with plant agriculture. Nowhere else was animal domestication nearly as big, integral, influential, and early as it was in the birthplace of the West. Nowhere else does it produce a herder subculture as it does in the Middle East. From there, large animal domestication and the herder subculture spread far and wide, to Europe, Africa, and the rest of Asia.

Second, I deliberately emphasize the animal side of agriculture because I believe writers tend to underemphasize it in discussions of our past. Much is being written these days about agriculture's being the "seed of alienation," and the "fall from grace." For most of these writers, farming is generic. Animal- or plant-tenders, farmers are one and the same: expansionist nature-busters. I'll admit that agriculture in general does bring on, to some extent, these two elements to culture, but, as I have argued, the animal side brings the lion's share of them. It also brings more of the male supremacy, hunter's hardness, and warriorism than does the plant side. As Peggy Reeves Sanday has shown in *Female Power and Male Dominance,* hunting, herding, and animal exploitation tend to be men's work while gathering, gardening, and horticulture tend more to be women's work. Men generally have more status and power in animal-based economies and women more in plant-based economies. Herding, then, was a conduit for the male supremacist hunter-warrior traditions to pour into Western agrarian culture—from its very beginnings and throughout its long, early, formative period.

Third, I believe that animal husbandry has had, on balance, much more impact on the human psyche (and hence on Western culture) than did horticulture. As we saw in Chapter 3, animals were and still are vital, stirring, moving—necessary—to the human mind. Animals, especially large ones, affect our emotions and our imagination like nothing else in nature. Animals, as we saw, give us a way to see order in the world, to feel continuity with it. Consequently, animals symbolize the rest of nature, and the way we see animals determines how we see the rest of nature.

I am tempted to speculate here about why the animal side of agriculture has been avoided or underrated. In the interests of space and the reader's patience, I will not do so. I would be repeating most of what has been said before—once when we looked at the man-the-mighty-hunter myth in Chapter 2 and again in Chapter 3, when we discussed the reluctance of psychologists and others to explain why animals are so prevalent in art, psychological tests, children's literature, dreams, and so on. There is a big irony here, and I will keep urging you to see it: Animals are so very important to the human mind and culture, and yet our nature-alienated culture has blacklisted them and made them marginal to our cultural evolution. Indeed, the entire subject is considered trivial, risible. The emotional dynamics involved in meat eating and institutionalized animal exploitation, I believe, have a great deal to do with it. Let's take this up again in the next chapter.

After all this emphasis, I may have created the impression that there were two separate societies in the ancient Middle East: herder and planter. This was not exactly the case. Let's take a moment, then, and try to put animal husbandry and herder society into perspective within the larger picture of early farming in the Middle East. Were the two societies separate? Yes and no. Some of the herder peoples stuck with nomadic pastoralism, living wild and free with their precious herds as long as they could. Typically, they were very proud of their nomadic way of life and looked upon settled farmers with scorn and contempt. These tribal pastoralists generally roamed around the edges of the settled regions, looking for water and grazing lands without having to make contact with the farmers. Relations between the two were mixed. They probably tried to maintain the peace in order to do some trading, but, given the mutual scorn and distrust, it must have been a very fragile peace.

But there were other herder people who were not so nomadic and warlike, and these probably lived more or less within the settled domains, trading animals, labor, and goods routinely. In time, of course, planters learned animal husbandry and began developing breeds to suit the needs of settled farmers. Goats and sheep provided milk, cheese, and, at feast times, meat after ritual sacrifice. Large, docile cattle pulled the plows of ancient farmers and provided milk and the occasional fatted calf for ritual sacrifice. Horses fought wars, mostly. They were the secret weapons and prized possessions of kings and warrior elites. It would be many centuries after their domestication in the Ukraine around 4000 B.C. before they were reduced to pulling plows in the fields of peasants. Very gradually, then, settled farmers acquired domestic animals and turned them into laborers and food on the hoof.

Controlling Nature: The Farmer's Livelihood

From the worldview of the nomadic forager, the living world was regarded as a partner and a provider and primal people never stored surpluses. For a sedentary farmer, however, surpluses were security and nature did not always provide them. Some have estimated that early farmers probably had one good, bountiful year in about seven. Farmers saw nature as part inferior, part adversary—in either case, a thing to be subdued, controlled at all times. As James Serpell puts it: "The farmer has no choice but to set himself up in opposition to nature. Land must be cleared for cultivation, and weeds and pests, which would otherwise restore his fields to their original condition, must be vigorously suppressed. Domestic livestock must be controlled and confined, using force if necessary, to prevent them wandering off and reverting to a wild state, or being eaten by predators. The entire system, in fact, depends on the subjugation of nature, and the domination and manipulation of living creatures."

Indeed, agriculture is the systematic manipulation of plant and animal reproduction, growth and other life processes for the benefit of human beings. From the outset, farmers have been nature-manipulators. If nature did not provide rain, people built irrigation canals to get water to their crops. If nature brought floods that destroyed croplands, people built dikes and dams to control the rivers. If farmers needed larger fields, they cleared forests and plowed prairies. In agricultural times, natural beings became obstacles. Human beings gradually ceased to look upon natural forces with awe; rather, they were increasingly frustrated by them and often left hungry. With larger populations settled in villages dependent on crop yields, a flood, drought, pestilence, or other natural event could bring massive starvation and suffering.

Granted that, over time, farming permitted food surpluses, settlement, urban centers, labor specialization, great arts and architecture, and generally fueled the rise of civilization. But it also drove a wedge between humanity and nature. Farming built huge, new insecurities into human existence. For the first time in human evolution, people could have too much to eat; but if nature was uncooperative, for the first time they could also have nothing at all. Gradually, agricultural societies came to see the living world less as a divinity and more as an enemy. Nature was not to be held in awe, it was to be subdued, outwitted, and controlled.

And besides increasing hostility, farming raised human arrogance toward the living world. In learning to control the growth of plants and animals, human beings demystified nature and set themselves up as her master. They put away the very old traditions of seeing themselves *in* nature, of seeing other beings as kindred in flesh and spirit, and they began to see themselves as godly.

These were major psychic changes, and to work through them people needed new ideas and new religions to help them along toward new ways. Serpell explains agrarian society's need for a new worldview in his book *In the Company of Animals:* "It is likely that this new relationship with animals and nature, with its conflicting combination of intimacy and enslavement, generated intense feelings of guilt; guilt which was reinforced by an uncompromising environment that could ruin a crop overnight or decimate whole populations of livestock. Faced with this conflict, new ideologies were required; ideologies that absolved farming people from blame and enabled them to continue their remorseless programme of expansion and subjugation with a clear conscience." The various agrarian centers found their way through varying ideologies, some more expedient than others. But, as Serpell says, "if the record of civilization is anything to go by, it was the most ruthless cultures . . . who prospered most of all."

Agrarian Religion—the Early Days

Let us recall the primal religion (which was, in the modern sense of the words, more a worldview than a theology) that prevailed on the eve of agriculture. We discussed it in Chapter 2. Anthropologist Robin Fox summarizes this worldview nicely. The aim of primal man, he says, "is to live harmoniously and successfully within the tribal framework. He is capable of both good and evil but is not particularly prone to either. Human nature is seen as a mixture of good and evil tendencies. If there is no notion of human beings as creatures born in sin against which they must struggle, neither is there any notion of them born essentially innocent and only later corrupted by the world. Thus there is no fall of man. In fact, man is seen as having evolved from a childlike state. . . ." Most tribes, Fox says, had some idea of an afterlife, but it was not very well defined; it was a hazy concept, and it was given little thought or discussion. Neither was the idea of "man's destiny"—a subject that becomes an obsession and a generator of much philosophical drivel in Western civilization after the Sumerians invented writing around 3200 B.C. If primal society had a sense of destiny or a philosophy, it was to live a happy, successful life in harmony with the natural and moral order as conceived by the tribe's culture.

But it is the primal views of the living world ("nature") that are most important to our understanding of the changes brought by agriculture and herding. Fox, Peter Farb, Ruth Underhill, Joseph Campbell, Paul Shepard, virtually all of the writers on the subject, are unanimous: The essential tenet of primal religions was a strong feeling of kinship or partnership with the living environment. For primal people, the world consisted of beings, souls, and powers; for the agriculturalist, it consisted of resources and pests.

Again, we must remember that this change did not come sharply or rapidly. For a very long time into the agricultural period, elements of the primal religion persisted. Some of these elements were carried on by societies that clung to their nomadic ways, refusing to settle down to farming and village life. Other elements were absorbed, with modifications, into the emerging agrarian worldview. We saw, for example, how hunt rituals and ideas about totem animals turn into war rituals, the notion of the Sacred Herd and animal sacrifice in the agricultural era.

In the agricultural era the scale of human society increased at all levels, which brought the need for mechanisms of social control. These include government, but also theologies and religious practices. Consequently, agri-cultural theologies, or religious ideas, were more formalized and rituals and ceremonies became increasingly complex and specialized. In primal times, "worship," or the exercise of one's religious beliefs, was more or less personal and immediate—an affair between the individual and the supernaturals. There were shamans, of course, who could help in spiritual matters, but they did not control the tribe's belief system. In the agricultural era, however, worship becomes more of a matter dictated by the state and its priests for political reasons. The priests are religious specialists, the managers of both religious dogma and flocks of worshipers. Religion loses genuine spirituality: that powerful—and empowering—feeling for one's belonging in the living scheme of things. It becomes less and less a medium for the human spirit and more and more a tool for social control.

When God Was a Woman

While the forager religions lasted well into the agricultural period, they were ultimately subsumed by the rising agrarian religions. Like the old forager religions, these venerated both male and female principles. Most writers agree, however, that the greater principles and deities were female—at least in the earlier millennia of agri-culture. God, as author Merlin Stone put it, was a woman. Unfortunately, that says it in monotheistic, anthropomorphic terms. It would be more accurate to say, at least in the first few millennia of the agricultural period, that the living world's greatest spirit-power was female. This veneration of a great mother-goddess had, as we saw in Chapter 2, very old roots in the old forager cultures. Big-breasted, wide-hipped "Venus" figurines show up in many Old World archaeological sites that date back well before 10,000 years ago.

This tradition of veneration of female principles naturally took off in the early millennia of agriculture. For one thing, women had most of the knowledge about plant cycles and did most of the work of gathering and horticulture. Some say, with good reason, that women probably "invented" the plant side of agriculture. For another, as Paul Shepard puts it, "the necessities of cultivation" are "inescapably feminine." The very nature of horticultural work—wedding seed to soil; tending to fragile, young shoots; and gathering the harvest—is in line with female traditions and principles. The new mysteries of plant fecundity and soil fertility also bolstered the beliefs of early farmers in a great female spirit of procreation, for the associations among seeds, germination, gestation, dormancy, birth, menstruation, fertility, growth, and death are striking. Female veneration was bolstered further by farmers' growing knowledge about the interconnected cycles of plant growth, the seasons, and the movements of the sun, moon, and stars. Bear in mind that these universal forces, cycles, and powers of creativity were *the* most impressive mysteries 10,000 years ago. They were the energies that moved early agricultural society along, and they were overwhelmingly female. Agriculture's essential and obvious femaleness, says Shepard, "dealt the male ego a blow so terrible that his vengeance may yet destroy most of nature. . . ."

Not surprisingly, then, archaeologists have found a great many figurines and other representations of the great female spirit-power, or mother-goddess, in early agricultural civilizations all over the world. In southeastern Europe alone, University of California archaeologist Marija Gimbutas reported 30,000 sculptures from a total of 3,000 sites. At Catal Huyuk, a very ancient city on the European side of the Middle Eastern region, British archaeologist James Mellaart found female figurines and shrines in all the earliest levels of excavation. Similar evidence has been found in Jericho, Syria, along the banks of the Tigris, and at other sites in the Middle East. More of the same have been found farther east in India, on Mediterranean islands, and in Europe and the British Isles. Female figurines are found in all of the agricultural centers, according to Joseph Campbell. In Mesoamerica, he says, "the most typical image is the stand-

ing female nude." Of these ceramic figurines, Campbell wrote: "There is
no point in pretending—like so many exact scholars of these matters—
that we do not know who she is. What we do not know exactly are the
uses to which her images were applied and by what names she was
invoked in her various manifestations and functions. But that she is the
great goddess-mother of us all and in the context of a planting culture's
inevitable order of interests was associated with the earth, we can surely
know." The popularity and wide dispersal of the ancient mother-goddess
religions has been thoroughly documented by Marija Gimbutas in her
book *The Goddesses and Gods of Old Europe 7000–3500 B.C.*

Denial of the Obvious

Modern, patriarchal society's scholars, of course, deny or denigrate the
importance of the evidence for ancient mother-goddess religions. They
tend to say things like, "we can't be sure what these female figurines
mean." This, says Riane Eisler in *The Chalice and the Blade,* is "the
invisibility of the obvious." The overwhelming evidence for a very old
veneration of the world's life force as female "is automatically excluded
under the prevailing worldview." When they encounter it, Eisler says,
"scholars suddenly go blank or quickly head in another direction."

Gerda Lerner, intelligently, has done what most scholars have not: She
explains the significance of the female figurines by looking at the rem-
nants of ancient myths, rituals, and creations stories about the great
mother-goddess. These, too, are evidence of a great female-oriented religion in the period of transition from foraging to farming, says Lerner in
The Creation of Patriarchy:

"The supremacy of the Goddess is also expressed in the earliest myths
of origin, which celebrate the life-giving creativity of the female. In Egyptian mythology the primeval ocean, the goddess Nun, gives birth to the
sun-god Atum, who then creates the rest of the universe. The Sumerian
goddess Nammu creates parthogenetically the male sky-god An and the
female earth-goddess Ki. In Babylonian myth the goddess Tiamat, the
primeval sea, and her consort give birth to gods and goddesses. In Greek
mythology, the earth-goddess Gaia, in a virgin birth, creates the sky,
Uranos. The creation of humans is also ascribed to her. In the Assyrian
version of an older Sumerian myth the wise Mami (also known as Nintu),
'the mother-womb, the one who creates mankind,' fashions humans out
of clay, but it is the male god Ea 'who opened the navel' of the figures,

thus completing the life-giving process. In another version of the same story, Mami, at the urging of Ea, herself finished the creative process: 'The Mother-Womb, the creatress of destiny/in pairs she completed them. . . . The forms of the people Mami forms.' "

Religion, as Eisler and many other authorities have noted, "supports and perpetuates the social organization it reflects." She, Marvin Harris, and others have shown that human societies during the early agricultural period were matrilineal—that is, they traced family descent through the female line. In these societies, especially when they idealized the supreme power in the universe as female, women, obviously, had considerably more status than they have had under the West's monotheistic, male-headed religions. In goddess-venerating societies, women would have had a very different self-image. As Eisler points out, with such a powerful role-model girls and women would naturally consider it their right and duty to fully participate in society and to take the lead in government and religion. "They would see themselves as competent, independent, and most certainly creative and inventive." Sure enough, there is ample evidence that women served as rulers and priests in most agrarian city-states well into the historical period.

That being the case, how did a matrilineal early agrarian society that venerated life, procreation, female principles, and female humanity come to be patriarchal, male-worshiping, misogynous, and hell-bent on war and conquest?

How did the Middle East's agri-culture start off seeing the living world full of great powers and spirits and end up seeing it as a pile of resources and commodities—chaotic and in need of human control?

Early agri-culture blended nicely with the older, forager tradition's ideas about the animal powers, the fecundity of the plant world, and the awesome creative powers of the female. By the end stage, after history had begun and the agrarian kings were busy building armies and empires, the primal worldview that saw souls and powers in the natural world was nearly dead. In sculpture, painting, pottery, and other art, the great spirits and mysteries of the living world show up less and less in animal form. More and more, gods and great heroes show up in human form. Human awe and veneration turn away from the living world and focus on human life alone.

5

Misothery and the Reduction of Animals and Nature

"What is not useful is vicious," declared Cotton Mather, the eminent Bostonian preacher whose sermons put forth the zeitgeist for colonial America. His remark sums up the views of agrarian civilizations toward animals and nature. Once human society elevated itself over all of nature, all other living beings fell into one of two categories: good and bad. Good things aided human life; bad things hindered human life.

Much of this worldview came from agriculture and the shift toward sedentary living in general, which created food insecurities and the social stresses of disease, larger groups, and larger-scale conflicts. These, in turn, brought desires to control nature and a need for new mechanisms for controlling human society. In settling down to farm, human society gave up freedom, a varied diet, a balance of power between the sexes, and a deep feeling of belonging in the living world. As farmers, people had to suffer slavery and royal oppression, large-scale warfare, poor diet and health, drudgery, sexism, and feelings of alienation from and contempt for the living world.

In this sort of world, people began to see everything as chaotic, in conflict. The agrarian worldview sees the natural order of things as sometimes disordered, sometimes hierarchical, sometimes dualistic, but ever in need of human intervention to bring about proper order.

The lion's share of these elements of the Western worldview came, however, from the animal side of agriculture—that is, the domestication and subjugation of sheep, goats, pigs, cattle, camels, and horses. The process of reducing these large animals from spirit-powers to slave-commodities had deep psychic consequences. Because animals represent nature in the human mind, because they inspire and stir such strong feelings, their reduction added an especially deep wound to the psyche of farmers of the ancient Middle East and to the Western culture they founded.

More than any other element, large animal domestication distinguishes early Western agrarian society from the other centers of civilization. All of the familiar, large farm animals were domesticated in the Middle Eastern center. All, that is, except for the llama and alpaca, domesticated in the Andean center by about 2500 B.C. In the Andes, however, the domestication of these species does not appear to have gone much beyond the Sacred Herd stage. The animals were not used to pull plows, they were not used militarily, and they did not produce a distinct herder subculture as did the species (especially cattle and horses) in the Middle Eastern center. Because it is so little discussed, it needs to be emphasized that the domestication and intensive exploitation of large herd animals are unique to the Middle East's early agrarian society.

Material Costs vs. Benefits

Western society enjoyed great material benefits from the harvesting and harnessing of these animals. Horse- and ox-powered plows gave Western agriculture a productivity and scale greater than any other center. Horses and camels carried people and heavy loads, giving greater power and range to Western warriors and traders. Although slaughtering was much less extensive than today, domestic animals provided a reservoir of food that could carry people through droughts and crop failures. Moreover, herd animals could be driven or led; they were not only food, but food on the hoof. This "walking larder" enabled people to carry on far-reaching trade with, or migration to, other regions. To a greater extent than those in any other center of civilization, the farmers of the Middle East were able to move, carry loads, explore, and fight over great distances—all the while staying fed on meat, milk, and blood.

All the writers recite these benefits, inadvertently crediting horses, cattle, and the other domestic animals with the material greatness and the glory of Western civilization. But this is not a balanced view. We ought to consider as well the costs of animal domestication.

Some of the costs are material, notably the destruction of fertile land by overgrazing. Theoretically, at least, sheep, goats, cattle, and other ruminants can create food for humans by eating tough grasses, weeds, brambles, twigs, and other plants inedible by humans. Goats will even scramble up the low-lying limbs of trees to reach leaves and tender twig-ends. By taking ruminants into deserts and mountains, the story goes, people were able to flourish in regions that would have offered sparse food for human beings.

That's the theory, anyway. In practice, however, farmers' animals probably destroyed more than they added to the land's food potential. The record shows that livestock very often turned fertile savannas and plains into infertile semi-deserts. Throughout the Middle East, archaeologists have found evidence of widespread abandonments of villages in ancient times. Some blame climate change, some blame increased use of plaster, the making of which took trees to fuel the lime kilns. But many blame sheep, who nibble grasses very close to the ground, and goats, who eat virtually everything that grows. And since wealth was measured in animal numbers, villagers tended to build up larger and larger herds. Very gradually, perhaps not even noticeably within a single lifetime, these herds changed the land around the villages. Trees disappeared because young seedlings and brush were eaten by too many goats. Grasslands disappeared because new growth and ground cover were eaten by too many sheep. Yields of wheat, lentils, and other food crops fell as croplands also deteriorated. These fields, when overgrazed during their pasture rotations, lay naked to the elements, leaving the sun's heat to suck away their moisture and rain and wind to sweep away their fertile soils. After many centuries, a community destroyed the farmland within its reach, forcing people to abandon their village and move to better land. Over many more centuries, the cycle was repeated over and over, and by many, many villages throughout the region.

It is true that a warming, drying period began after the last glaciers melted away, but did that cause *all* of the desertification around the Mediterranean and throughout the Middle East and Northern Africa? Surely it was greatly exacerbated by the hordes of herd-hoarders who dominated these regions for nearly eighty centuries.

Desertification and related impacts on the earth are practically irreversible. The material costs of animal domestication, then, are far greater than we were taught. We ought to teach the next generation that the glories of ancient Egypt, Sumeria, Persia, and Greece came, ultimately, from dirt—more specifically, from intensified agriculture and its stepped-up exploitation of that dirt. In learning about our culture's first great agrarian wealth, its "gold," we should understand that—ecologically speaking—it came from a kind of strip-mining. This would bring honesty, completeness—integrity—to our understanding of our heritage.

Cultural Costs vs. Benefits

It needs to be said over and over again, apparently, that there is more to life than material wealth. There are also psychic and emotional considerations—what some would call spiritual considerations. In affairs of the spirit, has domestication brought wealth or poverty? Has it brought people more peace of mind? Has it brought positive, loving views of the rest of the world that lives and breathes around us? Has it brought a calming, reassuring culture? Has it brought social peace? I think not. On the contrary, I think it has brought great damage to the human mind and culture, and, thereby, to the social fabric. Animal domestication has brought spiritual bankruptcy, if not poverty, to Western culture; it has spread, unfortunately, along with Western influence.

As we saw in the last chapter, herders were the father and planters the mother of agrarian culture in the Middle East. There, the herder culture's aggressive, expansionist, male-centered ways were integral to the gestation and birth of agrarian society. Its arrogance, toughness, and ruthlessness put a hard, cruel edge on Western agri-culture and enabled it to dominate other societies a great distance away. Western agri-culture was born domineering, and it grew up to swagger around the world conquering other lands and peoples.

This military edge, unfortunately, has often been mistaken for superiority. While the other agri-centers also fostered values on controlling nature, they did a relatively better job of resolving the conflicts it stirred up within the human soul. Most would agree that Hindus, Buddhists, Jains, and Taoists of India and the Far East see human supremacy as much less certain, much less absolute than do Jews, Christians, and Muslims. The latter come from the longest tradition of animal domestication—from the source of it, in fact. They "resolved" the conflicts by denying them. Their theologies put forth the idea that human beings are separate and apart from the rest of the living world. Thus there is no kinship, no continuity; consequently, there is no conflict in appropriating other life for human benefit. Indeed, it is according to God's plan. Therefore, exploitation is not just moral, it is godly. What other agri-cultures see as slightly sinful, Westerners see as wholly righteous.

And it must be emphasized that the hard, aggressive, domineering traits that characterize Western heroes (and thereby the Western value system) oppress a great many kinds of living beings. Sheep and cattle were not the only victims. They were merely the first in a long line of manipulated lives that include many members of the human species as well. When empathy for fellow beings was blocked, when kinship with them was denied by the Middle East's animal-domesticating, agri-culture, all life, including the human variety, would suffer all the more. After their God told them "the fear of you and the dread of you shall be upon every beast of the earth," they could more easily treat Others—human beings different from them—as beasts.

Animals—at the Heart of Nature

It goes without saying that the dominionism concocted by Western agri-culture greased the manipulation and oppression of a great many nonhuman animals, for that, after all, was its purpose. Because that is understood, we need not go on about it here. What needs to be understood is how this particularly Western idea caused human suffering as well.

The starting place is that, for the human mind, animals equal nature. Animals have always been our way of understanding the world. As we saw in Chapter 3, animals give us a handy way to "see" the vague, formless, chaotic rest of nature. They give form, shape, and personality to nature; they symbolize nature.

And we must remember that not all of nature is "out there"; some of nature is in us as well. For example, we tend to see our wilder passions—sexual lust, anger, and so on—and the various bodily functions as the animal nature within. Because we have such negative views of animal nature, though, we have to put this sense of our selves away somewhere. We put it away in our subconscious mind; Sigmund Freud called it the "id." At any rate, our vague, shadowy ideas about nature, whether within or outside us, are usually embodied in animals. Real and imagined, animals symbolize these ideas and give us a way to keep them tangible. As Yi-Fu Tuan wrote in *Dominance and Affection,* "When people want to express their sense of the force of nature, both in the external world and in themselves, they have found and still do find it natural to use animal images."

This is why, then, the reduction of animals from spirit-powers to slave-commodities has wrought such devastation to the human mind and culture.

Again, I emphasize that animal domestication did more to bring on that reduction than did farming in general. Let's see how the process unfolded.

When early herders and farmers intensified their uses of animals, they needed some ways to resolve their beliefs in the animal spirit-powers. They needed to move away from forager beliefs in animals as the First Beings and the souls of the living world. They needed new beliefs and cultural devices that would reduce animals from this status to one that would permit more control over the lives of animals, more deliberate exploitation. They needed also new ways to deal with the greater load of guilt that came with greater control and exploitation. They came up with a set of beliefs, which I call misothery, and a set of cultural devices, which James Serpell and others call "distancing devices." These replaced the older guilt-reducing rituals of the hunt and of animal sacrifice.

Misothery: Animal Hating

I have coined the word *misothery* (miz OTH uh ree) to name a body of ideas that we are about to discuss. It comes from two Greek words, one meaning "hatred" or "contempt," the other meaning "animal." Literally, then, misothery is hatred and contempt for animals. And since animals are so representative of nature in general, it can mean hatred and contempt for nature—especially its animal-like aspects. One writer, for example, has described nature as "red in tooth and claw"—that is, bloodthirsty like a predatory animal. In another version of the same idea, we say "it is a dog-eat-dog world." These are misotherous ideas, for they see animals and nature as vicious, cruel, base, and contemptible.

And, as noted, nature debasement bounces back on us when we consider our own human nature, because some of our ideas about human nature are misotherous. For example, one meaning of the word *animal* in a modern dictionary is: "an inhuman person; brutish or beastlike person; pertaining to the physical or carnal nature of man, rather than his spiritual or intellectual nature." Thus, we call someone an "animal" when we want to insult and debase him or her. It is an epithet applied to the cruelest, most heinous criminals. Serial killers are usually referred to as "animals" in the popular press. We describe horrible human beings as "animals," "beasts" or "brutes" (an old word for "animal") when we want to describe their egoism, insatiable greed, insatiable sexuality, cruelty, senseless slaughter of nonhuman beings, and the mass slaughter of human beings—all of the kinds of behavior that are, wrote John Rodman in his essay "The Dolphin Papers," "more frequently observed on the part of men than of beasts."

I deliberately constructed the word *misothery* for its similarity to the word *misogyny,* a reasonably common word for an attitude of hatred and contempt toward women. The similarity of the two words reflects the similarity of the two bodies of attitudes and ideas. In both cases, the ideas reduce the power, status, and dignity of others. Misogyny reduces female power/status/dignity and so it aids and abets the supremacy of males under patriarchy. Misothery reduces the power/status/dignity of animals and nature and so it aids and abets the supremacy of human beings under dominionism. Just as agrarian society invented beliefs to reduce women, it also invented beliefs—or ideologies—about animals that reduced them in the scheme of life.Collectively, these beliefs served to replace the awe and respect humans had for animals with contempt and loathing. Among these are the ideas that animals are too base and insensitive to feel physical pain or emotional suffering. There are many other such ideas in this set of beliefs that I put under the name misothery.

Bringing Animals Down Off Their Pedestal

Let us go back to the time when animal sacrifice prevailed in the agrarian centers of the ancient Middle East. That ritual, as we have seen, made meat available to town-dwellers who still believed (somewhat) in the animal spirit-powers and for whom hunting was less and less an option. Marvin Harris says animal sacrifice had to be phased out because it had outworn its usefulness as a redistributive feast. Society was getting too big, and the rulers simply could no longer provide meat for everybody as they did back when they were "big men" in tribal society. Animal sacrifice may have also ended because of agrarian society's growing body of ideas about property and ownership. Wealthy herders and farmers probably came to resent the priesthood's monopoly on slaughtering their animals. The practice was like a tax, and it hampered trade in animals. Herding and stockbreeding were a major part of the agrarian wealth, a major part of the farming business; it made no sense to have them restricted by old-fashioned religious ideas. Clearly, animals would have to have less spiritual value and more secular value. They would have to stop being gods if they were to serve as money.

The waning of animal sacrifice did not put animals in higher regard. On the contrary, wealth-building agrarian society's new requirements of them called for another wave of reductive new beliefs about animals and nature. In the Middle East, where exploitation of domestic animals was key to the wealth-building, agrarians invented misothery to ease the reduction. There, the builders of the bustling city-states preached misothery in their arts and their rising, new agrarian religions. In these, the essential message was to debase animals and nature and to elevate human beings over them. The effect, spiritually speaking, was to turn the world upside down: Before domestication, the powerful souls or supernaturals (or "gods") were animal, and primal people looked up to them; after domestication, the gods were humanoid and people looked down on animals. In primal culture all beings had souls, of which the greatest was the tribe's totem animal; in agri-culture, humans alone have souls and god is in human form. The agrarians' god might be a living Sumerian or Assyrian king, or it might be Zeus, Jupiter, Aphrodite, Venus, Artemis, Diana, or any of the other human-shaped gods of Greek and Roman polytheism, or it might be the super-man Yahweh, God, or Allah of Middle Eastern monotheism. At any rate, animal-using agrarians stripped animals of their souls and powers and put them in what they perceived to be their proper place: in the service of humankind.

It was some help to the process that the agrarian religions also had political agendas. They are sometimes called the first "universalizing religions" because they helped the growing nation state and empire end the divisions caused by tribalism and its many animal totems. These new agrarian religions put people of many tribes and languages under one god. Rulers wanted to get away from the temple slaughterhouse system in which priests and cult leaders controlled the people through the old rituals, fresh meat, treats, and entertainments at "ceremonial" feasts. The system divided people and distracted them from developing a national identity and loyalty to the ruling elite.

Dominionism and Disensoulment

As the Old Testament tells us, the leaders of the Hebrews were among the first to denounce these "heathen" festivals, urging their people to worship an all-powerful God—a sort of superman-god. This greater, new God set up a new order of life: a hierarchy of being with God and men at the top. It was like a ladder, with males the top rung, females second, "heathen" people third or lower, and animals and nature at the bottom. Above the ladder, next to men, sat God. This new order gave men dominion over everything below them. We will discuss its effects on women and other people in the next two chapters.

By giving them dominion over all of His creations, God gave men a broader license to kill and eat animals. The Western creation story in Genesis reveals that God wrestled with this violent aspect of dominion a couple of times before he made it explicit to Noah after the Great Flood. Even then, the license came with a great many restrictions—the dietary laws spelled out in the books of Leviticus and Deuteronomy. Restrictions notwithstanding, the grant of dominion made animal slaughter more accessible, more secular than ever before.

The very length and complexity of these dietary rules point to the emotional and psychic turmoil stirred up by this theological move. For this stripping away of the remains of the very old animal powers and souls was deeply unsettling, and it had to be done with the trappings of sanctity. Through these dietary rules, the Hebrews, to their credit, carried out their license to kill with ritual reminders of the gravity of their offense against nature. The borrowers of their theology were a bit more cavalier with slaughtering and meat eating: They adopted dominionism but without the inconvenient dietary laws. After this point, animals were meat on the hoof—agricultural commodities along with other products of the harvest.

This new view of animals as soulless, lowly beings helped the growing commerce in wool, hides, and meat that expanded in direct proportion to the growth of cities, trade, and specialization in the labor force. It enabled animal husbandry—the deliberate control of animal breeding—to produce more useful breeds and traits. It paved the way for herdskeeping to become the industry most vital to the colossal success of early Middle Eastern—or Western—civilization.

It was a great idea to reduce animals from spirit-powers to slave-commodities, but it took a lot to pull it off: It required the injection of a great many negative ideas about nature (which I have lumped under the term *misothery*) into Western culture. Unfortunately for animals and nature, and for human beings as well, this misothery poisons both our views of ourselves and our relations with the living world.

Early-Stage Misothery

One of the ways to see how misothery might have taken shape centuries ago in the Middle East is to look at people today whose cultures are going through the transition from foraging to farming. In *Thinking Animals,* Paul Shepard looked at three examples of "culture intermediate between totemic and domestic": the Thai, the Nuer, and the Balinese. The

Thai keep their domesticated buffalo and oxen under them, literally—in pens under their houses built on stilts. For them, the dog, a food scavenger and a nonworker, is held in very low, or negative, regard. To the Thai, the dog is a "low-life." They regard monkeys as degenerate human beings, and, according to Shepard, "the most feared and awful are the creatures of the remotest forest and wildest places." The Thai show two characteristic elements of misothery: contempt for animals under human control, and fear or hatred of those beyond their control.

The Nuer are African herders of cattle for whom life "is an endless pursuit of grazing advantage by means of individual political acumen," says Shepard. "Territorial rights through male initiative is the core of ideological life." Their society, he says, is "denatured" in that they no longer see animals as key to the order of things. The Nuer make an exception for cattle, with whom they are very nearly obsessed. They are the means of life, the source of song and affection, says Shepard, and in the classification of cattle horns and colorings there is a schematic ordering of humans and nature. For the Nuer, the rest of the world exists apart, "physically separated by the space necessary to keep hoofed animals." As cattle-keeping forces them to live in opposition to predators and other wild animals, they have little regard for the rest of nature. "The wild is external, accidental, inessential," says Shepard, while cattle are everything. The opposition of wild and domestic brings about a jarring alteration in worldview. Wild nature comes to represent everything "outside" —including other peoples, other animals. As a result, Shepard says, the Nuer are "truculent, aloof, isolationist and aggressive."

The Balinese show another transition from totemic to domestic culture. Here the animal domesticated is small—the red jungle fowl, known to us as the chicken. Yet its reduction brings sharp changes in a people's views of animals and nature. The Balinese obsession is with cockfighting, which may have begun as a ritual to resolve the animal powers left over from totemism. In the jungles, wild males fought to maintain bird homes, families, and flocks; but in the villages today, their domesticated descendants fight to provide entertainment for gamblers and onlookers.

The Balinese case shows us how animal reduction brings misothery, which brings negative ideas about humanity as well as animals and nature. The cockfight began as a ritual, became a tradition, and evolved into a game or sport. Today, the Balinese use the cockfight to carry on aggression and competition among villages. The loser in a cockfight, Shepard says, "literally tears his bird to pieces and gives it to the owner of the winning bird, who eats it."

Beasts, even small ones, fighting to the death over and over for public wagering and "sport" may appear to provide a "civilized" outlet for social conflicts, but it also provides a negative model for nature, both wild and human. Shepard notes that the Balinese "see animality as that which is reprehensible in man" and, predictably, Balinese demons have animal shapes. For them, the cockfight acknowledges the dark side of humanity and, less consciously, of nature. The cockfight may keep Balinese villagers from warring with each other, but it feeds the war within their psyches and their wars with the rest of the living world.

The Taming of Beast/Man—and of Nature

Another way to see misothery-in-the-making is to look at the mythologies of the ancient Middle East from the period of its struggles to overthrow the old animal powers and replace them with humanlike gods. One of the most revealing ones from Mesopotamia is the Gilgamesh Epic, the national epic of the Babylonian Semites, which was written down about 2000 B.C. Gilgamesh was a god/king of the first dynasty in Uruk, Sumeria, and a great culture hero to the Babylonians. Since the written form of the epic is the end product of a very old tale handed down orally, it reveals some of the ideas from the "old days" and tells us how myths were changed to suit the emerging animal-based agri-culture.

Gilgamesh is identified as a strong ruler through a personal history of acts of war and rape. According to Andrée Collard and Joyce Contrucci in *Rape of the Wild*, "he is presented as a hero of unbridled aggression and sexual appetite (he leaves 'no son to his father,' 'no virgin to her lover')." Outraged by his tyranny, the gods create a wild beast/man named Enkidu to bring the terrible king under control. Collard and Contrucci describe Enkidu:

"He is hairy like an animal, his hair 'sprouts like grain' and looks like a woman's. He 'eats grass with the gazelles,' drinks with them . . . and delights in his heart with them. He lives in open country. He is the scourge of hunters, filling their pits, foiling their traps, and in general protecting all animals from the harmful intentions of Gilgamesh's people. It is interesting to note that an armed hunter coming face to face with this peaceful, unarmed creature is 'benumbed by fear' at the sight of him, as if to hunt were to break taboo and incur guilt, as if the older law (represented by Enkidu) were still powerful enough to inhibit its violators."

The authors point out that Enkidu represents the older, totemic order in which humans lived in harmony with animals and nature. Gilgamesh represents the new order, based on aggression and control of women, animals, and nature. The transition from old to new is symbolized in Enkidu himself, who leaves his animality behind and becomes a hero, a god/man, and a friend of Gilgamesh. In this part of the legend, misogyny is so thoroughly interwoven with misothery that it is hard to tell one from the other. It does illustrate, though, how wild nature is symbolized by both animals and women.

A hunter persuades a temple harlot to take Enkidu away from his animal life in nature, and over to civilization. Whether via rape or seduction, Enkidu lays with the harlot for six days. The text says, "she treated him, the savage, to a woman's task." Now his wild animal friends are afraid of him, for "he now has wisdom, broader understanding." After she has civilized him through sex, the harlot takes Enkidu to Gilgamesh and the two become friends. Together they raid and rule, challenging and putting down the goddesses and their temples. Note the woman's role in taming nature, which is symbolized by the wild beast/man, Enkidu. This seems to credit, subtly and indirectly, women with the invention of agriculture. Did women domesticate nature and bring civilization? Perhaps Enkidu symbolizes that very old, persistent idea. But here that idea is twisted with the misogynist notion that sex is "a woman's task," and that whether by rape, deceit, seduction, or hire, it tames a man.

Eventually, Enkidu comes to regret his conversion and longs for his former life as an animal in nature. This probably reflects civilized humanity's longing for the older, preagricultural life-style. This same longing, as we noted in Chapter 1, shows up the Hebrews' creation story in Genesis. But the longing comes too late for Enkidu. He has insulted Ishtar, the once-great mother-goddess, and her curse kills him. Gilgamesh, for his part, resigns himself to his human mortality and puts his energies into strengthening the fortifications around his capital city, Uruk.

The misothery here is subtle, but we see it in Enkidu's taming and conversion to a civilized man. We are given the idea that he is made better by this conversion. The implication is that animal life and nature, although depicted as peaceful here, are beneath human civilization. The implication is that Enkidu, the animal, is improved by woman so that he will be useful in Gilgamesh's civilization.

Beast Fights in Sumerian Art

Finally, we can turn to ancient Middle Eastern art and see graphic evidence of animal reduction and misothery-in-the-making. Here animal reduction is painted, drawn, and carved. In Mesopotamia, the favorite motifs are scenes of animal processions, animals fighting, and man fighting animals. These scenes are found on temples, murals, and pottery and in sculpture. More of the same kinds of scenes, according to Francis Klingender, show up in great numbers on the famous Mesopotamian cylinder seals. In the days before writing, these small, carved, stone cylinders were rolled over pieces of clay. This "trade marked" glob of clay was then used to seal containers of wine or grain. Thousands of these cylinder seals exist, according to Klingender, and they "provide a continuous record of the changing fashions in Mesopotamian art for almost three thousand years, from the middle of the fourth millenium to the collapse of the Persian Empire in the fourth century B.C." (After writing appeared about 3200 B.C., the cylinders continued to be used to leave "signatures" on writers' clay tablets.)

In the earliest, protoliterate stage known as the Uruk period, the prevailing themes, according to Francis Klingender, were "serenely pastoral, in marked contrast to the later subjects of Mesopotamian art." Early on, the main theme was the sacred temple herd. The animals, cattle or sheep, are depicted in a peaceful procession, usually in natural settings. These are docile, domestic animals, moving in single file to the fields. These "animal-file" scenes evoke bucolic feelings of the calm and order of a well-to-do agrarian city-state.

Then, gradually, a second major grouping of scenes appears on the cylinder seals. In these "beast-hero" scenes, the animals are reared up, usually in confrontation, as on heraldic coats of arms. On some, a pair of heroes—possibly Gilgamesh and Enkidu—grapple with bulls or other beasts. On others, "a hero may grapple simultaneously with a beast on either side, thus forming a triad representing a kind of fighting antithesis to the tree-of-life," says Klingender.

Then a third major theme appears; this one "consists of a continuous frieze of fighting creatures, usually lions and other beasts of prey attacking cattle, with herdsmen defending their flocks." These themes, Klingender says, continue in the heraldic art of the Middle Ages in Europe. The whole feeling is one of dangerous animals, of violence and conflict in nature.

By the thousands, the cylinder seals illustrate Mesopotamia's changing views of animals and nature. In the process, Klingender says, "detachment was achieved" when the lifelike, naturalistic animals of the early period are shown distorted and stylized in later periods. "This probably reflects the taste of the barbarians who invaded Mesopotamia," he says. These "barbarians" would have been horse-mounted warrior peoples—the Kurgans, Aryans, or their equivalent—who burst out of the northern

Middle East in the third and fourth millennia B.C. By waves of raiding to the south, they left their mark on Mesopotamia, its art, and, apparently, its views of nature. (The Kurgans left their macho mark elsewhere, as we shall see in the next chapter.) Cylinder-seal artists, Klingender says, were "increasingly attracted by the beast-fight motif, now detached from its original setting; and the next few centuries of Sumerian seal-design are marked by ceaseless experiments in heraldic groupings to enhance the expressive power of this motif as a symbol of cosmic strife."

Klingender continues, describing the emerging view of animals and nature after the introduction of horse warfare and cattle breeding, when Sumeria was wealthy and powerful: "To emphasize his victory the hero may hold the beast [at once a real predator and a symbol of wild nature] upside down. . . . Intersecting rampant animals, twin bodies joined to one head, human torsos mounted on lions instead of legs, and other bold devices served to introduce further variety into the entanglements of fighting heroes, beasts and monsters, presented upon tightly packed friezes. . . ." Gradually, a theme emerged "more appropriate to the idea of embattled force," he says. "On the seals dating from c. 2500–2400 B.C., the period of the first all-Mesopotamian empire founded by Sargon of Akkad, true monumentality was achieved. The elementary heraldic groups, such as the triad, antithetic animals or intersecting rampant beasts, were now set off with striking effect against bland backgrounds, or placed, like heraldic supporters, to either side of inscribed panels. At the same time the animals themselves finally assumed those attitudes of force and violence frozen into immobility, which have served ever since, through later Mesopotamian and Assyrian art down to medieval heraldry, to symbolize the military virtues of strength and aggression."

Man Over Beast—and Nature

These "achievements" in art reflected a deeper psychic/cultural process: the reduction of animals from animated, ensouled, kindred beings in nature to frozen symbols of human power over nature. Once, they were believed to carry the spirits and powers of the living world; hereafter, they would be mere sign-carriers for human spirit and power over that world. In Mesopotamia, says Lord Kenneth Clark, "the sense of kinship with animals has been superseded by an overawed recognition of their strength, which can be used to symbolize the terrible power of the king." And the king, we might add, in his wealth and power, symbolized the entire agrarian society's mastery over plants, animals, and the land—what we have been calling nature.

Klingender says that "animal art of later civilizations in Western Asia was wholly under the sway of this [Mesopotamian] achievement." He notes that these rampant, fighting beast motifs in animal art show up on a gigantic scale in Hittite palaces and temples. More of the same at Assyrian sites and later still, at Nebuchadnezzar's Babylon and in the palaces of Persian kings at Suza and Persepolis. "Their influence on the other great styles is no less remarkable: they contributed decisive elements to the arts of early Greece, the later Roman empire, Sassaid Persia, Byzantium, the Muslim world and medieval Europe."

He means, of course, the motifs, themes, and scenes—the style of the art. But we know that art reflects a society's deepest ideas about the world, so the widespread popularity of these "styles" also tells us something about the spread of Middle Eastern agri-culture. Obviously, its ideas about the order of humans, animals, and nature had appeal far and wide wherever domestication had begun. And the Mesopotamians, with some help from hordes of horse-warriors to the north, furnished the graphics that best illustrated this new order. They were the first propagandists for misothery and hierarchy of being. These notions were thoroughly ingrained in the agri-culture of Mesopotamia by the time Abraham was born there, in the City of Ur, Sumeria, nearly 2,000 years before Jesus was born in Bethlehem, Palestine, 750 miles due west.

Distancing Devices

Agrarian society had to distance itself from animals because steady use required it. A plowman who felt genuine empathy or kinship with his oxen would probably do very little plowing. The village slaughterer could carry out the killing more comfortably under the belief that animals are not like humans and that they feel nothing. James Serpell has identified some of the mental gimmicks that agrarian culture invented to annul empathy for its animal slaves. He calls these "distancing devices." They go quite a few steps beyond the hunter's old guilt-reducing rituals.

Hunters, Serpell says, know a great deal about animal character and behavior, but they don't interact closely with an animal over time. Hunters, then, do not come to know, or get attached to, an animal. (The exception is the occasional animal brought back to the camp and tamed, not, as we have seen, killed and eaten.) Only at the moment of killing does the hunter exercise control over the animal. Until then, the animal remains an independent, respectable being with a life of his own. The domestic animal, on the other hand, lives a life of dependence under her owner. Day after day, the owner feeds her, leads her to water, milks her, and steers the plow behind her. Unless he puts up emotional barriers, the farmer may become too personally attached to his cow. If this happens, working, driving, whipping, and slaughtering her will inevitably cause feelings of guilt and remorse because, in human terms, they amount to a gross betrayal of trust. Farmers, Serpell says, "have learned to cope with this dilemma using a variety of essentially dishonest techniques." Unfortunately, he says, "these techniques have also been applied to wild animals and to the natural world in general." Borrowing from Hyam Maccoby's *The Sacred Executioner,* Serpell identifies four devices: detachment, concealment, misrepresentation, and shifting the blame.

Detachment is the main distancing device. Konrad Lorenz illustrates it in the opening paragraph of his book *Man Meets Dog*. He tells of eating some fried bread and sausage at breakfast one morning. Both the sausage and the lard that the bread was fried in, he wrote, "came from a pig that I used to know as a dear little piglet." Thereafter, Lorenz wrote, "to save my conscience from conflict, I meticulously avoided any further acquaintance" with pigs.

Rather than give up pork and lard, Lorenz chose to give up closeness to pigs. Multiply this emotional transaction thousands of times over thousands of years and we can understand why agri-culture views animals impersonally, indifferently. Consequently, Serpell says, "detachment and unnecessary brutality seem to be universal components of intensive animal husbandry, presumably because they help to distance the farmer from the mass suffering and slaughter for which he is either directly or indirectly responsible." This is made easier, of course, in modern, "factory" farms where the day-to-day care of animals is left to machines controlled by electronic sensors.

Hiding the Ugly Realities

Concealment is the natural partner of detachment. It results from agrarian society's conspiracy to hide slaughterhouses, dog pounds, and the other places where its uses of animals turn ugly. Today, even the farms are out of sight, as animals by the thousands are warehoused in windowless, anonymous, automated buildings. People drive by them on superhighways and mistake these "confinement" buildings for machine sheds. For the farmer, the concealment is in the numbers. With thousands at hand, there is no opportunity for familiarity with any particular animals. Finally, verbal concealment eases humanity's conscience. The words *beef, pork,* and *veal* have concealed the origins of animal muscle tissue for centuries. The flesh from chickens, ducks, or geese needs no euphemism because these animals are small and, as birds, more remote in degree of kinship.

Verbal concealment is a handy device for the other fields of animal exploitation as well. Thus, after the pet industry oversells puppy-mill puppies, the nation's dog pounds collect the rejected and abandoned ones and "put them to sleep." And to put the halo of science on the development of the new products, whether they be shampoos, oven cleaners, magic-bullet medicines, or heroic surgical procedures, experimenters "sacrifice" animals in laboratories.

Misrepresentation, Serpell says, is a cultural device that distorts the facts about animals so that their suffering and death seem necessary or deserved. The distortion can be deliberate or it can be unconscious. The great bulk of it is unconscious, for negative, hateful ideas about animals pervade the West's agri-culture. We grow up on these in art, literature, and film and they thoroughly color our attitudes about animals and nature. Though attitudes have improved very recently (at least for whales, wolves, and a select few animals), throughout history animals have been seen as dangerous and disgusting.

If animals inspire fear and loathing, it becomes morally easier to control, use, and kill them. Indeed, these become moral imperatives. And the nearer an animal comes to posing an actual threat to human welfare, as do rats and wolves, the more intense the misrepresentation. In our literature, these animals in particular are misrepresented as bloodthirsty, ravenous beasts snarling at the gates of civilization, cruelly intent on bursting through to ravage innocent humanity. Actually, farmers invaded their habitat and set out dinner tables loaded with flocks of sheep and fields of grain. Yet these animals are regarded as malicious creatures who deliberately mount attacks on human society. This makes them absolutely evil, which makes it absolutely necessary to eradicate them.

This idea of animal evil is a very handy tool for agrarian society—so much so that it is kept sharpened and accessible through Western folklore. The most obvious example is the legend of the werewolf, which fed generations of Europeans with a morally righteous hatred for the "beast of waste and desolation," the wolf. In a typical passage from his bizarre book *The Werewolf,* Montague Summers, a Jesuit, describes the beast as pure evil: "The werewolf loved to tear human flesh. He lapped the blood of his mangled victims, and with gorged reeking belly he bore the warm offal of their palpitating entrails to the sabbat to present in homage and foul sacrifice to the Monstrous Goat [Satan] who sat upon the throne of worship and adoration. His appetites were depraved beyond humanity. In bestial rut he covered the fierce she-wolves. . . ."

This is vintage misothery and a gross misrepresentation of real wolf behavior. Such views have fueled campaigns to exterminate wolves in both Europe and North America that very nearly succeeded.

Shifting the Blame

Blame-shifting is a leftover from the old rituals of hunting and animal sacrifice. We saw examples of it before, in the Ainu bear sacrifice and in the Babylonian temple sacrifices. There the rituals explicitly shifted blame for the killing to ancestors or the gods. Priests were the first to do the dirty work, and ever since division of labor has helped shift, or diffuse, the blame. For centuries, Serpell says, society has relegated the work, and the moral and emotional burdens, of killing animals for meat to butchers and slaughterhouse workers. He notes that "those directly responsible for killing animals have been regarded with a curious mixture of awe and disgust, not unlike that normally reserved for public executioners." Although people relish their meats and sausages, they regard those who work them up from the living animal, says Serpell, "as odious, merciless, pitiless, cruel, rude, grim, stern, bloody and greasy." This distances the meat-eater from both the killing and the killer. And it makes the killing seem somehow inevitable or natural because it puts it in the hands of the sort of persons who, by their very nature, do horrid things. The device allows the meat-eater to think, "I did not do the killing; that is the day's work of base, cruel people; the killings will go on in spite of me; therefore, I am not responsible."

Today, Serpell notes, responsibility for the killing of animals for food is completely diffused by the corporate bureaucracies that have taken over animal agriculture. One firm, or a division of it, may specialize in breeding animals, another in caring for young animals, and another in feeding them to market weight. Other business entities transport them to stockyards and auctions, where still others buy them and take them to the slaughterhouse. And dozens of others—packers, processors, and supermarket chains—reduce the carcasses to bloodless, shrink-wrapped packages that offer the consumer no clue as to their animal origins. The buck is passed around so many times that no individual or firm *feels* any responsibility for the reduction of a living being to packaged flesh. "In a sense," Serpell says, "everyone involved is guilty, but no one is obliged to shoulder the full burden of responsibility."

The various distancing devices work hand in hand with misothery to keep animal exploitation from being emotionally and morally troublesome. The devices were relatively simple back in forager times when the "trouble" occurred mainly at the moment of the kill. But then farming came along with ways to use animals from birth to death, and to use them intensively. This raised "a hideous moral dilemma," Serpell says. "Our highly developed social awareness enables us to understand and empathize with animals, just as we understand and empathize with each other. It also allows us to use animals and to manipulate them to our own advantage in precisely the same way that it allows us, up to a point, to exploit and manipulate other humans." This same empathy, though, brings us to identify with animals and to form close, emotional bonds with them. This will raise problems if the animals are to be worked, killed, or otherwise exploited for human benefit—activities that animal domestication institutionalizes. This raises the burden of guilt, Serpell says, "to the point where it can no longer be expiated through simple acts of ritual atonement." Consequently, agrarian society constructed an agri-culture in which it "created an artificial distinction between us and them" and it erected "a defensive screen of lies, myths, distortions and evasions, the sole purpose of which has been to reconcile or nullify the conflict between economic self-interest, on the one hand, and sympathy and affection on the other."

The immediate harm caused by these devices is the immense toll in animal suffering and death. This may not disturb the average reader, steeped as he or she is in the millennia-old agri-culture. But there is another harm or two, and these affect the human species. By loading our culture with misothery, we despise too much of the living world—including our animality and ourselves. By using distancing devices to prop up intensive animal exploitation, we build ruthlessness and detachment into our culture. What could be a more loving, whole human spirit is maimed; what could be a greater sense of kinship, of belonging in the world, is cut off. Consequently, our feelings for the world, and life in it, run more to the negative pole than the positive. We feel *dis*enchanted, despirited, *dis*illusioned. Our deepest feeling for this life is malaise, so we long for the next. Our deepest feeling for the living world is horror, so we strive to destroy it.

The Beast Within

Misothery does more than maim the human spirit and stunt our humanity so that we are half what we could be. It also pollutes the half that we are. And unfortunately, we are rarely aware of it. We do not think that our attitudes toward other animals affect us in any way, but they do, and the reasons have been spelled out in Chapter 3. Animals are central to our learning about the world, and they give form and shape to our vague notions about the world, about nature. If we hate animals, we hate just about everything in the world—including some part of ourselves. Our agri-culture's contempt for animals/nature runs so deep that it works unconsciously in ways that never occur to us.

The agri-culture makes us despise and try to control the animal within us. By this I mean our animality, which is several things. One is the simple, biological fact that we are animals—primates, in fact. If this amuses you or makes you uncomfortable, then you are illustrating my point: We don't like to think of ourselves as animals, or even as closely related to animals. Our animality includes also the body and its natural cycles and activities. These tend to remind us of our closeness to animals, so we control, hide, and deny them. When the body's natural functions break through our restraints, we are terribly embarrassed, humiliated. Then we are base, crude—like an animal.

In European society, Keith Thomas says, morals, religion, polite education, "civility," and refinement were all "intended to raise men above animals." An influential textbook on civility by Erasmus, says Thomas, "made differentiation from animals the very essence of good table manners, more so even than differentiation from 'rustics.' " Because all of the bodily functions had undesirable animal associations, "some commentators thought that it was physical modesty, even more than reason, which distinguished men from beasts." Thomas tells of Cotton Mather, the New England puritan preacher who wrote in his diary about an incident in which he was urinating ("emptying the cistern of nature") at a wall. At the same moment, a dog came along, heisted his leg and peed near him. Mather wrote: "What mean and vile things are the children of men . . . How much do our natural necessities abase us, and place us . . . on the same level with the very dogs!" Mather wrote that, from then on, whenever nature called to "debase me into the condition of the beast" he would "make it an opportunity of shaping in my mind some holy, noble, divine thought . . ." and to practice "thoughts of piety wherein I may differ from the brutes. . . ."

Keeping Our Distance

In a section entitled "Maintaining the Boundaries," Thomas gives many examples of European society's fear of animality. All bodily impulses were regarded "as 'animal' ones, needing to be subdued," and "lust, in particular, was synonymous with the animal condition." Words like "brute," "bestial," and "beastly" had much stronger sexual connotations than they do today. In bestiaries and emblem books, the moral textbooks of the Middle Ages, most of the animals that appear were intended to symbolize lasciviousness or sexual infidelity.

Besides "lust," European society saw many other reminders of human animality. John Stuart Mill stressed cleanliness because its opposite, "more than anything else, renders man bestial." Nakedness, too, was bestial. Men who had unduly long hair were considered bestial. It was bestial, Thomas noted, to work at night because that is the time when, as one period writer said, "beasts run about seeking their prey." It was bestial even to go swimming because it was a form of movement more natural to animals than to humans. And moralists frowned upon people dressing up in animal disguises, for that flirted with crossing the boundaries.

Most despised of all, however, was "bestiality," the crime of having sex with an animal, which remained a capital offense in many countries until very recently. In the Middle Ages, both the human and the animal were executed. It is telling of society's low regard for animals that the great offense was not the rape of the animal. "The sin," Thomas says, "was the sin of confusion; it was immoral to mix the categories." As one Stuart-era moralist put it, "it turns man into a very beast, makes a man a member of a brute creature."

Though Europe maintained strict boundaries between humans and animals, it allowed one strange exception: It routinely put animals on trial and sentenced them for their "crimes" against human beings. Several books have reported these animal trials, notably Gerald Carson's *Men, Beasts and Gods*. Dogs, pigs, cows, horses, rats—even slugs and flies—were tried and convicted in the regular courts, before judges and juries. Their offenses ranged from destruction of food or crops to "murder." Pigs were frequently offenders, usually for mauling or killing children. Carson reports that in 1386, in Falaise, Normandy, "a sow was dressed up in a new suit of man's clothing, mangled about the head and forelegs, and hanged—the penalty for maiming and killing a baby in a similar manner."

Condemned animals were executed by a variety of methods, according to Carson. "They could be lightly singed, then strangled; burned at the stake; buried alive; sometimes tortured before being strung up on a gibbet. Animals were even put to the rack in order to extort a confession. No confession was expected, but this act of cruelty made it certain that due form was being observed. Domestic beasts met the ignominious death of human criminals, for as intimate members of the human community, they were treated with the same public contempt as felons in a similar fix. If the wrongdoing occurred on a Friday, that fact constituted a serious aggravation of the offense."

Misothery and Pornography

Our agri-culture, then, sees all of animality as base, contemptible, wicked—often evil. So we strive to control, hide, and deny the "beast" within us. We struggle with ourselves so that we do not behave like the animals under our control. This is what we must do to be "civilized" human beings. And we must exert great effort to think of ourselves as very different from animals, as having nothing in common with the rest of the living world. A large part of the effort has been carried out in art, song, and literature, with much of the message exalting *human* over *lower* (animal) existence.

But try as hard as we might, we are still aware of our own animality. Aware, that is, at the lower levels of consciousness. We don't dwell on it, but we know that some parts of our self—our being, behavior, and body— are animal-like. The misothery in our agri-culture, then, produces a schizoid view of ourselves: It exalts some of ourselves while it debases the rest of ourselves. Misothery sets us up for inner conflict. For if human beings are exalted and animals and nature are base, then anything we have in common with other animals is base and something to be despised, controlled, hidden, and denied. Misothery in culture teaches us to hate/hide our bodies and our bodily functions. It teaches us to control the sexual, the sensual, the emotional, and the playful, for these are near the realm of nonhuman animal being and they must be humiliated, devalued, debased.

This outlook, this mind-set, produces some major destructive side-effects—notably pornography, which "entertains" by degrading women, human sexuality, love, and our bodies. In *Pornography and Silence,* her brilliant analysis of the pornographic mind, Susan Griffin asks, "What is it that is humiliated in this obscene [I would call it misotherous] mind? The child is humiliated; beauty is humiliated; the body is humiliated; the feminine and the animal are humiliated. And of all these we can say: Nature is humiliated"—by human agri-culture.

Griffin's genius is in pointing out the seemingly odd companionship between pornography and Western religion. It seems odd at first until we realize that both have, she says, "a profound distrust" of the animal/natural world and, by extension, the sensual, emotional, irrational, and physical realms. Our religion puts these aspects of life and nature down in one set of ways, pornography puts them down in another. Our religion teaches us to debase the animal/natural realm and, in doing so, sets up a mind that is "entertained" by scenes of debasement. Our religion, in other words, is the prep school for pornography.

Proper Places for Man's Seed and Sexual Energies

Agri-culture's values on sexual/emotional restraint combine well with many of its other values. For one, agrarian society values work, which is a Good Use of the body. The work ethic holds play, sensual pleasures, and idleness as sinful, thus channeling human energies into manual labor in fields and barns. Second, since agrarian society values the family as a labor force, more is better. Agri-culture wants large families as they supply more men *for* labor, more women *in* labor. It wants human sexual life for breeding only. Agri-culture's sex ethic, then, restrains (and distorts) the great, complex range of human sexuality. It is sinful for a man to "waste his seed" or for a woman to use birth control. All of that wicked lust, and therefore much of the wickedness of human existence, can be redeemed if people channel it entirely into making babies, who, incidentally, enlarge the family labor pool, which, in turn, increases the family wealth.

Princeton University professor of religion Elaine Pagels traces this ethic to old herdskeeping traditions in her book *Adam, Eve and the Serpent.* For over a millennium before rabbis wrote Genesis, she says, "Jews had taught that the purpose of marriage, and therefore of sexuality, was pro-creation. Jewish communities had inherited their sexual customs from nomadic [herder] ancestors whose very survival depended upon reproduction, both among their herds of animals and among themselves." The story of Abraham told in Genesis 22:17 promised the Hebrews descendants "as numerable as the stars in the sky and the grains of sand on the seashore." Jewish agri-cultural law, Pagels says, "banned as 'abominations' sexual acts not conducive to procreation, and the impurity laws even prohibited marital intercourse except at times most likely to result in conception." No wonder Job had seven sons and three daughters.

The Hebrews were just one of many sources of the agri-cultural sex ethic that binds us today. Susan Griffin, again, traces some of these. St. Paul, for example, declared: "It is good for a man not to touch a woman." Augustine, as we shall see, thought that humans were tainted with the sin of lust from birth. Judeo-Christian tradition aside, the West's other wellsprings of culture held many of the same views on sex. The Romans, for example, who founded their state on cattle breeding and extended it to an empire through war and slavery, gave us much in language and law. While Hollywood has portrayed Romans as living from orgy to orgy, Rome actually promoted asceticism and hatred of the body. Democritus, for example, defined a brave man as one who overcame not only his enemies, but his "pleasures." Epicurus, of all people, intoned that sexual feelings "never benefited any man." The Stoics warned against passion in marriage. Plotinus and his student Porphyry despised desire as evil. The neo-Platonists practiced celibacy as a virtue.

St. Augustine: Sex Ruined the World

The West's sex ethic works hand-in-glove with the deeper fear and loathing of our animal natures—the inner-directed misothery that despises and seeks to control the sexual beast within. The combination produces fanatically held sexual mores that suppress masturbation, homosexuality, oral/anal sex, and all forms of sexual pleasure that "waste a man's seed" and remind us of the sensual "beast within." These obsessively misotherous, anti-human-sexuality mores were carved in stone by the early Christian patriarchs—Clement, Irenaeus, and St. Augustine. They advanced the notion that sex was so generally evil (Satan borrowed the practice "from the irrational animals" to tempt Adam and Eve) that it is best avoided altogether. Celibacy was even better than Christian marriage, which had its sexual temptations. According to Elaine Pagels, Clement warned married couples: "not even at night, although in darkness, is it fitting to carry on immodestly or indecently, but with modesty, so that whatever happens, happens in the light of reason . . . for even that union which is legitimate is still dangerous, except in so far as it is engaged in procreation of children."

A couple of centuries later, Augustine, no doubt tormented by the conflict between his own impulses and restraints, advanced an idea on sex that was to become Catholic doctrine: Everyone is conceived through sexual desire, and sexual desire is transmitted to everyone through the very semen involved in conception. For Augustine, then, all humanity is tainted with sin "from the mother's womb." He thought, says Pagels, that "Adam and Eve's intercourse permanently corrupted human nature as well as nature in general." This fits with the larger idea that human original sin corrupted the world. "Nature," Augustine wrote, "which the first human being harmed, is miserable." This Augustinian elaboration on agri-cultural views of sex and nature tainted Christian thought from then on. Centuries later, Pagels wrote, "the Protestant Christian painter and engraver Dürer depicted the awesome power of Adam and Eve, as tradition had taught him, in vivid form. While they stand ready to take the fateful bite of that forbidden fruit, a cat waits at their feet, poised to pounce upon the unsuspecting mouse. Her [the cat's, read: nature's] capacity for murderous violence—and that of all living creatures—is about to be unleashed by human sin."

Augustine's idea that sex ruined the world still lives in Catholic orthodoxy. It stuck, Pagels believes, because it appealed "to the human need to imagine ourselves in control, even at the cost of guilt." Because sexual desire is constant, feelings of guilt are constant, and the need for control is constant. The effect, of course, was to bind sinners to the Church, where they could try to work off their guilt through prayer, ritual, and the Church's work.

A Sexual Straitjacket

The misothery in agri-culture, in all its forms and refinements, has straitjacketed human sexuality. Only two kinds of "sex" are allowed: none (celibacy) and marital breeding. The broader range of natural sexual feelings, on the other hand, evoke shame and self-hatred. These must be repressed, and the agri-culture has produced many kinds of "isms" over the centuries to do the job.

In the last century, it was some elements of the health and temperance movements who preached sexual restraint for its humanizing powers.

One of the most popular lecturers was Dr. Sylvester Graham, famous for the invention of the graham cracker. Although he had a lot of good ideas about diet, exercise, and rest, Graham believed that sexual "excesses" damaged the body's various organs, causing a great number of diseases. Sexual appetites, he thought, could be controlled by diet, which should be bland and devoid of spices and stimulants. Such ideas were in vogue on both sides of the Atlantic, and in the latter half of the nineteenth century some experts prescribed even stronger controls on sexuality. Youthful masturbation was considered one of the roots of all evil. According to George Leonard in *The Transformation*: "The fear of masturbation reached such hysterical heights that respected physicians in the United States and Europe regularly recommended clitoridectomy, circumcision, infibulation (putting a silver wire through the foreskin), wearing of locked chastity belts or spiked penil rings, blistering the penis with red mercury ointment, cauterization of the spine and genitals, surgical denervation of the penis and, in extreme cases, removal of both penis and testes." Some doctors prescribed penis-wiring for mental patients, others advised adults to sleep with their hands tied. Sexual repression reached such heights that households concealed the piano's legs with dust ruffles, says Leonard, "so that the sight of them should not excite the baser passions."

Sadomasochism vs. Sensuality

Ironically, those who act on the fuller range of sexual feelings and practice nonprocreative sex are considered "perverts" guilty of "crimes against nature." Such sexual behavior, especially the homosexual kind, is shrouded in sin and decadence, with torment and self-loathing falling to those who give in to their "beastly" bodies and urges. This sets up a conflict within: control sexual urges or take the punishment. For many people, whether homo- or heterosexual, sadomasochistic fantasies and practices offer a way to resolve the conflict. Sex practiced becomes the same as sex punished. One can have sexual pleasure only if control or punishment is involved; hence, sexual gratification becomes inextricably linked with pain, control, and domination. Scenes of such "sex" dominate S&M pornography, of course, for they, rather than sensuality, are what titillates and what arouses.

While not all of us are full-blown sadomasochists, we are steeped nevertheless in the constant association of sex with power and violence that pervades our culture. Hard-core pornography is plentiful, cheap, available, and a steady seller in most every community. Utter depravity and violence are considered sexy, as evidenced by "snuff" films, which show a woman's murder during a "sex" act. Lately, scenes of sexual abuse of children have been popular. Even in mainstream Hollywood films, sexuality is hard, tough, detached—more about domination than sensual feeling.

Many are set in "whorehouses," which, in a reversal of reality, are depicted as places where men can unwind and have fun. Actually, men go to the "whorehouse" for quick, impersonal sex—like a trip to the bathroom for one of the other bodily functions. For the John, the "whore" is a sort of sexual mechanic who can change his oil and give him a tune-up while-you-wait. "He wishes his sexual partner to act out coldness and harshness," says Griffin. "And in this one can sense the shadow of a whole culture."

Well outside hard-core pornography, our culture likes "hard," macho heroes. This century's most popular, celebrated writers are Ernest Hemingway and Norman Mailer, who in life as well as in their "art" exuded male toughness and violence. We got more of the same on film from heroes played by Marlon Brando, John Wayne, and Arnold Schwarzenegger. There are other types of male heroes, of course, but the perennial best-sellers are Rambo and James Bond types—cool, tough, impervious meat-hunks who seduce/rape women rapidly, repeatedly, facilely. Shades of the same mixture of macho sex and violence are common in the imagery of music videos on MTV and in titillating news coverage of rapes and serial sex murders. What we might call "pop" S&M shows up in some types of rock, rap, and other styles of commercial music as well as in magazine and television advertising. We also see it in fashion trends— notably the recent slash-and-safety-pin "pierced look" and in the leather-strapped, high-fashion "punk look."

For the excitement, the kick it gives, pornography has become a fixture of the mass media. Behind that kick, however, is the tumultuous pressure of sexual energies kept in constant conflict by misothery and its animal/self-hating sexual mores. The definitive examination of Western, nature-dominating agri-culture's fascination with sadomasochism and other forms of pornography is Susan Griffin's *Pornography and Silence: Culture's Revenge Against Nature*.

Alienated from animals and nature by misothery, our agri-culture puts us superior to, and distinct from, the living world. In that position, we can only despise and deny the animal and natural wherever we see it in ourselves or in the rest of humanity. Our anxieties about our animal-like characteristics cause us to project our fear and hatred onto not only other animals but other people whose differences we think places them below us—nearer to animals and nature than us. Throughout history, as we shall see in the next chapters, the "civilized" Westerner has used animals to symbolize lustful women, Jews, Africans, and various Others seen as close to nature.

6

Misogyny and the Reduction of Women and Female Power

In 1991, Charles Bowden, a popular nature writer, wrote an article about mountain lions for *Buzzworm,* a mainstream environmental magazine. In the course of his article, Bowden had occasion to describe mountain lions, nature, and/or women, we can't be sure which:

"Nature is this teeming, unruly bitch at the gates of our lives, ready at an instant to violate our humanity. She waits out there by the picket fence so white against the green lawn. You stroll out, open the gate, and suddenly she walks out of the desert, dressed smartly, the lips full and inviting, the eyes dangerous with desires. Her hair is black, the teeth very even, the cheekbones strong, the voice, well, you can hear no voice, you merely sense a kind of purring coming off her body. She moves toward you, seems almost to glide, you turn, smile, tip your head silently forward as if to say, hello. Her dress rustles, a soft silky kind of sound, the hair is long and stirs with the breeze. She is at your throat, the teeth tear and warm blood cascades down your body."

Bowden has painted a nightmare. Vivid images race toward us: a feline beast—sexy, stealthy, seductive . . . and vicious. But these are not merely scenes from a bad dream. These are very old, deeply ingrained views of women, animals, and nature. These have settled, like muck, in the channels of Western culture, and Bowden roils them up. Under these views, wild nature (like a woman) lures men, lulls them, and (like a predator) turns on them and kills them. She is treacherous, against which men are innocent. She is evil, against which men are good. Nature is always female, and she is always a beast to man. As usual, it is impossible to tell where misothery ends and misogyny begins, for they are so intertwined.

Nature is the ultimate criminal, thought the infamous Marquis de Sade, the "father" of sadomasochism and pornography: "I tell you, nature lives and breathes by [crime]; hungers at all her pores for bloodshed, aches in all her nerves for the help of sin, yearns with all her heart for the furtherance of cruelty. . . . Good friend, it is by criminal things and deeds unnatural that nature works and moves and has her being; what subsides through inert virtue, she quickens through active crime."

For examples of nature's crimes, de Sade wrote out a list: "she feeds with fresh blood the innumerable insatiable mouths suckled at her milkless breast; she takes the pain of the whole world to sharpen the sense of vital pleasure in her limitless veins; she stabs and poisons, crushes and corrodes; yet cannot live and sin fast enough for the cruelty of her great desire. Behold, the ages of men are dead at her feet; the blood of the world is dead at her hands; and her desire is continually toward evil, that she may see the end of things she hath made. Friends, if we would be one with nature, let us continually do evil with all our might" (cited in Karl Stern, *Flight from Woman*).

Again we see how tightly misothery and misogyny are intertwined around fear, loathing, and hatred for nature. But de Sade aside, even respectable philosophers have drawn on the same thinking and imagery to describe nature, or, as the case may be, the nature of women. There seems to be an equation: woman = nature = beast.

"Near the Animal State"

In the West's agri-culture, women have been clearly down the ladder of being. It has assigned them a place "near the animal state," according to Keith Thomas, who has surveyed European attitudes toward the natural world. "Over many centuries, theologians had debated, half frivolously, half seriously, whether or not the female sex had souls, a discussion which closely paralleled the debate about animals. . . ." Just as anthropologist Sherry Ortner theorized in a 1974 essay, women's status was determined by pregnancy, childbirth, and nursing. Throughout history, Thomas says, these "animal aspects of child-bearing" gave women a more obvious link to animality than men. These were like the other bodily functions, and were to be shunned and hidden. The upper classes, for instance, regarded infant care, especially breast-feeding, as debasing, so they farmed out their infants to wet nurses who carried out the dirty work.

This view of women as animal-like is not exactly old-fashioned. It still gets plenty of expression from misogynists. Norman Mailer, for example, wrote in *The Presidential Papers*: "Most men who understand women at all feel hostile toward them. At their worst, women are low, sloppy beasts." The critical praise for, and the popularity of, Mailer's writings tell us that many endorse his views.

How different this is from the much older, primal view of women, childbirth, and child care. Ironically, the very association with nature that once gave women social power and status served, in agri-culture, to reduce that power and status. Ironically as well, the agri-culture that has put a high value on female fecundity and large families regards women essentially as livestock—as breeders, domestic laborers, living property. If we want to improve understanding between the sexes, we need to understand the process by which women were reduced by the agri-culture.

The Creation of Patriarchy

It's an open game these days for theories as to how, when, and where male rule over society began. My own view is that male usurpation of female power came from the joining of three forces: first, male jealousies of female powers. These were long-standing and culturally institutionalized in things like menstrual taboos, secret hunt rituals, men's houses and cults, men's need for ceremonies and "offices," and others. As we have seen, the hunt itself served men with a way to compensate for female powers in that by killing animals, especially large, powerful ones, men "took" or appropriated their powers. As Richard Leakey has pointed out, the hunt gave men a spectacular and impressive way to put food on the table. At any rate, this institutionalized male envy carried over into the agricultural period, in which sedentary living, population density, and the growth of towns and cities made hunting less practical and successful. In this situation, hunting and its rituals gradually ceased to offer men means of compensation for female powers. Male envy then turned on the female principles (and on women) and worked to reduce and co-opt them and bring them under male control.

Second, female powers gradually eroded as agriculture demystified nature. These powers, as noted, had been based on women's association with the mysteries of procreation specifically and nature's mysteries in general. As society took greater control over nature through irrigation, clearing, plowing, and other methods of intensified agriculture, it came to regard nature—and thereby women—with less and less awe. In battling weeds, pests, predators, droughts, and capricious storms, farming society came to regard nature as more foe than friend. Farmers learned contempt for what they could control in nature and they learned fear and hostility for what they could not control. Insofar as women had been associated with nature, their powers, status, and essence tended to change accordingly.

Third, the discovery of fatherhood, I believe, struck the most overt blow to female prominence. As anthropologists have noted, forager society would have had no reason to associate men and coitus with procreation. Procreation, the most powerful mystery in nature, was therefore exclusively woman's. Then at some point in evolution these connections were made and ideas about male fertility began to emerge. Many think they emerged among animal domesticators and herding peoples unique to the Middle East and nearby regions where all of the major herd animals were originally domesticated.

In the Middle East and environs, then, all three of these forces were operating earlier than in any of the world's other centers of agricultural origin. As agriculture evolved there, these forces grew to a point when they reached a cultural critical mass and a synergy occurred. When it did, the male side of society took charge with a vengeance and began constructing the patriarchy.

Other Views

No doubt there are many other factors involved that other theorists stress, and they look mainly to psychological and economic activities. The psychologists see the socializing of boys as very different from that of girls. Girls grow up identifying with their mothers and with others, whereas boys reject the mother and define themselves as distinct and within rigid ego boundaries. This is thought to have made boys more prepared to run society as it grew more complex under agriculture. Freud himself thought male aggressiveness came from Oedipal rivalry with the father for the love of the mother. He suggested that this rivalry sexually frustrates males in childhood, so they compensate by going out in the world and building civilization. Simone de Beauvoir and many feminists have been greatly influenced by such ideas, which has led them to think that male rule is a product of male biology or psychology. In light of better information from both psychology and anthropology, however, this biological determinism seems crude and off the mark. The better theories of the past thirty years say that patriarchy is cultural and historical (and therefore changeable) rather than stamped into our genes.

One such approach is that of Marvin Harris, an anthropologist who believes women's devaluation began with male supremacy in hunter-warrior cultures. To regulate population and foraging territory, these cultures carried on tribal wars that put a premium on manhood and "macho" values. Males were desirable, females were not. The same values also made it easier to kill girl babies, which reduced the number of potential mothers. But can Harris explain the rise in female power, goddess cults, and matrilineality early in the agricultural period? Yes: Warfare among forager bands and tribes was local and brief, so men could go home at night and keep in charge of things. Warfare among settled agricultural communities took men long distances for weeks at a time, so their villages needed strong women in charge while they were away. Eventually, as agrarian wealth was consolidated and towns and city-states arose, classes and specialists emerged that permitted men to carry on both warfare abroad and rule at home. Harris's approach is called "materialist" because it sees a people's culture as a product of their economic activities—that is, their ways of securing the material needs of life.

Another such approach is that of Eleanor Leacock, also an anthropologist. She argues that male dominance came when the agrarian state began to trade in commodities, which led to wealth, specialization, and social hierarchies. Women lost out, she says, because men tended to control slaves, artisans, and the rest of the labor of commodities production. Moreover, the trade in commodities, especially cattle and farm animals, was in the hands of men. In this economic milieu, women's central role in kin- and village-based society was undercut and they were relegated to chores and children.

Sexual Commodities

A similar approach is that of Gerda Lerner, who argues in her book *The Creation of Patriarchy* that male rule grew out of the ancient practice of warfare and captive-taking, which, in the agricultural period, grew into a regular trade in female slaves. This trade, along with the traditional exchange of women among villages for marriage alliances, helped to reduce women to the role of breeders and housekeepers. "The sexuality of women," Lerner says, "was commodified even prior to the creation of

Western civilization." It occurred in the agricultural period because farmers "could use the labor of children to increase production and accumulate surpluses." Gradually, men came to have rights over women that women did not have over men. "Women themselves became a resource, acquired by men much as the land was acquired by men. Women were exchanged or bought in marriages for the benefit of their families; later, they were conquered or bought in slavery, where their sexual services were part of their labor and where their children were the property of their masters." According to Lerner, this process took about 2,500 years, from approximately 3000 to 500 B.C. Lerner shows us that the first steps toward male rule were taken at about the time writing (and history) began, and that it was consolidated by the time male-only "democracy" began in Athens, Greece.

I have no quarrel with Lerner's case that the female slave trade did much to devalue women and turn them into sexual and reproductive commodities. My only quarrel is that she and the other materialists discount the discovery of fatherhood as a factor in the rise of patriarchy. They mention it in passing now and then, and quickly dismiss it. Lerner does this in her book, referring to it as a "single-cause explanation." Those who base their arguments on the animal husbandry connection "are factually wrong," she says. "Animal husbandry [began] around 8000 B.C. and we have evidence of relatively egalitarian societies, such as Catal Huyuk, which practiced animal husbandry 2,000 to 4,000 years later. There cannot therefore be a causal connection." This jumps over a great deal of information to reach a conclusion. It is also a slight to Elizabeth Fisher, who, in *Woman's Creation* (1979), did a detailed analysis of the evidence at Catal Huyuk and other early agricultural settlements. Fisher showed that early Catal valued women in the numerous Venus figurines and other female symbols. But as sheep, goats, and cattle are introduced, there are signs that women's roles and status may have changed. Fisher believed, as I do, that animal husbandry brought a clear understanding of the male sex role to agri-culture, and that this severely undercut the very old idea that procreation is female.

Facts, Factors, and Fatherhood

Moreover, Lerner, too, is factually wrong in her statement that "animal husbandry began in 8000 B.C." Actually, true husbandry, which is the deliberate manipulation of the sexuality and reproduction of animals to achieve desirable horns, colors, sizes, temperament, and so on, appeared much later. The earliest domesticated animals were probably shaped more or less unintentionally by selective killing of semi-wild herds, either by hunting or in roundups. It is probable, then, that the animal "husbandry" at Catal was not advanced to the point where people clearly understood the role of males in procreation. We should remember, too, that female power and society's ideas about the great female life force were very old and had great inertia. Even after true animal husbandry and plow agri-culture bean, these notions held their own for a very long time.

Lerner, then, seems a bit mechanistic when she suggests that herds-keeping could not be a cause, otherwise patriarchy would have followed right after the first stage of animal domestication. In addition, she, like Marvin Harris and the other materialists, works from an often rigid ideo-logical base that has open disdain for the roles that psychic and emotional factors play in cultural evolution. For them, like Marx and Engels, eco-nomics is everything; labor and commodities production drive all history. Lately, some materialists have added environment, so now there are three forces that drive culture. The environmental factor should allow them to see what powerful informants and models animals are for human society, but there is a strange reluctance to look in such directions. Consequently, the materialists explain much less than they think they can. At the other extreme is Joseph Campbell and the Jungian school, who say that arche-typal ideas, mental pictures, emotions, and affairs of the mind drive cul-ture. Some of them recognize the powerful influence that animals, both real animals and animal symbols in art, have on the human mind and culture. Less sectarian thinkers can easily see that each side is about half right.

For me, feminist and author Kate Millett was right on the mark back in 1972 when she theorized about what might have happened to the ancient female-oriented powers and fertility principles. She suggested that "the circumstance which might drastically redirect such attitudes would be the discovery of paternity. There is some evidence that fertility cults in ancient society at some point took a turn toward patriarchy, displacing and down-grading female function in procreation and attributing the power of life to the phallus alone. Patriarchal religion could consolidate this position by the creation of a male God or gods, demoting, discrediting, or eliminating goddesses and constructing a theology whose basic postulates are male supremacist, and one of whose central functions is to uphold and validate the patriarchal structure."

Millett, however, did not speculate on how people "discovered" the male role in procreation. Is it not rather obvious that early farmers figured it out in the course of their work with domestic animals? Why, again, do we avoid any connection with the animal world—even when it would help understanding of our own problems?

Animal Exploitation: A Source of Male Power

Many writers have made the generalization that female principles are more important in plant-based societies and male principles are more important in animal-based ones. In *Man's Rise to Civilization,* anthropologist Peter Farb reasoned that males tend to determine residence and family lineage in hunting cultures because the men have to stay together for better hunting success. They need to learn the hunting grounds from their male elders, so it would not make sense for them, when they marry, to go off and live with the wife's family. On the other hand, in gathering/gardening cultures the work tends to be primarily women's or at least woman-led. In these groups, women's expertise, cooperation, and stability are valued. And they are better shared when the women stay together. In these matrilocal and matrilineal societies, the new husband goes to live with his wife's people and the children claim descent through the maternal line. Joseph Campbell and Lewis Mumford, among others, further generalized that the animal-based, or hunter/herder, societies tend to be northern where animals are the only source of food and materials year-round, while the plant-based, or gatherer/gardener, societies tend to proliferate in southern zones where all sources are available year-round.

Peggy Reeves Sanday measured the evidence for these generalizations and confirmed much of them. In *Female Power and Male Dominance,* she looked at marital residence, creation stories, parenting patterns, and various other features of culture in the Standard Cross-Cultural Sample of 168 societies. Of these, she looked at the creation stories of 112 groups. Her data showed that "Almost all of the animal-oriented economies are characterized by masculine origin beliefs, whereas the plant economies are characterized by feminine, couple, or masculine symbolism. The simpler plant economies (gathering and semi-intensive agriculture) tend toward feminine or couple origin symbolism, but the more advanced plant economies (shifting and advanced agriculture) are split nearly evenly between those displaying exclusively masculine symbolism and those displaying feminine or couple symbolism." Sanday also looked at patterns in infant care and parenting and how they relate to the base economy. In the animal-based societies, there was sexual segregation in work, with fathers spending less time with infants and leaving child care to women. These societies also tended to be more competitive, with males tending to be "distant, controlling figures" who are "too busy proving their maleness to spend time with children." These cultures are also marked by "macho" values on toughness and male supremacy as well as predator animal models and warriorism.

Sanday found also that these values and male dominance were strongest in societies where large animals were the main prey. And she found some other correlates: "Male dominance is associated with increasing technological complexity, an animal economy, sexual segregation in work, a symbolic orientation to the male creative principle, and stress. [Data] show that the sexes are most likely to be equal in gathering, fishing, and shifting cultivation economies. The sexes tend to be unequal in animal husbandry societies." She found also that female or couple origin myths are more frequent in sexually egalitarian societies, that sexual segregation tends to go with male dominance, and that sexual cooperation rarely goes with male dominance.

Sanday's empirical data reinforces the observations by many others that northern hunter/herders tend to have male dominant cultures whereas southern gatherers/gardeners and hunters of smaller animals tend to be more egalitarian. The latter also have more intersexual cooperation, male involvement with children, and a prevalence of female status and symbolism. This squares with what we discussed earlier in Chapter 4 about the herder culture that emerged in the agricultural period. There we saw how herdskeepers tend to be aggressive, violent, individualistic, and warlike with much emphasis on male toughness, strength, and supremacy. Much of the worst stuff of patriarchy is here without even getting to the factors of commodities exchange, female slave trading, and the hierarchy and class divisions of the agrarian state.

A Civilization Led by Soul-Damaged Men

These macho-man values are no mere coincidence; they have had a purpose. They furnished men with the distancing devices we talked about in the last chapter. Men in animal exploitative societies "needed" the emotion-disarming effects of these devices to enable them to carry out the often brutal work of hunting and herding. (I choose the word *brutal* here, by the way, for its interesting levels of meaning: "savage; cruel; inhuman; irrational; unreasoning; bestial; like an animal." When humans inflict pain, suffering, and death, they are brutal—like brutes.) But the macho values also produced some unintended destructive side effects. With both weapons and minds geared to the work of hunting and herding, men were more disposed toward warfare and the oppression of others—especially those regarded as closer to animals or closer to nature. Such behavior, as we know, has marked Western civilization since its beginnings in the Middle East. Given the economic importance of domestic animals and animal husbandry to those beginnings, it seems arbitrary, or worse, to simply ignore the role of the herder culture complex (the various groups who herded sheep, goats, cattle, horses, and camels) as a major forger of patriarchy and macho values in Western society.

If we can put our own culture and its built-in distancing devices aside for a moment, we should not have much trouble seeing that animal exploitation, particularly animal husbandry, has fostered values that have created generation after generation of hardened, detached, domineering, self-aggrandizing men. It has done great emotional and spiritual damage to the male half of humanity. As a result, ours is a wounded civilization—one made by soul-damaged men; one marked by their violence, individualism, emotional hang-ups, and male supremacist institutions. These have rung up enormous costs to girls and women, of course, but they have also put a great rip in the fabric of humanity.

But why do we have so much difficulty in seeing the connections between these problems and animal exploitation? My answer is that we are blinded by our own culture, which has been shaped by animal exploitation. The culture has a built-in blinding agent—misothery—that has institutionalized detachment, misrepresentation, concealment, and blame-shifting. Our agri-culture uses misothery to detach from the living world, to reduce it beyond moral consideration, and to defuse any feelings of guilt or conscience that might arise from our actions in exploiting it. When it is argued, then, that animal exploitation has benefited humanity, we need to ask: In what sense? We can say that it has benefited us materially, economically, but we must also take into account that it has damaged us psychically, spiritually, emotionally, and socially.

Using misothery, then, the agri-culture regards animals as unimportant, beneath consideration historically, morally, and every other way. This attitude has blinded scholars and caused them to miss—or perhaps avoid—the substantial influence that the herder culture complex has had on the evolution of Western civilization. Perhaps this is more of the "invisibility of the obvious" that we discussed at the end of Chapter 4 (in connection with the failure of scholars to see the evidence of goddess worship).

A Summary

That herder societies were the prime movers of patriarchal culture should be obvious. I would summarize the flow of cultural evolution as follows: Over the many centuries that it took to build agrarian society, male-dominant herding peoples with their values on expansion, aggression, and war-making naturally took over. When they conquered and annexed a region, they put their stamp of culture on it, and herder ways and views came to dominate the Middle East both geographically and culturally. Over time, herder culture provided the dominant threads in the agri-culture of the Middle East. Only in that center of civilization was such a powerfully male-supremacist worldview woven so early into the usual fabric of agricultural society. There, herder culture colored the entire process—from the early increase in the scale of society, to the emergence of classes, ruling elites, and labor specialization, and, finally, the building of the agrarian state itself with its taxes, bureaucrats, patriotism, and wars of conquest. Early on, it gave hue and pattern to the formation of Western civilization. Its motif was a world for males only, with every other kind of living being serving them. Since males were to rule over the entire living world, the system is known as patriarchy—literally, the rule of the fathers.

The Rise of Patriarchy in Mesopotamia

We can see much of this process unfold in the early history of Meso-potamia, which began about 3000 B.C. Gerda Lerner believes that this was the beginning point of a 2,500-year process in which female power and status gradually fell while male power and status rose. Before this process began, male-female relations were roughly egalitarian, although the greatest spirit-powers or deities were female; at the end of the process, men ruled over women as they ruled over their livestock and there was one deity—an all-powerful male god.

Again, my only quarrel with Lerner's analysis is that it misses some important factors that had been in place earlier. The oldest of these was the long-standing male jealousy of female power, which was institutionalized in culture in the form of men's cults and rituals. Men "stayed in their place" as long as female power was perceived to be strong, which it was in the early agricultural period. Then, two new factors kicked in to unleash this age-old male resentment: These are agricultural intensification and animal husbandry. Intensification of plant agriculture gradually demystified nature's cycles of life, growth, and reproduction and gave farming society a greater sense of control over nature. This slowly eroded women's power base, which had lain in their association with these mysteries and natural forces.

Animal husbandry, however, brought a couple of swifter kicks into the process of female power reduction. It brought knowledge of men's role in procreation, which undercut women's age-old "ownership" of this most powerful mystery. It also brought the herder cultural complex with its male supremacy, hardness, individualism, competitiveness, violence, and militarism. I suggest, then, that male society was already struggling for the upper hand in Mesopotamia by the time Western history begins there c. 3000 B.C. We know that the buildup of agricultural wealth and power in that region drew heavily from the husbandry of large herd animals, particularly cattle, horses, donkeys, sheep, and goats. So I think we can assume that the herder cultural complex and the knowledge of fatherhood had been at work in Mesopotamian society well before writing launches the historical period.

Strong Men Take Over Temples and Tradition

With this in mind, let us summarize Lerner's account of the process by which women and female principles were reduced and patriarchy was established in the ancient Middle East: She begins with what archaeologists call the Uruk V–Early Dynastic period—the few centuries on the eve of history. It was during this period that "military elites developed next to temple elites and soon became an independent and rival force in society," she says. "Military strong men would first become chieftains over villages and later establish their dominance over previously communally held temple lands and herds, gradually pushing the priests into the background. . . . Later the strongest of these chieftains would set themselves up as kings, usurping power over the temples and treating temple property as their own. In the ensuing centuries of intercity warfare, the strongest of these rulers would unite a number of such city-states into a kingdom or a national state."

Although Lerner does not say so, many writers believe that the herder cultural complex contributed these military strong men who made their way, through warfare, to the position of kings and emperors. We can be sure that their battles against the temples and priests (and priestesses) were more than fights simply for property and regional power. As in all wars, they were also battles over ideology; they were part of the larger war against the old great goddess religions and the peoples who practiced them. In simplest terms, this larger war was the war for male supremacy directed against the bastions of established female power.

But it was a long war, because old religious and social institutions die hard. Lerner says that in the next stage, the first 1,500 years of the historical period, women, at least in the upper classes, still served as queens, priestesses, and wealth-holders. What is clear, however, is that they became less and less autonomous, holding their offices and wealth as "standins" or deputies for men. Their powers were not as women, but as wives or close relatives of powerful men in the "patrimonial bureaucracy." According to Lerner, "Their influence and actual role in shaping events [were] real, as [was] their power over the men and women of lower rank whom they own or control. But in matters of sexuality, they [were] utterly subordinate to men." Increasingly during the early historical period, Lerner says, even elite women's power and status "depend[ed] on the adequacy of sexual services they perform[ed] for their men." Since rulers and elite men looked to their dozens of concubines, or sexual slaves, for sexual pleasure, the wife's sexual value was more as a breeder. She needn't be so "good in bed" as she needed to be a good producer of healthy children who could strengthen the family's wealth and power.

The Invention of Slavery and Concentration Camps

Lerner turns next to the changing roles of nonelite women in early historical periods. The crucial development here was the "invention" of slavery. Women's sexuality and reproductive potential had already become valuable commodities to be exchanged or acquired for male pleasure or for the betterment of the agrarian family. Women were already being valued, identified, and therefore circumscribed by these aspects of femaleness. As we saw earlier, the various wars among city-states of this period culminated in the massive slaughter of male captives and the abduction and enslavement of female and child captives. Eventually, males were taken captive and blinded, castrated, or otherwise mutilated so they would be less of a threat and then turned into slaves as well. Nevertheless, records indicate that a preponderance of the slaves in early Middle Eastern civilization were female.

Many of these female slaves were maintained in what we would call concentration camps where they worked at milling, weaving, and other manufacture. The Sumerologist Kuzuya Maekawa of Kyoto University has analyzed records of the Ur III period (c. 2100 B.C.) and found that some 6,400 female slaves served as weavers in the districts of Lagash, the capital of ancient Sumeria. These women were organized into "gangs" of twenty, each supervised by one or two seasoned female slaves, who in turn answered to a male leader. It appears that these women were also the sexual property of some of the men in the community, for, according to Maekawa, they "bore their children, male and female, even after being recruited to the weaving workshop." Possibly, although Maekawa does not say, they were deliberately bred, like livestock, to produce more slaves. At any rate, the system produced girls who were allowed to stay with their mothers and eventually added to the weaving and milling gangs. The boys, says Maekawa, "were separated from the mothers and were castrated just before they attained puberty when they were given 15 *sila* of barley. They were frequently assigned to lowly labor such as towing ships" and working in the livestock stables. Tellingly, the Sumerian word for these castrated slave boys, *amar-kud,* was also used for young castrated donkeys, horses, and oxen. Accordingly, Maekawa sees the management of livestock as a model for the management of slaves, with females kept in a work and breeding camp and the males castrated and trained to work as beasts of burden.

I still agree with Lerner, who argues that "the domestic subordination of women provided the model out of which [human] slavery developed as a social institution." Nevertheless, the more basic source was probably the animal husbandry model, for in Mesopotamia we can see that women's enslavement, commodification, confinement, and management as worker-breeders was very much a product of the views and values of the large animal herder cultural complex.

In any event, once female slavery became a common fixture of early Middle Eastern civilization, it caused women to be seen in a new way. They were no longer seen as equal human beings; instead, they became animal-like—that is, seen as tools and commodities for the benefit of men. All women, not just those enslaved, suffered a decline in power and status because they belonged to an easily identifiable group that could be dominated. During this period, females in general came to be seen as an inherently inferior class of human beings, while males in general came to be seen as inherently superior.

Misogyny: Patriarchal Propaganda

Patriarchy, like any other cause on the make, needed to have God and morality on its side. As we might expect, in the ideological warfare that ensued between the emerging male rule and the older female-empowered, egalitarian order, both religion and ethics were invoked to reduce women and to elevate men. Myth, as Kate Millett notes, "is a felicitous advance in the level of propaganda, since it so often bases its arguments on ethics or theories of origins." In Western culture, there are two leading origin-of-evil myths—that is, myths that purport to explain why the world is so full of toil and trouble. One is Hebrew, the other Greek—the two principal feeders of Western thought and culture. Both are crassly misogynist. Both have their taproots in herder culture.

The Greek story of Pandora's box credited woman with opening the box and releasing evil into the world. According to Kate Millett, the myth served two purposes: It discredited and reduced Pandora, who was probably one of the older fertility goddesses of the Mediterranean, and it promoted the idea of feminine evil and destructive influence. In his account of the myth, the Greek poet Hesiod described Pandora as the original of "the damnable race of women—a plague which men must live with." She introduced evil through what the patriarchal Greek mind saw as a uniquely female product: sexuality. In his *Works and Days,* Hesiod described Pandora as a dangerous temptress with "the mind of a bitch and a thievish nature." She had "the cruelty of desire and longings that wear out the body." She was full of "lies and cunning words and a deceitful soul." Pandora was a snare sent by Zeus to be "the ruin of men." Millet notes the hypocrisy and mendacity of the Greeks' patriarchal propaganda: "When it wishe[d] to exalt sexuality, it celebrate[d] fertility through the phallus; when it wishe[d] to denigrate sexuality, it cite[d] Pandora."

The Hebrew myth of the Fall from Grace, which we discussed in Chapter 1, is strikingly similar to that of Pandora. It is, however, much more central to the Judeo-Christian-Islamic tradition and therefore to our present worldview. Even for the nonreligious, says Millet, "this mythic version of the female as the cause of human suffering, knowledge, and sin is still the foundation of sexual attitudes, for it represents the most crucial argument of the patriarchal tradition in the West."

The story of Eve and the Fall in Hebrew tradition also suggests that Eve, like Pandora, may have been a fertility goddess in earlier times. At one point in Genesis, it says that Adam named her Eve "because she was the mother of all living things." So like the Pandora myth, the Hebrew myth was double-barreled propaganda: It demoted a female deity while it denigrated women in general. Millet explains that the monotheistic, patriarchal Hebrews lived in a continual state of war with the fertility cults of their neighbors. In this situation, the story of Eve and the Fall helped to solidify Hebrew identity against the wickedness and backwardness of their enemies. Another parallel to the Pandora myth is that woman's sexuality tempted man and brought about original sin, shame, and evil in the world. In the Eve myth, the sex act is disguised in language about eating forbidden fruit from the tree of knowledge of good and evil. Scholars have pointed out that the Hebrew word for "eat" can also mean coitus, and that throughout the Bible the word *knowing* is synonymous with the sex act—as in "carnal knowledge," or "he lay with her and he *knew* her." Again, as in the Pandora myth, a god-the-father figure punished his subjects for taking up sinful sex. Adam and men were condemned to endless toil and adversity, while Eve and women were sentenced to inferiority and the pains and sorrows of childbirth. As Millet notes, "the connection of women, sex, and sin constitute[d] the fundamental pattern of Western patriarchal thought thereafter."

We know that the culture of the Hebrews came from a long unbroken tradition as herders of sheep, goats, and cattle. The Greeks' began with mixed farming and fishing in the Aegean and an egalitarian, goddess-worshiping society. We shall soon see how that culture was overthrown by Indo-European invaders from the north who rode horses, lived by war and raiding, and brought their patriarchal worldview to the Aegean. It was after their influence on Aegean/Greek culture that the Pandora myth was created and, later still, reported by Hesiod.

The Shepherd Model for God and Dominionism

We saw in Chapter 4 how herders applied their shepherd-flock model to the ordering of human society. A good shepherd tended his flock of sheep; a good patriarch tended his family and clan. It is easy to see how this community model provided a model for the patriarchal nation-state: a good king tended his nation's citizens. As kingship and the nation-state evolved in the Middle East, the relationships between king and subjects followed this patriarchal model. The king had absolute authority over his people just as the shepherd ruled over his flock and the patriarch ruled over his kinfolk. The subjects owed complete loyalty and submission to the king just as the sheep obeyed the shepherd and the family and clan obeyed their patriarch. The relationship boiled down to one of complete power and authority in the leader on the one hand and, on the other, complete loyalty and submission in the flock or subjects. Under this relationship, humans become like sheep—docile, base, and obedient. Over time, as we have seen, this shepherd model elevated many Middle Eastern kings to the level of gods.

The next ideological extensions of the shepherd model were monotheism and dominionism. It provided the scheme for a great king of heaven and earth who tended to the great flock of the faithful. Just as the nation's subjects owed loyalty and tribute to their king, believers owed faith and worship to their almighty god. Just as the nation's subjects received the king's protection, his peace and the use of his lands, believers received their god's grace and dominion over his creation. Just as the nation's king had life-or-death authority over his subjects, the good Lord could, as the Bible says, "giveth and taketh away." One was not entitled to question the ways and works of either the king or the god almighty.

This Good Shepherd model is no mere theory; it is embraced in symbol, ideal, and practice by all three branches of the Middle East's monotheistic religion. The model is explicitly embraced, for example, by the Presbyterian Animal Welfare Task Force, the Midwestern church group referred to in Chapter 1 in the discussion of dominionism. In its paper, "The Treatment of Domestic Farm Animals," the group notes that "many of the references to animal husbandry in the Bible draw upon that branch of agriculture as an example to describe how political and religious leaders should serve their followers. Kings who fail in their responsibility are described as shepherds who scatter a flock, driving them away rather than keeping them unified, neglecting them rather than tending their needs." Like all political rulers, the Task Force says, "God is pictured as caring for people in the manner of a good shepherd." The paper gives the example of the Twenty-third Psalm, in which God is described as doing "what a good livestock producer does: providing adequate food and water as well as protection from danger." The Task Force's paper, like many similar religious tracts, goes on to give many examples from the Bible, especially the teachings and parables of Jesus, in which the Good Shepherd model is used to teach trust in God and righteous living.

From Flock Wether to Court Eunuch

Some will object and claim that the Good Shepherd model was merely a metaphor, a convenience for simplifying religious concepts so illiterate peasants could more easily grasp them. Even so, herder views and values—patriarchy, hierarchy, obedience, and all the rest—poured into the evolution of agri-culture and became the dominant worldview. I argue, however, that the Good Shepherd was more actual model than metaphor, more blueprint than teaching aid. Remember that animals, as we saw in

Chapter 3, feed the human mind and culture and give us ways to find shape and order in the world. Moreover, the work of Japanese anthropologist Yutaka Tani gives some evidence that herding models may have carried over into human affairs. Tani has spent years studying the herding peoples of southern Europe and Asia—the same lands where the major herd animals were domesticated millennia ago. Throughout these areas, shepherds castrate certain male sheep and goats, train them to obey simple commands, and use them to help control the rest of the animals in their herds. Tani believes that their ancestors invented these practices millennia ago and that they may have provided the model for the court eunuch, who served as a mediator, slave leader, and harem boss for early kings. He admits that there is no record of how and where the role of court eunuchs began, "but it seems possible that this kind of social control, using the castrated male, prepared the cultural background for the idea of the eunuch." The views of Professors Tani and Maekawa (the Sumerologist who has studied female weaver-slaves) are attracting the attention of other scholars. One is Juliet Clutton-Brock, the world authority on the domestication of animals. She has written that she thought Tani's hypothesis "farfetched" at first. "But since," she wrote, "I have come to believe that there was probably very little difference in the attitudes and treatment of animals and human slaves by the dominant members of those ancient human societies that kept slaves."

Can We Locate the Beginnings of Patriarchal Culture?

What, exactly, was this "herder cultural complex" and when and where did it arise? So far, we have been talking about its formation in the Middle East well before history began about 3000 B.C. Let's see if we can be more specific about times, places, and species of herd animals. Then we can follow the various migrations and invasions and see how herding people rapidly spread their patriarchal cultures throughout the Old World.

First, we need to get a better idea of the part of the world that I have been calling the Middle East. We think of this region today as made up of Israel, Syria, Iraq, Iran, and the countries whose internecine religious wars dominate the news. The geography is even more confusing because the borders and nation-names keep changing. Moreover, some scholars call this region the Near East while others call it southwest Asia. Let's start with the newsmedia picture of the Middle East—Israel and Iraq—and build from there. Around this center, all of the major herd animals were domesticated: sheep and goats (8000 B.C.) in northern Iraq; cattle (6000 B.C.) in western Turkey; horses (4000 B.C.) just north of the Black Sea in Ukraine; and camels (c. 3000 B.C.) in southern Iraq and Saudi Arabia.

Second, all of these places of domestication spawned herder subcultures—that is, pastoral, nomadic peoples whose cultures we described earlier as expansionistic, individualistic, militaristic, arrogant, male-dominated, and patriarchal. We do not know the details of their travels in the centuries before history began, but we have evidence that they went far and wide. And, according to anthropologist C. D. Darlington in his essay "The Silent Millennia in the Origin of Agriculture," pastoral societies moved their cultures faster than did settled cultivators. Add to their mobility and speed the aggressive, domineering nature of their culture, and we can assume that these prehistoric herder peoples were, to put it mildly, very influential in shaping the agri-culture all around the Middle Eastern center.

Finally, it is difficult to pinpoint dates and places because experts in the various specialties disagree on so much. There is disagreement, for example, over where cattle were first domesticated and when they were taken into Egypt and Africa. Scholars disagree by about 2,000 years on when horses were domesticated and when they were brought into Mesopotamia, and so on. About the best we can do under these circumstances is to relate the accounts of the various experts. Keep in mind, though, that their dates won't jibe. Perhaps we should lay all of them out and then take an average. In time, of course, as more and more experts take an interest in the role of herder cultures in the evolution of agri-culture in the Middle Eastern center, a more detailed and accurate picture can be drawn.

The Horse Warrior Complex

If we had to single out one animal and herder culture as *the* most influential, it would have to be the horse and its herders. Horses were probably the first animals to carry riders, and they carried them farther and faster than any of the other domesticates. Remember, too, that these first riders were also skilled hunter-warriors who had all the usual tribal enemies and territorial conflicts. This combination produced, as we shall see, much trouble throughout the Middle Eastern agri-center. Remember Cranstone's insight, discussed in Chapter 4: The more powerful and mobile the animal herded, the more warlike the herder culture. The horse's social and breeding patterns also gave these hunter-warriors of the northern steppes a well-defined macho model. In the wild, horses form two primary social units: bachelor bands and harems controlled by a single stallion. Wild horse life, besides grazing, consists of the most aggressive bachelor stallions making raids on the harem to steal a few females. Eventually, one of these stallions successfully makes off with a few mares and starts a harem of his own. Or he may successfully challenge the boss stallion and take the whole harem of mares. For the tribes who lived from these animals—first by hunting, eventually by herding them—this was a stark model for human society.

According to the leading experts on the horse, anthropologists David Anthony and Dorcas Brown, the animal was domesticated about 4000 B.C. just north of the Black Sea, in present-day Ukraine. After a long formative period, these people formed a herder subculture, based on the horse, that enabled them to range throughout the steppes, or plains, west of the Ural mountains. Then, between 3500 and 3000 B.C., these horse herders rapidly spread their culture first eastward toward present China and Mongolia, then westward into northern Europe. Anthony and Brown believe that "it took a very long time for the custom of riding to diffuse southward into the Middle East." They put the horse in the Mesopotamian Middle East about 2000 B.C., where it was ridden and used to pull battle carts.

Anthony and Brown have also studied the use of feral horses by seventeenth-century Amerind tribes of the Great Plains of North America. These horses descended from animals left by Spanish explorers and others who escaped from Spain's colonies in Mexico. Brown and Anthony see this Plains Indian culture as a model that can help understand how prehistoric Ukraine horse culture arose and spread. They say that "the acquisition of horses wrought a revolution in virtually every aspect of life of the Plains tribes." Horse riders were able to move three times farther and faster in a day than people on foot. Resources, enemies, allies, and markets that had been distant suddenly came within reach. Life in the tall grasslands had been risky and uncertain for pedestrian foragers, but on horseback it became safer and easier. From horseback, warriors could easily mount surprise raids into sedentary farming villages, taking captives and treasures with little opposition or fear of pursuit. According to Brown and Anthony, "Many of these villages were abandoned, and their occupants became mounted hunters in self-defense, as happened in the case of the Cheyenne, the Arapaho and the Crow." Warfare increased in intensity and social importance, they say, because horses came to be so valuable and they were so easily stolen. In addition, these mounted societies had to redraw ethnic boundaries that had been based on foot-travelers' distances. Trade systems rapidly reached farther, became more socially complex, and carried a greater volume of valuable goods.

Above all, though, the horse was a warrior's animal. On fast, well-trained horses, a group of warriors had a military advantage over just about any enemy force. Any people who had them were sure to rule over just about everyone else—as they did in what has been called the Bronze Age. This designation, of course, is the Cartesian mind-set updated by the Industrial age; it glorifies copper, bronze, and iron metallurgy, but it misses the real animal. Seeing through it, we know that it was horses who won the wars of the ancient world. They decided the battles until the introduction of gunpowder and firearms in the fifteenth century.

Back in the steppes of southwestern Asia in 3000 B.C., the horse herders, then, very probably had the upper hand in war, trade, migration, and cultural dispersal. Anthony, Brown, and other experts believe that they may well have been the source and the carriers of the Indo-European language group, the most widely dispersed family of languages in the world. The group includes Sanskrit, Homeric Greek, and Latin as well as the modern languages English, French, Russian, and Persian.

The First Cowboys

In his 1956 book *The Testimony of the Spade,* Geoffrey Bibby described some of these same horse herders when he wrote of the "battle-ax" people who poured into Europe "before 2000 B.C." bringing herds of cattle as well as horses. Europe's residents must have been disturbed by these "hordes of tomahawk-wielding horsemen from the east," Bibby says. "Driving their herds of cattle and seeking out the best pasture lands, these insurgents poured on to the Rhine, each tribe carving out an area for itself and settling down." Farther south, he says, the same battle-ax folk spread into Turkey and northern Mesopotamia, where they carved out the Hittite kingdom and the kingdom of the horse-taming Mitanni. "And these conquering tribes, we know, spoke and wrote languages recognizably Indo-European."

Paul Shepard described the horse herders' cultural complex when he wrote, in *Nature and Madness,* of what he calls the "Neolithic dialect," or the conflict between herders and settled farmers. He saw it as a conflict caused, in part, by "incursions of mounted pastoralists from the north, successively demolishing the theocracies of the soil" to the south. The demolishers often stayed, melded with the earth-centered traditions of the conquered peoples, and became farmers themselves—only to be invaded by new hordes from the north a generation or two later. "Such Semitic desert nomads," Shepard says, "invaded and ruled Sumer nearly four thousand years ago; the Hurrians from the Caucasus, led by aristocratic Indo-Aryan chariot-fighters; warrior-herding Hittites, coming into Turkey; and the Kassites, who worshiped the sun and wind, are but a few." The same sort of invasions and wars marked Greek history, according to Shepard. "The Mycenaeans, absorbed by the Minoan megaron culture after 1600 B.C., had themselves arrived from the north and were in turn overrun by Achaeans, allies of the Hittites, after 1300 B.C. and, a century later, by the pastoral warrior Dorians."

I agree with Shepard that this "Neolithic dialect"—the constancy of warfare and conflicts—was pressed primarily by aggressive, expansive herder cultures. Thus, the herder cultural complex set the tone of Western culture. As Shepard puts it: "The background of both classical Greece and the Jewish Bible lands, of Zeus and of Yahweh, was a turmoil of armed mounted invaders from the north and east."

Male Dominance Takes Over Old Europe . . .

The influence of these warrior-invaders on Western culture has been written about most recently by Riane Eisler in her popular book *The Chalice and the Blade*. Eisler draws heavily from the investigations of University of Southern California archaeologist Marija Gimbutas. They tell of "several migratory waves of steppe pastoralists or 'Kurgan' people" that swept across prehistoric Europe, disrupting older farming communities and displacing their egalitarian, goddess-worshiping cultures with patriarchy. According to Gimbutas, the first wave of Kurgans into Old Europe came about 4200 B.C. The second wave came around 3300 B.C., and the third wave came about 2900 B.C.

These Kurgans, Eisler wrote, "were of what scholars call Indo-European or Aryan language-speaking stock, a type that was in modern times to be idealized by Nietzsche and then Hitler as the only pure European race. In fact, they were not the original Europeans, as they swarmed down on that continent from the Asiatic and European northeast. Nor were they even originally Indian, for there was another people, the Dravidians, who lived in India before the Aryan invaders conquered them." Nevertheless, the term *Indo-European* has stuck. It is used to describe a long line of Eurasian nomadic peoples who carried on wars of invasion over long distances. Wherever they went, they carried with them their horses, cattle, and their male gods of war and mountains. And, wrote Eisler, "as Aryans in India, Hittites and Mittani in the Fertile Crescent, Luwians in Anatolia, Kurgans in eastern Europe, Achaeans and later Dorians in Greece, they gradually imposed their ideologies and ways of life on the lands and peoples they conquered."

. . . and the Aegean

Both Eisler and another writer, French historian of religion Monique Saliou, have traced the transformation of the ancient culture of Crete, an island in the Aegean Sea where Greek culture first began. In Crete, we can see how, during the historical period, a patriarchal herder culture invaded and took over an area with an egalitarian, goddess-worshiping culture. The invasions and the transformation occurred here considerably later than they did in the rest of the Middle East, and so the prepatriarchal culture in Crete was alive longer and able to develop further than it did in neighboring regions.

Before 2000 B.C., Saliou says, the people of Crete "lived on agriculture in a system of clan property (as is shown by collective tombs); clan ancestors were women, as is proved by the exclusive presence of female idols in the religious statuary. Matrilineality and matrilocality are established beyond doubt." Crete's early agrarian society accumulated surpluses, or wealth, from both horticulture and cattle as well as specialized spinning, weaving, and other crafts. In early Crete, as elsewhere, cattle-keeping does not automatically produce male-centered, patriarchal culture. Cattle, because of their mixture of uses and symbolism, are as often identified with females as they are with males.

Around 1500 B.C., however, the Minoan culture flourished on Crete and some changes were evident, says Saliou. "All we do know is that in terms of the relations between the sexes, Minoan society appears to be the product of contradictory tendencies." The trend was marked by an increase in the use of female labor, much of it by female slaves. In short order, the island was invaded by the first of Indo-European raiders who established the Mycenaean culture that lasted for several centuries after about 1450 B.C. Here, Saliou says, began the male domination of Aegean culture "through the clear predominance of female slavery, the sexual division of labor that gave the least valued tasks to women and through patrilocality." She notes that, as a concession to the locals, the new regime allowed royal women and priestesses to maintain their high status.

Then, in the twelfth century B.C., the Dorians, the last of the waves of Indo-Europeans, arrived and destroyed Mycenaean civilization "wholly and brutally." This caused emigration, disruption of trade, and the temporary disappearance of writing. The waves of "Indo-European invasions," Saliou says, "brought victors with increasingly patriarchal systems." Everywhere in the Aegean, these invaders came up against the much older, female-oriented core culture. "In reaction to the threat it represented to all patriarchal society, male superiority was constantly and vehemently asserted." It was asserted so constantly and vehemently that it forged a Greek culture that would turn out to be male chauvinist. By the age of democracy in the fifth century B.C., the character Creon, in Sophocles's *Antigone,* could say: "Our duty is to defend order and never endure that a woman has the upper hand." He spoke it on a stage where all actors were male, before an audience that was probably exclusively male, and in an age when the seclusion of women was the rule.

So we see that in 1,500 years, women's status in the Aegean went from goddesses and clan founders to being objects of ridicule before all-male audiences in the theaters of "democratic" Athens. Earlier, in the heart of the Middle East, the assault on female power and women's status had begun even before the beginnings of history. This may seem like a long way from the misogyny of today's pornographers and serial killers, but it is not. The reduction and degradation of women has proceeded in a straight line from the time patriarchy first reared its ugly, arrogant head nearly 6,000 years ago among the herder cultures in the regions around the Black Sea. As scholars learn that misothery, like misogyny, has blinded, and sometimes colored, their approach to cultural evolution and history, perhaps they will be able to provide better information about the role of animal domestication and the herder cultural complex in the creation of patriarchy.

And then we may see the roots of many of our problems growing out of the herder cultural complex. Its misogyny and, as Shepard says, its "jostling readiness to kill remind us that Western civilization has a heavy heritage of pastoral thought. From the Hun and Scythian horsemen, Mediterranean goat- and ass-keepers, Semitic cattle-breeders, Persian shepherds, and Arabian camel-lovers; from them and other animal-keepers the Western world obtained its premises of a world view."

Racism and Colonialism: Dominating Lands and Others

We need to sort out a few ideas. Chapters ago, we set out to understand the making of the Western worldview because many now believe that it is the main cause of our disastrous relations with the living world. In addition, I am suggesting that our worldview, which values hierarchy, domination, and exploitation, damages social, or human-to-human, relations as well. We just saw how it has wrecked male-female relations, and we will soon see how it affects relations with the Other—that is, people perceived to be markedly different physically and culturally.

So far, then, we have discussed dominionism, misothery, patriarchy, misogyny, agri-culture, and many other concepts. These tend to run together in the mind after a while if we don't keep putting them in perspective. Let us briefly review these ideas, which I see as the building blocks of the West's worldview.

Our worldview is the product of tens of centuries of agriculture, which is the manipulation of plants and animals for human wants and needs. With farming as the base of human subsistence, human effort and experience has been directed toward essentially two ends: harnessing the natural processes of domesticates, and subduing the natural processes of their competitors, the untamed natural world. Farmers, in other words, have striven to take the laws of nature into human hands. Generations of farmer experience have contributed dozens of views and values that have conglomerated into a worldview that sees nature as part slave, part enemy, and always a thing to be on top of.

Culture carries a human society's experience, views, and values—its worldview—from generation to generation. Our worldview, then, has come to us by way of an agrarian culture, which I have been calling the agri-culture.

Many of the views and values that make up the worldview work together in pairs. For example, a valuing of one's own group depends on a devaluing of another group. Thus, male supremacy depends on misogyny, a hateful ideology that places women in an inferior place to males. Similarly, human supremacy depends on misothery, a hateful ideology that places animals and nature inferior to human beings. These pairings work together to offer a basis for a system of control and exploitation. Thus, patriarchy operates from the pairing of ideas about male supremacy with misogyny, and dominionism operates from the pairing of ideas about human supremacy with misothery.

The Ladder of Being

The agri-culture, like any other culture, has striven to find order in an apparently chaotic, whimsical cosmos. It has constructed a worldview that sees every living thing ranked, according to historian Clarence Glacken, in "a hierarchy of being, in which, typically, plants exist for the sake of animals, animals for man, and man in order to contemplate God." The view, Glacken noted in his classic *Traces on the Rhodian Shore,* is strictly utilitarian: "Things are made for the sake of those who can use them." A living being's rank, or value, depends also on its distance from base, contemptible nature. Women, for example, are ranked "near the animal state" or closer to nature than men, but they are right below men because they are useful as breeders, child-rearers, and laborers for the patriarchal family and agrarian state.

A diagram of Western agri-culture's worldview would, as we have seen, look like a ladder, with God holding up the top. God placed men at the top rung, from which they are to hold hands with Him and serve as His stewards (or shepherds) over all below them in the hierarchy of being. This puts men in a godlike (shepherdlike) position of authority on earth, notes Glacken: "The theme that man, sinful though he be, occupies a position on earth comparable to that of God in the universe, as a personal possession, a realm of stewardship, has been one of the key ideas in the religious and philosphical thought of Western civilization regarding man's place in nature." Keith Thomas also notes the strength of the view that "man was the end of all God's works," and "central to the Divine Plan."

Despite the Fall, man's right to rule remained intact. He was still "the Vicegerent and Deputy of Almighty God." Under this scheme, notes Thomas, "Man's authority over the natural world was thus virtually unlimited."

On this ladder or hierarchy of being, women of one's own group are one step down. People whom we call "Others" are another step or two down, depending on their usefulness and their distance from nature. Male Others may outrank the women of one's group if they are "civilized"— that is, if they have a similar agri-culture with dominionism, patriarchy, royalty, wealth, monumental art, urban centers, and so on. If, however, they have few of these trappings of civilization, they will be seen as close to nature and therefore inferior. Until early in this century, they would be described as "savages," a word that derives from the older European words *sauvage* and *silvaticus* for "wild" and "of the woods." The Others will be seen as even closer to nature if their region is uncharted wilderness, for it represents raw, chaotic, menacing nature with all of its evil powers not yet brought under control by God's stewards, the West's civilized agrarian men. The Others will be seen as still closer to nature— far down the ladder of being next to animals—if their appearance and behavior are markedly different from ours. For if they are very physically *Other* they must be of another order in nature, they must be another kind of being.

Base, Evil Nature

On the rungs below Others stand animals, first those useful to men, then, farther down, all the others. At the bottom of the ladder is raw, chaotic nature itself, composed of invisible organisms and an unclassifiable mass of life that feeds, grows, dies, and stinks in dark, mysterious places. This is muck and swamp, and steamy jungle and all backwaters and wildernesses far from the pruned orchards and weeded crop rows of agrarian civilization; this is nature least useful, nature most mysterious, and therefore nature most hostile and sinister. This is the realm of nature described by Marlow, Joseph Conrad's narrator/hero in *Heart of Darkness*; it is "... all that mysterious life of the wilderness that stirs in the forest, in the jungles, in the hearts of wild men." This is nature at its lowest level, at the pole opposite God and civilized man and therefore evil and dangerous to men. As Marlow makes his way up the Congo river on a steamboat, a passenger gestures to "the forest, the creek, the mud, the river," which Marlow sees as a land with a "sunlit face," but loaded with "lurking death, . . . hidden evil," and a "profound darkness of its heart." It is wild nature so powerfully evil that it can suck away a man's civilization, as it did to Kurtz, the ivory trader's station chief in Conrad's story.

The vague, formless aspects of these lower reaches of nature are nevertheless symbolized by certain animals, like worms, snakes, and animals that slither about the ground, and bats, wolves, and animals that are active in the darkness of night. These frighten us inordinately because they are associated with the deepest, darkest, most dangerous reaches of terrible nature.

Similar views of a hierarchy of being running upward from base nature are expressed in Hindu and Buddhist thought, which are agrarian as well. But they show much less hostility toward the lower end of the ladder. Base nature is not as evil or sinister as it is in the West; lower lives are just not as enjoyable and valuable as human life.

For example, the Hindu yogi, as Freud noted, attempts to reduce suffering by taming the baser impulses, by mastering the lower, animal nature within. Yoga's ascetics practice control over pain, the senses, heart rate, and other bodily functions as tests of spiritual willpower over life's physical (animal) aspects. Having learned from the Hindus, Buddha taught that the soul "transmigrates" through the animal kingdom as a punishment for bad living. The implication, according to German sociologist and zoologist Richard Lewinsohn, is that "anyone who behaves like an animal during his lifetime will sink after death to the animal level."

This ideology of the transmigration of souls, or metempsychosis, was prevalent in ancient Egyptian culture, and it spread far and wide in the Old World during the sixth century b.c. In Greece, Pythagoras and his school of thought added the idea to Greek culture.

Though somewhat more benign than the Aristotelian and typically Western hard-core fear and hatred of lower nature, metempsychosis nevertheless reveals the disgust agrarians feel toward the dark, slimy, swampy living world. Buddha's sermons, Lewinsohn notes, tell of a natural world that clearly has its low-lifes: "There are animalized beings that are born in the dark, live in the dark and die in the dark: the beetles, moths and wood lice. There are others that are born, live and die in water: fishes, turtles and crocodiles. Then there are still other animalized beings that are born in filth, live in filth and die in filth, and those that are born, live and die in rotten fish or in soiled food or in pools and puddles. Each enumeration follows the same menacing formula: foolish men who do wicked deeds will become such and such creatures."

Agrarian Hierarchy

Bits of these ideas about a hierarchy of being seem to be common to all intensive agricultural societies, whether or not they have domestic animals. Even in the Americas, where population pressures had not made agriculture as intensive as in the Old World, there are some signs of the beginnings of ideas about hierarchy. Many of the familiar Amerindian tribal names, for example, are European bastardizations of derogatory words some tribes used for others. The horticultural, corn-planting Algonkians, for example, called one group of enemies "snakes" and referred to arctic hunting peoples as "eaters of raw meat" and "rude, uncivilized people." These Algonkian terms were reduced by the French to the tribal names with which we are familiar: Iroquois, Eskimo, and Naskapi, respectively. No wonder the present-day members of these groups resent these labels and seek to restore their original tribal names in their own languages: Hodenosaunee, or "people of the longhouse"; Inuit, or "the people"; and Neenoilno, or "the perfect people," respectively.

Perhaps farmers the world over soon learn contempt for nature and begin to see their enemies and Other groups as "lower" forms of life. In Mesoamerica, for example, where agrarian civilizations built teeming cities that fed on intensive horticulture and domesticated dogs and turkeys, we can see more signs of an idea of hierarchy in the natural world. The creation story of the Maya civilization, which flourished at about the same time as the Romans, is a case in point. It is told in the Popol Vuh, or "Council Book," also called "Our Place in the Shadows," and "The Dawn of Life." After making all the animals of the mountains and forests, the creators ordered the deer and birds to speak and to praise them. When the animals could not, the gods said, "It hasn't turned out well" and ordered them to "just accept your service, just let your flesh be eaten." The animals failed to perform as humans, "And so their flesh was brought low: they served, they were eaten, they were killed—the animals on the face of the earth." Another attempt to make humans failed as well: "They were not competent," says the Popol Vuh, "nor did they speak before the builder and sculptor who made them and brought them forth, and so they were killed, done in by a flood." These flawed people were then attacked by the animals and by their grinding stones and cooking utensils, who rebelled against their cruelty, shouting, "You caused us pain, you ate us, but now it is you whom we shall eat." The flawed people were "ground down, overthrown. The mouths and faces of all of them were destroyed and crushed." The story concludes: "And it used to be said that the monkeys in the forests today are a sign of this. . . . So this is why monkeys look like people: they are a sign of a previous human work." This view is similar to one expressed in medieval European art, in which monkeys and apes were used to depict degenerate or incomplete humanity.

Spin-Offs from Hierarchy: The Beast Within . . .

In the West, the idea of a hierarchy of being is very old. It was basic to many of the agrarian societies around Mediterranea and the Middle East, thus it was well developed early on and it was dispersed among many language and culture groups. Perhaps this is why it has spun off so many related ideas. We have just looked at two of the biggest ones: male supremacy and its companion, misogyny; and human supremacy and its companion, misothery. We noted how these two pairs of ideas are especially strong in Western culture because of the herder cultural complex, which has been a major contributor to the reduction of both women and animals. We saw also how these two pairs have, in turn, spun off still another round of ideas that pollute the West's views of life and nature. Let us review these, for they heavily infect views of human nature and the Other.

The first of these, as noted earlier, is the fear of "the beast within"—that is, sexuality, animality, and the physical body. This goes back at least to the Greeks. In *The Republic,* Plato wrote that when the appetitive part of the human soul got out of control, "then the wild beast within us . . . starts up." It is then that we become senseless, shameless, sexually wanton, he said, and we may commit every "conceivable folly or crime." The idea of a beast within came, of course, from misothery, which agrarians invented to reduce animals from their older near-deity status. Souls, creators, and ancestors before agriculture, animals are vicious, oversexed, deceitful, and evil by the time of Archaic Greece and the drafting of Genesis in 800 B.C.

. . . Evil Animality . . .

This soon produced another idea: If animals are so evil, then the animality in us is evil as well. Now no matter how hard humans tried to see themselves as above animals, the wicked beast was always just below, slavering and lusting like the dickens. A slip on the ladder of being could send one plunging into the jaws of animality. Or if the evil beast within were not kept constantly at bay, it would rise up and take over the soul and the higher self. And, of course, some human beings—women and Others—were already positioned down closer to the beasts; in them, the beast within was ever present and straining at its leash. Besides, the thinking goes, they probably didn't have souls or higher selves anyway.

Naturally, then, the idea of human evil would be cast in the form of animals. "It was no accident," notes Keith Thomas, "that the symbol of Anti-Christ was the Beast, or that the Devil was regularly portrayed as a mixture of man and animal." The classic image of Satan is a fire-red man with horns, tail, wings, and cloven hooves. And, says Thomas, "when people saw what they thought were evil spirits, it was usually in the guise of some animals: a dog, a cat or a rat" and sometimes a bull. Animals themselves were thought to carry evil spirits. In fifteenth-century Europe, a papal edict by Pope Innocent VIII declared that cats were possessed by the devil and some 100,000 women who kept cats were burned at the stake—along with their animals. Here again, misogyny and misothery appear to be one and the same idea.

. . . Evil Sex . . .

Second, we noted the very agrarian idea that sex is for procreation only. Any other kind of sexuality is evil, for it "wastes" the man's seed on idle pleasure instead of family enlargement. This idea has vilified just about the whole range of human sexuality and sensuality. Today, this tradition causes great suffering and injustice to homosexual men and lesbians, who must contend with hateful propaganda from self-righteous religious groups as well as the violent "bashings" it fosters. The bulk of this tradition comes directly from the Bible, but its roots go deeper to the herder culture of the Hebrews, the Sumerians, and many of the other ancient Middle Eastern agrarian groups who raged against every kind of sexual "indulgence" that did not result in child-making. In time, their repression of sexuality aided the idea that sex was evil as was the source of its desires, the human body.

. . . Breed Purity . . .

Finally, the agri-culture carries on a couple of ideas with such vigor that they might be called obsessions. One is an obsession with breeding, bloodlines, and breed purity—primarily in domestic animals, but also in human groups. Its companion idea is an obsession with manipulating and controlling beings down the ladder of life. The latter comes in part from man's self-styled role as God's steward, which gives him the "duty" to constantly prune, trim, weed, breed, castrate, and herd. It is a patronizing and condescending idea, this notion that "lower" forms of life need continual godly/manly management. But that is only the conscious side of this obsession—the side used in argument to rationalize the deeper, less conscious side, which is that wild, chaotic animals and nature tend to rise up and overwhelm humans and their civilization. Consciously, then, men are stewards of nature; less consciously, they are masters over a dangerous beast who must be kept ever under control.

. . . Playing God—"Improving" Nature

The former obsession, the one with breeding and bloodlines, probably derives in part from this steward/master notion and in part from long experience with "improving" strains of plants and animals for an ever-more intensive agriculture. Thomas notes that this obsession with breed "improvement" was particularly rampant in eighteenth-century Europe, when the "outlook was ruthlessly eugenic." Europeans exercised (in all senses of the word) their authority over creation by relentless manipulations of breeds and bloodlines, which, as Thomas notes, helped bolster "an extremely hierarchical attitude to domestic animals." In 1609, a bishop put out the order that he wanted no "riff-raff horses" in his market. A country gentleman observed that the "best-bred creatures, and of the truest race, are ever the noblest and most generous in their natures; that it is this chiefly which makes a difference between the horses of good blood and the errant jade of a base breed; between the game cock and the dunghill craven; . . . and between the right mastiff, hound or spaniel, and the very mongrel."

As always, this thinking, this model for human-animal relations leaked over to human-Other relations. It established deep values, as Thomas notes, that "Blood was important; there was a social hierarchy among animals no less than men, the one reinforcing the other."

There is another deeper driver of this obsession over animal breeding and blood purity. According to Harriet Ritvo, an authority on human-animal relations, "the whole enterprise of maintaining and improving breeds embodie[s] a metaphorical assertion of domination; the breeder assume[s] an almost godlike role in planning new variations." Animal breeders, of course, are barely conscious of this motivation and would hardly admit it if they were. But they nevertheless find great satisfaction in crafting animals and plants into the shapes and characteristics they like. "Success in these endeavors," noted Yi-Fu Tuan in *Dominance and Affection*, "gives people a godlike sense of power over life." He notes also that this power is often abused: "Breeders have created . . . goldfish with bulging eyes and dogs that are genetically defective, and dogs of exceptional ugliness such as the *shar-pei*, which has corrugated skins that fold over like an unmade bed."

It is elementary genetics that in order to create such breeds and to achieve ever greater refinements of them, animal breeders must maintain strict control of "blood" or "bloodline" or "purity" in their animals. Hence, the near obsession with purebreds and thoroughbreds, which are thought to be perfect because they match the human-made model and have none of chaotic, unpredictable nature in them. Indeed, it seems that the less "natural" they are, the less they resemble the original wild ancestor, the more valuable they become.

Racial Purity

These breeder's values, however, have a flipside. They have instilled in culture a horror of breed, blood, and species pollution. It meshes well with that old, deep fear of wild, base nature creeping in and corrupting hard-won civilization. For the breeder, then, the perfect, purebred, human-made race of animal must have no taint or corruption of genes that might have come from wild or mixed "stock." Such animals are "mongrels" or "mutts" and considered junk by pure-breeders.

Like so many other attitudes about animals and nature, these leak over into the realm of human relations. Predictably, they are applied to the Others down our ladder of being—those people perceived as close to nature. In the human realm, these deep fears, fed by breeder obsessions, manifest themselves in the thoroughly rotten ideology of human racial purity and supremacy.

This is why, despite all the efforts of science and civil rights campaigns, the racial hatred still lies, like a great aquifer, just beneath the surface of consciousness in our culture. On occasion, it wells upward and becomes a very conscious, very political cause.

Then it draws on the breeder's ideologies of bloodline and purity, as it did in Nazi Germany and the segregated South; as it still does today among neo-Nazis and white supremacists. The rhetoric of all these racists speaks of the breeder's obsessions, and the extremity of their actions speaks of the depth of their fear and hatred of "lower" nature: The Nazis ranted against Jews, gypsies, Poles, and other "mongrel races" and then methodically tried to exterminate them. Southern segregationists preached against "race mixing" and used lynchings, mob violence, and terrorist campaigns to keep people of color "in their place."

Unfortunately, these ideologies are alive and well today and are being zealously spread by various white supremacist and right-wing groups. The March 1992 issue of *The Truth at Last,* a Georgia-based tabloid newspaper ("mailed in a plain, brown, sealed envelope") features a center-spread article, "Senator Bilbo's Monumental Book: 'Take Your Choice— Separation or Mongrelization.' " The feature consists of excerpts from a 1948 book by Senator Theodore G. Bilbo, former governor of Mississippi and three-term U.S. senator. The text is one continuous diatribe against "race-mixing" and "mongrelization" of the "White Race." After a line about the "creative genius of the White Race," for example, the senator went on: "Any effort to destroy the blood of this creative race through contamination with the blood of Africa is an effort to destroy our nation and its future." Race-mixing, he wrote, has "always resulted in mongrelization which destroyed the White race and left a weakened and listless brown mongrel population."

Like racists then and now, Senator Bilbo drew heavily on bogus "science" and the lessons of animal husbandry. He cited this passage from the writings of a "famed anthropologist," Lothrop Stoddard: "Two things are necessary for the continued existence of a race; it must remain itself, and must breed its best. Hence, when a highly specialized stock interbreeds with a different stock, the new less stable, specialized characters are bred out, the variation, no matter how great its potential value to human evolution, being irretrievably lost, and of course, the more primitive a type is, the more potent their genes. This is why crossings with the Negro are uniformly fatal. Whites, Indians or Asiatics—all are vanquished by the potency of the more primitive, generalized and lower Negro genetic make up."

The Potency of Evil Nature

We can see here all too well the writer's fear of the "potency of the primitive," and the fear that "lower nature" can rise up and "vanquish" the "highly specialized"—in other words, the civilized, refined white race. Just about any blatantly frank, hard-core racist rhetoric speaks in such terms, but with a passion that can be driven only by the very deep agrarian fears and hatreds of animals/nature that I wrap together under the term *misothery*.

This may seem farfetched to many, but then who among them ever bothers to think about the sources and connections of racism? I submit that it will seem farfetched only because "white" Europeans habitually avoid probing too deeply into the racism they carry—whether they are conscious racists or not. Of course, they don't actually *think* they fear and hate some physically different Other because he or she is close to nature. But they come very close in their racist jokes and jibes about people of color being "animals" from "the jungle." Beyond question, most people's conscious, racially prejudiced thoughts revolve around the idea that some Others are subhuman, like animals. In full-blown racist ideology, of course, this idea is usually very explicit.

Although most ideologies are passionately held, the racist's is in a class by itself—as Nazis and Southern lynch mobs have so terribly demonstrated. I suggest that the racist is driven by (aside from problems with self-esteem) unusually intense feelings because of the depth of fears of dangerous animality and evil, base nature.

These have probably driven racism for a very long time and will continue to drive it until our culture comes to better views of animals and nature. The age of the fear is expressed in an old legend, which explained how "wildness"—meaning decay, corruption, immorality, and so on—returned to the world after the purifying flood of Noah's time in the form of Ham, who passed on wildness and the "Negro race."

The depths of the fear were probed by African-American author Toni Morrison in her novel *Beloved*: "Whitepeople believed that whatever the manners, under every dark skin was a jungle. Swift unnavigable waters, swinging screaming baboons, sleeping snakes, red gums ready for their sweet white blood. . . . But it wasn't the jungle blacks brought with them to this place from the other (livable) place. It was the jungle whitefolks planted in them. And it grew. It spread. In, through and after life, it spread, until it invaded the whites who had made it. . . . Made them bloody, silly, worse than even they wanted to be, so scared were they of the jungle they had made. The screaming baboon lived under their own white skin; the red gums were their own."

Hatred of the Other

Alienated from nature and loaded with the misothery in our agri-culture, we strive to stay above and distinct from animals and nature. We despise and deny the animal and nature wherever we see it—in our bodies, our selves, our fellow human beings. So we have great anxieties about our animality, which cause us to project our worst fears and hatreds onto animals and Other people. Throughout history, we have used animals to symbolize the lust, danger, and deceitfulness we saw in ourselves, but especially that which we saw in women, Jews, Africans, and various Others seen as down the ladder of being.

Beryl Rowland's *Animals with Human Faces* catalogs the animals of the medieval bestiaries and what they symbolized. Remember that these books were used in an age when few people could read and write, so animals were convenient and powerful messengers. Most of the animals, Rowland notes, symbolized some human sexual or sensual trait, usually lust, lechery, or promiscuity. A few animals, especially bulls, goats, camels, boars, and apes, were much more loaded with human sexual projections than others. The hare portrayed female sexuality, usually as libidinous, wanton, or willing—"nearly always perjoratively," Rowland says. She explains that human-to-animal transformations, as in werewolf and vampire legends, were a common device for expressing sexual anxieties. A transformation symbolized either the yielding to or the resisting of bestial sexual urges, depending on the type of animal in the legend and whether the human turned into an animal or the reverse. Beyond their use to carry ideas about sex, Rowland says that animals are used throughout the bestiaries to symbolize Jews and the various anti-Semitic beliefs about Jewish sensuality, greed, pride, and deceitfulness.

Animals dominate many of the scenes of feminine evil that were common in late nineteenth- and turn-of-the-century popular art, as we can see in Bram Dijkstra's book *Idols of Perversity*. Here we can see how Paul Klee depicted women as bestial in the painting *Woman and Beast*. The same theme shows up in the paintings of many lesser-known artists. One, *The Muting of Animalism,* shows a warrior/man in armor holding down a tiger who has the head of a woman. Another shows the evil woman Eve holding a huge, menacing snake. Another shows a woman turning men into evil beasts of desire. One in particular shows the tight relationships among beast-hatred, racism, and misogyny: *The Temptation of St. Anthony* by J. C. Dollman shows dark, hulking figures, vaguely Semitic or African, who join female forms in symbolizing beasts of desire nipping at the saint's soul.

Dijkstra's illustrations and commentary turn to the vampire theme, popularized in Bram Stoker's *Dracula*. Fascination with this story, he says, grew out of the misogyny and anti-Semitism that were rampant in Europe in the nineteenth century. With his heavy accent and his exotic looks and dress, Dracula personified the dark, sinister stranger to European society. He was from faraway Transylvania, a wild place between civilized Europe and the Jewish homelands to the east. He seduced women, turned them into his servants, and sent them out into the night to prey on men. Beyond subtle anti-Semitism, the message, says Dijkstra, was a warning to modern men "not to yield to the bloodlust of the feminist, the New Woman," for "she is the personification of bestiality, forever crawling."

Anti-Semitism

Sadly, the misothery of the early Hebrews came back to haunt and oppress their descendants in Christian times. To Europeans, the Jews were a different people—physically, culturally, and geographically. Early in the Christian era, they fell victim to an apartheid imposed by the Catholic church. Raul Hilberg traces the evolution of this anti-Semitism in his book *The Destruction of the European Jews*. In his view, it began as a missionary effort to "convert [an] obstinate jewry" to Christianity. Beginning with the Synod of Elvira in A.D. 306, the Roman church prohibited sexual intercourse, intermarriage, and sharing meals between Christians and Jews. In 535, the Synod of Clermont forbade Jews to hold public office. In 538, the Synod of Orleans ordered Jews off the streets during Passion Week and forbade them to employ Christian servants. Century after century, Christian Europe passed laws and spread ideas to keep Jews down and out of their society. It was the Papal See itself that set up the first ghetto, which it maintained in Rome until the city's occupation by the Italian army in 1870.

While Hilberg argues that these devices were employed to pressure Jews into adopting Christianity, it is evident that many of them smack of racial prejudice—the hatred of the Other that lies embedded in Western agri-culture. Hilberg, however, notes more of the racist element in the anti-Semitism of later centuries. Much of it showed up in Martin Luther's tract *About the Jews and Their Lies,* which reads like a primer for the Nazi ideology of the 1930s. For Luther, Jews were "thirsty bloodhounds and murderers of all Christendom." Jews, Luther noted, "were often burned to death upon the accusation that they had poisoned water and wells, stolen children, and torn and hacked them apart, in order to cool their temper secretly with Christian blood."

According to Hilberg, Luther's ideas were common in Europe at the time, and they were a harbinger of things to come. Luther described

Europe's Jews as "a plague, pestilence, pure misfortune." Later, in 1895, an anti-Semitic faction of the Reichstag proposed to stop Jewish immigration because of the "racial qualities" of Jews. "Gentlemen," a speaker said, "the Jews are indeed beasts of prey." They "operate like parasites," they are "cholera germs." These characterizations surfaced again a few decades later when Nazi leaders described Jews as "cancer," "vermin," "lice," and other epithets that drew from the acquifer of deeply felt ideas about evil, insidious nature.

The Legend of the Wild Man

Many of the misotherous ideas of the West's agri-culture were solidified in the legends of Wildness and the Wild Man that ran throughout European literature in the Middle Ages. These imaginary Wild Men were not exactly animals, but they were closer to the animal state than Europeans. The Wild Man is still alive today in the form of beliefs in the existence of "Big Foot" or "Sasquatch," a beast-man who lives in the rain forests of the Pacific Northwest, and the "Abominable Snowman," who is said to live in the Himalayan mountains.

In the Middle Ages, the legend was used over and over again to reinforce the idea that without God and agrarian civilization's discipline and order, humans would decay and lapse morally. This emphasized the need for constant Good Shepherding, without which we would slice downward into impulsive, animal existence.

While the Wild Man's antics kept these ideas lively in the earlier literature, they lived on to provide many good stories about bad beast-men in recent literature as well. In them, the idea is very explicit that nature's restless beast can easily take over if people leave the controlling forces of civilization or if they fail to repress all traces of the animal within. Probably its most blatant expression is in Robert Louis Stevenson's story of *The Strange Case of Dr. Jekyll and Mr. Hyde*. Variants of the theme show up again and again in Jack London's stories. It provided the basis for William Golding's *Lord of the Flies* and, as we noted, Joseph Conrad's *Heart of Darkness*.

The roots of the idea of Wild Men go back, according to Cambridge historian Anthony Pagden, to ancient Greece—for some, the early Western world's highest civilization. In *The Fall of Natural Man,* Pagden explains how the Greeks of the seventh and sixth centuries B.C. coined the word *barbaros,* or barbarian, to describe foreigners. At first, the term implied no disrespect, but by the fourth century B.C. it implied cultural backwardness or other types of inferiority. For the Hellenistic Greeks, it meant a babbler—someone who did not speak Greek. This soon came to mean a person who lived outside Greek thought and civilization and then, rapidly, a person devoid of reason and humanity. Thus Aristotle described the Achaeans, the Henoichi, the Thracians, and other neighbors beyond the fringes of Greece as barbarians and "hardly different from an animal."

In Roman times, some animals were mistaken for Wild Men by naive conquerors who could be counted on to bring back fabulous reports. Pliny wrote of a race of wild, hairy, shrieking *silvestres,* who were probably eastern gibbons. According to historian Richard Bernheimer in *Wild Men in the Middle Ages,* the Romans knew too little about the great anthropoid apes to identify them as animals, "so that they were usually described as hairy, speechless humans and thus, by implication, as wild men." Roman writers and geographers described what were probably gorillas in one equatorial region, calling them "hairy women," and chimpanzees in another, calling them tribes of "Ethiopian seed-eaters." If this seems quaint or odd to us today, we must remember that these observers had no knowledge of zoology or anthropology. These were first encounters for them, and they described strange, new creatures largely in terms of their confused ideas about the differences among living beings.

Barbarian Beasts Abroad

By the Christian era such ideas about exotic beasts and "barbarians" became even more confused. We might even say they became *fused.* Then, says Pagden, "in most respects the barbarian was another animal altogether." He was one of the *Sylvestres homines,* men of the forest, or Wild Men, who lived far from civilization and rational men. Under this worldview, the cities in which Europeans lived were outposts of order and reason amid a world that was hostile and threatening. According to Pagden, "Wild men were creatures who lurked in woodlands and mountain passes ready to seize upon the unwary traveller." They were, like the older mythological fauns and satyrs, a kind of half-human/half-beast creature.

Richard Bernheimer has taken a more complete study of this creature in *Wild Men in the Middle Ages.* In graphic arts, the Wild Man was usually depicted as a hairy man with both human and animal features; however, he was more man than ape. According to Bernheimer, this figure was much more important in the thinking of the Middle Ages than we realize today. "His presence is like the running commentary with which a man's half-conscious imagery accompanies his conscious ideals and aspirations: a reminder that there are basic and primitive impulses clamoring for satisfaction." The Wild Man gave the Middle Age mind a way to express vague, complex ideas about repressed desire, animal instincts, and the pull of nature.

The picture drawn was very largely a negative one. Beyond his hairy, bestial appearance, the Wild Man had a number of what we in the age of psychology would call behavioral traits: He lived in nature, usually alone in the forest. He had "bestial strength" and was fiercely aggressive. He had none of the powers of reason or speech, and he had no religion, for he probably had no soul.

He did have some qualities, Bernheimer notes. The most striking of these was the Wild Man's kinship with animals, which he used, in his better moments, to help poor peasants find lost sheep. But this same trait was often depicted as a mastery over animals, due as much to his strength and fierceness as to his natural affinities with them.

Does this sound like Enkidu, our hero of the Gilgamesh epic of ancient Sumeria? It does, although the European of the Middle Ages had never heard of him. The connection is psychological; it is in the way of thinking of agri-cultural people: This beast-man is a figment of our imagination, a figuration of our deep worries and ambivalence about kinship versus alienation, about being *in* the world versus mastering it, about being *of* nature versus being *over* nature, and about the rest of the can of worms of human-animal-nature relationships.

Of course there was a Wild Woman, too. She seems to have been more representative of the natural environment, says Bernheimer, because she varied from place to place. In the grand, wide open spaces of the Alps, she was a giant. In tamer, forested regions she was a hairy old woman who lived in the underbrush. As we might expect, her most persistent trait was her lustiness. She craved ordinary men and would go out of her way to get them. Next in order—again, predictably—was the Wild Woman's deceitfulness, for she could change her appearance to entrap innocent men. In other words, as Bernheimer says, "The wild woman [was] thus a libidinous hag" and he suggests that she may as well be called a witch. Indeed, he says, in the demonological tracts of the Middle Ages, Wild Women were frequently equated with witches. The linkage is bolstered by the Wild Woman's reputation for knowledge of herbs and the healing arts.

Wicked Witches Within

Volumes have been written, of course, on the mass hysteria of Europe's campaigns to exterminate witches. In his *Encyclopedia of Witchcraft and*

Demonology, author Rossell Hope Robbins called the era a "shocking nightmare, the foulest crime and deepest shame of Western civilization, the blackest of everything that *Homo sapiens,* the reasoning man, has ever upheld."

There are a number of explanations for the witch-craze, but they all point to some kind of a crackdown—that is, a violent assertion of social control. The witch-hunts were a crackdown on independent women, their crafts, trade, and culture; on a resurgence, real or imagined, of female power; on vestiges of paganism in peasant culture; on vestiges of female principles in peasant culture; on the power of folk/herbal remedies as competitors with the Church, faith, and prayer; on medievalism's laxity and tolerance in people's views toward animals and nature. No doubt it was a wide-ranging crackdown on all these things, all of which the witch symbolized. Since records reveal that 85 percent of the victims were women and since the witch is usually portrayed as a woman, it seems rather obvious that it was, fundamentally, a crackdown on women in particular and female principles in general.

Although the threats were vague and wide-ranging, they were still seen as very active, Robbins says. The witch threat was "a powerful subversive force working day and night to destroy true religion and to prevent the establishment of God's kingdom." It was an international movement so insidious, so evil that it called for the suspension of justice and the infliction of cruel tortures. The most common torture, for example, was the *strappado,* which the authorities used to extract "confessions" and names of accomplices. The torturer tied a prisoner's arms behind her back with a rope attached to a pulley, then hoisted her from the floor. She hung there until the interrogators got the answers they wanted. If the victim refused to talk (probably because of sincere faith, ironically), the torturer could turn up the pressure with *squassation,* a variant torture in which she was hauled up, dropped, and then jerked to a stop within inches of the floor. Once a proper "confession" was obtained, the severely injured victim was put out of her misery with a public burning at the stake.

Gynocide in the Age of Reason, the Enlightenment

Aside from the extreme cruelty of the tortures, the wide range of the hysteria throughout Europe, the maniacal zeal with which the authorities departed from conventions of law and order, and the huge toll in victims (from a low of 200,000 to a high of several million burned at the stake over 300 years), what is most shocking about the witch-hunts is the age in which they occurred.

The fires of extermination raged from 1450 to 1750—from the early Renaissance into the Age of Reason and the Enlightenment. They burned during the Reformation, and during the Age of Discovery and colonial expansion. Mind you, witch mania occurred not in the Dark Ages nor in the Middle Ages, but during the great flowering of European art, thought, and progress. It was the very ugly underside of a period often touted as the high point of European cultural glory.

Almost unbelievably, the infamous *Malleus Maleficarum,* the "hammer of witches," was first printed in 1486—only six years before Christopher Columbus reached the Americas. This handbook for witch-hunters was reprinted and republished in thirteen more editions by 1520, when Michelangelo Buonarroti had not yet begun to paint the Sistine Chapel ceiling. Another sixteen editions went out by 1669—when William Shakespeare had been in the grave for decades and when Isaac Newton was sitting down to write his laws of physics.

What does it say of the Western state of mind that Europe's first holocaust—an official terror and extermination campaign—could go along so swimmingly even as Europeans were putting forth huge claims and displays of high civilization? Francis Bacon, René Descartes, and the other fathers of Reason were alive and kicking (and thinking and writing) in that age. If they had been truly the greatest minds of their time, we should know them today for their efforts against the witch-hunts instead of as inventors of the philosophical lobotomy known as modern thought. Indeed, Bacon, as Lord Chancellor of England, presided over Britain's witch-hunting courts for three years before a bribery scandal forced him from office.

Europe's Cultural Cargo

Witches, Wild Men, barbarians, savages, and various Others: to the Europen mind of the fifteenth century, the world outside was full of strange, inferior beings—many of them evil and dangerous. Even more terrifying was the idea that they were very close to human and thus we might have some of these bad traits—sex, deceitfulness, bloodthirstiness, and so on—in common. These were but a part of the very old, very odd mythological bestiary that, as many a writer has noted, Europeans carried as they voyaged about the world. It was a zoo of imagined beasts, and the most terrible of the lot were the beasts within.

So were Europeans equipped to sail out to new continents and meet new people. Naturally, the weight of this cultural and emotional baggage put a great strain on the encounters.

They also carried with them volumes of Greek and Roman ideas on hierarchy, natural slavery, and Western man's supremacy. The Church's old friend, Aristotle, had taught them that there was nothing morally wrong with enslaving people who did not "possess reason," practice virtue, or participate in political affairs. "Slaves and animals," he wrote, "do little for the common good, and for the most part live at random." And since every being existed for the purpose of those above it, the purpose of the natural slave was clearly, then, to be a slave. This is pure Aristotle, who also reasoned that slaves were incapable of deliberate choice or moral action. According to Anthony Pagden, Aristotle saw the slave's "position in the hierarchy of nature . . . at the bestial end of the human scale. . . . [The slave's] role in the household would seem to be similar to that of the domestic animals. He is condemned to a life of perpetual servitude, his obligations are indistinguishable from those of the beast of service and his acquisition may be likened to hunting."

When they set out in ships around 1500, then, Europe's explorers, traders, and colonists had quite a cultural cargo: misotherous ideas about themselves and the Other; obsessions with breed purity and manipulation; fears of species decay and pollution; beliefs in races of wild beast-people; and obsessions with order and control lest potent, evil, chaotic nature overtake human civilization. In addition, they had tons of experience with slavery and large-scale wars of conquest. And they were all fired up by the flames of their holy war against the nature-friendly ideas symbolized by witches. On top of it all, they had tons of certainty about their supremacy and their God-given rights to the world. For the peoples of Africa, the Americas, and the Pacific, it made for a bad time to be "discovered." All these things considered, it was inevitable that they would be judged savages at best, beasts at worst, and treated accordingly.

Early Encounters

In Columbus's accounts of his very first voyage he did not rave on about the bestiality of the native peoples of the Caribbean islands. The bulk of his statements of first impressions are good and kind. He does, however, mention rumors of cannibalism. There are no reports of violent incidents, but the Spanish rather casually took prisoners—much as one picks up souvenirs—back to show to their king and queen. Could Columbus have tempered his account of the trip as part of his machinations for future voyages?

A year later, on the second voyage, the encounter was marked by violence and conflict. The Spanish made contact with cannibals and some crew members were lost in a skirmish. Columbus formed some bad impressions of the island Amerinds, and he wrote that they were of a "bestiality greater than any beast on earth." In this and in the accounts of his next voyages, the most frequently appearing word is "gold." The Spanish were clearly impressed by the amount of gold ornaments worn by native people and by their nonchalance about it. Again, natives were taken back to Spain ostensibly for their religious conversion and education. Columbus was becoming more open about his views of the people of the New World; he wrote that "they will be better than any other kind of slaves." During the 1495 voyage, he sent 550 Amerind slaves back to Spain, 200 of whom died on the trip. Most of those who reached Spain died shortly of European diseases.

Within a couple of decades, Spain was sending shiploads of explorers back and forth to the Americas. These early voyages and the prospects for continued exploitation raised a great debate back home over the humanity of the native Americans. Most were convinced that they were subhuman beasts, others were not so sure and felt that they should be treated fairly just in case. Out of this early debate arose the famous *Requerimiento,* a document drafted in 1514. It was an injunction, or message, to be read by explorers to all Amerind peoples they encountered. It was a European attempt at fairness, but its very conception is wholly arrogant. It began with a brief history of humanity up to the appearance of Christianity. It declared Jesus Christ "master of the human lineage" and explained that he had turned over authority to St. Peter and the popes who followed him. The text then explained that the present pope had granted Spain authority over the American continent.

The *Requerimiento,* then, was to inform Amerinds of the legal situation and to give them a choice in the matter. They could accept Spain and the Church as their masters or they could be punished. In the manner of Don Corleone, the godfather of movie fame, Spain made the Amerinds an offer they could not refuse.

To the European mind, refusal was a rejection of God, which was evil; therefore the natives were subhuman and deserved to be enslaved or killed. Said the *Requerimiento:* "But if you do not do this, and wickedly and intentionally delay to do so, I certify to you that, with the help of God, we shall forcibly enter into your country and shall make war against you in all ways and manners that we can, and shall subject you to the yoke and obedience of the Church and of their Highnesses; we shall take you and your wives and your children, and shall make slaves of them as their Highnesses may command; and we shall take away your goods, and we shall do all the harm and damage that we can as to vassals who do not obey and refuse to receive their lord, and resist and contradict him."

According to Fernandez de Oviedo y Valdez, a Spanish historian of the time, many of the conquistadors who read this warning did not even bother to use the language understood by the native peoples, nor did they seek interpreters. Many people, wrote Oviedo, "had no opportunity to reply, being immediately carried away prisoners, the Spaniards not failing to use the stick on those who did not go fast enough."

Humans or Animals?

The debate over Amerind humanity boiled down to one between adventurers and conquistadors, who wanted an official license to take wealth, and Spanish professors and priests, who wanted to make sure they followed established rules. The former would have treated Amerind people much as animals, the latter would have treated them as inferior humans. Not even the humanists thought the natives were on a par with Europeans. One wrote that "although these barbarians are not altogether mad, yet they are not far from being so." They were not capable of governing themselves, he said, "any more than madmen or even wild beasts and animals, seeing that their food is not any more agreeable and scarcely better than that of wild beasts."

Another humanist, the Dominican Tomas Ortiz, wrote to the Council of the Indies and offered a litany of evidence of Amerind inferiority: "They are more given to sodomy than any other nation. . . . They go naked . . . have no respect for love or for virginity . . . are stupid and silly . . . have no respect for truth . . . unstable . . . brutal . . . no obedience among them . . . are incapable of learning." He noted also that they had none of the human arts or industries, they ate worms and insects, and showed no interest in the Spanish religion. "The older they get the worse they become. About the age of ten or twelve years, they seem to have some civilization, but later they become like real brute beasts. I may therefore affirm that God has never created a race more full of vice and composed without the least mixture of kindness or culture. . . . The Indians are more stupid than asses, and refuse to improve in anything."

Those who were intent on enslaving natives and taking their lands and gold went even further. For them, Amerinds were bestial, evil sinners— quite possibly agents of the devil. This, of course, made it all the more necessary and righteous to conquer them.

In their documents, the true spirit of the Age of Discovery (and of Reason) stands out against the pious rhetoric of the priests and professors. In one, a proposal to invade Florida, to enslave or kill its indigenous people, and then to occupy it with 1,500 colonists, Dr. Pedro de Santander flattered the king and queen of Spain with this florid passage (full of our old friend, the Good Shepherd model): "It is lawful that your Majesty, like a good shepherd, appointed by the hand of the Eternal Father, should tend and lead out your sheep, since the Holy Spirit has shown spreading pastures whereon are feeding lost sheep which have been snatched away by the dragon, the Demon. These pastures are the New World, wherein is comprised Florida, now in possession of the Demon, and here he makes himself adored and revered. This is the Land of Promise, possessed by idolators, the Amorite, Amalekite, Moabite, Canaanite. This is the land promised by the Eternal Father to the faithful, since we are condemned by God in the Holy Scriptures to take it from them, being idolators, and, by reason of their idolatry and sin, to put them all to the knife, leaving no living thing save maidens and children, their cities robbed and sacked, their walls and houses levelled to the earth." The letter is dated July 15, 1557, and it goes on in detail with proposals to build several cities, including one at Tampa Bay, where Dr. de Santander believed many slaves could be taken.

Treated as Animals

Spain's pro-slavery faction could see no need for restraints on their ruthlessness. For them, the situation was quite simple: The natives were clearly inhuman and the Spanish, being close to God, had clear rights to master them. Such thinking was to give Amerinds "the status of an object," noted Tzvetan Todorov in *The Conquest of the Americas*: "their flesh is used to feed the surviving Indians or even the dogs; they are killed in order to be boiled down for grease, supposed to cure the wounds of the Spaniards." In the course of such treatment, he notes, the natives "are identified with animals for the slaughterhouse; all their extremities are cut off, nose, hands, breasts, tongue, sexual organs, thereby transforming them into shapeless trunks, as one might trim a tree." Some suggested that their blood could be used to irrigate the fields. The humanist Bartolome de Las Casas reported that the price of a female Amerind slave rose according to whether or not she was pregnant, as with cattle, and he told of a "godforsaken man" who "worked as hard as he could to get Indian women with child," for they would bring more "when he sold them as slaves."

The debate raged into the 1570s, when the Council of the Indies ruled largely in favor of Las Casas and the other priests and professors. The Council issued ordinances banishing slavery and violence, except in cases of *extreme necessity*. They attempted to redefine Spains' activities in the Americas, pushing colonialism and missionary work over outright slavery and conquest.

Perhaps they did temper excesses and set a nicer tone for exploitation, but the ordinances were also a whitewash and masterpiece of Renaissance public relations art. The gist of them was to clothe Spain's exploits in the Americas in the garb of Christian missionary work. The text declared that "discoveries are not to be called conquests" and that explorers should gather information about the tribes and make alliances "with the lords and nobles who seem most likely to be of assistance in the pacification of the land." Priests and missionaries are ordered to wear robes and carry "the Cross in their hands" at all times. "The preachers should ask for [Amerind] children under the pretext of teaching them and keep them as hostages; they should also persuade them to build churches where they can teach so that they may be safer. By these and other means are the Indians to be pacified and indoctrinated, but in no way are they to be harmed, for all we seek is their welfare and their conversion."

With the Council of the Indies and its ordinances, Spain chose Christian paternalism to lead militarism in the march to dominate and annex the New World. It was a strategy for the long haul. After eighty years of forays for gold, silver, and slaves, France, England, Portugal, and other nations were getting in on the act and the situation was becoming more complex; it called for Spanish presence in the new lands, which would be best aided and defended by a docile, supportive native population.

French and English Treatment

The other colony-building nations started with the same basic European view that the Amerinds were somewhere between savages and beasts. All shared the belief in races of Wild Men and Women, all shared the Hebrew/Greek worldview, all had plenty of their own bestiaries within. Each nation had its own variations on these basic themes. Seventeenth-century French writer Pierre d'Avity described five degrees of "brutishness," based on diet, eating habits, nudity, housing, and absence of government. After many early descriptions of the Amerinds as wild, hairy, naked beast-people, France knew them only as a stereotype. Early English explorers described them as "beasts," subhumans "who eat any kind of flesh," and as "bestial, cannibalistic, and sexually abandoned," according to Gary Nash, in *Race, Class and Politics.*

All of Europe saw plenty of evidence that Amerinds were far down the ladder of being. Europeans, after all, were dedicated masters of nature, but the Amerinds were not. This was a strike against them for George Louis Leclerc Buffon, the eighteenth-century French naturalist, who argued that they were brutes and passive beings, "mired in animality" because they did not subdue animals and nature.

These early stereotypes merged into others as the Europeans established their various commercial and national interests. In the Caribbean and South America, the Spanish and Portuguese quickly built their sugar plantations and began bringing over African slaves. They were in the Americas to get rich and go back to Europe so they did not bring wives and families. These Iberian men looked down on relations with "inferior" African and native women, but they winked and carried them on anyway. Eventually, their situation made them even more pragmatic about race, and the intermarriages established a large population of people with European, African, and Amerindian ancestry. There, racial prejudice came to make little sense.

The French, by most accounts, had the best relationship with native American peoples because their commerce in furs depended heavily on good dealings with Indian trappers. Their treatment may have been helped, too, by the French idea of the "noble savage," a romanticization of the Amerind as an innocent, childlike "natural man." Michel de Montaigne was the leading advocate of this view by the 1570s when Spain was still arguing beast versus savage and slavery versus colonization.

Early on at least, the English also saw Amerinds as trading partners who were dumb and backward but friendly. Relations deteriorated after 1620 when the English began building their colonies in North America, and the earlier savage-beast image was resurrected. The English interest was not so much in short-term trade profiteering as it was in religious refuge and establishing a beachhead of successful colonies. English settlers, then, had little incentive to get along with the natives, whom they saw as beastly residents of a "dreary waste," a "howling wilderness." They de-

234 An Unnatural Order

scribed Amerinds as "beavers upon our streams," as "mad dogs," "wolves," and "tigers." One commentator called them "game" for the colonists. The Anglo-Americans, then, treated native peoples pretty much the way they treated other "lower" living beings: They shut them out and kept their distance. The relationship was one of alienation and polarization.

Francis Parkman wrote that Spain crushed, England scorned, and France embraced America's native peoples. We may see these differences another way: Spain came for their gold and their souls, England came for their land, and France came for their animals. Europeans felt that all of this was entirely fair; it was "trade," and for their end of the deal the Amerinds got plenty—in Christianity, God's Forgiveness, and Eternal Salvation.

A Terrible Toll

Despite the Council of the Indies and its look-alikes, despite all the ordinances, papal edicts, and royal decrees, actual dealings with Amerind peoples usually fell far short of any civilized ideals. The rules and regulations were made back in Europe, in courts and cathedrals where such matters counted; but the physical encounters between European and Amerind took place in the Americas, in the wilderness—in the dark, so to speak. The rules were made by official window-dressers who stayed back in the comfortable seats of civilization. But the explorations were carried out by weary soldiers, and the colony-building by hungry merchants and adventurers—society's least idealistic and empathetic people. What few ideals and strands of empathy they had to begin with were surely dissipated after months at sea and years of isolation, deprivation, loneliness, and terror in the American wilderness. Consequently, their self-interested actions took a terrible toll on America's native people.

The Spanish took a material toll. According to historian Olive Patricia Dickason in *The Myth of the Savage*, they took, between 1500 and 1650, 181 tons of gold and 16,000 tons of silver from the Americas. The Amerinds' cups, bowls, jewelry, religious articles, and other objects of art were collected, melted down into ingots, and shipped to Spain. In Canada, the material toll was in furs, and according to historian Calvin Martin in *Keepers of the Game*, the fur trade played a role in undermining northern hunting people's totemic worldview. Animals rapidly ceased to be sacred when they could be so readily traded for blankets, firearms, liquor, ironware, and other material goods.

The Europeans also took a heavy cultural toll on America's indigenous people. In Mesoamerica, where a succession of native agrarian civilizations had built cities with palaces and libraries, Spain's soldiers looted temples and its priests smashed "pagan" art. In the process, "hundreds of hieroglyphic books were tossed into bonfires by ardent missionaries," wrote Boston University professor of anthropology and religion Dennis Tedlock in the introduction to his translation of *Popol Vuh,* the Mayan "bible." Only four of these books survive today, and three of them are in Europe—in museums in Paris, Madrid, and Dresden. The fourth survives in Mexico only because it was recovered there recently.

We cannot measure the rest of the cultural damage, for it is in formless things such as destroyed chiefdoms, leveled cultural centers, crushed spiritual traditions, and broken lifeways. Together, these put out the lights of Amerind cultural evolution. It was a culture ended by violent death, said historian Oswald Spengler, one "murdered in the full glory of its unfolding, destroyed like a sunflower whose head is struck off by one passing." The Amerindian march of human progress, one that had spread over two continents, was largely stopped and what little of it that remained was co-opted and corruped by European presence. Europeans, of course, *had* to put their heavy-handed stamp on the Americas, for they needed to obliterate the "pagan" culture there as well as that of "witches" back home.

"Microbe Shock"

The rest of the toll amounted to genocide, carried out with three levels of intent, according to Todorov. There was direct murder, which was carried out in warfare, torture, and massacres—much of it conducted to "clear" a region of its native population. There was bad treatment, which claimed the lives of natives who were imprisoned, housed on reservations, or otherwise kept in dependency by Europeans. They suffered starvation, exposure, disease, and the sort of treatment usually offered slaves: hateful neglect.

Finally, the greatest toll on native lives was that taken by what Todorov calls "microbe shock"—that is, huge epidemics caused by European diseases to which Amerinds had never been exposed. When an infection occurred, natives died in massive numbers. And the epidemics spread through native trade networks much more rapidly than did the explorers themselves. According to Alfred Crosby, smallpox "played as essential a role in the advance of white imperialism overseas as gunpowder—perhaps a more important role. . . ." The disease, he says, spread early from the Caribbean and was devastating the Aztecs even as Hernán Cortés captured their capital in 1521. Smallpox raced ahead of the conquistadors into Peru, where it killed off a great number of people including the Inca (ruler) himself and the successor he had chosen. This set off civil war and chaos, into which Francisco Pizarro entered and turned to his and Spain's advantage. Wherever it hit, smallpox favored Europeans who were largely immune. When it hit the Amerinds of the Massachusetts Bay Colony in the 1630s, Governor John Winthrop reverently wrote that "the natives, they are all near dead of small Poxe, so as the Lord hath cleared our title to what we possess."

The authorities disagree on the number of native people in the Americas on the eve of European contact, but they tend to agree that it fell by at least 90 percent in the two centuries after contact. In *Interpreting Colonial America,* historian James Martin estimates that there were about 50 million people in North, Central, and South America before Columbus; by the end of the 1600s, he says, Amerinds numbered about 5 million. Todorov estimates about 80 million Amerind people before Columbus; by 1550, he says, there were only 10 million. In Mexico, he puts the native population at 25 million on the eve of European contact, and at one million in 1600. Whatever the population was before contact, Jerald Milanich and Susan Milbrath, authors of *First Encounters,* say it fell by 90 to 99 percent in the 200 years after Columbus.

In our ignorance, we wonder why early European colonists bothered to haul over Africans for slaves when they had Amerind people right here. For one thing, they *did* rapidly enslave Amerinds for plantation work in the Caribbean and South America. European slave raiders first picked the islands clean of the Amerinds who survived the epidemics. Then they turned to Mexico and the southeastern United States, where sedentary corn-planter tribes were easily plundered. Following the pattern set by their cultural ancestors in the ancient Middle East, the slave raiders massacred Amerind leaders and took captives to sell to the plantations. For another thing, slavery and disease just as rapidly wiped out the Amerinds, which is why the plantation complex turned to Africa's people and began the infamous Atlantic slave trade.

Disease, Sugar, and Slaves

Throughout the sixteenth century, hundreds of adventurous, footloose Spaniards flocked to the Caribbean in search of fortunes. Many of them operated from Hispaniola, where they organized "war bands" to search the far islands and the mainland for gold and Amerind captives to be sold for slaves. By the end of the sixteenth century, wrote historian Philip Curtin in *The Rise and Fall of the Planatation Complex,* "virtually all of the Indians of the tropical lowlands were dead except the Caribs," who had successfully fought off the Spanish long enough to begin to develop immunities to the disease epidemics. The Caribbean was essentially "cleared" for colonization, and the English, Dutch, French, and others moved in for island footholds and trade bases.

Meanwhile, the Portuguese, who had built a sugar industry in Madeira with African slave labor, moved operations to Brazil, where they used Amerind slaves. As Amerinds died out from the epidemics, the Portuguese brought over more and more Africans. By 1600, Brazil's sugar industry was the world leader, producing an average of 130 tons a year for a mostly European market. In Europe, demand for sugar skyrocketed as the price fell, which put the coveted product within the reach of nearly all Europeans. The jump in demand for cheap sugar drove the spectacular growth of the New World's first huge industry, which pushed up demand for cheap slave labor to work the fields and mills.

The Dutch, who specialized in shipping and trade, saw a chance to increase their own business in the burgeoning sugar trade. They had had experience in Brazil, where they learned the techniques of the sugar plantation and mill complex. In the late 1630s, Dutch traders taught these techniques to colonists on Barbados and nearby French and English islands. The sugar plantation complex, with its cheap labor base of African slaves, spread throughout the Caribbean. Entire islands were devoted to cane fields and sugar estates. On Barbados, for example, 40 percent of the island was planted in sugar by 1645; by 1767, cane fields occupied 80 percent of the island. This planting pressure, of course, created a great demand for slaves, who soon vastly outnumbered their owners and others. On the typical sugar islands, according to Curtin, 75 to 95 percent of the population were slaves, and many of the free people were of African ancestry.

From the islands, the plantation complex, the slave system, and the slave trade spread to the United States, where it grew to become the basis of the Southern economy after 1700. Half of all the U.S.'s African slaves were brought in by 1770. It is interesting to note, in contrast, that the median date of arrival for Irish, German, Italian, and other European groups was 1900. This makes African-Americans "more American" than the European ethnic "minorities" by over a century.

On the African side, the slave trade drew heavily on that continent's peoples and cultures. For roughly four centuries, the outside world preyed on them to meet its demands for slave labor. The slave trade's pressures led to kidnappings, political intrigues, civil wars, collapsed empires, and decimated populations in Western Africa. Capture and shipment there began before 1500, when the Portuguese began trading in slaves to work their sugar plantations on the islands along the coasts of West Africa. Although abominable on any scale, the African slave trade was meager until after 1650, when the sugar boom took off in Brazil and the Caribbean. The great bulk of the Atlantic slave trade occurred between 1650 and 1850. In the eighteenth century alone over 5.5 million Africans were sent to the slave traders, in whose custody they did not fare so well. Curtin estimates that, on the average, between 30 and 50 percent of captives died in the holding compounds or on the slave ships.

All of this for cheap sugar. It is a sad commentary on Western *civilization* that Europe, its bastion at the time, could inflict this much brutality on human beings just for an addictive sweetener. But, of course, Europe saw them as savages and beasts, which made it all right.

The Black Other

Some authors have argued that there was little racism toward Africans on first contact, that racism was a by-product of the plantation complex. Nevertheless, many believe that Europeans saw Africans as subhuman from the start and that this view merely intensified with slavery. This, as we have seen, was the normal progression of attitudes after first contact with Amerinds. Initial fascination and curiosity gradually turned into hostility and contempt as Europeans drew upon their deep-seated misothery to explain the Other's looks, habits, and differences and to justify their exploitation. There is proof enough that Europeans saw Africans to be far down the ladder of being, as they did Amerinds, in that they saw them as proper candidates for slavery. From the European's point of view, Africans fully met Aristotle's criteria for "natural slaves"—that is, they were non-Europeans and they appeared to live, as did Amerinds, close to nature.

Africans, however, had something else, too. They were "black." As historian Winthrop Jordan pointed out in his classic *White Over Black,* for Europeans that color was loaded with intense meaning. In England and northern Europe especially, black was an emotional color, a symbol of baseness and evil, a sign of danger and repulsion. White, on the other hand, connoted purity, virtue, and benevolence. Like other native peoples, Africans were seen as savage, wild humans close to animals, but their blackness caused them to be perceived with much more fear and anxiety than Amerinds and other non-European people.

This fearsome image was made even worse by European attitudes about the African continent. They called it the "dark" continent, for it was an especially mysterious and dangerous wilderness. Europeans and their cultural ancestors, the Romans and Greeks, knew Egypt and Africa above the Sahara, but the great desert cut off contact with the rest of the continent until about A.D. 1000 when camel caravans opened up trade into West Africa. Even then, Europeans and other northern peoples found tropical Africa an impossibly inhospitable place. European attempts to explore and settle were wiped out by malaria, yaws, river blindness, liver flukes, and other parasitic diseases. Until relatively recently, Africa's tropical disease environment was as effective as the Sahara in sealing off Africa from the great, ancient flow of trade and cultural exchange among Europe, the Near East, and the Far East. For Europe, Africa was off limits and a land full of huge dangers and mysteries; naturally, then, its human residents would be seen correspondingly.

The Black Beast

Europe's very old Western misothery furnished the perception of Africans as Others—inferior beings characterized by sexuality and wildness. For the white European, the African "Negro" was truly a bête noire—a black beast, and a fearsome one. With this perceived nature, African people would be dealt with severely by the white shepherds of the slave system. Many slave colonies and states prescribed castration as a punishment for runaway slaves and for slave assaults against white people. Castration and other forms of dismemberment, such as cutting off a slave's foot, were considered a "necessary" means of control. According to Winthrop Jordan in *The White Man's Burden: Historical Origins of Racism in the United States*: "Castration of blacks clearly indicated a need in white men to persuade themselves that they were masters and in all ways masterful, and it illustrated dramatically the ease with which white men slipped over into treating their negro slaves like their bulls and stallions whose [wild animal] spirit could be subdued by emasculation."

The slave system acted out all of the old agrarian obsessions about bloodlines, breed purity, and the need for civilized control over chaotic nature. Euro-Americans built bulwarks in the form of rules and laws to keep the African population "in its place" lest superior white society be polluted and corrupted by its dark, animal essence. Race mixing would darken white hopes and strivings for mastery over the continent. As Jordan notes, "a darkened nation would present irrefutable evidence that sheer animal sex was governing the American destiny and that the great experiment in the wilderness had failed to maintain the social and personal restraints which were the hallmarks and the very stuff of civilization. A blackened posterity would mean that the basest of energies had guided the direction of the American experiment and that civilized man had turned beast in the forest. Retention of whiteness would be evidence of purity and of diligent nurture of the original body of folk."

Bloodlines and breed purity had to be maintained, for Western civilization was riding on it. Clearly, the "white," civilized Euro-American population had to control the black, "bestial" one—but with even more force than it used to control its domestic animals because the threat was so much greater.

More Fear of the Beast

As noted before, much of the whites' need to control "the Negro" stemmed from their perception of Africans as animal-like and the rest of it stemmed from their anxieties about the sexual beasts within—both pure misothery. Unfortunately, many of the discussions of the dynamics of racism pay little attention to these sensitive but basic factors. Jordan, for one, sees them as major elements in the Euro-American's felt need to impose the controls of the slave system.

Obviously, any slave system needs strict controls on its involuntary labor force, but the Euro-over-African master-slave relationship had this extra element of sexual-racial fear. This is why the controlling relationship was extended to "free Negroes" and why it has lasted so long after the abolition of slavery.

Jordan explains this need to maintain control over "the Negro" further: "Above all, the white man had to sustain his feeling of control; in restraining the Negro, he was at the same time restraining and thereby reassuring himself." Jordan says that whites feared both race mixing and insurrection, and in advancing these as the principal reasons for "curbing the free Negro . . . white Americans were expressing—in the language in which such things are expressed—how greatly they feared the unrestrained exercise of their most basic impulses. Neither danger existed in anything like the proportions they saw; the proportions were much more theirs than the Negro's. In this sense, white men were attempting to destroy the living image of primitive aggressions which they said was the Negro but was really their own. Their very lives as social beings were at stake. Intermixture and insurrection, violent sex and sexual violence, creation and destruction, life and death—the stuff of animal existence was rumbling at the gates of rational and moral judgment. If the gates fell, so did humanness; they could not fall; indeed there could be no possibility of their falling, else man was not man and his civilization not civilized. We, therefore, do not lust and destroy; it is someone else."

The agri-culture's very deep misothery, then, supplied much emotional intensity to white society's urge to confine and control "bestial" black Africans. That control required even more emotional intensity than did the control of their domestic animals, for the threat and the stakes were so much higher. But the wells of misothery are deep, and they were able to feed passionate hatred against Amerinds, Africans, and all Others. The wells had fed their ancestors' control over Amerinds, whom they tried to eradicate as any other agricultural pest. It was agrarian work according to the agrarian order. To understand it in frank imagery, to white Euro-Americans, Africans were livestock and Amerinds were wildlife—predators or "vermin." But they were much more dangerous because of the twin threats of sexual attraction and race pollution. These were extra dangerous beasts, these beasts within.

8

Rituals of Dominionism— Then and Now

In pens near the town, the bulls have gone without food for days. Starved to a frenzy, they are driven into the streets by gangs of young men wielding whips, knives, and clubs. Other townspeople join in and the mob chases the bulls through the streets, slashing, clubbing, and tormenting them in every conceivable way. Some of the people throw fireballs at them; others try to slash their eyes out; still others try to cut off their tails. Wounded and exhausted after three days of torment, the bulls are finally killed and eaten.

As night falls in another town, the young men fasten balls of wax and resin to the horns of three bulls, then light them and release the bulls into the streets. Crazed and nearly blinded by the blazing fireballs, the terrified animals race through the crowd-lined streets. Crowds join the young men in jabbing the bulls with long, spiked poles and by pelting them with rocks and bottles. Someone throws a burning shirt across one bull's horns and eyes. After nearly four hours of torture, the mob of young men kills the bulls and they are dragged away to be slaughtered and eaten.

In other towns not far away, similar celebrations of animal torture and death take place during religious holidays. In one town, a live female goat is thrown from the church bell tower. She falls to the plaza below and struggles to get up on her broken legs. In another town, a troupe of young men dressed as clowns entertain children by tormenting and slowly killing a group of young calves. In another town, live chickens and geese are hung upside down by ropes and left dangling. Young men and women on horseback ride by and try to pull off one of the bird's heads.

In what century did these festivals occur? 3000 B.C.? A.D. 500? A.D. 1300? These are Spain's *sanguinary fiestas populares,* or popular fiestas with acts of blood, and they occur today. In fact, there are more of these fiestas in Spain today than there were thirty years ago. Brazil's coastal state of Santa Catarina conducts similar fiestas to celebrate Easter Week, New Year's Day, and, increasingly, weddings and various special events.

What is the point of these gruesome festivals? The most popular—and erroneous—explanation is that these "provide outlets for repressed aggression that are not overtly socially dysfunctional," in the words of one psychologist. In other words, people torture and kill these animals to blow off steam that might otherwise be turned against each other. What is wrong with this psychologism is that it assumes human aggression and hostility to be innate rather than learned, to be biological or "natural" rather than cultural. It harks back to some of the outdated and grossly misunderstood theories of Konrad Lorenz and others who suggested that we are driven by raw aggression, that violence is in our genes.

No doubt some *potential* for aggressive behavior is floating in the human gene pool, but we ought to accept that war, racism, rape, and most of our other penchants for violence, dominance, and hate are strictly cultural. The belief that beast-torturing releases pent-up, genetic aggression, then, depends upon some terribly erroneous and negative views about the nature of the human animal. Moreover, it apologizes for beast conquests and other kinds of stupid violence against animals and nature on the ground that they are in some way "necessary." We should admit that they are in no way necessary and that, in fact, they tend to encourage violence, suffering, detachment, ruthlessness, and mastery—the very values that twist and harden the human soul.

Cultural Exercises, Symbolic Statements

This, of course, is why beast-busting festivals got started in the first place: They helped foster the values "needed" by tough, male-supremacist, nature-busting agrarian society. We have built such festivals (and, as we shall see, other activities) into our culture over the centuries in much the same way that we have built religious rituals: to remind us that we are on top and in command of the world. Rituals, as anthropologists know, serve to express, remind, reaffirm, and perpetuate a society's worldview and ways of life. Ritual, according to Cambridge social anthropologist Edmund Leach, makes "symbolic statements about the social order." As we have seen, "the social order" in the broadest sense is dominionism—a view of the world that places animals, nature, and Others on a ladder or hierarchy of being. If we want to come to a better view of the living world, one with ideas of kinship and belonging, we need to identify the rituals that serve to "express, remind, reaffirm and perpetuate" that old-fashioned, hierarchical, dominionist worldview.

Dominionism, which puts humans at the top of the ladder of being, requires a number of assumptions and myths about the nature of nature. And as we have seen, animals represent the nature of nature—that is, various animals symbolize the power, aggression, danger, evil, whimsy, deceit, sexuality, fertility, and other traits that we think we see in nature. Animals, in other words, give bodies and images to the intangible aspects of nature.

This requires animals to perform essentially two kinds of chores for humanity: material chores and ritual chores. We use animals primarily as tools for material and practical benefit, as in pulling plows, carrying warriors, supplying meat and leather, and so forth. We also use animals as ritual tools to reaffirm the body of assumptions and myths that make up dominionism. In other words, we use animals in rituals, ceremonies, and entertainments that, in themselves, give no actual material benefit, but they provide a means for society to celebrate and reaffirm its mastery over animals and thereby the whole of nature that they represent.

Thus, the Spanish corrida, or bullfight, for example, when stripped of its pretensions of cultural tradition and art form (called a "sacred sport," "stylized ballet," and a "religious ceremony" by an American promoter) is a ritual contest in which men demonstrate mastery over beastly nature. Never mind the claims of aficionados who say the corrida is an even match; if it were, the death ratio of men to bulls would be near fifty-fifty. As we shall see, the deck is stacked against the bull in a number of ways so that the ritual comes out right in public.

Man Over Beast (and Nature)

At first glance, it seems ironic that a society would use spectacular brutality to celebrate its civilization and its rise over brutal nature. If we look more carefully, however, we find it telling rather than ironic. The bullfight aficionado apparently needs to believe that the forces of nature are dangerous and evil and that progress against them is, by necessity, violent and bloody. Thus, the bullfight celebrates the manly bravery required to subdue beastly nature. The ideal matador is the complete macho man: cool, controlled, hard, tough, and fearless in the face of pain, injury, mutilation, and possible death. His performance defines civilization as a patriarchal accomplishment—one produced by the male heroics of warriors and strong men.

Contrary to popular belief, the corrida as we know it is not an ancient ceremony. Historians suspect that it grew out of organized hunts to exterminate wild cattle, called aurochsen. Standing over six feet high at the shoulders and carrying a massive pair of horns, these animals were dangerous and difficult for Europe's farmers. They broke down fences, invaded fields of crops, and mated with domestic cattle, thereby "polluting" their specialized bloodlines. Consequently, extermination campaigns were widespread throughout Europe during the Middle Ages; they ended in 1627, when the last few aurochsen were killed by a party of hunters in Poland. In Spain, mounted horsemen hounded the aboriginal herds, sweeping them from the plains and making way for ranching and agrarian civilization. These wild cattle hunts appear to have been ritualized in the *Toro de la Vega* or "Bull of the Plain," one of Spain's *fiestas populares* in which men on horseback and in trucks chase bulls through the countryside toward the fiestas in town. There, with the help of the crowds, men and boys slash and poke the animals with spears, knives, tridents, sharpened sticks, and other weapons. The fun and festivity culminate when the mob kills the bulls, usually by spear thrusts.

The bullfight, or corrida, reached its present form in 1725 when Francisco Romero invented the muleta, a small red cloth mounted on a short stick used to "work" the bull and ready him for the kill. Romero and others defined the matador's basic maneuvers and techniques during the eighteenth century and they have changed very little since. Stylization and rigidity mark the proceedings, which makes the corrida all the more ritualistic—like a high mass. It must not change, or it might veer too far from the necessary symbolism, thereby losing its meaning. Splendor and formality also add to the ritual purpose, for they shroud the event in both festivity and solemnity—two essential ingredients for any sacred ceremony.

A Drama of Dominion—in Three Acts

The corrida's ritual of death unfolds in three acts, called *tercios*. It begins precisely at four in the afternoon with a blast of trumpets and a colorful parade of the day's participants into the arena. Men on horseback lead the procession. Then come the matadors on foot, each strutting in a gaudy, tight-fitting "suit of lights," each a picture of male condescension and narcissism. Behind each matador is his cuadrilla, the team of men who will "work" the bull until he is ready for the kill. Two of them, the picadors, are mounted on horseback. Three others, called banderilleros, are on foot.

Once the parade is over and the arena is clear, the officials release the first fighting bull. Until this moment, he has been with other animals and for the last few hours he has been in a dark pen under the grandstand. This guarantees an exciting entrance: suddenly, he is isolated from the security of his herd, blinded by sunlight, and frightened by the roar of the crowd and the blare of trumpets. Alone in strange territory, the bull rants about the arena in confusion and terror, looking for all the world like a "brave bull." The banderilleros and the matador test him with their colorful capes, noting his moves and charging habits. Bullfight officials send in the picadors on their horses, and they "work" the charging bull. They must spear the bull in the neck at least three times during the first *tercio.*

At the sound of the trumpets, the picadors retire and the three banderilleros enter the arena. During the second *tercio,* their job is to plant short, barbed spears, or banderillas, between the bull's shoulder blades so that he will be properly enraged (but with painful, weakened muscles) for the matador in the last *tercio.*

That done, the trumpets sound and the matador enters the arena. Using his muleta, he teases and entices the bull to charge, bringing him dangerously close while he, the matador, stands firm, proud, aloof. This displays complete domination over the bloody, exhausted animal and sets him up for the kill. Some matadors add one final act, the *displante,* to emphasize their mastery and the bull's degradation. With pure macho bravado, the matador shows contempt for beasts by stroking the bull's horns or nose, usually with an arrogant gesture to the audience that shows his disdain and fearlessness. "*Displante,*" Matador Gabriel Gonzales told a reporter, "is my way of showing the crowd I have conquered the bull. Killing *toros bravos* [fighting bulls] is only part of the art. Domination is everything."

Conquest and Humilation

After both matador and crowd are satisfied that the living bull has been subdued, it is time for the "supreme moment" or "moment of truth," the ultimate act of domination—the kill. Ideally, the matador is supposed to ram his three-foot sword between the shoulder blades into the bull's heart; ideally, the bull drops dead instantly. Ordinarily, the sword misses, hits a bone or slices into the lungs instead. Then the bull staggers about the arena, blood pouring from his mouth and nose until he can be put out of his misery by more sword thrusts. With domination settled, the matador and the crowd often humiliate the dead "brave bull" before a mule team drags the body from the arena. With arrogant gestures and body language, the matador may clean his bloody sword by wiping it across the animal's body. Or if his performance has pleased the crowd, they may "award" him some of the bull's body parts, one or both ears, the tail— some trophy of his heroism over the dangerous beast.

The entire corrida, then, is a ceremony for the exercise of agrarian society's values on subduing wild, dangerous nature. It parades its fine, brave men with their horses and weapons before the entire community. It displays the fearsome, dangerous bull—the beast of nature. It enrages the bull to emphasize his wild, evil nature, which symbolizes the wildness and evil of the rest of nature. This emphasizes, in turn, the righteous need to control and dominate that nature. And into this arena steps the matador, the elaborately dressed, rationally controlled representative of human civilization. Coolly, fearlessly, he faces the beast (and beastly nature), subdues it, and degrades, dominates, and humilates it in cooperation with the entire community.

The Cowboy: Outrider for Agrarian Civilization

The corrida is to Iberian culture what the rodeo is to Anglo culture: a popular man-beast contest and ritual that reinforces the dominionist worldview—in both cases a worldview heavily colored by ancient herder values.

The rodeo and the American cowboy culture, as every schoolchild knows, grew out of the Spanish ranching tradition in Old Mexico. There, in the seventeenth and eighteenth centuries, Spanish colonists and missionaries built up huge herds of cattle on the wide plains that stretched into North America. Cattle and ranches became so numerous that they encroached upon Amerind lands and peoples. Weakened by epidemics and cultural collapse, native people struggled in vain against priests, soldiers, and ranchers. To survive the European onslaught, many young Amerind men joined the ranching system as low-paid mounted herdsmen—the first cowboys in America. This they saw as glorious, prestigious work, for they had been forbidden to ride horses earlier in the Conquest Period when horses were crucial to military advantage. Now they could ride on horseback and wear spurs, like their conquerors. Now they could be vaqueros, the only station of some power and prestige for young men of a colonized society. At first, they were Amerindian, but gradually, according to environmentalist and author Jeremy Rifkin in his book *Beyond Beef,* they were "blacks, mestizos, mulattos, and poor whites, a semiprivileged group among the working poor, distinguished by their mounts and their iron footgear."

This American herder culture complex came by way of Spain, the Moors of northern Africa, and the ancient Middle East. It became what we know as the Western cowboy tradition around 1820, when Anglo adventurers began to roam Texas (when it was still Mexico) stealing Mexican cattle, horses, lands, watering sites, and, in the process, Mexican cowboy—vaquero—culture.

Although they were few in number and their heyday was short relative to trappers, miners, loggers, and other Euro-American nature-tamers, the cowboys sparked a fascination in the Western mind that has never stopped growing. The glory days of the trail ride lasted only twenty some years—from about 1865 to the mid-1880s, but the cowboy is America's reigning frontier hero far and away from the others.

He looms more important than the others, according to authors Joe Frantz and Julian Choate in *The American Cowboy,* because the cowboy symbolizes so many heroes and values of Western civilization: He is the "rider at the edge of civilization," a strong, manly figure who goes into the wild frontier and makes it safe for others to come. He is also the mounted herdsman who lives a nomadic life wild and free under the stars. Half utilitarian businessman and half romantic dreamer, the cowboy is an ambivalent figure, and thus one who best symbolizes Western culture's tensions between civilization's order and nature's freedom. He is the perfect figure for the brave and visionary vanguard who helps civilized society extend its outposts, its reach into new lands and new wealth.

Rodeo—the Cowboy Culture Carrier

In America, the rodeo replays the cowboy's work out on the range; it offers a slice of the mounted herder's life, his work in wrestling large animals and making the land safe for settlers and civilization. The rodeo displays the cowboy's skills, but also his society's values on fearlessness, violence, strength, domination, and obliviousness to pain.

Tufts University anthropologist Elizabeth Atwood Lawrence has explored the rodeo's ritual value in her book *Rodeo.* She notes that the modern rodeo is an end-product of a long history of herder values and culture. In his moments in the arena, the rodeo cowboy passes them on again. He is patriarchal culture's heir apparent, and he is father of the future generations. Even out of the arena, the rodeo cowboy carries the hard, heavy mixture of macho traits common to stock-herding cultures the world over: exaggerated male sexuality, self-containment, "bravery, fortitude, and the ability to withstand pain and hardship." Lawerence notes that other anthropologists have described the herder tradition as "proud, arrogant, and tending toward aggressive, often hostile, sometimes violent behavior." Like all herders, she says, rodeo cowboys are highly individualistic and competitive and they love proving their manhood with feats of "endurance, stoicism, bravery, propensity for risk-taking, aggressiveness and violence." They are pragmatic, egalitarian (within their group), and they push rugged individualism as far as they can without breaking the code of group conformity.

Rodeo also serves as ritual for another huge sector of patriarchal culture. It is a major initiation rite of passage into the masculine elite. "Stoicism is a prime requisite," Lawrence says, "and like the cowboys of old, rodeo participants avoid complaining. It is not an infrequent occurrence for one of them to break an ankle in the chute and go on to finish his ride. Many compete with broken limbs in casts or their entire chests taped because of fractured ribs." She tells of seeing a rodeo in which a contestant broke his leg on a ride, went to the hospital, and returned to ride about the arena with his leg in the new cast. She saw him soon after at another rodeo with his arm in a cast. Lawrence observed many examples of seriously injured cowboys returning to the chutes to take another ride.

At the rodeo, it appears that hard men enjoy exchanging power and pain with large animals; thus, rodeo amounts to a male cult of sadomasochism, but in broad daylight and in public. Fathers take their sons, put them in the saddle, and spur them into the macho model of manhood. Even the corporate cattlemen of the beef business embrace the ritual, apparently, for the magazine *Beef Today* went to a "School of Hard Knocks," a Kansas school for rodeo cowboys. There the reporter noted that "young men's bodies did indeed fly in all directions and land with gut-wrenching thuds and stifled cries of pain." The reporter saw a lot of Bibles, prayers before rides, and grace before meals. He also watched fathers goad their sons into the man-beast conquest contest. One, who claimed, "I always liked rodeo myself," brought twin teenage sons for initiation. One flunked out the first day—after suffering a concussion from bronc-riding. On the third day of school, the other got gored by a bull while still in the chute. "Blood flies all over, and he's helped to the ambulance," says *Beef Today*. " 'Looks like that one broke his jaw,' says his father with a touch of pride in his voice." Even the reporter is grossed out. "Machismo," he wrote, "is one obvious reason these young men are here."

Rodeo is ritual on a number of levels. But "on its deepest level," Lawrence wrote, it "is essentially a ritual addressing itself to the dilemma of man's place in nature, exploring the boundary lines between people and other forms of life. It deals with the major theme of human supremacy over nature, and specifically with man's relationship to the animals which he conceives of as existing both within and beyond his sphere of control."

Rodeo has appeal because it gives people such a large, quick dose of cowboy culture, such a heavy "hit" of herder values. It reminds and exercises just about all of the West's principles for living at the top of the ladder of being. According to Lawrence, it reaffirms the superior position that we like to take in all the important relationships in the world: human-animal, male-female, predator-prey, civilization-nature. Rodeo is the West's saga in that it celebrates over and over the subduing of wild, chaotic nature. In wrestling, roping, and tying down large, dangerous beasts, it celebrates domestication and the victory of human culture over nature.

Hunting—or Man Is Just Another Predator

The quintessential man-beast contest, hunting, is a ritual assertion of supremacy over animals and the right to kill and eat them. Hunters, although rarely frank and insightful, occasionally slip and admit as much, as did one who wrote a letter to the editor of the *Greenwich* (Connecticut) *News* in defense of hunting: "What it comes down to is that man is the leading and controlling species on earth. We encroach on wildlife every day by developing everything in sight; we tell wildlife where to live and not live; we choose which animals we domesticate and eat most often. In essence, we have total power over them." Under this worldview, man (especially men) is *the* dominant predator on earth, and hunters are merely carrying out their natural duties.

Lord Kenneth Clark, the art historian, thought, like so many others, that hunting "started as a necessity" as "primitive man hunted in quest of food." As I suggested in Chapter 2, however, this belief in primal necessity is the invention of a modern society apparently guilty over its unprecedented appetites for cows, pigs, chickens, and turkeys. The magnitude of the killing requires huge rationalizations and reassurances. A major reassurance is the belief that our ancestors hunted and lived on meat "from the beginning of time," as it is usually put.

This is the popular belief despite archaeological evidence that shows that plant foods have provided the overwhelming bulk of the human diet throughout evolution. As we saw, the most recent evidence suggests that any meat in our distant ancestors' diets came from scavenging and opportunistic kills until about 20,000 years ago when *Homo sapiens sapiens,* fully modern humans, began true, organized hunting. Even then, the hunt was shrouded in rituals. Indeed, as I suggested, the hunt itself was largely a ritual activity by which men tried to take spirit-powers from nature in order to balance the powers and status of women, who were believed to have inherent powers from their closeness to nature. If I am right, hunting is human society's oldest man-over-beast ritual.

At any rate, most human societies became "hooked" on meat, seeing it as a favorite food and seeing hunting as a prestigious activity. Then, according to Lord Clark, once animal domestication came to supply dinner tables more reliably, "hunting became what it has remained ever since, a ritualized display of surplus energy and courage." He noted that hunting "has always been closely identified with social status." Kings and emperors used hunting as a display of privilege, as a practice for war, and as an excuse to annex vast areas of land for game preserves. Naturally, then, hunting was coveted by the other levels of society who took it up as a badge of status, as a mark of having "arrived," once European revolutions and the colonization of the Americas broke up the old feudal privileges.

Myths of Necessity, Nature, and Manhood

Today, hunting reaffirms essentially two beliefs, which I abbreviate as Necessity and Nature. These seem to require constant bolstering through the many forms of the sport—for example, bow hunting, big-game hunting, trophy hunting, trap-and-release shoots, live-bird shoots, "canned" hunts, contest killings, and the great seasonal ritual, the fall deer hunt.

While a small minority of society actually hunts, the larger society tacitly supports hunters who perform the ritual on society's behalf. Like the matador and the rodeo cowboy, the hunter keeps dominionist values alive and handy for all of society. Everyone cooperates in the ritual. As one writer put it, "the opening of deer season remains a secular day of obligation." Schools and factories close, restaurants offer "sportsman's plates," local media sponsor Big Buck contests, and the standard greeting is, "Get your deer yet?" As a *New York Times* headline writer put it, "The Rite of Autumn Is the Song of the Rifle."

In these very civic ways, society embraces the belief of Necessity, which serves to eliminate any question of choice and hence morality. The hunt is necessary, society believes, as a feeder of people and a controller of nature. Without hunting, people would starve; also, animal populations would explode, spreading disease and starvation and posing a menace to human existence. These are the beliefs that make up a very popular myth—one strongly held and deeply seated in the bedrock misothery at the bottom of our agri-culture. Through this myth, the hunter becomes society's hero, its man against the teeming elements of vicious nature; his work saves us all from a fate worse than death.

The other belief, Nature, sees the living world as a meat-hungry, snarling mass of predators, with man-the-fittest surviving at the top. The *Greenwich News* letter writer calls it "Mother Nature's basic life plan" and argues that "everybody is eating everybody to survive." This view of nature handily exonerates hunting and, by extension, all killing of animals for food.

Small wonder, then, that the hamburger-hungry general public tacitly supports hunting through a tax-supported game management bureaucracy that controls the nation's wildlife and our parks, refuges, and wilderness areas. No other sport is as pampered and privileged, for no other sport does so much to champion the myths and values of meat-hungry, dominionist society. Indeed, it has elevated hunting beyond the realm of sport into that of the sacred. Hunters have the run of the woods and anyone who interferes with them can be arrested under the new "hunter harassment" laws passed hastily by dozens of states to keep hunt protestors at bay. No ordinary laws would do, it seems; special ones were needed to protect a very special activity. Hunting's sanctity turns ridiculous, of course. In Iowa, a father-son team will, for $500 plus expenses, pack a deceased hunter's cremated remains into shotgun shells and fire them at his favorite game animal.

In addition to these ritual services, hunting, like rodeo, is a major rite of passage into the patriarchal model of manhood. Hunting clubs and magazines echo the National Rifle Association's advertisements that urge men to bring their sons (and, increasingly, their daughters) up properly—on the virtues of the "outdoorsman" and the "sportsman." A rare few women do hunt, to the delight of the historically all-male hunter cult. Token women hunters do not significantly encroach on male cultural territory and they are good P.R. devices against the protest that hunting is a cruel, macho sport. Nevertheless, as the *Times* writer noted, "women hunt, but it remains a beer-and-boys sport, both in the woods and the deer camp." Pro-hunt P.R. aside, hunting is still pitched as the doorway to manhood, to adult male maturity and responsibility.

But that is only the stated part of the initiation, the socially acceptable part. The other part of the ritual is to condition young men to the stoicism, the steely toughness believed to be necessary by our herder-rooted agri-culture. The hunt gives a boy the experience of cold-blooded killing and the opportunity to choke down naturally strong feelings using his culture's beliefs in Necessity. Judging from accounts by ex-hunters, hunting maga-zines, and other sources, even macho men balk on the verge of a kill. By all accounts, many of those who pull the trigger feel shame and remorse as they approach their animal struggling in its death-throes. But this is the greatest moment of the ritual, for it is the moment that brings into play all of the values, myths, and other bits of culture that rationalize the killing as a Necessity. This is the moment that makes a man a real man because it tests and exercises his cultural and mental "muscle"—that is, his strength of will in controlling soft, "feminine" (and very natural) feelings of empathy. He is now a hard man, a heartless man, a manly man. He is now equipped to dish out pain and to take pain. On every occasion, he will be able to mutter the standard platitude: "A man's gotta do what a man's gotta do."

The Circus—a Show of Power

Not all of the agri-culture's man-beast conquest rituals feature spectac-ular violence. Some use spectacular humiliation. The violent rituals tend to reinforce myths about vicious animals and evil nature; the humiliating ones tend to reinforce myths of animal stupidity, inferiority, and willingness to submit to human dominion. The circus hones dominionist values by re-ducing animals to toys and clowns, and hence nature is reduced to a play-thing, an object of human whimsy. In elaborate dress and trappings and strictly conditioned by severe training techniques, circus animals perform highly controlled and unnatural behaviors designed to amuse a human au-dience. In our laughter and amazement we accept their buffoon status, their simplicity, their utility. Their contrived performance teaches children and reminds adults that human beings are the masters over the living world.

The circus's career as a degrader of animals and nature began long before the Christian era when ancient Egyptians trained animals and kept collections of animals in parks like our zoos. The Greeks first taught lions, bears, and horses to dance, bow, and do other tricks. The Greeks also put together the first traveling menagerie, which took nature-debasement out to the countryside where the urban elite thought it was most needed.

The Romans, however, put the circus on the West's cultural map, so to speak. Rome raised the limits of extravagance in the display of human supremacy over the rest of creation. At its glory, Rome's Circus Maximus accommodated nearly 200,000 spectators who watched chariot races, gladiatorial combats, and *venationes*—combats between wild animals. The frequency, scale, and bloodiness of these entertainments are legendary. By the mid-fourth century A.D., 175 days each year were official holidays celebrated by public spectacles of violence.

But not without good reasons: hard-core amusements helped control a decadent Roman citizenry. More important, they gave militaristic emperors an excellent showcase for their wealth and power. Each emperor felt compelled to outdo his predecessor in amassing collections of exotic animals and then choreographing their destruction in the arena. When the Colosseum was dedicated, 9,000 animals were killed in a hundred-day show. To celebrate Trajan's triumph over other peoples and their lands, 11,000 animals were mass-murdered in the ring before thousands of spectators.

These public mass killings also served as a celebration of self-aggrandizing Rome's power over distant regions, their peoples and their wild animals who in older, forager times had stood for the powerful forces of nature. Rome, in other words, was celebrating its sense of civilization.

Nature—Tamed and in Chains

Christianity brought an end to public mass killings, although animal combats on a smaller, more discreet scale continued to be popular into modern times. People continued to be fascinated with exotic animals, with freaks, and abnormalities—whether in humans or in animals. As the new religion settled across Europe, entertainment involving animals turned from the visceral thrill of seeing them mass-murdered in public to the amusement in seeing them dance, do tricks, and be teased and duped by humans. As did the bloody mass destruction in the arenas of agrarian Rome, the new forms of circuses helped secure agrarian, newly Christian Europe's dominionist worldview: Humans were superior and in easy control over inferior, malleable animals/nature. The new spectacle was less cruel and violent, but it served the same purpose; to laugh at the dancing bear or the clown-suited monkey was to reduce them, to debase them into their proper place in the dominionist Divine Plan.

While feudal Europe set about destroying its native wildlife to protect its crops and to advance its efforts with domestic animal breeding, it grew more and more fascinated with bizarre animals from other lands. Jugglers, minstrels, mountebanks, and other itinerant entertainers roved from town to town with their performing leopards, bears, and monkeys. By the Middle Ages, towns, trading, and urban ways were established.

European culture had long been agrarian and nature-alienated, but as it became more and more urbanized and separated from the natural environment people's very deep and emotional attachments to, and needs for, the natural world were severely strained. Urban Europe, like city-state Rome, Greece, and Egypt before it, craved something of nature—particularly animals, as they were nature's most outstanding representatives. Roving entertainers with their animals met this need and were always popular. Little by little, bands of these entertainers grew into circuses and brought pieces of nature, albeit tamed and trained, to the populace.

In a different vein, displays of large, dangerous, exotic animals impressed and subdued the citizenry, for they indicated imperial wealth and power. On another level, the royal menageries probably symbolized the agrarian nation's dominion over wild, chaotic, dangerous nature. Elephants in chains and lions in cages displayed both menacing nature and humanity's mastery over it. Well into the nineteenth century, when the first European public zoos were founded and the great circuses had their heyday, the wealthy nations boasted their agrarian empires through animals. Today, the circus, like the zoo, is a relic of a nature-alienated culture. Worse, both serve as rituals for the reinforcement and recycling of human supremacy, mastery over beasts, victory over nature, and the other cornerstones of dominionism.

Pets for People

It may seem odd that widespread pet-keeping and pet-breeding arose in the nineteenth century just as Western society was beginning to wake up to its impact on nature. The developments appear to have no connection. Yet they do, for the surge in popularity of these hobbies reflects Europe and America's growing ambivalence about their increasing mastery over the living world. Wilderness, which had been seen traditionally as dangerous and evil, was beginning to be seen as a thing of beauty and serenity to be protected from destruction by commerce. In the same period, the first laws against cruelty to animals were enacted by the British Parliament. Western society was not reversing dominionism, but it was moderating it into a form of benevolent dictatorship.

In this milieu, "the safe, captive, and loyal pet was an obedient and subservient symbol for the appropriate relationship between humankind and the natural world," wrote Tufts University professor of environmental studies Andrew Rowan in a chapter note to his book *Animals and People Sharing the World*. "Control of the breeding of pets allowed owners to shape their animals' form and behavior." People were still controlling and dominating the living world, but they were doing so with affection and with the belief that they were "improving" it. It was an attitude of "dominance and affection," according to geographer and author Yi-Fu Tuan in his book of the same name.

The nineteenth century also brought a middle class and a nontitled elite who wanted to have all of the playthings of the rich and powerful. And pets, like meat, horses, and weapons, best symbolized having arrived because for centuries they had been the exclusive possessions of the ruling class. World conquerer Alexander the Great loved not only his famous horse, Bucephalus, but he hand-reared a favorite dog, Peritas, and named at least one town in Asia after him. Europe's great kings treated their royal pets with conspicuously lavish affection, and included them in many royal portraits. Chinese empresses doted on miniature dogs as early as the first century A.D., carrying them about the palaces in the sleeves of their elegant robes. Britain's eighth earl of Bridgewater, who was known for lavish parties, often dined at the table with his favorite dogs. "Human menials in rich livery were made to serve his animal pets, also lavishly attired," according to Yi-Fu.

Black "Boys" in Collars

In many cases, the ruler's pets were human beings. Before the days of democratization and notions of civil rights, the rich and the powerful used Africans, dwarfs, and other extraordinary (for Europeans) human beings to provide novelty to their armies of servants. As with pet fanciers today, there was a fascination with interesting specimens. After about 1550, African servants became a fad in Europe's noble households because of their rarity and exotic appearance. According to Yi-Fu, young African boys "were openly offered for sale in shops, warehouses and coffeehouses." Newspapers carried advertisements such as, "a Pretty little Negro Boy, about nine Years old, and well limb'd." The fad spread to all of Europe, and London was the best place to "shop." In 1769, the czarina of Russia sent her agent to London to find a "number of the finest best made black boys." According to Yi-Fu, these young slaves were often dressed in elaborate costumes and made to attend to their owners in drawing rooms, theater boxes, and at other public functions. Clearly, as he says, they "occupied a special position as exotic ornaments and pets."

Far more telling of their true status, though, were the collars and padlocks many of them were forced to wear. Many of these were made gaudy and elaborate—like the rhinestone doggie collars of today—in an attempt to make a pathetic situation seem funny and therefore acceptable. A London goldsmith got into the act, advertising "silver padlocks for Blacks or Dogs; collars, etc."

Then as now, "a pet is a diminished being, whether in the figurative or in the literal sense," says Yi-Fu. "It serves not so much the essential needs as the vanity and pleasure of its possessor." The pet exists to bolster the ego and to heighten the station of the owner. They may be doted on and given conspicuously lavish treatment if the owner wants to display wealth and privilege. Just as often, however, they may be humiliated and teased because these treatments reaffirm the hierarchical relationship. When you can get away with playing with another's life and being, you can feel pretty sure of your superiority.

For most pet owners, this treatment is not overtly abusive or physically harmful, but in the wrong sort of person it can be extremely so. For most of us it is mild, and is probably seen as just play. Even so, humiliation and teasing maintain the gulf and the respective positions between owner and pet. We cannot see this so much in our relations with pet animals because the West's agri-culture has assigned animals the status of inferiors and objects, but we can see it in Yi-Fu's examples of the treatment of human pets. It begins with naming, which can strongly indicate either respect or disrespect. Since Roman times, for example, owners have referred to their slaves as simply *por,* after *puer,* "boy."

Improper Names

An inferior being has no dignity, no identity, and hence no need for a proper name. But sometimes names were deliberately given to amuse the superiors at the expense of their slave-pets. Giving slaves ridiculous names was clearly a playful, but abusive, way of demonstrating the hierarchical relationship. In America as in Europe, African slave-pets were given absurdly serious names such as Pompey, Socrates, and Plato as well as absurdly trivial names such as Starling, Tallow, Little Ephraim, or Robin John. Yi-Fu tells of a clergyman who was sent to a Mississippi plantation to baptize forty slave children with names such as Napoleon, Queen Victoria, and

Madame de Stael. The names had originated in the "merry brain" of the owner's sister, and the baptismal ceremony had been staged for the amusement of white neighbors and guests. The Chinese Imperial elite also practiced name-humiliation by giving their domestics fanciful pet names such as Butterfly, Emerald, Lotus, Sunset, Happy, Joker, Cheerful, and Lively. Naming, though nonviolent and seemingly playful, can be one of the most effective rituals of dominance and control over one's "inferiors."

More clearly abusive is the tradition of deliberately shaping a living being in order to make a more interesting pet. This also bolsters agri-cultural values, for it shows human power over natural forces of growth and procreation. A very old favorite is miniaturization, the making of toy-sized trees, dogs, horses, and other living beings. The pocket-sized being has a double stamp by humanity: it is more obviously human-made (as opposed to natural) and it signals triviality, "toy-ness"—a plaything well under control.

Were there attempts to produce small and deformed people for amusement of the elite? "The answer would seem to be yes," says Yi-Fu. He explains the Greek word *gloottokoma,* which refers to boxes used to lock up little children with the aim of shaping their growth for a lucrative career as circus dwarfs. The Roman Longinus wrote in the first century A.D. of the practice of caging people in order to stunt their growth. Romans were known to have disfigured children so they would make more pathetic and effective beggars. Yi-Fu suggests that they may have also used forced malnutrition in order to stunt or deform children's growth to produce dwarfs, jesters, and fools for the entertainment of the elite.

Whether these techniques worked or not, elite society managed somehow to maintain its collections of exotic human pets. Europeans carried on the tradition until well after the Renaissance. A cardinal of Rome gave a banquet in 1566 at which thirty-four dwarfs served the guests. In eighteenth-century Russia, Peter the Great kept a stable of fools and dwarfs, feeding them a hundred at a time in a dining hall. He encouraged them to marry and breed and he often sponsored their weddings and balls; of course, he and select noble guests attended for amusement, watching the festivities from the sidelines.

Pets for the Modern Age

"Dominance," says Yi-Fu, "normally takes the form of straight exploitation. When it takes the form of condescending playfulness, it expresses the belief that women and slaves, fools and blacks are immature and naive, animal-like, and sexual. Men of power, arrogating to themselves the attributes of mind and culture, find it pleasing to have around them humans of a lesser breed—closer to nature—on whose head they may lay an indulgent hand." But human beings, fortunately, are more and more off limits these days as candidates for pethood and objects for the display of power and privilege. Unfortunately, this leaves nonhuman animals wide open for the job.

And the pressures for pethood are greater than ever before. There is tremendous ambivalence about our species' impact on the rest of the living world, which, as noted above, translates into dominance tempered by affection. There are, in other words, more people now who want to be benevolent dictators. In addition, now the vast majority of society enjoys powers and privileges formerly held by a tiny elite, and they, too, want to demonstrate their new godlike position in the hierarchy of being. Thus, the human population is in a frenzy for pets, more pets, exotic pets, and purebred pets. Pet shops proliferate, as do the puppy mills and the back-yard breeders who supply them. The sport of dog-breeding and -showing is at an all-time high in popularity; and cats, who had been largely spared from the breed-nut's designs on their sex lives and body shapes, are no longer. For in crafting new dog and cat breeds, the owner/breeder can, as Yi-Fu and MIT humanities professor and author Harriet Ritvo note, achieve a "godlike sense of power over life." That sense of power is, of course, unconscious and it is tempered by strong, conscious feelings of affection. To hear the breeders tell it, they are simply "crazy about" their poodles, shi-tzus, golden retrievers, ragdoll cats, and so on.

They also go to great lengths to "improve" their breed—with the most emphasis on the animal's look and shape. As any honest veterinarian can tell you, this has produced many physical problems. The chronic hip dysplasia in German shepherds, for example, is the result of decades of selective breeding for a dog with a low-to-the-ground rear end. The de-sired "look" was one of aggression—an animal that always looked as if it was about to spring in attack.

One can go from breed to breed and list the problems caused by breeding for a "look." Pekingese and other "pug" breeds have problems with their eyes, teeth, and noses because of their unnaturally foreshort-ened skulls. Collies have another family of head problems because their skulls have been made long and skinny. English bulldogs must be deliv-ered by Caesarian section because the puppies' heads are too large for the pelvic opening due to selective breeding for that big-headed bull-dog "look." People still seek the "look," even though the potential health problems are obvious: dachshunds and Great Danes are prone to back problems and disc diseases, the wrinkled Shar-Peis are prone to skin problems, and the giant breeds have one foot in the grave by the time they are six years old.

The Rape of Lassie

Well behind the scenes, of course, are the selective breeding techniques. One is not supposed to know too much about the sort of handling needed to make animals breed by the numbers. Yi-Fu says that the literature on the subject "reads at times like a laboratory manual and at times like pornography." As we might expect, the breeder's craft is one of very bizarre practices. Much of it begins, it must be said, in the bizarre mind of the sort of person who enjoys manipulating nature, one who has, as Yi-Fu says, "that compelling desire to intervene decisively in the life of another."

With a certain dog "look" in mind for a blueprint, the breeder's job is to decide which nearly perfect male will mount and fertilize which nearly perfect female. After generations of such forced breeding, the ideal-looking dog should be achieved. (Dogs, by the way, don't give a damn about looks in their sex partners, they go mainly by smell.) A problem arises if either dog has someone else in mind. One may not like the other's "looks" (smells). Needless to say, the breeder is working against the grain of natural instincts and behaviors, so force must be applied. Yi-Fu reports one breeding expert's advice: "Get a good firm grip on her ears. Someone else should then put a hand underneath her to steady her for the dog. With the other hand, a little helpful push at the right moment behind the dog might make all the difference. Steady him whilst he is tying the bitch; then when you are quite sure that the tying has taken place, gently turn him round, back to back with the bitch."

Some breeders force the sex act by putting Vaseline or other lubricant on the female's vaginal opening and then man-handling the male into copulating with her. To prepare him, the breeding expert advises, take the male dog's penis "into the palm of one's hand and exert a slight warming pressure." At some kennels, strongly resistant females are muzzled and hung in a sling so they cannot refuse the males. In humans, of course, such an activity would be called a gang-rape and it would be a felony.

Dog (and now cat) breeding, however, is anything but a felony. It is one of the rituals by which modern humanity displays and reaffirms its mastery over the living world. It is another of our rituals of dominionism.

As Harriet Ritvo says, it offers breeders "the chance to stamp canine raw material with designs of their own choosing; it [is] a continually repeated symbol of the human ascendancy over nature."

As with the rituals of bullfighting, rodeo, and hunting, however, the society-at-large is a participant along with the matador, the cowboy, the hunter, and the breeder. We glorify their sports even if we do not compete in them. We attend them, applaud them, and make them financially successful. Indeed, where pet-breeding is concerned, we are rather major participants, for we, too, are hooked on the various "looks" of the pure-breds. If enough of us are "crazy about" miniature schnauzers, the breeders will keep on "improving them" and filling the pet shop windows.

Cutting Up Life

Many a reader will balk at my suggestion that experimentation on animals—what the Victorians called simply "vivisection"—is in any way a ritual. That is taking this thing too far, one thinks. And 80 percent of the American public believes in its Necessity, in its heroic accomplishments for the benefit of the human species. Nevertheless, beliefs in the rightness of human slavery and the existence of witches were just as popular in their day and they are now just as widely rejected. Which is to say that we could be just as wrong about vivisection today, that our delusions about it have not yet worn off.

Many who are clearly not fanatics have been saying as much, only to be regarded as were the opponents of human slavery and witch-hunts. One was Dr. Henry J. Bigelow, a professor of surgery at Harvard University Medical School, who said, "There will come a time when the world will look back on vivisection in the name of science as they do now to burning at the stake in the name of religion." Another is Dr. Roger Ulrich, a research professor of psychology at Western Michigan University: "Faith in the ability of animal research to guarantee the continuance of human-kind on earth is nothing less than pure superstition. Indeed, we are faced with a situation in which over 100 years of animal research may have left our culture further behind in the search for wisdom than when the research started."

What makes one suspect so strongly that vivisection may be a mass delusion and a very sophisticated, modern ritual of dominionism is the vehemence, the near fanaticism with which it is promoted. It has about it the strong smell of a secular religion, one pushed by a cult (albeit a large and complex one) of people who need to feel heroic and superior to not only the living world but to all of us. Those of you who have had personal dealings with heart surgeons will get my meaning.

The scientific professions have had this ego problem ever since the Age of Reason, when they began to compete with the Church as the main institution of human salvation. But the medical profession has been the most successful, for its proffered benefits have been much more direct and personal than the chemist's or the geologist's. The doctor will make us feel better; the doctor will save our sick child. And, like the Catholic system of the Middle Ages, we can do just about anything we want as long as we go to the doctor and trust him and take his medicines. Americans today are virtually obsessed with doctors' appointments, drugs, therapies, and heroic surgeries. "Going to the doctor" is the ritual of the modern age and we do it perhaps with even more frequency and blind trust than our ancestors went to priests centuries ago. We go more eagerly and we pay more dearly because we are more convinced that we will be saved.

The believers believe that vivisection—literally, the "cutting up of life"—is a practical, rather than ritual, activity. It is pure science, it is carried out by the most noble members of our species, and it saves lives. This popular belief has been carefully shaped by the pharmaceutical industry and its clients, the allopathic medical profession and the constellation of disease foundations who provide most of the public pressure for funds for research toward "magic bullet" medicines and "miracle" surgeries. These interest groups appear to depend exclusively on animal experimentation as their tool of progress; when alternative methods are suggested, they are most vehement in saying "there aren't any." (If this is the case, we should demand changes, for true science would not so narrowly restrict its methods.) One fights back the blasphemous thought that the medical establishment has stealthily created a system in which the big money is in high-profile research, impressive surgeries, high-tech diagnostic machines, expensive drugs for patient maintenance, and costly long-term care rather than in effective prevention and treatment.

The Power of the Animal Model

But why do they need to experiment on animals? Can't they just go in heroic circles without blinding cats and strapping monkeys into restraining chairs?

Perhaps they could, but the circles would not seem nearly as heroic.

Perversely, we need to see extreme measures taken to convince us that science is leaving no stone unturned in its fight to conquer disease. Perhaps less invasive, less manipulative approaches would not appear so glorious; hence, they would not attract public support, funding, and the best reseachers. Medical research is, after all, just another attempt to conquer some force or process in nature, and, as we have seen, animals are potent symbols of nature. Perhaps Claude Bernard, the "father of vivisection," knew this intuitively when he wrote: "With the help of these active experimental sciences, man becomes an inventor of phenomena, a real foreman of creation; and under this head we cannot set limits to the power that he may gain over nature through future progress in the experimental sciences."

If animals are the most potent representatives of nature, then drastic invasions and manipulations of animals, even under the guise of science, send the strongest signals that great efforts to conquer nature are under way. Just as the bloody animal sacrifices of old impressed the masses and heightened the prestige of a god, its temple, and its priests, animals are "sacrificed" in our medical laboratories to impress us and raise the prestige of medicine, its corporations, universities, and researchers.

The actual research is not carried out so publicly because the procedures appall today, nevertheless the public knows that they are generally gruesome. As with slaughterhouses, one does not have to actually see the laboratories to know that the research on animals there would shock and disturb. We know enough; we are impressed sufficiently to vote more tax dollars for research and pay more for life-saving products and procedures.

One of the best examples of this system was the head-injury research on baboons conducted in the laboratory of Dr. Thomas Gennarelli at the University of Pennsylvania in Philadelphia until public protests apparently moved the Secretary of Health and Human Services to cut off his funding in 1986. For more than thirteen years, Gennarelli's laboratory spent a million dollars a year of the public's money slamming baboons' heads in attempts to duplicate the kinds of brain damage humans suffer in boxing matches, football games, and auto accidents. For one thing, as critical scientists pointed out, the long-headed baboon is not a very good model for traumatic brain injury in spherical-headed humans. For another, there had been years of human autopsy findings that already explained how violent movement of the brain within the skull caused widespread "shearing" damage to nerves and brain tissue. Nevertheless, Dr. Gennarelli did what respectable scientists feel they must do: re-create similar injuries in animals in the controlled setting of the laboratory. In this way, he provided experimental "proof" that violent blows to the head cause the soft brain to slam about in the skull, tearing neurons, irreparably damaging brain tissue, and leaving the victim in a comatose or vegetative state. Gennarelli's main accomplishment, according to veterinarian Brandon Reines, was to coin the term "diffuse axonal injury" (DAI) to describe the widespread damage to brain nerve cells already observed in human autopsy studies. Because the experiments were able to reliably cause both DAI and coma in baboons, they would, according to Reines, "help to set the DAI hypothesis in concrete: to make it dogma."

And, of course, they focused credit on Dr. Thomas Gennarelli and the University of Pennsylvania. As Dr. Reines observed: "The baboon experiments . . . catapulted him to the top of the head-injury field. Gennarelli not only became a full professor at the University of Pennsylvania but now preaches the gospel of DAI in leading textbooks of neurosurgery and at dozens of conferences around the world." (Reines and others report that Dr. Gennarelli's most recent head-injury experiments use specially bred miniature pigs—a species even less relevant to human brain injury than baboons but one not so objectionable to the public.)

Such is modern animal sacrifice, and its heroic nature-wrestling has a deep-seated appeal to the public. Another example is the addiction research of Dr. Ronald Wood at New York University. The research facility has a $14 million rodent laboratory in a city that can't afford housing for homeless people. As a *Village Voice* reporter noted, "in New York City, there are 480,000 heavy drug users and 38,718 treatment slots. Meanwhile, Dr. Ronald Wood's monkeys are smoking close to $200,000 in taxpayer-financed crack a year." The medical establishment has apparently convinced the government that counseling, jobs, and rehabilitation are "socialistic" and that researchers can come up with a "magic bullet" cure for drug addiction. Never mind that addictions are known to have social causes, the big research race is for a patentable product that can be sold for huge sums of money. Consequently, funding to addiction research such as Dr. Wood's increases while funding to treatment programs dwindles.

In other addiction research funded by our tax money, researchers found that dogs' breathing rate changed when they were forced to smoke cigarettes. Researchers cut nerves and repositioned them to allow better study. The dogs vomited repeatedly from being forced to smoke. This research cost $387,271 a year in 1988, but the grant had been renewed twenty-six times for a total cost of $4,729,114 over the life of the research.

Big Costs, Dubious Benefits

No doubt many practical benefits have been extracted from the methodical manipulations of animals in the laboratory, but the medical community has overstated its case by so much that it has a credibility problem. Among its current propaganda efforts is a statement to the effect that "every single major medical advance in this century has come from animal research." An honest look reveals how false this is. It is almost common knowledge that the major killer diseases of the early 1900s were pneumonia, influenza, tuberculosis, typhoid, and other infectious diseases. The death rates were brought down by better public water systems, sewage management, nutrition, and general improvements in living conditions. Tuberculosis, for example, killed 200 people per 100,000 in 1900. Decade after decade, the death rate fell steadily and by the 1950s, when the first effective antituberculosis drugs became available, the annual death rate was already below 20 per 100,000.

The elimination of typhoid followed much the same pattern, so that by the time effective drugs and vaccines became available it was already a rare disease. According to medical writer Steven Tiger, "In fact, medical intervention—the clinical application of research data—is the least important of the four factors that determine anyone's state of health." Tiger notes that the Centers for Disease Control analyzed data on the ten leading causes of death in the United States and concluded that life-style was by far the most important determinant. Life-style had a 51 percent influence, followed by environment (20 percent) and biologic inheritance (19 percent). Medical intervention had the least influence at 10 percent.

A famous study by John and Sonja McKinlay of Boston University looked at health and the medical profession between 1900 and 1973. Over the period, they found that there had been a 69 percent decrease in the overall mortality in the country and that almost all of it was attributable to the fall in the rate of infectious disease. A group of diseases including diphtheria and polio became less lethal after medical measures were introduced, but this group accounted for only 3.5 percent of the overall reduction in the death rate. The McKinlays attributed the remaining 96.5 percent reduction to improvements in the standard of living. An interesting graph in their study showed that the sharp rise in medical care expenditures came when nearly all (92 percent) of the modern decline in death rates had already occurred. As medical writer Dr. Hugh Drummond noted, "Medicine has about as much to crow about as Mozart's Papageno in defeating an already dead monster."

But crow it will because it knows it has a public obsessed with fears of cancer and other killer diseases, a public willing to believe in medical miracles, a public willing to foot the bills. These diseases are easily preventable by changes in life-style and environmental policy, but that would be to acquiesce in the laws of nature, and, besides, it would not produce as many patentable products.

So the approach is pure dominionism: Attack nature's diseases and the body's deterioration with potent medicines and exotic procedures. Conquer illness, aging, and perhaps even death. These are the last battles in the age-old war to conquer nature, we think, and winning them will place human beings in a paradise on earth.

The trouble is, the thinking is a delusion. When we believe in myths, we follow the wrong paths and seek the wrong solutions. We support directions in medical science that are wasteful, ineffective, and unrealistic. The medical community cannot deliver our order so it "makes busy," desperately trying to preserve a profitable situation. Having convinced us of its heroism, it must carry on with as much heroicity as possible.

As usual in our agri-culture, the mastery of beasts provides the best display of heroics, the strongest show of power in the struggle to dominate nature. While the matador and the rodeo cowboy carry on this struggle in a dusty, public arena, the medical scientist carries it on in the clinical seclusion of the laboratory.

Pornography: Ritual Reduction of Women

Dominionism requires many rituals to maintain its myths and beliefs in the hierarchy of being. Animals, as we have seen, bear the brunt of these rituals because they are such potent symbols of the natural forces and processes that humanity thinks it must dominate. But they are not the only symbols, or representatives, of the lower rungs of nature's ladder of being.

As we saw in Chapter 6, women and female powers must also be subdued and held in check if the patriarchal system is to function well. Patriarchy, recall, is our dominionist agri-culture's system for the control of hierarchal relations between men and women. It maintains order in those relations just as dominionism maintains relations between human beings and the rest of nature. Patriarchy, as we saw, depends greatly on various myths about the natural inferiority, evil, deceit, and so on of women. Taken together, these ideas have one common denominator: misogyny, or hatred and contempt for female people and principles.

Misogyny is kept alive and well in many forms these days, but pornography is the most obvious. Pornography is a ritual. It is one of the chief rituals of patriarchal control because it is so effective in teaching (and reaffirming) misogyny and a male-centered view of sex roles. We have touched on this before, so we can be brief here. Susan Griffin puts it best: "For above all, pornography is ritual. It is an enacted drama which is laden with meaning, which imparts a vision of the world. The altar for the ritual is a woman's body. And the ritual which is carried out on this altar is the desecration of flesh. Here, what is sacred within the body is degraded."

Pornography trashes what used to be venerated: procreation and female principles. Pornography degrades the very features of femaleness that once gave women status, power, and self-esteem. Through pornography, woman's genitals—the source of life itself, the organs of procreation—are reduced to a "cunt." Through pornography, woman's breasts, which sustain infant life, the organs of nurturing, are reduced to "tits."

The chief purpose of pornography is to destroy the possibilities that femaleness can be seen with dignity, that femaleness can be power, that it has important status. Pornography reduces femaleness to erotic tidbits, to things for male sexual pleasure, to dismembered body parts. Pornography dismantles female wholeness, which is female being, identity, and self-esteem—the collective power of which would threaten the shape of the patriarchal order. Pornography, to put it bluntly, is the ritual that keeps women in their place on the ladder of being.

Female Control: Genital Mutilation

In many parts of the world where patriarchy has spread, women are kept on their rung through more direct physical violence. In old China, a common proverb said: "A wife married is like a pony bought; I'll ride her and whip her as I like." In European custom, a man could beat his wife with a stick no bigger than his thumb. Not so long ago, Chinese patriarchy valued women with feet made tiny by painful binding. In India, widows were expected to express grief on their husband's death by throwing themselves into the flames of his funeral pyre. Throughout eastern Asia, girl babies were abandoned or neglected to death because the patriarchal families valued sons so highly.

Some of these old traditions linger today. In India, young brides are still clandestinely murdered by their husbands if her parents don't ante up enough dowry money. In the more fundamentalist parts of the Islamic world, the father still carries out his right of "honor death"—that is, to kill his sexually sinful daughter for bringing shame to the family (and ruining her bride price). In parts of Africa, the Middle East, and Southeast Asian islands, millions of Muslim women and girls have been subjected to genital mutilation, euphemistically known as female circumcision. According to Lori Heise, senior researcher at the Worldwatch Institute in Washington, D.C., these "operations" are crudely done by members of the family, who hold the girl while one of them cuts her. In the mildest form, called sunna, they remove the prepuce—the "foreskin" of the clitoris. In a more radical version, they cut away the entire clitoris and the labia minora. In the most radical version, they add infibulation—that is, they sew most of her vulva shut, leaving a small opening for urine and menstrual flow. According to the World Health Organization, more than 80 million women have suffered these mutilations in Africa alone. Women's groups there are fighting this practice, which seems to be dispersed along the Muslim belt nations of the sub-Sahara.

It is a touchy subject, castigating impoverished and colonized societies for their violations of basic human rights. But some kinds of institutionalized abuse and violence transcend nationality, ethnicity, race (if there is such a thing), and even religion. We ought to identify them without indicting an entire people and their culture. We can separate one bad tradition from—while being careful to value—the larger culture.

There are dozens of other rituals of dominionism, some old, some current. Not long ago, bull- and bear-baiting were popular European entertainments; today, cockfighting is popular across the world. There are still predator-control and extermination campaigns, which reorganize natural systems to accommodate agriculture. Perhaps more than a few still exist to reaffirm beliefs about the inferiority of some Other human group. Not long ago in this country, minstrel shows reduced African-American people through public humiliation while lynchings reduced them through community-supported mob violence. In every case, the activity is a ritual in that it reminds, reaffirms, and carries on dominionism's view of the living world as ordered in a hierarchy, or ladder, of being.

9

Beyond
Dominionism

As I write this, delegates from governments around the world are gathered in Rio de Janeiro at the first Earth Summit. There, they are discussing global threats of climate change, species extinction, and the other impacts on the planet caused by human economic and population growth. Not since the Club of Rome twenty years ago have world leaders met to discuss the question of the limits to growth. Despite official denials of the problem and George Bush's shucking and jiving about attending the Earth Summit, world opinion is that human development is taking a dangerous toll on the rest of the world.

Biologically speaking, human beings have been too successful at the expense of other species. For one thing, our numbers have swollen quite recently. The global human population first reached a billion about 150 years ago; it reached 2.5 billion only forty years ago. Our numbers are expected to pass 6 billion in the year 2000. Even if we started now to put the brakes on world birthrates, experts predict that the human population will swell to 10 to 12 billion people before it levels off around the year 2050. For another, the average human being today uses dozens of times more energy and materials than ever before. We have become very materialistic animals. We boast of our affluence barely realizing that, ultimately, all of our wealth consists of stuff taken from the environment.

There is, of course, a great disparity in materialism and affluence among societies around the world. An average American, for example, has a home full of furniture, appliances, and clothing—not to mention two or more cars and various toys, tools, gizmos, and gadgets. Americans have as

much impact on the planet as 50 × 270 million, or over 13 *billion,* Bangladeshis. Compared to this, Bangladesh's human population of 112 million is a trifle. "Viewed in this light," say the Ehrlichs, "the United States
is the world's most overpopulated nation."

Dominionism in the Food Chain

Americans use about twice as much energy and materials per capita as
the Japanese and Europeans, which doesn't exactly let them off the hook,
either. When we add up the environmental "take" of all the nations with
the highest standards of living, it is no wonder that there is not enough to
go around, and why many other nations are left poor and the planet
mutilated. Rich and poor nations combined, human beings have appropriated to their own use about 40 percent of all the energy produced by
the earth's plant life. This leaves less and less for other animals—all of
whom depend ultimately on plants to live.

Consequently, human voracity has set off a chain reaction of destruction in the world's food chains. Since we began steadily intensifying
human food production through agriculture 10,000 years ago, we have
just as steadily wiped out species after species. Now Michael Soule and
other biologists fear that human impact is setting off mass extinctions that
could wipe out a fourth of the world's remaining species in the next fifty
years. Already, one in three primate species, our closest kin on earth, are
endangered because human development in tropical regions is destroying their habitats.

Unprecedented Hunger and Poverty

Finally, this acceleration in human development has been so lopsided
that it has brought unprecedented human misery as well. When there is
too little to go around, the stronger take from the weaker. Today, one
billion people, about a fifth of the world population, are desperately poor
and living on inadequate diets. They live, barely, in the "third world,"
now called the "developing world"—those nations struggling to over-
come centuries of colonialism during which Euro-America extracted the
wealth from their environments. Euro-Americans in general take their
affluence for granted, yet it has been built on centuries of expansionism
and military power, the main features of the West's herder-influenced
agri-culture.

When we look at the imbalance of power and wealth in the world, we see clearly that the most dominionistic societies have the lion's share of both. This, of course, leaves less for the countries whom they exploit, so we have a burgeoning world underclass. Our notion of "modern progress" is either cruel or moronic when our "development" has created more people poor and hungry today than ever before in history. If this sounds like a sweeping statement, just think for a minute: This earth didn't even have a billion people until the early 1800s. Even then, not a fifth were poor and hungry because people in those days still had access to land and the means to produce their own food. Go back further—before agriculture, which is thought to have fed more people. Tribal forager peoples did not suffer massive famines and chronic starvation. They may have had a bad season and lost some weight, but they did not go hungry year in and year out. We know this from archaeological evidence, from bones, teeth, and other remains, which reveal no signs of the malnutrition and wasting diseases we see today in the children of the poorest countries in Africa, India, and Asia. We know this, too, because we understand foragers' extensive knowledge of the environment and their easy mobility within it. Strange, isn't it, that the whole of human society was better off, and probably a great deal happier, *before* we began intensifying food production.

Whether the Earth Summit in Brazil will accomplish anything of substance is anybody's guess. But at least it is another step. At least it shows that there is worldwide concern about the fate of the earth. It shows that people of all stripes are aware that human economic *progress* is threatening all life on earth. A great number of us now believe that human beings must reexamine their ideas about progress and human supremacy.

The Dysfunctional Family of "Man"

There are reasons to reexamine these ideas aside from our suicidal pressures on the planet. Even if we balanced the power and wealth among nations, we would still have our alienation and a string of other problems in our relationship with the living world. Even if we wrestled another round of technological innovations that could intensify food production and reduce environmental impacts, we would still have our malaise and our discontent with the world we have so selfishly wrought. These deep, brooding concerns are much less flashy warning signs than are strip mines, clear-cut forests, and rivers afire with toxic pollution, but they are very much with us. They eat at us every day, and yet we are barely aware of them. They corrode our souls, drive us to drink and drugs, deform family life, and rot the social fabric. Even if we had control of our population and our environmental problems, we would still have to deal with race, sex, nature, and the meaning of human existence.

As I write this, the Earth Summit in Rio de Janeiro is but one show in town featuring the excrescences of *Homo sapiens sapiens*. There are also the ethnic and religious wars among Jews, Christians, and Muslims in the Middle East, which have become so business-as-usual that they might as well have a slot of their own, like the weather, on the six o'clock news. With the breakup of the Soviet Union, whole new regions are renewing centuries-old ethnic feuds. Czechs and Slovaks hate each other so much that they are parting ways as a nation. Yugoslavia has disintegrated into a six-sided ethnic riot, which is turning into a chronic war in the Middle Eastern style. There is more of the same in the outlands of the former Soviet Union—in Azerbaijan, Ukraine, Georgia, Kazakstan, Russian Armenia, and the others.

And all across eastern Europe and into Russia, there are new revelations about mass murders carried out by both Russian and Nazi forces during the 1930s and 1940s. Towns and villages are exhuming the remains of Jews, Poles, Russians, and others who were marched into trenches, stripped naked, and shot in the head. When their bodies stopped quivering, another group was stripped and forced to lie down on the corpses to receive their bullet in the head. When the trenches were full, bulldozers pushed dirt over the corpses. According to Christopher Browning in *Ordinary Men*, some of the soldiers who participated in these massacres became nauseous from the splatter of blood and brains and asked to be assigned to other duties.

An Unprecedented Scale of War and Genocide

The scale of war and massacre has increased with the scale of both technology and society. In sheer numbers, the twentieth century has been the bloodiest in history. According to R. J. Rummel, professor of political science and a student of genocide in the twentieth century, the statistics are "monstrous." In our century alone, nearly 36 million have been killed in battle in the various wars. An incredible 120 million more have been killed by the various genocidal programs carried out by governments. Rummel says he was shocked to find that "the total killed by government in cold blood was almost four times that of war. *It was as though a nuclear war had already occurred.*" The biggest contributor to the century's mass-murdered millions was, of course, the Communist Soviet Union, especially under Joseph Stalin. Rummel puts the Soviet's total at 61,911,000 people, pointing out that it is the "most probable tally, in a range from a highly unlikely low figure of 28,326,000; to an equally unlikely high of 126,891,000." The range of uncertainty in counting the mass-murdered, he notes, is just under 100 million people.

Human devastation this huge, this constant, must have some basic causes, which the West avoids looking too deeply for. Our intellectual community blames "totalitarianism," with those on the right blaming communism and those on the left blaming facism. Others claim to see intrinsic evil and darkness in the heart of humanity. The former blame a couple of twentieth-century ideologies, the latter blame nature.

For me, the former explanations are superficial, the latter scientifically wrong. As we saw earlier, the "heart of darkness" mythology grows out of misothery—hatred and contempt for nature. Applied to humanity, it becomes misanthropy, or hatred of humankind. Since some see so much evil and darkness in nature, they tend to see the same in themselves and then that explains why human beings do such evil, dark things. Their thinking is, "this is our nature, we can't help ourselves." This thinking, by the way, is often used in self-serving ways, as when one wants to rationalize an evil deed. One can simply say, "like all humans, my heart is dark; I couldn't help myself."

For me, the concept of totalitarianism is an insufficient explanation. I agree that a handful of men with a passionately held ideology can run a police state that, in turn, can effectively control a huge population. Just to put a label on their success, however, does not explain enough. We should want to know more about the roots of totalitarianism, the strains in our culture that make it work. We know, for example, that in each of its forms it is the work of paternalistic, militaristic males who want to dominate and control the world much as they would a flock of sheep. They want to rework humanity in much the same way they would rework nature by clearing, cutting, cultivation, and husbandry. In their very agrarian view, some people are weeds that must be eradicated in order to grow better crops of others.

They tend to get away with this scheme because it accords with the worldview of us all. It appeals to many values that run deep in Western patriarchal culture. "We are not the weeds," we think, using that ladder of being in our minds. "The weeds are Jews, Slavs, Gypsies, independent peasant farmers, homosexuals, people of color, etc." The hierarchy of being built into our worldview makes it extremely easy to dehumanize these "pests," these Others, and hence extremely easy to exterminate them as we do any other animals. Thus, our agrarian culture's worldview guarantees that enough of us will fall for the early promises and rhetoric of totalitarian schemes to put that first handful of bastards in power. From then on, they have us all by our most sensitive and private parts.

The Modern Malaise—Rooted in Old Traditions

Richard Rubenstein has explored the role of Western traditions in the Nazi holocaust. The main theme of his short book *The Cunning of History*, is that the West's religion, or worldview, promotes such detachment from the world that we are able to mass destroy it and each other with neither emotional nor moral qualms. Our agrarian (he calls them Judeo-Christian) cultural traditions set us up to mass-destroy life, says Rubenstein. "When one contrasts the attitude of the savage who cannot leave the battlefield until he performs some kind of appeasement ritual to his slain enemy with the assembly-line manufacture of corpses by the millions at Auschwitz, we get an idea of the enormous religious and cultural distance Western man has traversed in order to create so unique a social and political institution as the death camp."

This scale of human misery and environmental destruction has brought a pall upon twentieth-century society, one that we try to relieve with drugs, alcohol, television, spectator sports, and other commercially available distractions. Many who have looked carefully at modern society agree with George B. Leonard that "an uncommon and persistent malaise afflicts the advanced industrial nations." Leonard says it dates at least from World War I. In twentieth-century art, film, and poetry, the feeling is expressed that modern life in the high-technology civilization is, after all, sad, lonely, meaningless, and seemingly hopeless. "Here is the hidden price of the material surplus," wrote Leonard in *The Transformation*. "We have been taught in school that increasing human control of the nonhuman world has brought us leisure and art and culture and freedom from want. We have not been taught that control over nature has also meant an equivalent control over individual human beings. We have not been taught that whatever we have gained in dominance has been paid for with the stultification of consciousness, the atrophy of the senses, the withering away of being."

Other writers have seen much of the same in modern, "developed" society. Max Horkheimer, the founder of the Frankfurt School of philosophy, wrote of the "regression of what once was called civilization," and predicted that drug epidemics would come to the totally administered society because "it will be so boring." Writing in the 1940s, Horkheimer predicted that in the Leisure and Machine Ages meaning would disappear from the world, and "with no spiritual life, people's need for dreams will be met pharmaceutically."

Sigmund Freud explored this malaise in *Civilization and Its Discontents*. We have had a deep and long-standing dissatisfaction with the state of civilization and we have built on and made it worse, Freud wrote. As a result, "we are disappointed, and all our efforts have only produced more stress, more threats, more unhappiness." Much of it, he noted, arises from our sense of control over the rest of the world: "Men have gained control over the forces of nature to such an extent that with their help they would have no difficulty in exterminating one another to the last man. They know this, and hence comes a large part of their current unrest, their unhappiness, and their mood of anxiety."

More recently, Paul Shepard explored the same themes in his book *Nature and Madness*. Millennia ago, our early agricultural civilizations "fostered a new sense of human mastery and the extirpation of nonhuman life." This ethos, he believes, has had serious repercussions for the animal- and nature-informed human mind: "A kind of madness arises from the prevailing nature-conquering, nature-hating and self- and world-denial." Shepard, as we have seen, stands out among other thinkers on the problem in that he sees animal domestication in particular as the main culprit because it provides powerful models of slavery, exploitation, and monotony of being. In exterminating wildlife to make room for our clone-like food machines, we have mangled diversity in the animal world, and in doing so we have mangled both our model for existence and our link with the living world.

Calls for Change: "Radical," "Fundamental," and So On

As awareness of our global social and environmental messes grows, we are seeing a torrent of thoughtful books, papers, and editorials, many of which suggest new directions. When reading through this literature, one is struck by how many writers call for "radical" (or words to that effect) changes in our Western worldview. Such words and thoughts are coming from high-ranking political leaders as well as respected scholars.

In March 1992, Vaclav Havel, president of an ethnically divided Czecho-slovakia, a former political prisoner of the Communist regime, and thus one who should know, wrote in the *New York Times* of the social turmoil of the modern era and of impending environmental disaster. "Man's atti-tude to the world must be radically changed," said Havel.

Twenty years earlier, California law professor Christopher D. Stone used substantially the same language in a now-famous law review article that has become one of the "bibles" of the environmental movement. In "Should Trees Have Standing?," Stone wrote of the need for "a radical new conception of man's relationship to the rest of nature." Stone thought this could help in solving our material planetary problems as well as in "making us far better humans."

Another "bible" of modern environmentalism is the 1967 essay by his-torian Lynn White, "The Historical Roots of Our Ecologic Crisis," in which White urged a "rethinking" of "fundamentals," suggesting that we "find a new religion, or rethink our old one." He proposed "the greatest radical in Christian history since Christ, Saint Francis of Assisi," as the "patron saint for ecologists."

Many theologians also echoed this call for radical new views. J. Barrie Shepherd, who wrote *Theology for Ecology,* called for a "totally new attitude" about the world around us. His colleague of the cloth, Larry Rasmussen, called for a "new ethic," one "less anthropocentric" and "more humble."

Other professionals continue the rhetoric. Lord Kenneth Clark, the art historian, wrote that "What is needed is . . . a total change in our atti-tude of mind." Amerindian writer Vine Deloria continues this line of thought and rhetoric in *God Is Red*: "We face an ecological crisis com-pounded by a spiritual crisis. We need a radical shift in our world out-look."

The list could go on and on. One can see part of the litany of famous names and famous books in *A Search for Environmental Ethics,* pub-lished in 1980 by the Smithsonian Institution. Most of its entries indict in some way Western civilization's secular and religious traditions for our messed-up relations with nature. Whether one reads the complete works of Marston Bates, David Brower, Rachel Carson, Barry Commoner, Rene Dubos, Anne and Paul Ehrlich, Aldo Leopold, John Muir, Roderick Nash, or any of the other environmentalist writers, the message is the same: Humanity needs *fundamental* changes in its relationship with nature. Their views, in general, can be summed up in the few simple words British science journalist Colin Tudge wrote for *New Scientist*: "As an evolutionary strategy, exploitation has had its day."

Blind Spot for Animals

After having laid down such strong rhetoric, however, the movers and shakers of conservation and environmentalism, with rare exceptions, stop dead in their tracks when they approach the Animal Question—the whole sticky mess of human views toward, relations with, and uses of animals. This part of the Nature Question is oddly off limits. Should one of them step on it accidentally, he or she usually jumps back to safety in the remoteness of discussions about trees or the abstractions of biodiversity and species.

The Animal Question is regarded as illegitimate, silly, peripheral. Those who address it are regarded as emotional, sentimental, neurotic, misguided, and missing the bigger picture of human relations with the living world. One's bigness and seriousness as a thinker on the Nature Question is measured, in part, by how well one steers clear of the Animal Question.

I do not belittle Professor Stone's contribution to environmental and legal thought; I simply want to show that something major is wrong here. Perhaps I can illustrate it by posing this question: How would Stone's landmark article have been received if he had entitled it "Should Chimpanzees Have Standing?" We can be sure that his reputation would be very different today. Very obviously, Professor Stone and the great majority of our other ponderers of the Nature Question are more comfortable in their relations with trees than they are with animals. This is a sorry state of affairs in both science and law, for in either discipline the case for extending legal protections to chimpanzees is far stronger than it is for trees.

And so here is another of those big, red flags that we have been noting throughout this book; they mark the areas of anthropology, psychology, biology, ethics, humanities, religion, and other disciplines where the Animal Question should be addressed, but isn't. It can hardly be a coincidence that this troublesome area should be skirted by so many professionals and scholars. Their response would probably be that it *is* trivial, or peripheral, to the larger Nature Question and so they ought to avoid it.

On the contrary, the Animal Question is the very heart of the Nature Question. As we have seen, animals have always been the soul, spirit, and embodiment of the living world. To exclude discussion of relations with animals from the discussion of our relations with nature is to exclude the most important part of the discussion. Emotionally, culturally, psychically, symbolically—just about any way you want to measure it—animals are the most vital beings among all the beings of the living world. They are fundamental to our worldview; they are central to our sense of existence in this world.

We are fooling ourselves if we think we can deal with the big picture, the mangled mess of our relations with nature, without a soul-searching examination of our dealings with animals. That would be about as fair and productive as an attempt to work out a family matter in which one refuses to consider either a spouse or the children.

Let us pose the following question to our list of important thinkers who have proposed, for example, "radical" and/or "fundamental" changes in our worldview and our relations with nature: What does a "radical/fundamental" change in worldview/relations mean if it avoids animals—the central, essential beings in nature, the beings who embody and symbolize the whole of nature?

If the call is for a sweeping overhaul of the West's agri-cultural worldview, then how can we just skirt around this huge, thorny thicket of issues?

I'll admit that the Animal Question is the biggest and the most disturbing part of the Nature Question, but this is the very reason we have to tackle it. For if we try to steer around the Animal Question, then of course we leave it in place, forever to trouble our relations with nature. If we avoid it because it is difficult, then I submit that we will continue to have difficult relations with the living world. If, as the leading thinkers and writers suggest, we must get to the bottom of this matter with nature, then we must wade into the Animal Question. The very first step is one of recognition—one of seeing how basic and, therefore, important it is.

Barriers to Approaching the Animal Question

The next step is to feel out the barriers, cultural and emotional, that fend us away from the deeper parts of the Animal Question.

When we get our feet wet and wade into it, what fears and questions come up? We need to identify these and explore their sources. When we do, we will see that many of them stem from the misothery deeply embedded in our agri-culture.

Is this misothery at work, ever trying to keep us a safe distance away from loathsome, bestial nonhuman beings? We need to listen to what our agrarian culture is telling us as we enter these murky, forbidden waters.

Is it telling us to keep away from a reunion with animality? Why do we fear that?

Do we fear our own collective Beast Within, that it may get loose, run wild, and destroy civilization?

Do we fear the recognition that we have much in common with animals? Is that because it might take away from our comforting notions of human uniqueness and supremacy?

Do we fear coming to terms with the scale of violence and injustice now institutionalized in our uses of animals?

These are just a few of the questions and fears our agri-culture raises in our minds as we try to probe the Animal Question. If we seek a genuinely *fundamental* overhaul of our thinking about our place in the living world, then these must be faced and eventually resolved.

Many of our questions will be materialistic, many others pragmatic. We wonder: What about hamburgers, Thanksgiving dinner, leather jackets, and other things we enjoy that come from animals? What about the use of animals to find cures for AIDS, cancer, and other terrible diseases?

We worry a lot about what we may have to give up if we give the Animal Question too much thought, we worry about how much worse our lives might be.

We need to identify these fears and questions, for they, too, are significant barriers to our path of exploration into the Animal Question.

One can simply note them here, without answering them, so that it is possible to move on and map out the whole terrain. They may seem like the biggest barriers at the moment, but they may not seem so once we have the bigger picture in view. When we have it, then we will be better able to reexamine all of the cost/benefit thinking that crops up whenever use of animals is brought into question.

With a list of these materialistic, pragmatic questions in hand, then, we move on to a round of questions about them.

Which are realistic? Which are irrational?

To what extent is the agrarian culture's ladder-of-being mind-set screwing up the evaluation process?

How do we put culture aside as we delve into our own culture? How do we put existing habits and values aside and try to move impersonally, objectively along the path into the whole of the Animal Question?

We will probably stumble over fears and questions every step of the way. The point here is to identify them, but not to let them be barriers to exploration and discussion of the whole area. This is what I believe we must do if we want to get into the Animal Question, the key to the entire Nature Question.

Reexamining the Human Spirit

This is why we *must* go all the way into the thicket of issues about our views of, and relations with, animals; these are at the heart of our outdated, dominionist views of, and relations with, nature.

Let me tell you why it would be *good* to do so as well. We start with the recognition that our worldview includes views of not only the living world around us, but of ourselves as individuals, as sexes, "races," and our species as a whole. This part of our worldview includes our ideas about human nature and human existence. Here is where we harbor our ideas about the nature of the human animal, *Homo sapiens sapiens*. Here we keep all of our basic notions about the nature of human sexuality, maleness, femaleness, physical differences (as in "races"), and other physical aspects of life. It includes as well our notions about instinct, temperament, and the part of human behavior we inherit, irrespective of culture and learning. Are we by nature aggressive and selfish? Or are we by nature empathetic and social? Or are these the extreme ends of a range of possibilities that are shaped by experience and culture?

Notions like these determine our identity as a species, our sense of humanity. These answer the age-old questions: Who are we, what are we, and how do we naturally behave in this world?

The aggregate of these notions is the big notion of the human spirit. This does not mean "spirit" in the sense of a ghost or a soul—some filmy, white essence that rises out of our body and goes to heaven. This is "spirit" more in the sense of spirit of the times or spirit of a nation; it means essential character or nature.

The human spirit in this sense depends, then, on the various notions of which it is made up, many of which are notions about animality—our own and that of animals who inform us and give us models. If we see the animal/natural world as we have—that is, full of vicious, oversexed, predatory beasts driven by raw, selfish instinct—then these models will shape our sense of ourselves, our human being, and they will make up the bulk of our bigger notion of the spirit of humanity, or simply, the human spirit.

Clearly, we need to stop avoiding the Animal Question. We very much need a "radical" or "fundamental" reexamination of our dominionist, agrarian culture's entire set of views of animals and animality. We need to do so because they are so basic to our worldview. We need to do so because our ideas about animals and animality determine so much of our views of *life*: human life, the life around us, and our place among it.

The Problem of Human Uniqueness

In his editorial for the *New York Times,* the one in which he wrote that "man's attitude to the world must be radically changed," Vaclav Havel also urged that "human uniqueness, human action and the human spirit must be rehabilitated." While I respect Havel's views and agree with the overall message stated in that editorial, I would rewrite his latter urging to say: "the notion of human uniqueness is a big part of our problems, the human spirit must be reconstructed, and then *humane* action can move us in better directions."

First, the whole idea of our species' uniqueness is biologically bogus. Every species is unique, by definition. The cheetah, *Acinonyx jubatus,* is unique, for if there were another group of animals just like it they would be cheetahs, too. The idea of human uniqueness makes no sense scientifically, for it is not something that exists in the real, living world. For these reasons alone, it should be rejected, for it gives us a false basis for our place in the world. If we want to come to terms with nature, we must be honest about the realities in nature and honest about ourselves as real animals in it.

True, we have unique qualities, but so does every other animal. Some humans (not including myself) have the ability to understand the inner workings of the atom, yet many kinds of animals can find their home territory from hundreds of miles away without aid of maps or instruments. We can build supersonic airplanes, yet birds can fly and cheetahs can run fifty miles an hour on their own. We, or some of us, can play the violin, yet elephants can either pick flowers or pull up trees with their noses. If we are going to claim some kind of uniqueness, then we ought to admit that it is, in the grand scheme of things, pretty relative.

Psychologist Paul Chance explored this obsession with human uniqueness in an essay for *Psychology Today.* We seem to be driven to find something, he says, that "sets us apart from the beasts of the field, the slimy things that swim in the seas and the creepy things that hide under rocks." The obsession has a long history, Chance says. It began with the ancient Greeks, who said that reason separated us from brute beasts. Then, about a hundred years ago, psychologists found that some animals, notably chimpanzees, can do simple reasoning, too. So the human community switched horses and said that creativity separated us from beasts. Then, in the sixties, psychologists found that porpoises (and many other animals) are inventive, especially in their play behavior. So humans switched again, claiming tool-making as the distinguishing ability. Then, rather quickly, Jane Goodall and other scientists found that apes and other animals make and use simple tools. Human chauvinists switched horses again and said that language makes us unique, whereupon science soon found that apes can learn to use sign language. Almost immediately, language experts redefined language in such a way that only human beings can have it.

Every step of the way, humanity has shown an obsession with finding some trait tht gives us claim to uniqueness, Chance says, "though we seem to have directed the search toward more trivial distinctions." Why do we feel compelled to do this?

Chance hits the nail on the head: We want to feel superior to animals and nature. We want to be able to point to a trait and say, he wrote, "this is what proves that we are, somehow, not really animals at all." We are trying to prove our humanhood, just as some men are forever trying to prove their manhood. The trouble is, in both cases the approach is infantile and insecure. There are enough good things about humanhood and manhood to choose for one's identity and self-esteem without having to resort to phony claims of uniqueness and superiority.

Much of the rest of the obsession with human uniqueness is pure misothery. Our agri-culture carries such hate and contempt for animals and nature that we don't want to have anything in common with them. We insist on being in a class by ourselves, special and apart from the rest of the living world. Such views and values, of course, keep us on top, in dominion over nature. If we want a radical overhaul of our worldview, then we had better address this misotherous notion of human uniqueness.

New Paradigm for the Human Spirit

We need a better, healthier sense of who we are as a species and of how we ought to carry on here among the other living beings in the world. That much all of the more thoughtful environmentalists already seem to be saying. Some of them, however, call for stewardship, which is hardly a fundamental or radical change in worldview. As we have seen, the stewardship model is paternalistic, and it still presumes a ladder of being with humans running the world in a kind of benevolent dictatorship. Stewardship, many believe, is simply a euphemism for dominionism; it is old wine in new bottles. Its hierarchical nature can be demonstrated by applying the model to human relations. Ask a native American or African-American woman if she would accept the stewardship of males or Euro-Americans.

Animals and nature, of course, can't be asked about such things; but human beings go ahead anyway, falling back on conceit and presumption, and some apply stewardship as the new model for living on earth.

A better model, or paradigm, for the human spirit would begin with biological realities. It would square well with what actually goes on in the world in which we live. It would help keep us grounded in and bonded with the living world, for only then will we have a worldview and a spirit of living that is truly natural—that is, *of* nature.

Under this principle, then, we would have to throw away the ladder of being, get down off our high horse, come down to earth, and live in kinship with other beings. We are, biologically speaking, creatures of this living world. We are animals, one evolutionary result among millions of other kinds of animals. Phylogenetically speaking, we are the youngest children of the great family of animals and it would do us good to behave accordingly and grow up a bit.

Kinsip is the biological reality here on earth, yet our dominionist culture, especially its misothery, denies it. It denigrates our evolutionary next of kin, makes us hate them and have contempt for them, and it keeps us apart from them. It puts us all alone—*over* the living world, not *in* it. It gives us a lonely station over a despicable chaos of animals and nature. No wonder we destroy the world and suffer a malaise about the state of humanity.

The Persistent Predator Paradigm

Some will object: What about the biological reality of aggression; animals kill and eat each other. Isn't that the way we are? This thinking draws from the wells of misothery in our culture. It is the popular mythology that looks to baboons, predators, and man-the-mighty-hunter as models for human existence. It is not a fair and honest view of the whole family of animals and nature.

If we look at the entire spectrum of life, we note that the overwhelming majority of beings are neither baboons nor predators. If we were to be democratic about it, we should go with the majority.

Popular views of aggression are also far off the track of current science. In the popular, mainstream mind, we are the aggressive killer ape whose violent and oppressive ways are true to our genes, our biology. This idea is a popular perversion of ideas advanced by Konrad Lorenz in the 1960s. Although Lorenz's actual theories are still misunderstood by the public, the perversions are nevertheless popular because they appear to "make sense" in this violent, misotherous culture of ours.

Lorenz's "psychohydraulic" model of aggression is mechanistic and overly simplistic, explain authors Felicity Huntingford, a zoologist, and Angela Turner, a science editor, in *New Scientist*. Lorenz thought that aggression was an instinctive "drive" that builds up, like water pressure, and has to be released. "People have taken to heart his view of an accumulating drive for aggression and many believe that humans need an outlet for aggression, such as playing violent competitive sports," say Huntingford and Turner. They point out that there has been an enormous amount of research on aggression and instinct since Lorenz. Science has now rejected the psychohydraulic theory that aggression comes from a "drive" that inevitably builds up. While the research indicates that testosterone and other hormones do influence aggression in human beings, it reveals that many other factors, including learning and culture, do as well. The authors note, for example, that several studies have shown that people become more aggressive after bouts of verbal or physical aggression and competitive sports or after watching other people behaving violently. "This modern view of the biology of aggression," note Hunter and Turner, "suggests that there is much more scope for reducing human aggression than Lorenz believed." And, we might add, more than the popular mind still believes.

In a similar survey of both the popular and scientific ideas about aggression, Melvin Konner, an anthropologist and physician, wrote for the *New York Times* about the role of testosterone. If, as it seems, men are more prone to aggression because of this hormone, then, he suggests, perhaps we ought to consider them "testosterone poisoned." This is all the more reason, Konner suggests, to have "steady, massive infusions of women into positions of power, in a balanced way, throughout the world." This, he suggests, should "reduce the risk that irrational factors— 'come on, make my day' sorts of factors—will bring about an end to life on earth."

Perhaps Konner is kidding, but not entirely. Yet it is a thought-provoking idea. Remember not long ago when it was argued that women should not hold positions of power because they become "irrational" for several days during their monthly period? If, as it now appears, men's hormones make them prone to irrational aggression and violence at all times, then men should be the ones excluded from positions of power. Logically, we should give the power to women, for they are rational most of the time and they have too little testosterone to make them constantly dangerous.

After all of the surveys and studies are considered, it can be seen that the popular view of innate human aggression is not only wrong but dangerous. We should be taking pains to teach the public the truth about "aggressive genes." Pehaps this can be understood through an analogy with a more familiar behavior, like sexual behavior. We inherit the potential for aggressive urges and behavior just as we inherit the potential for sexual urges and behavior. How we carry them out is largely determined by learning, experience, and culture. Our "genes" may prime us for these behaviors, but culture can either dampen or exaggerate them.

With this better understanding of our human nature, of ourselves, we are no longer resigned to a destiny of violence and aggression. When we understand the biological realities and the true nature of aggression, we are more free to behave otherwise.

In addition, we discover new responsibilities: to cut down on the levels of aggression and violence in our culture and to stop passing it on from generation to generation. These, too, are matters better guided by a human spirit of kinship than one of dominion. Dominion thrives on aggression and violence; kinship abhors them.

Discovering the Rest of Our Genes

Under a kinship model, we would be more interested in fulfilling our potential for *helping* behavior than in trying to rationalize our habits of oppressive, hurting behavior. There is just as much scientific evidence of innate empathy as there is of innate aggression, but the dominionist popular culture continues to believe what it wants to believe.

As noted in Chapter 3, Aaron Katcher and other psychologists believe that humans, like many mammals, inherit capacities for empathy and helping behaviors. These capacities are no accident; they evolved because they tend to strengthen the social group, which gives the species another edge on survival. In the 1970s, scientists at the National Institutes of Health found that the potential for empathy can be enhanced by learning. In a paper entitled "Learning Concern for Others," the scientists worked with groups of preschool children over a period of several weeks. The adult caretakers provided some groups of children with "high-nurturant behavior"—that is, helping, comforting, giving attention, and showing affection. Adults for the other groups offered low- and nonnurturant behavior—that is, "indifference, lack of attention and care, punitiveness."

The results were just as we might expect: The children in high-nurturant groups learned altruistic behavior and greater sympathy for others than did the children in the low- and nonnurturant groups. The highest degree of learning occurred in the nurtured children where the caretaking adults both explained caring values and modeled altruistic behaviors.

So it appears that we have genes for aggression and genes for empathy. And if we have a "selfish gene," as suggested by the book by the same title, then we also have an altruistic, or helping, gene. While these are our biological potentials, it appears that learning, experience, and culture are the greater determinants of how we ultimately behave. As things are in this agri-culture, however, we have promoted selfishness and aggression over empathy and altruism because the former better fit the dominionist worldview.

If we want to get away from the dominionist worldview and its component behaviors, we will need to invert these priorities. As I have suggested, this direction will be clearer if we have a sense of kinship as a guide. With kinship as the guiding spirit of humanity, we will *want* to promote empathy and altruism over selfishness and aggression, we will want humane action instead of domination and exploitation.

Undoing the Rituals

We could make a start with the rituals of dominionism discussed in the previous chapter. It will be hard to move away from a dominionist worldview if we keep reaffirming it and perpetuating it through *fiestas populares,* corridas, rodeos, hunting, circuses, roadside zoos, pornography, and the other popular entertainments that have ritual effects. The problem is, how do we phase out activities that are popular and provide livelihoods to many people? Efforts to ban them through legislation usually fail on these grounds.

In the case of pornography, attempts at bans and restrictions have been met with howls of protests by (mostly male) civil libertarians who consider this a "free speech" issue. Never mind that constitutional law provides that speech can be restricted when it is destructive and dangerous— for example, libelous speech or yelling "fire" in a crowded theater. Many are convinced of the extreme destructiveness of pornography, of how it destroys respect for women, the human body, and sexuality. But proof of the destructiveness is made difficult by the very patriarchal, dominionist mind-set of courts and juries. Proof is also made difficult by the sheer subjectivity of pornography: When is a picture pornographic? Reasonable men and women will disagree; but then, that is the purpose of juries—to stand in for the community and make such decisions.

Since legislatures show little inclination to ban pornography and impose criminal sanction, two women have launched an effort to make pornographers civilly liable for any rape, assault, harassment, or similar behavior caused by their pornographic materials. Writer Andrea Dworkin and legal scholar Catherine McKinnon have produced a model ordinance for adoption by municipalities. Their concept is similar to that of "dram shop" laws, which make bars liable for damages caused by drunken customers.

None of the efforts against pornography will be very successful until a greater critical mass of men and women recognize it for what it is: a ritual disguised as an entertainment that works to promote humiliation and degradation of primarily females, but also human sexuality and animality in general. Pornography treats women the way the dominionist culture treats animals. Its very popularity indicates just how acceptable such treatment is under our dominionist worldview.

As for fiestas, corridas, and rodeos, they will cease to be entertaining, and hence popular, as people cease to see animals and nature as things to be dominated and humiliated. Circuses, sleazy zoos, and live animal acts will also die on the vine for lack of popular support. In the short run, those who earnestly seek better relations with the living world—namely environmentalists, bird-watchers, ecologists, and nature-lovers of all stripes—had better recognize the ritual effect of these entertainments and how they serve to perpetuate all the destructive, old, dominionist ideas about our living world.

With that recognition, they could do much more to reduce the level of public acceptability of these rituals of dominionism. They could, for example, persuade Coca-Cola, Budweiser, and other companies to get off the rodeo circuit and to promote their products in more globally responsible ways. The nature/environmental organizations could also use their influence to discourage conscientious members of the public from attending such events. In any community, a few concerned citizens can discourage, say, a Kiwanis club from bringing the circus to town to "entertain," or should we say "brainwash," its children. Such efforts are already achieving success. In the past year, the municipal governments of Toronto, Vancouver, Victoria, and other cities passed ordinances prohibiting circuses and other entertainments that include live animal acts.

In the same way, communities and organizations can reexamine the schools, nature centers, youth groups, and other local institutions that are passing on dominionism on a daily basis. If the dominionist message is not explicit in lessons and textbooks, it is implicit in the reductionism of studies of pickled pigs and pithed frogs rather than in the wholism of ecosystems and biological interdependence. If your community has a nature center, look into what it is teaching about animals and nature. Chances are it has a few squalid cages or pens containing some of the local wildlife, which teach that animals are things to be plucked from their homes so that humans can get a closer, momentary look at them. Or it may have glass cases full of birds' nests and stuffed squirrels, which teach that animals and nature are dead objects, things on display, like jewelry or antique curios.

Less Hunting, More Companionship

Environmental and nature organizations generally support sport hunting, preferring to see it as a "management tool" rather than as a ritual of dominionism. One has to wonder sometimes whether they are not willing participants in the traditions and rituals of dominionism. When we look at their predominantly male leadership, their corporate connections, and their "resource" orientation, we have to wonder which side they may be on in the worldwide effort to come to terms with nature. About all one can do with such organizations is refuse to support them until they show more verve and commitment to changing the status quo. Their support of hunting or their silence about it may be one of the best indicators of their mind-set and the kind of visions, if any, they have for better relations with animals and nature.

Hunting, by the way, may already be on the way out, so maybe the paternalistic, Old Guard nature groups don't want to kick a colleague on the way down. A Midwestern sociologist who is also an avid hunter says that numbers of Wisconsin deer hunters will reach zero by 2050. Tom Heberlein used data from surveys by the U.S. Fish and Wildlife Service, which shows that hunter numbers are declining by 5 percent each decade.

The hunting community is, of course, alarmed by the prospect of its own death. Its efforts to reverse the trend reveal the ritual nature of hunting: The hunting establishment, according to the *Chicago Tribune,* is trying "to get hunting instruction into Wisconsin schools" so they can "pass outdoor skills to succeeding generations."

Pet breeding and the mania for "pets," unfortunately, show no signs of waning. We can have mixed feelings about this. Exploitative and wasteful of life as it is, the trend shows, as we have seen, people's ambivalence about the living world. People want to be around animals, but the problem is they do so with a dominionist mind-set, one loaded with misotherous ideas about animal nature. People do not think, for example, that animals have any social needs, any need for interaction with members of their own species. So a family gets a dog, a highly social canid, puts him or her in an apartment or a pen in the backyard, and goes off about their business.

Misothery also guides people's choices of a "pet." Macho men tend to want killer dogs, while others want cute "baby" dogs. Some people, and more and more of them, want exotic pets—pythons, ostriches, llamas, ferrets, and so on. On a conscious level, they want an unusual animal, one out of the ordinary. On a less conscious level, they are choosing an animal for its symbolism, which may be aggression, helplessness, sexiness, or some other trait that the animal may not necessarily have, but we have imposed on it. Not often do these pet lovers reject their misothery and related cultural prejudices about the animal; in fact, more often than not those ideas are the ones at work when the person made the selection.

Only in the most superficial sense, then, is the pet lover getting in touch with animality and nature. Most of the time, he or she is so steeped in the dominionist mind-set that the animal is a "pet" rather than a companion, a slave rather than a fellow kindred being. Proof that there is no real bond, but merely a one-sided, utilitarian relationship shows up in the numbers abandoned or neglected to death. Too often, when the new wears off, or when the animal begins to seem less exotic, or when some new priority in life takes over, the "pet" either wastes away or is dumped.

We want to be around animals because that, too, is in our genes. But the current pet mania is a perversion of our deeper and older bonds with animals. It is also a promoter of dominionist views and values, and we must reexamine the whole business. Perhaps we can use our desire to be around animals as an exercise to help us work from a dominionist to a kinship worldview. It would help us learn some things about animals, ourselves, and the kind of relations we ought to have with the rest of animals and nature—even if they all can't be brought into our homes.

We can ask ourselves these questions: Are we seeking a purebred animal for its "look"? Are we supporting the breeding of animals for interesting shapes and sizes that cause suffering? Are we learning to recognize the social and emotional needs of animals? Are we supporting the taking of animals from their natural habitats? Are we choosing an exotic species unsuitable for our climate and environment? Are we learning to acquire an animal as a kindred being and to provide for him or her as such? If we can become more conscious and considerate caretakers of our companion animals, then we will have a very personal, daily way to work from dominionism to kinship.

Reexamining Costs and Benefits

When we come to the laboratory and the slaughterhouse, the calls for a "radical" or "fundamental" overhaul of relations with the living world suddenly go silent. Indeed, no reasonable person challenges these bastions of dominionism. Those who do so are pegged as the "lunatic fringe," which is a handy way of disposing of them and their troublesome ideas. The overwhelming perception is that these uses of animals are well justified in that they confer great benefits to the human species. That perception is, of course, both the source and the lasting strength of dominionism.

If we want a truly "fundamental" overhaul of our dominionist worldview, then we are going to have to deal with the most difficult issues, which are meat eating and animal experimentation. Many, of course, will refuse to step onto these sacred grounds. They will simply fall back on familiar dominionist axioms and stand their ground. To be charitable, we must excuse them, for many, if not most, people are simply not inclined toward soul-searching and changing their habits. Age, subculture, and other circumstances tend to instill a certain inflexibility in many people, and it is probably best not to bother them. But for others who genuinely want to help reconstruct our worldview, our sense of ourselves, and our human spirit, nothing can be off limits for reexamination and soul-searching.

For a starting point, I suggest that we carefully reexamine the whole business relationship between animal exploitation and benefit. We aren't getting very far away from dominionism if we cling to the self-serving idea that it is all right to advance our lives at the expense of other beings— especially the closely kin, sentient ones. And there is an important practical consideration: We may not be getting as much advance, as much benefit, as our alienated, dominionist minds have tricked us into thinking.

On the contrary, the massive scale of killing animals in laboratories and slaughterhouses may be doing us more harm than good. In spite of what we have been taught (through nutritional charts and classroom aids provided, coincidentally, by the meat and dairy industries) to believe, there is overwhelming evidence now that a diet centered around animal foods is not good for our health. Similarly, a growing number believe that a medical system centered around animal experimentation, with its emphasis on heroic cures, is not so good for the overall public health.

In other words, we had better look again at the cost-benefit ratios that the dominionist worldview has attached to the traditions of animal experimentation and slaughter. I am going lightly and briefly here, mindful that many cannot read details about such matters. Anyhow, the point here is not to persuade you of the magnitude of the gore and the suffering, for it goes without saying. The point is simply to raise some of the hard questions and considerations that a kinship-minded humanity must address.

Steps Toward Ending the Killing of the Spirit

If, as it appears, animal killing for food and other benefits has always caused guilt and emotional qualms, why do we continue to do it now that we know better? Especially now that we know the realities about animals' lives—their capacities for pain and fear; their sentience, sociality, and emotionality; their physical and evolutionary kinship with us.

Might all the rituals, belief systems, misothery, distancing devices, and the other institutionalized guilt-reducers be cluttering our culture with unnecessary restraints on our natural empathy and altruism?

Might these habits of animal exploitation carry so many emotional burdens and cultural compensators that they keep us from recognizing our kinship with the rest of the living world?

True, we do not have to actually see the killing. We enable our animal industries to hide their bloody activities far from the public view so that consumers do not have to associate steaks and other products with living animals. We have institutionalized the killing, turned it over to corporate bureaucracies and thereby insulated it from our senses. So the animal-slave system does not bother us directly; still, it takes its toll on our culture, on our beliefs about animals and nature. It takes its toll in what it requires us to believe about the living world, which amounts to a worldview distorted by misothery—hatred and contempt for animality, ours and theirs.

If we want to move away from dominionist views, we will need to do something about the animal-slave system in its entirety, for it will continue to feed us beliefs and views on animality and nature that are incompatible with the construction of a human spirit of kinship.

We will need agriculture, of course, as we are not likely to return to a forager way of life. But it must not be an agriculture guided by dominionist, nature-busting values. We will need new technologies of agriculture guided by new cultural values, such as our kinship with other life and the sanctity of the living world. Our agriculture, and our agrarian culture, must give up their strategies of relentless control of nature and of ceaseless intensification of agricultural systems and methods. From now on, our overriding strategy should be to control, instead, human population growth and to intensify the systems and methods that can do it successfully and humanely. A secondary strategy, which our new agriculture must incorporate, should be to improve the quality of life of the whole living world—not just the human part of it.

Fortunately, these better directions are already making headway against the mainstream of machinery- and chemical-intensive corporate agriculture. In recent years, the organic agriculture movement has grown by leaps and bounds and has gained acceptance in the marketplace. More recently, there has been a surge of interest in sustainable agriculture, which endeavors to use natural cycles and to minimize mechanical and chemical inputs. Both of these directions put more of a priority on soil health and food quality than they do on bushels per acre and other bean-counter measures of productivity.

Men, Women, and Sexual Ethics

In the huge area of relations between men and women, we have many fields ripe for change. The patriarchal system, which the West has spread far and wide through its invasions, migrations, missionaries, and colonialism, has distributed inequality, abuse, and a range of human rights violations around the world. Patriarchal culture now overlays the older culture of many formerly egalitarian societies. Beyond the injustices it inflicts on women around the world, it deprives humanity of half its energy, talent, and experience in an age when we need all the help we can get.

In addition, patriarchy's relegation of women to the role of breeders and child-rearers works against efforts to reduce birth rates and to reverse world population growth. For those who have not made the connection already, feminism *is* environmentalism in the world of today.

Feminism and environmentalism in this sense must include efforts to bring economic and political stability to developing countries where high birth rates and population densities maintain the cycle of poverty—the

"Downward Spiral" that we discussed in Chapter 1. In the poorest nations, it has been shown that high birth rates are linked to high infant mortality and the insecurities of living in an impoverished human community. As families in such regions come to enjoy adequate nutrition, health care, and economic security, birth rates drop dramatically.

My proposal will not be pleasing to wealthy, developed societies, but they are going to have to return some of the wealth they have stolen from the poorest regions during the colonial/imperial period. This sharing of wealth will be a key factor in building the global political stability and economic security needed before we can bring human numbers and material demands down to levels at which our species can once again live in balance—in kinship—with the rest of the living world.

What then remains, of course, is the task of stripping away patriarchal culture, with its models for sexuality, manhood, and womanhood. The traditional agrarian values, which favor strict gender roles, large families, and taboos against nonprocreative sexuality, must now be seen as not only unjust and unnatural but as ecologically insane. If, as the record shows, some 10 to 15 percent of the human population is naturally, normally homosexual, then the hate campaigns and witch-hunts against these people are the big sins, not the "homosexual acts" themselves. In the spirit of kinship with the living world, heterosexual human beings would embrace their brothers and sisters who are able to be passionate and loving without increasing human numbers. Although mainstream environmental organizations are now reluctant to speak out on this controversial, hate-laden issue, our society's treatment of gay men and lesbian women is as antinature, as ecologically stupid, as clear-cutting or toxic pollution.

As for heterosexual men and women, they need to get away from the agri-culture's patriarchal model that has pinched the broad range of human sexuality and gender types into the narrow dualism of father-leader versus mother-breeder. Our agrarian tradition holds that a man needs a woman's (sexual and household) services and that a woman does not "fulfill her destiny" unless she bears children. Single people and childless couples are harassed and pressured, with the result that too many people breed children they don't really want. This keep-up-with-the-Joneses style of parenthood is probably a major factor in today's epidemic of dysfunctional families and child abuse. Those who work in the schools, hospitals, and juvenile courthouses know that our society has an enormous number of families, rich and poor, in which the children are unwanted, unloved, and given about as much attention as the furniture. While most people do want to rear children, I suspect that a great many, if fully free from patriarchal models and peer pressures, would probably choose not to do so.

Steps Toward the New Ethic

The first step is the implementation of swift and active efforts to remove the old agrarian clamps on our broad, natural human sexuality—remove prejudices against same-sex love, the taboos on nonprocreative sex, and the mom-dad dualism that push the breeding of unwanted children. Beyond that, we need deeper consideration of some of the ideas on human sexuality that have been discussed for years but avoided because they are too "radical" or controversial for the mainstream media. British ecologist Frank Fraser Darling brought many of them up in "Wilderness and Plenty," a series of six lectures given in the United Kingdom in 1969; he explained how a new human sexuality must be a part of the process of our coming to terms with nature—both within and around us. In his lectures, reports Anne Chisholm in *Philosophers of the Earth,* Darling criticized the emphasis major religions placed on reproduction in the midst of a global human population problem. He called for a "new ethic of sexuality" that would be "joined with an ethic of the wholeness of life, giving us a reverence for lower forms. . . ." These two ethics should work together synergistically to "influence the attitudes of the West towards our exploitation of land and animal life," Darling said.

Much of the direction toward a new sexuality is already being provided by the feminist and gay rights movements. In response, however, many heterosexual men are expressing a collective feeling of resentment about being branded villains and being excluded from the new directions. This male resentment has created a whole new consumer group for the workshops, ritual sweats, and other ego therapies of the Men's Movement. Fathered and purveyed to by Robert Bly, poet and author of the bestseller *Iron John;* by Sam Keen, author of *Fire in the Belly,* another bestseller; by Douglas Gillette, author of *King, Warrior, Magician, Lover;* and many lesser poets, the Men's Movement offers men a place to "talk about their pain," according to *Newsweek,* and a chance to redefine masculinity.

While we can see the male resentment, the need to talk about pain, and the need to redefine manhood, the Men's Movement reveals more than a tad of defensiveness, not to mention an awful lot of reactionary "mythopoesy." Bly's *Iron John,* for example, takes us through a 260-page fairy tale about a beast-man of that name who is befriended by the son of a king. Through a steady stream of Jungian interpretations, Bly explains that the problem with men today is that they have inadequate initiation—rites of passage—into manhood. In his view, this situation is caused largely by the Industrial Revolution, which has made fathers absent in one way or another—through workaholism, alcoholism, or simple emotional indifference.

Bly's reliance on old fairy tales and folklore makes for an entertaining read, but it gives the not-so-subtle impression that our solutions lie in reverting to an older patriarchal order, its dualized male/female roles, sex separation, initiation rites, and so on. If Bly were willing to consider feminist ideas on patriarchal culture, he would understand that it has always produced cold, distant fathers—men who are always busy hunting, herding, preparing for war, or otherwise preoccupied with their "man's world"; men who carry disdain for the "woman's world" of child-rearing, food production, and household maintenance. Poor fatherhood is no recent phenomenon. It may have been made worse by the workaday life-style imposed by the Industrial Revolution, but its roots are much older.

The Men's Movement, we hope, will see that fatherhood suffers because of many aspects of the agrarian patriarchal culture: a misogynist disdain for the "woman's world" and "woman's work"; men-only groups, which set men apart from women and young children; values on stoicism and hardness, which keep fathers, even when home, emotionally unavailable to others in the family. The list could go on through the many facets of patriarchal culture's ideal man—the cool, tough, bellicose, controlling macho hero.

But men, I must take pains to emphasize, are not thoroughly rotten as they are often portrayed in the lore of the antihero. I do not bash all of men, maleness, and manhood. I am suggesting that we focus on those few values and ideals of the old patriarchal culture that have made men grow up tough, mean, and distant. These are hardly needed today. We don't need to be turning out hunters, warriors, and herders in this day and age. These strands of male culture are irrelevant and destructive, and a progressive men's movement would pluck them like weeds. But this sort of weeding will be difficult for men, many of whom are unwilling to give up the power and control conferred by these strands of male culture. These men know from experience that tough, macho men often get their way in the world. It will be up to the rest of us to teach them that the bully's days are over.

What makes Bly and the rest of the Men's Movement offerings so popular, of course, is the strong appeal of simplicity and familiar tradition in an age when sex roles and sexuality seem in turmoil. Moreover, this "movement" offers ego relief to men who are being made to feel responsible for the world's ills. Finally, it doesn't call on men to do very much other than to reaffirm their masculinity with drums, bonfires, and sweat lodges at weekend retreats. For $250 a pop, a man can revisit the camaraderie of ancient hunter/warrior rituals and presumably feel like a real, old-fashioned powerful male again.

New Models for Manhood

Trendy though it is, this sort of men's movement misguides the male resentment and offers a Band-Aid for the deep wounds patriarchy has inflicted on the body of human sexuality and sexual identity. We should strive for a scientific rather than "mythopoetic" approach, one that goes to the primal source of male resentment: the perception that women are closer to the powers of nature. Embedded in primal culture, this notion expanded into the rise of female principles, female power, and the great mother-goddess religions of the early agricultural period. In time, as we saw, the discovery of fatherhood and other factors brought on male principles and power with a vengeance. Ever since, there has been a "war between the sexes." Ever since, the patriarchal system has dictated rigid roles for men and restricted roles for women.

From this approach, men can understand the mistakes of the past and how they congealed into traditions that warp our culture today. Men today needn't feel responsible for the mistakes of both men and women who lived 5,000 years ago. Men do have a huge responsibility, however, to participate in the processes of restoring female principles, status, and power to society and of building an egalitarian sexual ethic. These are difficult tasks, of course, and no group that has long enjoyed supremacy and privilege of any kind has ever relinquished them gladly.

These and other chores offer plenty of opportunities for men to find and build on their humanity, as opposed to carrying on boyish displays of macho manhood. In the past, men showed bravery in the hunt or in battle; they showed "strength" in taking pain and dishing it out without feeling.

Instead of macho displays, the modern man can show genuine *human* bravery and strength. He can be brave enough to tackle the thorny strands of tradition that warp human society and threaten the living world.

Men can have the strength to accept an equal role in the house, at work, in bed, and in society as a whole.

Men, the predominant makers and users of pornography, can have the bravery and strength to dismantle this industry that degrades women, the human body, sexuality, and nature.

Men, whose traditional masculine culture values stoicism, detachment, and control of others, can use their strength to uproot those values and to build a culture that values empathy, altruism, and kinship with all Others—regardless of sex, "race," size, or species.

Religions and the Spirit of Kinship

In reading for this book, one insight struck me especially deeply: We are coming full circle around to the kind of awareness held by primal human society. We see the awesome web of life in the world; we see the human place among it all. We see the cycles of birth, life, death, and rebirth that keep all of nature alive and evolving. We see the living world as a First Being made up of many lesser beings, of which we are one. We see the miracle of living existence animated and given character by animals. We feel for animals, whom we see as kindred beings; they give us a sense of belonging here, of membership in the Great Family of life in this world. Our ancestors gained this worldview through real experience; we are gaining it, ironically, through science.

This emerging global view conflicts with many of the main beliefs of the West's agrarian religion, which sees this world as a temporary testing ground for humankind, as a lowly way station full of soulless beings whose despicable existence offers temptations to sin and evil. It will be interesting to see if religion's various branches can accommodate the emerging understanding of humans as beings kindred with others in the living world. If they cannot, they will become increasingly irrelevant. If they are unable to join the rest of us in coming to terms with nature and finding kinship among the life around us, they will cease to provide spiritual guidance and comfort and they will fall away as religions have done before.

I am pessimistic that the West's monotheistic religion will be able to move forward in the spirit of kinship, based as it is on a theology of human dominion. Nevertheless, its established churches and sects are major carriers of culture from one generation to the next and, as such, we would be wiser to try to alter their directions than to stop them. Perhaps the best that the progressive faithful can do is search for and revive their own long-suppressed traditions that come closest to embracing a spirit of kinship with the living world. The Christian religion has its St. Francis of Assisi, whose legacy is, unfortunately, rather mixed with good but patronizing views of animals and bad views of women. Less well known is Julian of Eclanum, who was St. Augustine's rival in the debate over the evils of sex and nature. No doubt there are many, many other long-suppressed ideas in the Judeo-Christian-Islamic religion that would, if revived, contribute some healing to the spiritual, sexual, and environmental crises we now find ourselves in. One hopes that the progressive faithful can find them and successfully revive them.

In addition to the search for relevant views within its own tradition, Western religion needs to come to terms with its ancestor religions—the "idolators," "pagans," goddess-worshipers, and the other belief systems that the monotheists so ruthlessly tried to stamp out. Many traces of these are alive and well today in the developing world despite centuries of mostly Christian and Islamic missionary campaigns. Judaism, to its credit, never sought to impose its theology and its God on other peoples and cultures. If Christianity and Islam can get beyond their current phase of strict fundamentalism and their obsessions with the "revealed word of God" on the printed page, they could bring massive mending to the spiritually torn fabric of humanity. When they recognize that human spirituality began with awe of life on earth and that humanity has always found comfort in a sense of kinship with the living world, perhaps they will see the need for, and the wisdom in, coming full circle to the primal worldview.

My own view is that the primal worldview, updated by a scientific understanding of the living world, offers the best hope for a human spirituality. Life on earth is the miracle, the sacred. The dynamic living world is the creator, the First Being, the sustainer, and the final resting place for all living beings—humans included. We humans evolved with other living beings; their lives informed our lives. They provided models for our existence; they shaped our minds and culture. With dominionism out of the way, we could enjoy a deep sense of kinship with the other animals, which would give us a deep sense of belonging to our living world.

Then, once again, we could *feel* for this world. We could feel included in the awesome family of living beings. We could feel our continuum with the living world. We could, once again, feel a genuine sense of the sacred in the world.

References

Anglemyer, Mary, Eleanor R. Seagraves, and Catherine C. LeMaistre. *A Search for Environmental Ethics: An Initial Bibliography.* Washington, D.C.: Smithsonian Institution Press, 1980.

Anthony, David, Dimitri Y. Telegin, and Dorcas Brown. "The Origin of Horseback Riding." *Scientific American,* December 1991, pp. 94–100.

Anthony, David W. *The Domestication of the Horse.* Vol. 2 of *Equids in the Ancient World.* Edited by Richard H. Meadow and Hans-Peter Uerpmann. Wiesbaden, Ger.: Ludwig Reichert Verlag, 1991.

Arciniegas, German. *America in Europe: A History of the New World in Reverse.* New York: Harcourt Brace Jovanovich, 1983.

Ardrey, Robert. *The Hunting Hypothesis.* New York: Atheneum, 1976.

Aristotle. *On Man in the Universe.* Roslyn, N.Y.: Walter J. Black, 1943.

Bacon, Francis. *Novum Organum.* Edited by Joseph Devey. New York: American Home Library Co., 1902.

Beck, Alan, and Aaron Katcher. *New Perspectives on Our Lives with Animals.* Philadelphia: University of Pennsylvania Press, 1983.

———. *Between Pets and People: The Importance of Animal Companionship.* New York: Putnam Publishing Group, Perigree Books, 1984.

Belleme, John. "Animal Research Under Fire." *East West,* March 1989, p. 59.

Berger, Peter. *The Sacred Canopy.* Garden City, N.Y.: Doubleday, 1967.

Bernheimer, Richard. *Wild Men in the Middle Ages.* New York: Farrar, Straus & Giroux, Octagon Books, 1979.

Bettelheim, Bruno. *Symbolic Wounds: Puberty Rites and the Envious Male.* Glenco, Ill.: Free Press, c. 1954.

Bibby, Geoffrey. *The Testimony of the Spade.* New York: Knopf, 1956.

Bilbo, Theodore G. See: "Senator Bilbo's Monumental Book . . ."

Blount, Margaret. *Animal Land: The Creatures of Children's Fiction.* New York: William Morrow & Co., 1975.

Bly, Robert. *Iron John*. Reading, Mass.: Addison-Wesley, 1990.

Boulding, Elise. *The Underside of History: A View of Women Through Time*. Boulder, Colo.: Westview Press, 1976.

Bowd, Alan. "Young Children's Beliefs About Animals." *Journal of Psychology* 110 (1982):263–66.

———. "The Understanding of Animal Suffering by Young Children." *Humane Education Journal* 4 (1982):5–7.

Bowden, Charles. "Love Among the Lion Killers." *Buzzworm: The Environmental Journal*, Autumn 1989, pp. 41–45.

Braidwood, Robert J. *Prehistoric Men*, 7th ed. Glenview, Ill.: Scott, Foresman and Company, 1967.

Brandon, William. *New Worlds for Old: Reports from the New World and Their Effect on the Development of Social Thought in Europe, 1500–1800*. Athens: Ohio University Press, 1986.

Brown, Joseph Epes. *The Sacred Pipe*. Norman: University of Oklahoma Press, 1953.

Browning, Christopher R. *Ordinary Men: Reserve Battalion 101*. New York: HarperCollins, 1992.

Caldicott, Helen. *Missile Envy: The Arms Race and Nuclear War*, rev. ed. New York: Bantam Books, 1986.

Campbell, Joseph. *The Way of the Animal Powers*. Vol. 1 of Historical Atlas of World Mythology. New York: Harper & Row, Perennial Library, 1988.

———. *The Way of the Seeded Earth*. Vol. 2 of Historical Atlas of World Mythology. San Francisco: Harper & Row, 1988.

Canny, Nicholas, and Anthony Pagden. *Colonial Identity in the Atlantic World, 1500–1800*. Princeton, N.J.: Princeton University Press, 1987.

Carson, Gerald. *Men, Beasts, and Gods*. New York: Charles Scribner's Sons, 1972.

Casas, Bartolome de las. *The Devastation of the Indies: A Brief Account*. Translated by Herma Briffault. New York: Seabury Press, 1974.

Cassell, Eric J. "The Limits of Modern Medicine." *Wall Street Journal*, August 2, 1977, p. 12.

Chance, Paul. "Apart from Animals." *Psychology Today*, January 1988, p. 18.

Chisholm, Anne. *Philosophers of the Earth*. New York: E. P. Dutton, 1972.

Chodorow, Nancy. *The Reproduction of Mothering: Psychoanalysis and the Reproduction of Mothering*. Berkeley: University of California Press, 1978.

———. "Family Structure and Feminine Personality." In Rosaldo and Lamphere, *Woman, Culture and Society*.

Clark, Grahame. *World Prehistory: A New Outline*, 2nd ed. London: Cambridge University Press, 1969.

Clark, Joseph. *Beastly Folklore*. Metuchen, N.J.: Scarecrow Press, 1968.

Clark, Kenneth. *Animals and Men*. New York: William Morrow & Co., 1977.

Clutton-Brock, Juliet. *A Natural History of Domesticated Animals*. Cambridge and London: Cambridge University Press and British Museum (Natural History), 1987.

———. *The Walking Larder: Patterns of Domestication, Pastoralism, and Predation*. One World Archaeology Series No. 2. London: Unwin Hyman, 1990.

——. "How The Wild Beasts Were Teamed." *New Scientist,* February 15, 1992, pp. 41–43.

Cohen, Mark Nathan. *Health and the Rise of Civilization*. New Haven, Conn.: Yale University Press, 1989.

Cohen, Michael J. *Prejudice Against Nature*. Freeport, Maine: Cobblesmith, 1983.

Collard, Andree, with Joyce Contrucci. *Rape of the Wild: Man's Violence Against Animals and the Earth*. Bloomington: Indiana University Press, 1989.

Columbus, Christopher. *Four Voyages to the New World* (Letters and Selected Documents). Edited and translated by R. H. Major. Gloucester, Mass.: Corinth Books, 1978.

Cook, Joan Marble. *In Defense of Homo Sapiens*. New York: Farrar, Straus & Giroux, 1975.

Coontz, Stephanie, and Peta Henderson, eds. *Women's Work, Men's Property*. Thetford, Norfolk: Thetford Press, 1986.

Cornforth, Maurice. *Historical Materialism*, vol. 2: *Dialectical Materialism: An Introduction*. New York: International Publishers, 1971.

Costello, David F. *The Prairie World*. New York: Thomas Y. Crowell Co., 1969.

Cranstone, B. A. L. "Animal Husbandry: The Evidence from Ethnography." In Ucko and Dimbleby, *Domestication and Exploitation*.

Crosby, Alfred W. *Ecological Imperialism: The Biological Expansion of Europe 900–1900*. Cambridge: Cambridge University Press, 1986.

Curtin, Philip D. *The Rise and Fall of the Plantation Complex*. Cambridge: Cambridge University Press, 1990.

Curtis, Patricia. *The Urban Dog*. New York: Bantam Books, 1986.

Dahlberg, Frances, ed. *Woman the Gatherer*. New Haven, Conn.: Yale University Press, 1981.

Daly, Mary. *Gyn/ecology: The Metaethics of Radical Feminism*. Boston: Beacon Press, 1978.

Darling, Frank Fraser. *Wilderness and Plenty*. Boston: Houghton Mifflin, 1970.

Darlington, C. D. "The Silent Millennia in the Origin of Agriculture." In Ucko and Dimbleby, *Domestication and Exploitation*.

DeBeauvoir, Simone. *The Second Sex*. Translated by H. M. Parshley. New York: Knopf, 1953.

Debo, Angie. *A History of the Indians of the United States*. Vol. 106 of The Civilization of the American Indian. Norman: University of Oklahoma Press, 1970.

——. *Prairie City*. Tulsa, Okla.: Council Oak Books, 1985.

de las Casas, Bartolome. See: Casas, Bartolome de las.

de Sade, Marquis. See: Sade, Marquis de.

Descartes, René. *Discourse on the Method of Rightly Conducting the Reason*. Translated by Elizabeth S. Haldande and G. R. T. Ross. Vol. 31 of Great Books of the Western World. Chicago: Encyclopaedia-Britannica, Inc., 1971.

Diamond, Irene, and Gloria F. Orenstein, eds. *Reweaving the World: The Emergence of Ecofeminism*. San Francisco: Sierra Club Books, 1990.

Diamond, Stanley, ed. *Primitive Views of the World*. New York: Columbia University Press, 1960.

Dickason, Olive Patricia. *The Myth of the Savage: And the Beginnings of French*

Colonialism in the Americas. Edmonton, Canada: University of Alberta Press, 1984.

Dijkstra, Bram. *Idols of Perversity: Fantasies of Feminine Evil in Fin-de-Siècle Culture*. Oxford: Oxford University Press, 1986.

Doughty, Charles M. *Travels in Deserta Arabia*. Gloucester, Mass.: Peter Smith, 1968.

Drummond, Hugh. "Pocketa Pocketa Machines." *Mother Jones,* January 1978, p. 32.

"Drums, Sweat and Tears." *Newsweek,* June 24, 1991, p. 46.

Dudley, Edward, and Maximillian E. Novak. *The Wild Man*. Pittsburgh, Pa.: University of Pittsburgh Press, 1972.

Dworkin, Andrea. *Pornography: Men Possessing Women*. New York: G. P. Putnam's Sons, Perigee Books, 1981.

Eisler, Riane. *The Chalice and the Blade: Our History, Our Future*. San Francisco: Harper & Row, 1987.

Ehrenfeld, David. *The Arrogance of Humanism*. New York: Oxford University Press, 1978.

Ehrenreich, Barbara, and Deirdre English. *For Her Own Good: 150 Years of the Expert's Advice to Women*. Garden City, N.Y.: Anchor Press/Doubleday, 1979.

Ehrlich, Paul R., and Anne H. Ehrlich. *The Population Explosion*. New York: Simon & Schuster, 1990.

———. *Healing the Planet: Strategies for Resolving the Environmental Crisis*. Reading, Mass.: Addison-Wesley, A Robert Ornstein Book, 1991.

Emery, Glenn. "Big Game Hunters Call the Shots." *Washington Times,* August 8, 1988, p. E1.

Engels, Frederick. *The Origin of the Family, Private Property and the State*. New York: International Publishers, 1975.

Farb, Peter. *Man's Rise to Civilization: The Cultural Ascent of the Indians of North America,* rev. ed. New York: E. P. Dutton, 1978.

Ferris, Robert G., ed. *Prospector, Cowhand and Sodbuster*. Vol. 11 of the National Survey of Historic Sites and Buildings. Washington, D.C.: National Park Service, U.S. Department of the Interior, 1967.

Fisher, Elizabeth. *Woman's Creation: Sexual Evolution and the Shaping of Society*. Garden City, N.Y.: Anchor Press/Doubleday, 1979.

Fox, Robin. *Encounter with Anthropology*. New York: Harcourt Brace Jovanovich, 1968.

Frantz, Joe B., and Julian Ernest Choate. *The American Cowboy: Myth and Reality*. Norman: University of Oklahoma Press, 1955.

Freud, Sigmund. *Civilization and Its Discontents*. Translated by James Strachey. New York: W. W. Norton and Co., 1961.

Fried, Morton, ed. *Readings in Anthropology,* 2d ed. New York: Thomas Y. Crowell Co., 1968.

Gill, S. D., *Beyond the Primitive: Religions of the Non-Literate Peoples*. Englewood Cliffs, N.J.: Prentice-Hall, 1982.

Gimbutas, Marisa. "The First Wave of Eurasian Steppe Pastoralists into Copper Age Europe." *Journal of Indo-European Studies* 5 (Winter 1977):277.

————. *Goddesses and Gods of Old Europe, 7000–3500 B.C.* Berkeley: University of California Press, 1982.

————. *The Language of the Goddess.* London: Thames & Hudson, 1989.

Girard, Rene. *Violence and the Sacred.* Translated by Patrick Gregory. Baltimore: The Johns Hopkins University Press, 1977.

Glacken, Clarence J. *Traces on the Rhodian Shore: Nature and Culture in Western Thought from Ancient Times to the End of the Eighteenth Century.* Berkeley: University of California Press, 1967.

Gray, Elizabeth Dodson. *Green Paradise Lost.* Wellesley, Mass.: Roundtable Press, 1981.

————. *Patriarchy as a Conceptual Trap.* Wellesley, Mass: Roundtable Press, 1982.

Gregg, Susan Alling. *Foragers and Farmers: Population Interaction and Agricultural Expansion in Prehistoric Europe.* Chicago: University of Chicago Press, 1988.

Griffin, Susan. *Woman and Nature: The Roaring Inside Her.* New York: Harper & Row, 1978.

————. *Pornography and Silence: Culture's Revenge Against Nature.* New York: Harper & Row, 1981.

Guggisberg, C. A. W. *Man and Wildlife.* New York: Arco Publishing Inc., 1970.

Hammond, Dorothy, and Alta Jablow. *Women in Cultures of the World.* Menlo Park, Calif.: Cummings Publishing Co., 1976.

Harris, Marvin. *Cannibals and Kings: The Origins of Cultures.* New York: Random House, 1977.

Havel, Vaclav. "The End of the Modern Era." *New York Times,* March 1, 1992, op-ed page.

Hawkes, Jacquetta. *Man on Earth.* New York: Random House, 1955.

Hawkes, Jacquetta, and Sir Leonard Wooley. *Prehistory and the Beginnings of Civilization.* Vol. 1 of History of Mankind: Cultural and Scientific Development. New York: Harper & Row, 1963.

Heise, Lori. "Crimes of Gender." *World Watch.* March/April 1989, pp. 12–21.

Hersey, John. *Hiroshima.* New York: Knopf, 1946.

Hilberg, Raul. *The Destruction of the European Jews.* New York: Holmes & Meiter, 1985.

Hildebrand, John. "Get Your Deer Yet?" *Harrowsmith/Country Life,* September/October 1990, p. 12.

Hilgartner, Stephen, Richard C. Bell, and Rory O'Connor. *Nukespeak.* San Francisco: Sierra Club Books, 1982.

Holbrook, Stewart H. *Machines of Plenty: Pioneering in American Agriculture.* New York: Macmillan, 1955.

The Holy Bible. Authorized (King James) Version.

Horkheimer, Max. *Dawn and Decline.* New York: Seabury Press, 1978.

Hultkranz, Ake. *The Religions of the American Indians.* Translated by Monica Setterwall. Berkeley: University of California Press, 1979.

Huntingford, Felicity, and Angela Turner. "Aggression: A Biological Imperative?" *New Scientist,* August 4, 1988, p. 44.

Husar, John. "Sociologist Says Deer Hunting to Vanish." *Chicago Tribune,* January 12, 1992, p. 22.

The Interpreter's Bible, vol. 1. Nashville, Tenn.: Abingdon Press, 1952.

Jerome, Norge W., Randy F. Kandel, and Gretel H. Pelto. *Nutritional Anthropology: Contemporary Approaches to Diet and Culture.* Pleasantville, N.Y.: Redgrave Publishing Company, 1980.

Jordan, Winthrop D. *White Over Black: American Attitudes Toward the Negro, 1550–1812.* Chapel Hill: University of North Carolina Press, 1968.

———. *The White Man's Burden: Historical Origins of Racism in the United States.* Oxford: Oxford University Press, 1974.

Kellert, Stephen. "Affective, Cognitive, and Evaluative Perceptions of Animals." In *Behavior and the Natural Environment,* edited by Irwin Altman and Joachim F. Wohlwill. New York: Plenum Press, 1983.

Klingender, Francis. *Animals in Art and Thought to the End of the Middle Ages.* London: Routledge and Kegan Paul, 1971.

Konner, Melvin. "The Aggressors." *New York Times Magazine,* August 14, 1988, p. 33.

Lamberg-Karlovsky, C. C., and Jeremy A. Sabloff. *Ancient Civilizations: The Near East and Mesoamerica.* Prospect Heights, Ill.: Waveland Press, Inc., 1979.

Lame Deer, John, and Richard Erdoes. *Lame Deer, Seeker of Visions.* New York: Simon & Schuster, 1972.

Lawrence, Elizabeth Atwood. *Rodeo: An Anthropologist Looks at the Wild and the Tame.* Chicago: University of Chicago Press, 1984.

———. *Hoofbeats and Society.* Bloomington: Indiana University Press, 1985.

Leacock, Eleanor Burke. *Myths of Male Dominance: Collected Articles on Women Cross-Culturally.* New York: Monthly Review Press, 1981.

Leakey, Richard E., and Roger Lewin. *Origins.* New York: E. P. Dutton, 1977.

Lee, R. B., and I. DeVore, eds. *Man the Hunter.* Chicago: Aldine, 1968.

Leeds, Anthony, and Andrew P. Vayda, eds. *Man, Culture and Animals: The Role of Animals in Human Ecological Adjustments.* Washington, D.C.: American Association for the Advancement of Science, 1965.

Leiss, William. *The Domination of Nature.* New York: George Braziller, 1972.

Leonard, George B. *The Transformation: A Guide to the Inevitable Changes in Humankind.* New York: Delacorte Press, 1972.

Lerner, Gerda. *The Creation of Patriarchy.* New York: Oxford University Press, 1986.

Lesy, Michael. *The Forbidden Zone.* New York: Farrar, Straus & Giroux, 1987.

Levinson, Boris M. *Pets and Human Development.* Springfield, Ill.: Charles C Thomas, 1972.

Lewinsohn, Richard. *Animals, Men and Myths.* New York: Harper and Bros., 1954.

Lopez, Barry. *Of Wolves and Men.* New York: Charles Scribner's Sons, 1978.

———. *Arctic Dreams: Imagination and Desire in a Northern Landscape.* New York: Charles Scribner's Sons, 1986.

Lorenz, Konrad. *Civilized Man's Eight Deadly Sins.* New York: Harcourt Brace Jovanovich, 1972.

Lumbreras, Luis G. *The Peoples and Cultures of Ancient Peru.* Translated by Betty J. Meggers. Washington, D.C.: Smithsonian Institution Press, 1974.

MacNeish, Richard S. "Ancient Mesoamerican Civilization." In Fried, *Readings in Anthropology.*

Madson, John. *Where the Sky Began.* Boston: Houghton Mifflin, 1982.

Maekawa, Kazuya. "Animal and Human Castration in Sumer." Part I: Cattle and Equids. *Zinbun* 15 (1979):95–140. Kyoto, Japan: Research Institute for Humanistic Studies, Kyoto University.

———. "Female Weavers and Their Children in Lagash—Pre-Sargonic and Ur III." *Acta Sumerologica* 2 (1980):81–125.

———. "Animal and Human Castration in Sumer." Part II: Human Castration in the Ur III Period. *Zinbun* 16 (1980): 1–55. Kyoto, Japan: Research Institute for Humanistic Studies, Kyoto University.

Martin, Calvin. *Keepers of the Game: Indian-Animal Relationships and the Fur Trade.* Berkeley: University of California Press, 1982.

Martin, James Kirby. *Interpreting Colonial America.* New York: Harper & Row, 1978.

McFarland, Cole. "Death in the Afternoon." *The Animals' Voice,* Premiere Issue, no. 1 (1988):32.

———. "Of Tourism and Torment." *The Animal's Voice,* Premiere Issue, no. 1 (1988):41.

McLuhan, T. C. *Touch the Earth: A Self-Portrait of Indian Existence.* New York: Outerbridge and Dienstfrey, 1971.

Mellaart, James. *The Earliest Civilizations of the Near East.* New York: McGraw-Hill, 1965.

———. *The Neolithic of the Near East.* London: Thames & Hudson, 1975.

Merchant, Carolyn. *The Death of Nature: Women, Ecology and the Scientific Revolution.* San Francisco: Harper & Row, 1980.

Midgley, Mary. *Beast and Man: The Roots of Human Nature.* Ithaca, N.Y.: Cornell University Press, 1978.

Milanich, Jerald T., and Susan Milbrath. *First Encounters: Spanish Explorations in the Caribbean and the United States, 1492–1510.* Gainesville: University of Florida Press, 1989.

Millett, Kate. *Sexual Politics.* Garden City, N.Y.: Doubleday, 1970.

Morgan, H. Wayne, and Anne Hodges Morgan. *Oklahoma: A Bicentennial History.* New York: W. W. Norton and Co., 1977.

Moss, Ralph W. *The Cancer Syndrome.* New York: Grove Press, 1980.

Mourant, A. E., and Frederick E. Zeuner. *Man and Cattle.* London: Royal Anthropology Institute, 1963.

MSS 87-83. "John Burnett's Birthday Letter." Cherokee, N.C.: Museum of the Cherokee Indian Archives, n.d.

Mumford, Lewis. *Technics and Human Development.* The Myth of the Machine. New York: Harcourt, Brace and World, 1967.

———. *The Pentagon of Power.* The Myth of the Machine. New York: Harcourt Brace Jovanovich, 1970.

Nash, Gary B. *Red, White, and Black: The Peoples of Early America.* Englewood Cliffs, N.J.: Prentice-Hall, 1974.

———. *Race, Class and Politics: Essays on American Colonial and Revolutionary Society.* Urbana: University of Illinois Press, 1986.

Nash, Roderick. *Wilderness and the American Mind,* 3rd ed. New Haven, Conn.: Yale University Press, 1982.

Newhouse, John. *War and Peace in the Nuclear Age.* New York: Knopf, 1989.

Nissen, Hans J. *The Early History of the Ancient Near East 9000–2000 B.C.* Translated by Elizabeth Lutzeier with Kenneth J. Northcott. Chicago: University of Chicago Press, 1988.

Nitecki, Matthew H., and Doris V. Nitecki, eds. *The Evolution of Human Hunting.* New York: Plenum Press, 1987.

Ortner, Sherry B. "Is Female to Male as Nature Is to Culture?" In Rosaldo and Lamphere, *Woman, Culture and Society.*

Osgood, Ernest Staples. *The Day of the Cattleman.* Chicago: University of Chicago Press, 1929.

Pagden, Anthony. *The Fall of Natural Man: The American Indian and the Origins of Comparative Ethnology.* Cambridge: Cambridge University Press, 1982.

Pagels, Elaine. *Adam, Eve, and the Serpent.* New York: Random House, 1988.

Palmer, Stanley, and Dennis Reinhartz, eds. *Essays on the History of North American Discovery.* Arlington, Tex.: Texas A & M University Press, 1988.

Parkman, Francis. *Pioneers of France in the New World.* Vol. 1 of France and England in North America. New York: Viking Press, 1983.

Passmore, John. *Man's Responsibility for Nature,* 2d ed. London: Gerald Duckworth & Co., 1980.

Patrico, Jim. "School of Hard Knocks." *Beef Today,* June/July 1989, pp. 28–31.

Pearce, Roy Harvey. *The Savages of America: A Study of the Indian and the Idea of Civilization,* rev. ed. Baltimore, Md.: The Johns Hopkins University Press, 1965.

————. *Savagism and Civilization: A Study of the Indian and the American Mind.* Berkeley: University of California Press, 1988.

Pfeiffer, John E. *The Emergence of Society: A Prehistory of the Establishment.* New York: McGraw-Hill, 1977.

Piaget, Jean. *The Child's Conception of the World.* New York: Harcourt Brace, 1929.

Plato. *The Republic.* Vol. 2 of The Dialogues of Plato. Translated by B. Jowett. New York: National Library Company, n.d.

Pond, Roger. "Iowa Men Offer Bizarre Final Rests." *Farmweek* (Knightstown, Ind.), May 13, 1992, p. 2.

Popol Vuh: The Mayan Book of the Dawn of Life. Translated by Dennis Tedlock. New York: Simon & Schuster, A Touchstone Book, 1985.

Presbyterian Animal Welfare Task Force. "The Treatment of Domestic Farm Animals." A report prepared by five Presbyterian congregations in South Dakota, May 1984. Mimeographed. (Available from: Livestock Conservation Institute, 239 Livestock Exchange Building, South St. Paul, MN. 55075.)

Price, T. Douglas, and James A. Brown, eds. *Prehistoric Hunter-Gatherers: The Emergence of Cultural Complexity.* New York: Harcourt Brace Jovanovich, Academic Press, 1985.

Randolph, Richard, David Schneider, and May Diaz, eds. *Dialectics and Gender: Anthropological Approaches.* Boulder, Colo.: Westview Press, 1988.

Redman, Charles. *The Rise of Civilization: Early Farmers to Urban Society in the Ancient Near East*. New York: W. H. Freeman, 1978.

Reines, Brandon P. "The Trouble with Gennarelli's Animal Models." *The AV Magazine*, April 1992, page 12.

Reitman, Judith. "Monkey Business at NYU." *Village Voice*, April 23, 1991, p. 37.

Rifkin, Jeremy. *Beyond Beef: The Rise and Fall of the Cattle Culture*. New York: Penguin Books, A Dutton Book, 1992.

Ritvo, Harriet. "The Emergence of Modern Pet-Keeping." In Rowan, *Animals and People Sharing the World*.

Rodman, John. "The Dolphin Papers." *North American Review*, Spring 1974, pp. 13–26.

———. "The Liberation of Nature." *Inquiry*, 20 (1977):83–145.

Rollins, Phillip Ashton. *The Cowboy*. New York: Charles Scribner's Sons, 1936.

Rosaldo, Michelle, and Louise Lamphere, eds. *Woman, Culture and Society*. Stanford, Calif.: Stanford University Press, 1974.

Rowan, Andrew N., ed. *Animals and People Sharing the World*. Hanover, N.H.: University Press of New England, 1988.

Rowland, Beryl. *Animals with Human Faces*. Knoxville: University of Tennessee Press, 1973.

Rubenstein, Richard L. *The Cunning of History: The Holocaust and the American Future*. New York: Harper & Row, Harper Colophon Books, 1978.

Rummel, R. J. *Lethal Politics: Soviet Genocide and Mass Murder Since 1917*. New Brunswick, N.J.: Transaction Publishers, 1990.

Sade, Marquis de. *Justine; or, The Misfortune of Virtue*. New York: Castle Books. 1964.

Sagan, Eli. *Cannibalism: Human Aggression and Cultural Form*. New York: Harper & Row, Harper Torchbooks, 1974.

Saliou, Monique. "The Process of Women's Subordination in Primitive and Archaic Greece." In Coontz and Henderson, *Women's Work, Men's Property*.

Salloum, Habeeb. "Stampede Lives Up to Childhood Dream." *Toronto Globe and Mail*, March 30, 1991.

Sanday, Peggy Reeves. *Female Power and Male Dominance: On the Origins of Sexual Inequality*. Cambridge: Cambridge University Press, 1981.

"Senator Bilbo's Monumental Book—'Take Your Choice—Separation or Mongrelization.'" *The Truth at Last* (Marietta, Georgia), no. 355, n.d.

Serpell, James. *In the Company of Animals: A Study of Human-Animal Relationships*. London: Basil Blackwell, 1986.

Service, Elman R. *Primitive Social Organization: An Evolutionary Perspective*. New York: Random House, 1962.

Sharp, Henry S. "The Null Case: The Chipewyan." In Dahlberg, *Woman the Gatherer*.

Sheehan, Glenn W. "Whaling as an Organizing Focus in Northwestern Alaskan Eskimo Societies." In Price and Brown, *Prehistoric Hunter-Gatherers*.

Shepard, Paul. *The Tender Carnivore and the Sacred Game*. New York: Charles Scribner's Sons, 1973.

———. *Thinking Animals: Animals and the Development of Human Intelligence*. New York: Viking Press, 1978.

————. *Nature and Madness.* San Francisco: Sierra Club Books, 1982.

————. *Man in the Landscape.* College Station, Tex.: Texas A & M University Press, 1991.

Shepard, Paul, and Daniel McKinley, eds. *The Subversive Science: Essays Toward an Ecology of Man.* New York: Houghton Mifflin, 1969.

Shostak, Marjorie. *Nisa: The Life and Words of a !Kung Woman.* New York: Vintage Books, 1983.

Siebert, Rudolf J. *Horkheimer's Critical Sociology of Religion.* Washington, D.C.: University Press of America, 1979.

Singer, Peter. *Animal Liberation,* 2d ed. New York: New York Review of Books, 1990.

Skinner, B. F. *Walden Two.* New York: Macmillan, 1962.

Soule, Michael E. "Conservation: Tactics for a Constant Crisis." *Science* 253 (1991):744–50.

Spring, David, and Eileen Spring, eds. *Ecology and Religion in History.* New York: Harper & Row, Harper Torchbooks, 1974.

Steiner, George. *In Bluebeard's Castle: Some Notes Toward the Redefinition of Culture.* New Haven, Conn.: Yale University Press, 1971.

Stern, Karl. *The Flight from Woman.* New York: Farrar, Straus & Giroux, 1965.

Stevens, Henry Bailey. *The Recovery of Culture.* New York: Harper & Row, 1963.

Stevens, William K. "Humanity Confronts Its Handiwork: An Altered Planet." *New York Times,* May 5. 1992.

Stoller, Kenneth P. "The Secret of NIH." *The Animals' Voice.* June 1989, p. 56.

Stoltenberg, John. *Refusing to Be a Man: Essays on Sex and Justice.* New York: A Meridian Book, Penguin Books, 1989.

Stone, Christopher D. *Should Trees Have Standing?* New York: Avon Books, 1974.

Stone, Merlin. *When God Was a Woman.* New York: Harcourt Brace Jovanovich, 1976.

Summers, Montague. *The Werewolf.* Secaucus, N.J.: Citadel Press, 1966.

Tani, Yutaka. "The Geographical Distribution and Function of Sheep Flock Leaders: A Cultural Aspect of the Man-Domesticated Animal Relationship in Southwestern Eurasia." In Clutton-Brock, *The Walking Larder.*

————. "Two Types of Human Interventions into the Sheep Flock: Intervention into the Mother-Offspring Relationship, and Raising the Flock Leader." In *Domesticated Plants and Animals of the Southwest Eurasian Agro-Pastoral Culture Complex,* edited by Yutaka Tani and Sadao Sakamoto. Kyoto, Japan: Research Institute for Humanistic Studies, Kyoto University, 1986.

Thomas, Elizabeth Marshall. *The Harmless People.* New York: Vintage Books, 1965.

Thomas, Keith. *Man and the Natural World: A History of the Modern Sensibility.* New York: Pantheon Books, 1983.

Tiger, Steven. "Misplaced Priorities." *The Animals' Voice,* June 1989, p. 52.

Todorov, Tzvetan. *The Conquest of America: The Question of the Other.* New York: Harper & Row, 1984.

Tuan, Yi-Fu. *Dominance and Affection: The Making of Pets.* New Haven, Conn.: Yale University Press, 1984.

Tudge, Colin. "Exploitation and the Art of Survival." *New Scientist,* July 8, 1989, p. 73.

Ucko, Peter J., and G. W. Dimbleby, eds. *The Domestication and Exploitation of Plants and Animals.* Chicago, Ill.: Aldine Publishing Co., 1969.

Ulrich, Roger E. "Animal Research: A Psychological Ritual." *The Animals' Agenda,* May 1991, p. 40.

Underhill, Ruth. *Red Man's Religion: Beliefs and Practices of the Indians North of Mexico.* Chicago: University of Chicago Press, 1965.

van Andel, Tjeerd H., and Curtis Runnels. *Beyond the Acropolis: A Rural Greek Past.* Stanford, Calif.: Stanford University Press, 1987.

Vermont Journal. "The Rite of Autumn Is the Song of the Rifle." *New York Times,* November 21, 1989, p. A14.

Vita, Eugene. "Which Animals Live, Which Animals Die?" *Greenwich News,* Letters to the Editor, August 17, 1989.

Walker, George Benjamin. *Man and the Beasts Within.* New York: Stein & Day, 1977.

Watts, Alan. *Nature, Man and Woman.* New York: Pantheon Books, 1969.

White, Lynn, Jr. "The Historical Roots of our Ecological Crisis." *Science* 155 (1967):1203–1207.

Whyte, Martin King. *The Status of Women in Preindustrial Societies.* Princeton, N.J.: Princeton University Press, 1978.

Williams, David R. *Wilderness Lost: The Religious Origins of the American Mind.* Selingsgove, Pa.: Susquehanna University Press, and London: Associated University Presses, 1987.

Wilson, David. *The New Archaeology.* New York: Knopf, 1975.

Wing, Elizabeth S. "Domestication of Andean Mammals." In *High Altitude Tropical Biogeography,* edited by Francois Vuilleumier and Maximina Monasterio. Oxford: Oxford University Press, 1986.

———. "Use of Animals by the Inca as Seen at Huanuco Pampa." In *Economic Prehistory of the Central Andes,* edited by Elizabeth S. Wing and Jane C. Wheeler. BAR International Series 427. Oxford: B.A.R., 1988.

Woman of Power, no. 9 (Spring 1988). (Various essays on feminism, spirituality, and politics.)

Worldwatch Institute. *State of the World: 1992.* New York: W. W. Norton & Co., 1992.

Yarrow, Marian Radke, Phyllis M. Scott, and Carolyn Zahn Waxler. "Learning Concern for Others." *Developmental Psychology* 8 (1973):240–60.

Yildiz, Fatma, and Kazuya Maekawa. "Animal and Human Castration in Sumer." Part III: More Tests of Ur III Lagash on the Term *amar-KUD. Zinbun* 18 (1982):95–121. Kyoto, Japan: Research Institute for Humanistic Studies, Kyoto University.

Young, Patrick. "Going to the Goats." *Science News* 137 (1990):142.

Zeuner, Frederick E. *A History of Domesticated Animals.* New York: Harper & Row, 1963.

Index

aboriginals, Australian, 58, 69, 74, 88
About the Jews and Their Lies (Luther),
   222–23
Abraham, 181
Adam, Eve and the Serpent (Pagels),
   180–81
advertising, 41–42, 96
Aesop's fables, 98
Africa, 75
   European attitudes toward, 239
   pre- and proto-humans in, 53–54, 57
aggression, 283–84
agriculture, agricultural societies, 118–57
   as beginning of man's alienation from
      nature, 11
   definition of, 21
   expansionism and, 136–37
   intensive, 119
   ladder of being in, 211–15
   mind and culture as affected by, 21–33
   sexuality in, 180–84, 215
   social effects of, 124–32
   technology of, 16–17
   transition from foraging to, 51–52,
      119–24
Ainu people, 110, 148
Alexander the Great, 256
Algonkians, 214
alpacas, 159
amar-kud, 199
Ambio, 44
ambition, 37
American Cowboy, The (Frantz and
      Choate), 248
Andes, 159
animal domestication, 98, 251
   beginning of, 122–23, 191–93, 203–4
   cultural costs vs. benefits of, 161–62
   material costs vs. benefits of, 159–61
   social effects of, 137–47, 149–51, 161–
      162
Animal Land (Blount), 104–5
Animal Question, 12–13, 277–79, 280
animals, 91–117
   in art, 95–97
   in children's games, 106–7
   in children's literature, 104–6
   in children's therapy, 91–93

as "embedded figures," 103–4
on factory farms, 118–19
foragers' view of, 64–65
as heart of nature, 162–63
human thought processes shaped by,
   93–95
importance of, 12–13, 116–17
language and tool abilities of, 281–82
as machines, 37–38
man as steward over, 30–31
medical and scientific research with,
   261–66, 290–91
as pets, 111–15, 255–56, 258–61, 288–90
psychic importance of, 100–103
ranking of, 212
religious basis for man's domination
   over, 27, 28
ritual use of, 244
sacrifice of, 148–49, 164
secular arguments for man's dominion
   over, 33–34
secularization of, 164–65
selective breeding of, 260–61
symbolic use of, 96–100, 213, 215–16,
   221
torture of, 242–47
trials of, 178–79
Wild Man's kinship with, 225
in worldview of foraging societies, 90,
   107–9
see also herding societies; hunting;
   misothery
Animals, Men, and Myths (Lewinsohn),
   139, 142–43, 144
Animals and Art and Thought (Klingender), 147
Animals and People Sharing the World
   (Rowan), 256
Animals with Human Faces (Rowland),
   221
animism, 52
Anthony, David, 205, 206
Antigone (Sophocles), 209
anti-Semitism, 219, 221–23
apes, 67, 78
Arctic Dreams (Lopez), 86
Ardrey, Robert, 70, 71, 73, 78
Aristotle, 33–34, 48, 224, 228, 238

art:
    animals, 95–97
    cave paintings, 57, 65, 69, 75–76, 83, 96
    feminine evil in, 221–22
    misothery in, 169–72
    Naked Goddess sculptures, 69–70, 155–156, 191
    royal status asserted in, 130–31
Aryans, 207–8
Aschmann, Homer, 141
Associated Press, 18
Athens, 191
atomic bombs, 42–44
atrocities, 272
Augustine, Saint, 181, 182
aurochsen, 245
Australia, aborigines of, 58, 69, 74, 88
autistic children, 91–92
awakening of awe, 56
Aztecs, 133, 134–35, 236

baboon model, 77–79, 80
baboons, 263–64
Bacon, Francis, 35–37, 48, 227
bacteria, 15
Balinese, 166, 167–68
Bantus, 74
Barbados, 237
barbaros, 223–24
Barsanas, 111
bears, 110–11
Beastly Folklore (Clark), 97
Beauvoir, Simone de, 189
Beef Today, 249–50
Beloved (Morrison), 220
Bernard, Claude, 263
Bernheimer, Richard, 224–25
bestiality, 178
bestiaries, 96, 98
Bethsabee, 91–92, 93
Bettelheim, Bruno, 85
Beyond Beef (Rifkin), 248
Bibby, Geoffrey, 206
Bible, 26–28, 29, 34, 202, 216
    authors of, 31–32
Bigelow, Henry J., 261
Bilbo, Theodore G., 219
binding of feet, 267
Binford, Lewis, 77
birds, 16
"Birth Stories," 98
"black blizzard," 18
blacks, 238–41, 256–58
blame, shifting of, 123, 175–77, 195
Bloom, Harold, 31
Blount, Margaret, 104–5
Bly, Robert, 294–96

bone piles, 76–77, 83
Book of J, The (Bloom), 31
Bowden, Charles, 186
brain:
    evolution of, 55
    imprinting of, 101–2
Brazil, 237, 238, 243
breast-feeding, 187
breeding, 216–19
Bronze Age, 206
Brown, Dorcas, 205, 206
Brown, James A., 73–74
Browning, Christopher, 272
Buddha, 98
Buddhism, 98, 213
buffalos, 167
Buffon, George Louis Leclerc, 233
bullfights and runs, 242–47, 287
business world, 41–42, 79, 96
Buzzworm, 186

Caldicott, Helen, 43, 44
Campbell, Joseph, 15, 56, 70, 75, 77, 83–84, 86, 88, 89, 109–11, 132–33, 154, 155–56, 193
Canada, 68, 74, 75, 234
cannibalism, 86, 89, 132, 133, 135, 228–29
Cannibals and Kings (Harris), 59, 141
Caribbean, 236–37
Carson, Gerald, 178–79
castration, 131, 199, 239
Catal Huyuk, 191, 192
cats, 216
cattle, 123, 167
cave paintings, 57, 65, 75–76, 83, 96
celibacy, 181
Centers for Disease Control, 265
Chalice and the Blade, The (Eisler), 156, 207–8
Chance, Paul, 281, 282
Chenchus, 111
Cherokee Strip, 14
Chicago Tribune, 288
childbirth, 68, 69, 70
children:
    animal stories for, 104–6
    animals used in therapy with, 91–93
    in foraging societies, 66, 68
    "high-nurturant behavior" by, 285–86
    "playing animal" by, 106–7
    sexual abuse of, 184
chimpanzees, 78, 82, 281
Chipewyans, 68–69
Chisholm, Anne, 294
Choate, Julian, 248
Christianity, 23, 254
    creation myth in, 25–27, 166

Christianity (*cont.*)
  sexuality and, 181–82
Christian Rebirth, 24
Chukchis, 140, 143
Churchill, Sir Winston, 44
Cicero, 34
circuses, 253–54, 287
Civilization and Its Discontents (Freud),
  275
clan property, 208
Clark, Joseph D., 97–98
Clark, Lord Kenneth, 95, 96, 148, 149, 171,
  250, 251, 276
class structure, 127
Clement I, Pope, 181–82
Clutton-Brock, Juliet, 203
cockfighting, 167–68
Cohen, Mark Nathan, 59, 125, 126
Collard, Andrée, 168
colonialism, 228–38
Columbus, Christopher, 228–29
commodities trade, 190
concealment, 173–74, 195
concubines, 198
Condoret, Ange, 91
"confinement" buildings, 118
Conquest of the Americas, The (Todorov),
  231
Conrad, Joseph, 212–13, 223
Contrucci, Joyce, 168
corn, 17
Cornforth, Maurice, 40
Costello, David, 17
cotton, 17, 18
covenant, 28
cowboys, 247–50
Cranstone, B. A. L., 140
creation myths:
  Biblical, 25–27, 166
  comparison of, 193
  Mayan, 214–15
  secular, 79–82
  in totemic cultures, 107–9
Creation of Patriarchy, The (Lerner), 131,
  156, 190–91
Crete, 208–9
Cro-Magnons, 56
Crosby, Alfred W., 119, 123, 139, 235–36
culture, origin of, 55–57
Cunning of History, The (Rubenstein), 274
Curtin, Philip, 237
Curtis, Natalie, 108

Darling, Frank Fraser, 294
Darlington, C. D., 204
Dart, Raymond, 71
Darwin, Charles, 72, 79

d'Avity, Pierre, 233
death, consciousness of, 56
Debo, Angie, 13
Deere, John, 16
Deloria, Vine, 276
Democritus, 181
dental loss, 125
de Sade, Marquis, 187
Descartes, René, 35, 37–38, 48
Deserta Arabia (Doughty), 140
desertification, 160
Destruction of the European Jews, The
  (Hilberg), 222
detachment, 173, 195
Dickason, Olive Patricia, 234
diet:
  Biblical laws for, 166
  of foragers, 58–60, 66, 82
  vegetarian vs. meat, 82–83
"diffuse axonal injury" (DAI), 264
Dijkstra, Bram, 221–22
disease, 125, 235–36
dogs, 167, 259–61
Dollman, J. C., 221
"Dolphin Papers, The" (Rodman), 164
dolphins, 92
Dominance and Affection (Yi-Fu), 162,
  218
Domination of Nature, The (Leiss), 25–26
dominionism, 21–49, 210–99
  as ambition, 37
  as crusading ideology, 39–40
  definition of, 25
  environmental destruction and, 45–47
  in Industrial Age, 35–36
  moving beyond, 269–98
  nuclear age as expression of, 42–45
  origin of, 32–33
  in other cultures, 30
  political spectrum and, 40–42
  religious and secular blend in, 34–35
  religious basis for, 23–30, 41
  rewards of, 36–37
  rituals of, 242–68
  secular influences on, 33–34
  shepherd model for, 201–2
  stewardship as apology for, 30–31
Dorians, 209
Doughty, Charles M., 140
Downward Spiral, 47–48
dowry murder, 267–68
Dracula (Stoker), 221–22
Dreamer religion, 50
droughts, 18
Drummond, Hugh, 265
Dubos, Rene, 35
dust storms, 18–19

Jericho, 127, 130
Jesuits, 135
Jews, 137, 180–81
    see also anti-Semitism
Jordan, Winthrop, 238, 239, 240–41
Julian of Eclanum, 298

Kalahari desert, 60, 74
Katcher, Aaron, 91–92, 95, 115, 285
Keen, Sam, 294
Keepers of the Game (Martin), 234
Kellert, Stephen, 95, 99
Klee, Paul, 221
Klingender, Francis, 96, 98, 147, 170, 171, 172
Konner, Melvin, 284
!Kung San, 58, 59–60, 74, 82, 87
Kurgans, 207

Lakota Sioux, 84
land, overgrazing of, 159–60
Lane, John, Sr., 16
language, 57, 281–82
Las Casas, Bartolome de, 231–32
Lawrence, Elizabeth Atwood, 248–49
Leach, Edmund, 243–44
Leacock, Eleanor, 190
Leakey, Richard, 87, 188
"Learning Concern for Others," 285
Lee, David, 115
Lee, Richard, 59–60, 66
Leeds, Anthony, 140, 141, 143
Leiss, William, 25–26, 35, 39–40
Leonard, George B., 52–53, 183, 274
Leopold, A. S., 22
Lerner, Gerda, 131, 156, 190–91, 192, 196, 197, 198, 199
Letakots-Lesa, Pawnee chief, 108
Levi-Strauss, Claude, 95
Lewinsohn, Richard, 111, 139, 141, 142–43, 144, 213
life expectancy:
    agriculture's effect on, 125
    in foraging societies, 59
Lima State Hospital for the Criminally Insane, 115
Limbaugh, Rush, 79
literature:
    animals in, 104–6
    Wild Man in, 223
Little Boy, 43
llamas, 159
London, Jack, 223
Longinus, 258
Lopez, Barry, 86, 110
Lord of the Flies (Golding), 223
Lorenz, Konrad, 71, 173, 243, 283–84
Luther, Martin, 222–23

Maccoby, Hyam, 173
McKinlay, John and Sonja, 265
McKinley, Daniel, 42
McKinnon, Catherine, 287
MacNeish, Richard S., 83
Madson, John, 15, 16, 17
Maekawa, Kuzuya, 198–99, 203
Mailer, Norman, 184, 188
Malleus Maleficarum, 227
mammals, 16
Man, Culture and Animals (Leeds and Vayda), 140, 141
Man and the Natural World (Thomas), 21, 141–42
Man and Wildlife (Guggisberg), 70
Manifest Destiny, 24
Man Meets Dog (Lorenz), 173
Man's Rise to Civilization (Farb), 134, 193
Martin, Calvin, 234
Martin, James, 236
Marx, Karl, 40, 192
Masai, 145
Massachusetts Bay Colony, 236
Master Animal, 110, 147
masturbation, 183
Mather, Cotton, 145, 158, 177–78
matrilocal and matrilineal societies, 193, 208
Mayans, 214–15
Mead, Margaret, 69
Mellaart, James, 155
men:
    hunting as enhancement of powers of, 84–86, 188
    mighty-hunter myth of, 70–72, 75, 80–84
    new models for, 296–97
    as predators, 250–51
    "testosterone poisoning" of, 284
Men, Beasts and Gods (Carson), 178–79
Men's Movement, 294–96
menstrual taboos, 85, 188
Mesopotamia, 129, 130, 131, 168–70, 196–197, 199
metempsychosis, 213
Milanich, Jerald, 236
Milbrath, Susan, 236
Mill, John Stuart, 178
Millett, Kate, 192–93, 200, 201
miniaturization, 258
misogyny, 186–209, 267
    beginnings of, 188–89
    definition of, 164
    misothery and, 164, 186–87, 215, 216
    rise of patriarchy and, 188–89, 196–98, 199–201, 203–4
misothery, 158–85, 220, 241, 273, 278
    in art, 169–72

misothery (*cont.*)
  definition and etymology of, 163
  distancing devices used in, 172–77,
    194–95
  early stages of, 166–68
  effects of, 166, 176–77, 179–80, 184–85
  misogyny and, 164, 186–87, 215, 216
  in mythology, 168–69
  pornography and, 179–80
  sexuality and, 180–84
misrepresentation, 173, 175–76, 195
Missing Link, 71
missionaries, 108
Moi, 111
monarchies, 128–29
money, 142–43
mongongo nuts, 59
monkeys, 82
monotheism, 202
Montaigne, Michel de, 233
Morgan, H. Wayne and Anne Hodges, 13–
    14, 18
Morris, Desmond, 71, 73, 78
Morrison, Toni, 220
Mumford, Lewis, 23–24, 36, 37, 38, 42,
    130, 132, 193
murder, ritual, 267–68
Myth of the Savage, The (Dickason), 234
mythology:
  of hunting, 70–72, 75, 80–84, 251–53
  misothery in, 168–69
  origin of evil, 200–201
  see also creation myth

Nagasaki, 44
Naked Goddess, *see* Goddess religions
Nash, Gary, 233
Nash, Roderick, 146
Naskapis, 110
national ambition, 37
National Institutes of Health, 285
National Rifle Association, 252
Native Americans, 85–86
  "civilizing" of, 50
  conquering and enslavement of, 229–34
  European diseases and, 235–36
  horses and, 205–6
  industries owned by, 19
  land taken from, 13–15, 22–24
  missionary influence on, 108
  pets kept by, 114
  population of, 236
  religious beliefs of, 50–52
  tribal names of, 214
nature:
  agriculture as beginning of man's alien-
    ation from, 11

  animals as heart of, 162–63
  baseness of, 212–13
  as evil, 219–20
  as female, 36, 41, 186–87
  man as distinct from, 37–38
  man's dominion over, *see* dominionism
  in primal religions, 51–52
  social problems caused by man's alien-
    ation from, 12
  see also animals; misothery; plants
Nature and Madness (Shepard), 206–7,
    275
Nature Question:
  Animal Question as central to, 12–13,
    277–78
  definition of, 11
  process of answer to, 12
Nazis, 218–19, 223
Neanderthals, 55, 56–57, 77
"Neolithic dialect," 206–7
Netherlands, 237
Newhouse, John, 43
New Scientist, 276, 284
New York Times, 60, 82, 252–53, 276, 280–
    281, 284
Nez Percé, 50
Nitecki, Matthew H. and Doris V., 76,
    77
Novum Organum (Bacon), 36
nuclear stockpiles, 44
nuclear war, 44–45
Nuer, 166, 167

Oedipal rivalry, 189
Of Wolves and Men (Lopez), 110
oil, 18
Oklahoma:
  description of grassland of, 15–16
  destruction of grassland of, 17–18
  as Dust Bowl, 18–19
  etymology of name of, 15
  industrialization of, 19
  land runs in, 13–15
  as microcosm of U.S., 15, 19
  statehood of, 15
Oklahoma: A Bicentennial History
    (Morgan and Morgan), 13–14
Oklahoma Farmer-Stockman, 18
Ordinary Men (Browning), 272
origin-of-evil myths, 200–201
Ortiz, Tomas, 230
Ortner, Sherry, 187
Others:
  hatred of, 220–22
  ranking of, 212
overgrazing, 159–60
Oviedo y Valdez, Fernandez de, 230

Pagden, Anthony, 223, 224, 228
Pagels, Elaine, 180–81, 182
Pandora's box, 200–201
parenting roles, 193–94
Parkman, Francis, 51–52, 234
Parr, Charles, 17
patriarchal societies, 85
    ideology of, 199–201
    origins of, 144–45, 188–89, 196–98,
        203–4
Paul, Saint, 181
Pawnees, 89, 108
Pentagon of Power, The (Mumford), 23–24
personal ambition, 37
person-demand, 46–47
Peter the Great, 258
pets, 111–15, 255–56, 258–61, 288–90
Pfeiffer, John E., 54–55, 57, 58, 61
Philosophers of the Earth (Chisholm),
    294
Picasso, Pablo, 96
pilgrims, 22, 24
plants:
    domestication of, 121–22
    in foragers' diet, 66
Plato, 33, 215
Pliny, 224
Plotinus, 181
plows, 16–17
Politics (Aristotle), 33–34
Popol Vuh, 214–15, 235
population:
    global, 46, 127, 269, 271
    of Native Americans, 236
pornography, 179–80, 187, 266–67, 286–87
Pornography and Silence (Griffin), 180,
    184
Porphyry, 181
Portugal, 238
poverty, 47, 270–71, 292–93
power, 37
prairie, 84, 118
    biodiversity of, 15–16
    destruction of, 16–19
pre- and proto-humans, 53–54
Presbyterian Animal Welfare Task Force,
    29, 30–31, 202
Presidential Papers, The (Mailer), 188
Price, T. Douglas, 73–74
Primal Man: The Killer Instinct, 71
primal religions, 51–52, 153–54
primal societies:
    definition of, 52
    see also foraging societies
primitive, use of term, 52
Primitive Social Organization (Service),
    83

prostitution, 184
proteins, 67
protozoans, 15
Psychology Today, 281
Pythagoras, 33, 213

Qur'an, 29

race, breeding and, 216–19
Race, Class and Politics (Nash), 233
racism, 218–19, 238–41
rape, 131
Rasmussen, Larry, 276
Reagan, Ronald, 41
Red Man's Religion (Underhill), 51, 108
Reines, Brandon, 264
religion:
    moral imperative for domination given
        by, 23–30, 41
    myths as origin of, 32
    of Native Americans, 50–52
    pornography and, 180
    primal, 51–52, 153–54
    sacred texts overemphasized in, 32
    universalizing, 165
    see also Goddess religions
Renaissance, 34–35
Republic, The (Plato), 215
Requerimiento, 229–30
Rifkin, Jeremy, 248
right wing, worldview of, 79
Rise and Fall of the Plantation Complex,
    The (Curtin), 237
rituals, 242–68
    animals in, 244
    genital mutilation, 267–68
    hunting, 250–51
    pornography, 267, 286–87
    purpose of, 243–44
    suicide and murder, 267–68
    undoing of, 286–87
Ritvo, Harriet, 217, 259, 261
Robbins, Rossell Hope, 226
Rodeo (Lawrence), 248–49
rodeos, 248–50, 287
Rodman, John, 163–64
Roman Catholic Church, 34, 182, 222
Rome (classical), 34, 48, 181, 222, 224,
    254, 258
Romero, Francisco, 245
Rorschach tests, 104
Rowan, Andrew, 256
Rowland, Beryl, 221
Royal Swedish Academy of Sciences, 44
royalty, 23
Rubenstein, Richard, 274
Rummel, R. J., 272

Sacred Bull or Ram, 147
Sacred Executioner, The (Maccoby), 173
sacrifice:
  animal, 148–49, 164
  human, 89, 132–33, 134–36
sadomasochism, 183–84, 187
Sagan, Eli, 133, 136
Saint-Simon, Claude Henri, 40
Saliou, Monique, 208–9
saliva, 67
Sanday, Peggy Reeves, 68, 85, 144, 150,
  193–94
sanguinary fiestas populares, 242–43
Santander, Pedro de, 231
Satan, 216
savages, derivation of term, 212
schizophrenia, 104
science:
  animals used in name of, 261–66, 290–91
  bias in, 72–73
  dominionist philosophy in, 35–36, 42
Sea of Grass, 15–16
Search for Environmental Ethics, A, 276
Sears, Paul B., 35
Serpell, James, 111, 113, 148, 149, 152,
  153, 172
  on distancing devices, 173, 174, 175, 176
Service, Elman R., 83
sexual aggression, 36
sexuality:
  in agrarian societies, 180–84, 215
  in Christianity, 181–82
  ethics and, 292–94
  evil and, 201, 216
  symbolism and, 221
Sharp, Henry S., 68–69
Sheehan, Glenn W., 89
sheep, 122–23
Shepard, Paul, 42, 140, 154, 155, 209, 275
  animals in theories of, 65, 93–94, 95, 96,
    99, 100–104, 105, 106–7, 206–7
  on cultural transition to farming, 166–68
Shepherd, J. Barrie, 276
"Should Trees Have Standing?" (Stone),
  276
Siberia, 74
"Silent Millennia in the Origin of Agriculture, The" (Darlington), 204
silver, 234
Singer, Peter, 38
Skinner, B. F., 41
slavery, slaves, 23, 41, 127, 131–32, 190,
  198–99, 203, 228, 237–38, 256–58
smallpox, 235–36
Smith, Betsy, 92
Smithsonian Institution, 276
Smohalla, 50, 53, 60

"snuff" films, 184
Social Darwinism, 79–80
social structure, 127–29
soil erosion, 16–19
Soule, Michael, 48, 270
Soviet Union, 272
  atrocities in, 273
  nuclear stockpile of, 44
Spain, 57, 77
  bullfights and runs in, 242–47
  as colonial power, 228–32, 234, 235,
    236–37
spearheads, 73
species extinction, 47–48, 270
speech, 56
Spengler, Oswald, 72, 77–78, 81, 235
squassation, 226
Stalin, Joseph, 272
Stern, Karl, 187
Stevenson, Robert Louis, 223
Stoddard, Lothrop, 219
Stoics, 181
Stoker, Bram, 221
Stone, Christopher D., 276, 277
Stone, Merlin, 154
stone tools, 54, 55, 83
*Strange Case of Dr. Jekyll and Mr. Hyde,
  The* (Stevenson), 223
strappado, 226
Straus, Lawrence Guy, 83
Subversive Science, The (Shepard and
  McKinley), 42
sugar industry, 237, 238
suicide, ritual, 267
Sumeria, 32, 129, 170–71, 199
Summers, Montague, 175
sunna, 268
"survival of the fittest," 79
Symbolic Wounds (Bettelheim), 85
Synod of Elvira, 222

Tani, Yutaka, 203
Tanner, Nancy Makepeace, 66, 67, 78, 79,
  80, 81
taphonomic studies, 76
technology:
  agricultural, 16–17
  animals and, 281
  of early humans, 53–54, 55, 73, 77, 83
Tedlock, Dennis, 235
teeth, 125
Teleki, Geza, 82
Temptation of St. Anthony, The (Dollman),
  221
Tennyson, Alfred, Lord, 79
Testimony of the Spade, The (Bibby), 206
testosterone, 284

Texasgulf, 42
Thais, 166–67
Theology for Ecology (Shepherd), 276
Thinking Animals (Shepard), 65, 93–94,
    103, 105, 140, 166–68
Third World, 270
    diet in, 60
    life expectancy in, 59
    personal energy consumption in, 46
Thomas, Elizabeth Marshall, 58
Thomas, Sir Keith, 21, 22–23, 26, 38, 141–
    142, 144, 177, 178, 187, 211, 216, 217
Thomas Aquinas, Saint, 34, 48
Tiger, Lionel, 71, 73
Tiger, Steven, 265
Time, 14
Todorov, Tzvetan, 231, 236
Tomei, Donny, 92–93
tools, *see* technology
Torah, 28
Torralba, 77
torture, 89, 226
    of animals, 242–47
totalitarianism, 273
totemism, 107–9, 147
Traces on the Rhodian Shore (Glacken),
    211
tractors, 17
Transformation, The (Leonard), 52–53,
    183, 274
"Treatment of Domestic Farm Animals,
    The," 202
Trinkaus, Erick, 77
Truth at Last, 219
Tudge, Colin, 276
Turner, Angela, 284
Twenty-third Psalm, 202

Ulrich, Roger, 261
Underhill, Ruth, 51, 108, 154
United States:
    cowboy culture of, 247–50
    European immigration to, 15, 17
    global impact of, 269–70
    life expectancy in, 59
    nuclear stockpile of, 44
    Oklahoma as microcosm of, 15, 19
    personal energy use in, 46
    pet industry in, 111–12
    racism in, 218–19
    slavery in, 237
universalizing religions, 165

vampires, 221
Vayda, Andrew, 141
Veblen, Thorstein, 112
vegetarian diet, 82–83

Village Voice, 264
virgin land, 22
vivisection, 261–62

Walden Two (Skinner), 41
Wallace, Alfred Russell, 79
war, 272–74
War and Peace in the Nuclear Age (New-
    house), 43
warrior states, 129–31
Watt, James, 41
Way of the Seeded Earth, The (Campbell),
    132
Werewolf, The (Summers), 175
werewolves, 174–75, 221
wet nurses, 187
wheat, 17, 18, 121
Where the Sky Began (Madson), 15
White, Lynn, 26, 276
White Man's Burden (Jordan), 239
White Over Black (Jordan), 238
"Wilderness and Plenty" (Darling), 294
Wild Man, 223–25
Wild Men in the Middle Ages (Bern-
    heimer), 224–25
Wild Woman, 225
Williams, Michael, 92, 93
Winthrop, John, 236
witches, 225–27
wolves, 174–75, 213
Woman's Creation (Fisher), 191
women:
    foraging by, 60, 65–68, 87
    Genesis written by, 31
    genital mutilation of, 267–68
    infanticide and, 89, 190
    life expectancy for, 59
    pornography and, 179–80, 187, 266–67
    as power base in foraging societies, 68–
        70, 85–86
    ranking of, 211–12
    sacrifice of, 89
    as slaves, 190–91, 198–99, 232
    in war, 131
    see also misogyny; sexuality
Wood, Ronald, 264
workdays, 60
Works and Days (Hesiod), 200
World Health Organization, 44, 268
Worldwatch Institute, 47
writing, 32–33

Years of Decision (Spengler), 78
Yi-Fu Tuan, 162, 218, 256, 257–59, 260
yoga, 213

zoos, 255, 287